HAMPDEN COUNTY

1636 — 1936

THE AMERICAN
HISTORICAL SOCIETY, INC.
1936

A Facsimile Reprint
Published 1999 by

HERITAGE BOOKS, INC.
1540E Pointer Ridge Place
Bowie, Maryland 20716
1-800-398-7709
http://www.heritagebooks.com

ISBN: 0-7884-1196-9

*T*HIS set, "Hampden County, 1636-1936," by Clifton Johnson, is one of a series produced over the past half century by noted historians and educators, each work a distinct entity, but joined with the others to form a library of regional history that stands without parallel in the publishing field.

THE AMERICAN HISTORICAL SOCIETY, INC.

SUNRISE ON THE CONNECTICUT, 1650

HAMPDEN COUNTY

1636 - - - - 1936

By

CLIFTON JOHNSON

Historian and Author

VOLUME I

THE AMERICAN HISTORICAL SOCIETY, INC.

NEW YORK

1936

INTRODUCTORY NOTE

A people which takes no pride in the achievements of remote ancestors will never achieve anything worthy to be remembered by remote descendants.

—T. B. MACAULAY.

THE plan in these volumes has been to write a readable account of the most interesting and important events which have taken place here since William Pynchon made his first settlement by the Great River in 1636. Long and frequent quotations from poorly-spelled, ancient records might interest the historian but would only bore the average reader, so they have been omitted. Lists of names and pages of statistics are also left out as unsuited to a general history.

The information in these volumes has been drawn from many sources, too many to be acknowledged individually. I wish to express my indebtedness to the historians of the past and my grateful appreciation to the many still living who have contributed to the preparation of this history.

CLIFTON JOHNSON.

CONTENTS

ILLUSTRATIONS

PUBLISHERS' NOTE

THIS history of Hampden County appears at the close of the county's tercentennial year. We place it in the hands of the public with confidence in their enjoyment of it, and quote the comments of Frank Walcott Hutt, Secretary of the Old Colony Historical Society, Taunton, Massachusetts, upon reading advance sheets:

"You will never have a more interesting history in your hands than the present Hampden County story. . . . . It will be read and be memorable, for it is popularized already with memories, personalities, countless incidents of the every-day life of successive times and people."

To the author the publishers express appreciation of effective and prompt coöperation, while grateful recognition is likewise made to the Advisory Council which served with him throughout the preparation of the work, as follows:

Springfield: A. G. Baker, W. G. Ballantine, George G. Bulkley, Waldo L. Cook, Rt. Rev. Thomas F. Davies, D. D., Carlos B. Ellis, Dr. James G. Gilkey, Hon. Wallace R. Heady, Frederic M. Jones, Dr. Charles F. Lynch, John MacDuffie, Horace A. Moses, Samuel Price, John C. Robinson, Mrs. Meta M. Seaman, Dr. Frederick B. Sweet, A. B. Wallace; Holyoke: Nathan P. Avery, Robert E. Barrett, Mrs. Minnie R. Dwight, Joseph Skinner, William F. Whiting; Westfield: Harold T. Dougherty, Miss Lucy Gillette, Hon. Robert E. Parker; West Springfield: John R. Fausey; Palmer: D. L. Bodfish; Chicopee Falls: N. P. Ames Carter; Chicopee: Preston C. Pond; Wilbraham: Ralph E. Peck.

Winfield Scott Downs, Litt. D.,

Managing Editor, The American Historical Society, Inc.

Hampden County and John Hampden

CHAPTER I

Hampden County and John Hampden

Hampden County is a fairly young civil division of Massachusetts, which with all the rest of the western part of the State was originally included in Hampshire County. This was established by an act of the General Court in 1662 and had only three towns, Springfield, Northampton, and Hadley. The committee then appointed to have charge of county affairs was Captain John Pynchon, Henry Clarke, Captain Aaron Cooke, Lieutenant David Milton and Elizur Holyoke. The first year Springfield was the shire town. The following year they decided that the shire meetings should be held alternately in Springfield and Northampton. This plan prevailed until 1794, when for the convenience of the inhabitants generally Northampton was made the shire town, and all public records and properties were transferred to that place.

The removal of the seat of justice from Springfield to Northampton was not favored by the people living in the south part of the county and naturally they complained that the change was injurious to their interests. But it was not until February 25, 1812, that Hampden County was set off by itself. It included the towns of Springfield, Longmeadow, Wilbraham, Monson, Holland, Brimfield, South Brimfield, Palmer, Ludlow, West Springfield, Westfield, Montgomery, Russell, Blandford, Granville, Southwick, Tolland and Chester. Springfield was made the shiretown. Its population was then only 2,700, a little more than that of Northampton, and the population of the whole new county of Hampden was only 25,000.

John Hampden, for whom Hampden County is named, was a soldier and an English statesman, a cousin by marriage of Oliver Cromwell. He laid down the two conditions under which resistance to the King became the duty of a good subject. Those conditions were an attack on religion and an attack on the fundamental laws. Hampden was an opponent of episcopacy, and distrusted the bishops as he

HAMPDEN COUNTY

Scale of Miles
0 1 2 3 4 5 6 7 8 9 10

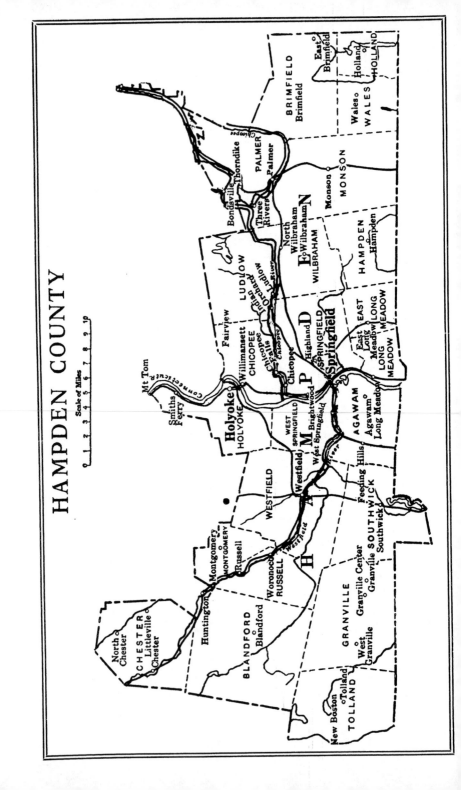

distrusted the monarchy. In 1637 his resistance to the payment of "ship-money" gained for his name a lustre which it has never since lost. This tax was first planned to be levied on the maritime counties alone and only in time of war, so when Charles I demanded ship money from the whole country and in a time of peace it aroused a great deal of opposition. Moreover, this was done without the sanction of Parliament and increased the growing belief of the people that the King was determined to dispense with government by that body altogether. John Hampden, then a wealthy Buckinghamshire landowner, refused to pay the tax and the case was taken to court, where the trial lasted for six months. Seven of the twelve judges gave a verdict for the crown, but not long afterward an end was put to such practices. Hampden struggled, not so much to win his own case, as to establish the supremacy of the House of Commons.

As a military officer in the war between King and people, Hampden raised a regiment of his own Buckinghamshire men for the parliamentary cause. Wounds received on Chalgrove Field brought about his death in 1643.

Geology of the Region

CHAPTER II

Geology of the Region

The Story of Hampden County as Nature Has Written It in the Rocks and Streams

For a long period a nameless valley here, devoid of human inhabitants, was the savage playfellow of the elements. The primeval rocks formed and wore away, and reformed again and again. There was internal fire and vast upheavals. It was no place for people and indeed they could not have existed during the desolation of most of the slow formative era.

The Connecticut Valley, from the northern border of Massachusetts to the sea, is not an ordinary river-channel, but is, in fact, a wide trough between two systems of mountains. On the west lie the worn-down remnants of the once lofty Berkshire Mountains; on the east, the yet more worn-down ridges that we may call the Central Massachusetts set of mountain ranges. These old mountains were elevated at different times. That on the east was probably the first to begin its upward movement in very ancient days. The elevation of the Berkshire chain most likely began at a little later date. As these mountain chains grew they left between them a broad trough, from ten to thirty miles wide, extending from the sea to some distance north of Springfield. The trough probably assumed something like its present form just after the close of the coal-measures. During the coal-making time this valley was most likely a region of forests, but shortly afterward the thick and extensive beds of sandstone were laid down directly on the surface of the old crystalline rocks which then, as well as now, were the valley's sides and floor.

This sandstone extends from near the north line of the State to the shores of Long Island Sound. It is a good building stone, and there are extensive quarries at East Longmeadow. Evidence obtained from borings for artesian wells indicates that the entire deposit of sandstone is from three thousand to ten thousand feet in thickness. Sometimes the sandstone layers show interesting traces of ancient life in the region. Slabs have been found imprinted with the feet of animals that probably were akin to the reptiles and amphibians of the present day. In other instances there are the traces of insects, impressions by waves and ripples, mud cracks caused by the drying of the deposits, and marks of rain drops made by passing showers on the plastic material.

Edward Hitchcock, professor of geology in Amherst College, and afterward president of the college, made an extensive collection of the impressions, and recorded the results in a report published in 1858.

In general the surface of the valley is level, but there is one noteworthy exception in the ridges of hills associated with Mount Tom and Mount Holyoke. In Hampden County the ridges pass through the western part of Holyoke, West Springfield and Agawam. Their structure can be effectively observed on the line of the Boston and Albany Railroad between Mittineague and Westfield. From there two distinct ridges are in sight. One is lower than the other and has a cutting through it just west of Tatham station. The rock is dark gray in color and is compact and crystalline. Some of it is a porous, spongy sort of stone, and has cavities that often are filled with quartz.

About three-fourths of a mile west is the higher ridge which is of traprock, and in it a large quarry has been opened. Great quantities of this rock are used in road-building. The quarry walls are distinctly columnar in character, and both ridges are the result of successive outflows of lava. Probably the lava flowed over the muddy bottom that intruded from the sea, and then was covered by more layers of mud and sand. Finally these hardened into stone, and there was a second, but smaller, lava flow which in turn was covered by sandstone. The tilting and faulting of the region and the subsequent erosion, causing the trap ridges to stand out in bold relief on the southern slopes of Mount Tom, are distinct evidences of volcanic action, and lava plugs and other remains of ancient volcanoes have been mapped by students of local geology.

During this time there was formed a shallow arm of the sea, extending nearly as far north as the present Vermont line. It probably received a number of large streams rising in the hills to the east and west, and at its head was the delta of the upper Connecticut. This period of the New Red Sandstone occupied a long portion in the earth's history, and saw many great changes of climate. More than once it was a region of extensive glaciers that discharged a great deal of pebbly sediment into their Connecticut basin. These pebbles were sorted and arranged in strata, and now appear in the extensive reddish-colored pudding-stone beds that abound in the valley.

Enough is known of other regions to make it pretty certain that at the outset of the glacial period there was a climate here not very different from that now prevailing in this region. Many large animals existed then that are no longer found, including the elephant, called the mammoth, and his smaller kinsman, the mastodon, himself as large as an ordinary elephant.

The last one of the glacial periods came suddenly, but what caused the change we do not know. It is probable that without any great change in the average temperature of the year, the summers became much cooler and the winters less cold, while the deposit of water in the form of snow was greatly increased, so that the cool and short summer could not melt it away. Even with our present warm summer, if the snowfall were to be increased so that the winter fall gave a depth on the average of ten feet, the likelihood is it would stay unmelted on the highlands of the Berkshire and Central Massachusetts mountain ranges, and reinforced by the snowfall of the following winter, give us glaciers that would creep down the valleys and slowly possess the lowlands.

Be this as it may, the glacial sheets grew in this country until the Connecticut Valley was filled far above the tops of the hills on each side. At its time of greatest thickness this sheet was probably about a half mile deep. It flowed slowly, a few feet a day, down the valley to the sea. The ice stream was not peculiar to this valley, but was part of a great sheet that covered nearly all the northern half of North America. In New England the ice extended south to beyond Long Island, and ended in a vast sea-wall of ice that stretched as a vast rolling icy plain far to the north. It swept over the top of Mount Washington in the White Mountains, though that mountain rises three-quarters of a mile above the general level of the country on which it stands.

From the valley of the Hudson, where the ice was even deeper than in the Connecticut basin, it flowed over the Berkshire Hills, increasing the tide of frozen water. As this enormous weight of ice ground its way to the sea, it wore down the rocks over which it moved. The soft red sandstones and shales gave way readily, and a large part of their beds that were in the Connecticut Valley before the glacial period were ground away by the ice-mill. Where there were thick masses of lava, a much denser and harder rock, these parts remained projecting, and formed the sharp ridges such as Mount Tom. The pudding-stones were also solid enough to resist better than the sandstones, and so frequently stand up in ridges while the softer rocks were worn down on either side of them.

After a long period of desolation, during which our region was in the condition that Greenland is now, the ice vanished as mysteriously as it came, leaving a vast amount of rocky waste strewn over the region. One of the peculiar features of the glacial period was that all the regions covered by the ice sheet seem to have been pressed downward to a depth proportionate to the thickness of the ice that had lain on their surfaces.

When the ice left, the land crept slowly up to something like its old level; but for a while the valley, in common with the neighboring regions, was much depressed. The sinking seems to have been greatest near its head. In the Long Island Sound vicinity it probably did not exceed a hundred feet; while as far up as Bellows Falls, the sinking was probably more than three hundred feet; so that, for a while after the glaciers disappeared from the valley, it seems to have returned to the conditions of the period when it was a broad but shallow arm of the sea.

With the disappearance of the ice there was left a land surface deeply covered with a rubbish of sand, clay and boulders. The heavy rainfall that marked this ice period continued to exist, though probably in a less intense form, after the ice had retreated toward the North Pole, so that much of this glacial trash was carried away by the streams; and from the hill region of the Connecticut Valley a vast amount of the lighter part of the waste that the streams could easily handle was swept out into the Connecticut Valley, and laid down beneath the water that covered the surface. The falling of glacial waste, transported and rearranged by the action of water.

THE CONNECTICUT RIVER AT SPRINGFIELD
Viewed from the west shore

formed a very thick sheet in the Connecticut Valley. It was at least a hundred feet deep near the mouth and over three hundred feet thick in the region near the New Hampshire line.

Sometimes the glacial deposits are piled up in rounded hills known as drumlins, or they may be left in long ridges of gravel. McCarthy's Hill in East Longmeadow is a good example of a drumlin, and an example of the gravel ridges can be seen at Monson, east of the village.

Soon after the filling-in of mud, sand, and gravel was completed, the floor of the valley was lifted above the sea, and the river began to wear away the waste. It is the manner of rivers to swing to and fro in their valleys, cutting first against one bank and then the other. In these swings the Connecticut has crossed its valley at Springfield nearly from side to side, leaving here and there scraps of the old stratified drift in the form of terraces. They have been left at different heights above the river's present level, and the highest are the oldest, the smallest in area, and the most ruined by the action of frost, rain, and snow.

The most prominent and extensive of these terraces in the Springfield vicinity is at the height of about a hundred and eighty feet above the level of low water in the river.

If a person will go to some convenient hilltop that commands a wide view of the valley, and in his mind restore the vast mass of sand and gravel included below the level of the highest terraces and the present level of the river, he will then see how great has been the work done since the close of the post-glacial period. If he will remember that this post-glacial period probably occupies not over one five-hundredth part of the time that has elapsed since the building of this valley began, he will get a better idea of the wonderful changes that have been witnessed by it, only a small part of which have been recorded.

William Pynchon Comes to the Connecticut Valley

CHAPTER III

William Pynchon Comes to the Connecticut Valley

Springfield, in its evolution, has been, not simply a town or city, but a controlling factor in the development of Western Massachusetts. At first, it was just a village in the wilderness, with Indians for close neighbors. Next it was a town, and after that a mother of towns. From such a start it has gone on and on until now the embryo hamlet is the mother of cities.

But to begin at the beginning, we must cross the Atlantic to another Springfield which is the parent of ours. It is in Essex, an eastern county of England, bounded on the north by Cambridgeshire and Suffolk, east by the North Sea, and south by the river Thames. Essex has always been an agricultural county, and a writer in 1594 describes it as "most fat, fruitful, and full of profitable things." It continued rustic in spite of its nearness to London, which intimately associated it with all the great historical struggles. Several of the Essex men were concerned in the Gunpowder Plot and during the Civil War of the seventeenth century the county rendered valuable aid to the Parliament.

As we look back for a few hundred years we find an Old World weary of its burden of customs that had been the growth of centuries of ignorance and oppression, yet beginning to reach forth toward a new and better state of things. The discoveries of voyagers had revealed to Europe this continent in the west as an open field for its enterprise, and at once the Old World began to seek a better home in the New. Old systems of government were distrusted and old forms of religion began to be discarded. Men craved a change which would give them more hopeful conditions. As a consequence those who chafed under arbitrary government, and wanted greater freedom in religion, and more security in their persons and property, were eager to seek a new home west of the Atlantic. With that object in view, several influential English gentlemen solicited and obtained from King Charles I a charter that gave to them all the lands in New England from a line running westerly three miles north of the Merrimac River to a line running westerly three miles south of the Charles River and extending to the west from the Atlantic Ocean.

After much debate, it was decided the charter should be transferred with the colony to New England and the government of it settled there.

When King Charles II dissolved his third Parliament with the avowed purpose of ruling without it, thus putting his heel on the statute liberties of England, there dwelt in an Essexshire hamlet a warden of the established church.

He was thirty-nine years of age, and of gentle birth, acute, restive, and singularly self-assertive. He had seen some of the stoutest men in the realm break into tears when the King cut off free speech in the Commons, and he had seen ritualism, like an iron collar, clasped on the neck of the church, while the Duke of Buckingham, a young, jeweled courtier was accepted as the King's favorite. A colonial enterprise backed by some Lincolnshire gentlemen had been noised abroad, and the warden joined his fortunes with them. Thus William Pynchon, of Springfield in Essex, England, became one of the incorporators mentioned in the royal charter of the Massachusetts Bay Company in America. When we trace back the lineage of the family we find a sturdy quality that flourishes in the fastness of Wales, yet they were not strangers to the graces of the gentry and the pride of family. It seems that one of them, whose name at that period in its development was Pinco, instead of Pynchon, came to England accompanied by "his sworn brother" in war, and the two of them campaigned with William the Conqueror at the time of the Norman Conquest. As a reward they received, among returns for their services, a village in Lincolnshire.

Various spellings of the Pynchon name continued to arrive, and finally the first *William Pynchon* appeared. He is said to have been an "oppulent butcher," and from him descended a line of important Baronets and Squires of high degree, one of whom was Nicholas Pynchon, who became High Sheriff of London in 1533. After a few more generations there was another William Pynchon, and he was the Essex Pynchon, founder of Springfield, Massachusetts.

Such photographs of his home region as have found their way to America suggest a very appealing, idyllic charm—"a land flowing with milk and honey," and it would seem that leaving the Mother Country must have given a cultured, sensitive man like William Pynchon many a heartache.

He was a person of broad and aggressive thought who loved both money and adventure. Besides, he loved the gospel in its purity and loathed political corruption, but at the same time distrusted the phase of Puritanism which drifted away from royalty.

After King Charles had risen from his bed, where he had fallen in unkingly tears on hearing of Buckingham's assassination, he resolved to continue the fight for the divine right of kings by adopting two notable policies, and in the very month when he dissolved the Parliament that had bolted its doors against the royal messenger, he signed the famous Massachusetts Bay charter. The eagerness of His Majesty to be well rid of his Puritan subjects explains the liberal terms he gave when he transferred the Massachusetts wilderness to Endicott, Pynchon, and other associates. They and their heirs and assigns forever received from the King, in the territory of Massachusetts Bay, "all lands and woods, havens, rivers, waters, mines, minerals, jurisdictions, liberties, inheritences," and so on, using some words which in spelling or quaintness are distinctly puzzling. The chief consideration was a payment of "one-fifth part of the gold and silver ore which from time to time, and at all times hereafter, shall be there gotten."

Every person joining the corporation was required to take the freeman's oath, swearing "by the great and dreadful name of the ever living God" to maintain and preserve all the "liberties and privileges" of the colony; and did not doubt his right to exclude freemen who developed heretical opinions. John and Samuel Brown, who found themselves in trouble for using the book of Common Prayer, were sent back to England from Salem, and it was arranged that the dispute should be put out for arbitration. The Browns nominated Mr. Pynchon, among others, to deal with this problem, and in the end it is believed they were paid a small sum for their financial losses in America.

Mr. Pynchon's importance in the enterprise of transferring the charter from England to Massachusetts was evident from the beginning, and he was named by the King as assistant, pending organization. He was at the meeting in England in May, 1629, when he paid his "adventure money" to the treasurer, and in October was placed on the committee in charge of taking the historic charter across the ocean. The fleet of four vessels which sailed in April, 1630, carried the charter with the seal of England attached to it by strings of braided silk, and it carried Mr. Pynchon and his feeble wife with four children, Ann, Mary, John, and Margaret. Another son was left in England and later went to the Barbados. Most of the immigrants had families with them.

When the fleet left its anchorage England and Spain were at war, with the hostilities mostly carried on at sea. It was understood that cruisers were lying in wait for the emigrant vessels destined for New England, and it became important that the four ships should find ways for mutual aid and defence. They were armed, and to each was assigned a special post of duty. There was little favorable weather before the 8th of April, when the fleet weighed anchor. On the morning of April 9 there was quite an alarm. Eight sails were in sight astern that seemed to be Spanish cruisers from Dunkirk waiting for the emigrant ships, and as Winthrop says in his journal, "we all prepared to fight them." To the "Arbella," named after Lady Arbella, wife of Isaac Johnson and of high rank in England, was assigned "the place and title of Admiral." The Lady Arbella and other women and children were removed to the lower deck that they might be out of danger.

"All things being thus fitted we went to prayer on the upper deck." "It was a pleasure to see how cheerful and comfortable all the company appeared, not a woman or child showed fear, though all thought the danger was great." Soon afterward it was discovered the ships were not Spanish cruisers.

The emigrants suffered from the high winds and extreme cold the greater part of the voyage. There was some sickness among the passengers, especially among the children. "They lay groaning in the cabins, and we fetched out a rope which we stretched from the steerage to the mainmast, and made them stand, some on the one side, and some on the other, and sway it up and down until they were warm. By such means they soon grew well and merry."

June 7 Winthrop says they put their ship "astays" and with a few hooks in less than two hours caught sixty-seven codfish, most of them very great fish, some a yard and a half long. This was a very seasonable supply for the passengers who had now been sixty-eight days on shipboard. June 8 they saw land about ten leagues distant, which proved to be Mount Desert. They now had "fair sunshine," Winthrop says, "and so pleasant a sweet air as did much refresh them, and there came a smell off the shore like the smell of a garden." June 11 they were all day within sight of Cape Ann and on Saturday some of them landed at their destined port, which was Salem, and were visited by John Endicott, the founder of the town, and by its minister.

On their return to Salem these gentlemen had with them Governor Winthrop and some others. There, Winthrop says, "we supped with a good venison pasty and good beer, and at night returned to our ship, but the greater part of the voyagers went on shore at Cape Ann, which lay very near, and gathered a store of fine strawberries." The new colonists began at once to look for good places near Massachusetts Bay for planting settlements. Pynchon selected Roxbury for the site of his home, and became the founder of that town. Without any question "Rocksbury's" name was descriptive of its substance.

His wife died soon after landing and left one son and three daughters. Not long afterward Mr. Pynchon married a second wife, who is described in the Roxbury church records as a grave matron of the church at Dorchester.

Mr. Pynchon aided in establishing a church at Roxbury and was active in other public affairs. He attended the first General Court at Charlestown, and was made treasurer of the colony. Curiously enough, the court fined him and two assistants a "noble apiece" for being tardy. He had to cross the river and no doubt there was some good reason for being late.

It seems fairly certain that early plans were made for an extensive beaver trade and for some commerce by sea. The General Court authorized Mr. Pynchon to receive various goods as a gift to the plantation, and that naturally implies wharfage facilities. Certainly, in later years, he owned a wharf at Boston. Mr. Pynchon secured a license to trade in beaver skins with the Indians, but trade was disappointing, nor was the outlook encouraging for the town of Roxbury.

One pioneer, John Pratt by name, probably expressed the feelings of many when he wrote back to England lamenting the barrenness of the soil. The Bay authorities heard of it and Pratt was forced to make a public retraction, giving the climate and soil a certificate of good character. Mr. Pynchon was one of the court chosen to examine Pratt's retraction. It would be interesting to know what he as a "gentleman of learning and religion" thought when he was signing his name to the acceptance of the retraction, in which Pratt acknowledged under the counter pressure of necessity that

> "As for the barrennes of the sandy grounds I spake of them as I supposed them to be, and now by experience of my own, I find that such ground as before I accounted barren, yet, being manured and husbanded doth bring forth more fruit than I did expect."

The poor condition of the so-called soil at Roxbury, from which even proper husbandry could not, under the circumstances, supply encouragement to the tiller, led to a dispute about taxes levied on the several towns by the General Court, and in 1635 Mr. Pynchon refused to pay his part of the assessment. For his resistance he was fined five pounds.

The strangest instance of discipline connected with Mr. Pynchon's name arose in connection with the beaver trade. The laws as to giving firearms to the Indians were very strict. But the Indians were good hunters, and the temptation to lend them guns for a day or week, with perhaps an Englishman going along to supervise, was hardly to be resisted.

In the spring of 1634, Mr. Pynchon and an associate applied to the Court of Assistants for a special permit and it was granted, but shortly afterward the General Court levied a fine of ten pounds, half to be paid by Pynchon and his associate for breach of the law, and half by the Court of Assistants, "who gave them leave thereunto."

A theological cloud was now gathering over the Boston and Salem churches, and Mr. Pynchon concluded it was time to have a still deeper taste of the American wilderness. This led to a resolve to settle in the Connecticut Valley, and marks the beginning of the history of Springfield.

Soon after the colonists arrived in New England, an Indian chief from the Connecticut River called on Governor Winthrop at Boston, and urged that some of the English should visit the valley of the Connecticut and settle there. He described the soil as fertile, and promised to give eighty beaver skins yearly to settlers who came to the valley. This invitation, though not accepted at the time, produced an impression on some of the colonists. And now, when the most desirable places about the Bay had been taken by emigrants, they felt cramped, and there was a longing for new plantings and perhaps better ones, for themselves and their increased stock of cattle. From many of the towns about Boston there came petitions to the General Court for authority to remove "themselves and their estates to the River of Connecticut," of whose attractions so much had been said.

CHICOPEE FALLS

One consideration that led William Pynchon and his associates to leave Roxbury and settle in the Connecticut Valley was the prospect of better trade. Another was his dislike for Boston's tendency to limit the qualifications of freemen, while at the same time the privileges of those in authority were expanded. Many other persons were similarly disturbed by this setting up of the "standing council for the term of life."

There had been much concern shown by the Bay authorities when the first suggestions were made to settle in the Connecticut Valley. They had even dismissed with a show of impatience Plymouth's proposal to join in a western trading expedition. They frowned, too, on the adventurous John Oldham with his visions of extraordinary gain. However, it seems quite possible that Mr. Pynchon gave Oldham substantial aid in exploring the Connecticut Valley. This is based on the fact that when Oldham's estate was settled it showed a considerable indebtedness to Mr. Pynchon.

There is little doubt that Mr. Pynchon came to the valley as early as 1635, to satisfy himself that it was a region such as he and his followers would take permanent pleasure in for a future home. Until he had made certain the advantages of the place for his beaver trade, it is hardly probable that a man of Pynchon's caution would hazard a venture with so much peril as the removal of his family and property from the Bay to the river involved.

John Cable came here from the Bay in 1635 with John Woodcock and built a small house on the west side of the Connecticut and south of the Agawam River, in a meadow, which, for that reason, was long known as "House Meadow." These men occupied the house for a time, and the "old Indian ground" about it, but abandoned it later.

The Springfield pioneers have been represented as coming to their new home by way of the "Old Bay Path," but some historians claim this path to Boston was not opened until 1673, nearly forty years later. Old records show that in 1647 the board of townsmen instructed the surveyor to "open a Horseway over the meadow to the Bay path." This indicates that probably the Indians did have a trail to the Connecticut at Agawam at the time Pynchon first came to the region.

English explorers of that early period discovered that the site of Woodstock, Connecticut, was in a rich corn region, where the grain was stored in Indian "barns" or cellars with baked clay walls. From Woodstock old trails branched off in all directions. It was an Indian trail center. Governor Winthrop, of Massachusetts, was supplied with corn in 1630 by Indians, who carried it in skins on their backs to the Bay. This early supply train proceeded from Woodstock past the sites of such places as Grafton and South Framingham, and along the north bank of Charles River, after which they continued to Cambridge and Boston. These Indians did not break through an untrodden forest. They took the trail known later as the Old Connecticut Path, which had been developed from an English bridle path for horses and cattle.

One trail from the Woodstock center continued from there to Springfield, and another to the Falls on the Connecticut above Holyoke. There was also an Indian trail which was an offshoot from the Old Connecticut Path, and among other places ran through what is now Springfield, Brimfield, Warren, and West Brookfield. Pynchon may have used this branch but it is generally agreed that when Mr. Pynchon approached the Connecticut Valley on his preliminary expedition in 1635, he came by the Old Connecticut Path. With him he had an Indian interpreter and one other companion.

It was at once apparent to him that he would not be content to settle his Roxbury company below the other Connecticut plantations, and he decided to prospect. So he ascended the "grate" river until he came to the mouth of the Agawam, where he found Indians that were skilled beaver hunters. He was unaware that he had pushed far enough north to be outside of the Connecticut jurisdiction, and he struck a bargain with these Indians, who had a fort on a hill overhanging the east bank of the river, and who had extensive planting grounds on the west side of the Connecticut south of the Agawam River.

This bargain was completed in July, 1636, by a deed from two ancient Indians of Agawam for themselves and other Indian proprietors, conveying to William Pynchon and others, and their heirs and associates forever, a large part of the territory now occupied by Springfield, Longmeadow, West Springfield and Agawam. The signing of the deeds was quite a ceremony, with a company of at least thirteen Indians who put their marks on paper for the first time. As they crowded about the table they seemed to have no difficulty in thinking of designs to stand for their signatures. For instance, one drew a canoe, and another a bow and arrow. Besides the Indians apparently two of the white men could not write and had to make their marks to serve in place of signatures, just as the savages did. This deed was fully explained to the Indians by Haughton, an Indian interpreter from the Bay, who was perfectly understood by them.

They received an adequate consideration according to the values of that time, and were never dissatisfied with the bargain. For the lands sold by the Indians they received eighteen fathoms of wampum, eighteen coats, eighteen hatchets, eighteen hoes, and eighteen knives; and reserved to themselves the ground then planted, and liberty to take fish and deer, ground nuts, walnuts, acorns and a kind of wild peas. If any of the white men's cattle spoiled the Indians' corn they were to pay its worth. One of the other specifications was that hogs were not to cross the Agawam River except in acorn time. Wrutherna, one of the Indians, received from Mr. Pynchon two coats as an extra consideration. Of the fifteen articles in the agreement signed by the planters the first three have a special significance. They read:

"Firstly—We intend, by God's grace, as soon as we can with all convenient speed to procure some godly and faithful minister with whom we purpose to join in church covenant to walk in all the ways of Christ.

"Secondly—We intend that our town shall be composed of forty families, or if we think after to alter our purpose it shall not exceed the number of fifty families, rich and poor.

"Thirdly—Every family shall have a convenient proportion for a house lot, as we shall see meet for every ones quality and estate."

By the limitation of the town to forty families it is evident that the original planters intended to make the town a compact settlement and not one of scattered farms, separated from each other by long distances. This was essential for mutual safety, living as they did in the midst of an Indian neighborhood, and so remote from the protection of the older settlements.

Each head of a family was to have a house-lot and an allotment of planting-grounds, pasture, meadow, marsh, and timber land. Taxes were to be levied on land only. William Pynchon, John Burr and Henry Smith were given forty acres of meadowland south of the "End Brook," to be exempt from taxation on account of money paid out by them in founding the town. No man but Pynchon was allowed to have ten acres in his house-lot. Henry Smith, whose wife was Pynchon's daughter Ann, drew up the agreement. He seems to have been a man of notable character and reliability.

Mr. Pynchon left his men to plant and to build a house in the meadow about half a mile above the mouth of the Agawam River on the south side. He himself hastened back to the Bay. The house was built at the common expense and cost six pounds. It sheltered some of the first arrivals in 1636 and was still standing forty years later. When the rest of the settlers came a few probably traveled overland, but with practically only an Indian trail to follow it is probable that most of them with their families and goods came in the large shallops, sailing vessels of those times that could be sailed and poled up a shallow river like the Connecticut. It was not simply the danger from floods that induced the settlers to change the proposed site of their town, as some traditions have it. It was also because the Indians had cornfields on the west side which would be trespassed on by the live stock of the new settlers. Another difficulty was the Indians' demand of a large sum for their right in the lands on the west bank and insisting they should have a great shallop which the English needed.

The year 1636 was a busy and trying one for Mr. Pynchon. Besides being on the General Court Board of Commissioners to govern for one year the plantations that might be started in the Connecticut Valley, he had to take full charge of the transportation of his party and their household goods, and he advanced a large part of the money needed.

The March session of the General Court was full of excitement. Lack of security on account of the restless Indians was one thing, and special religious meetings of certain uneasy spirits in their houses of worship was another. This year, 1636, may be called the exodus year to the Connecticut Valley. Parties from the east were plodding through the wilderness to establish new homes at Hartford, Windsor, Springfield and Wethersfield all that spring and summer. Governor Winthrop's "Blessing of the Bay" sailed from Boston for the Connecticut River late in April, and about the same time most of the Roxbury pioneers betook themselves to the Massachusetts woods. Both the "Blessing of the Bay" and a vessel that belonged to John Winthrop, Jr., carried goods for the Roxbury party, and the first of the band to reach the journey's end arrived between April 26 and May 14. This instalment included at least a dozen families, and there was a horse litter which was the only practical vehicle for the aged or indisposed amid the forest tangles. Cows and pigs were included in this pioneer procession, while the armed outpost led the way over the pine plains or down sylvan ravines to clear away obstructions or scout for savages. As for the red men, there is no reason to doubt that the party was well received at the Indian villages along the trail.

The General Court early passed a law that all dwellinghouses should be built within half a mile of the meetinghouse, and first settlers, except in a few special cases, condensed the population within what they thought safe limits. The street on which the houses were built followed the general course of the river, and the house-lots were on the west side of the street, and with some exceptions, were eight or ten rods wide. All of the house-lots extended from the street to the river, and each had an allotment on the east side of the street of the same width as the house-lot.

Construction of the first Springfield houses probably followed along lines with which the early settlers were familiar in England. The roofs were thatched with the best materials for that purpose which could be found and the sides were of saplings set upright, with twigs woven through them and daubed with clay. This served until boards could be sawed. Sometimes the houses were set against a hill and so received more protection from the weather.

The land east of the street and adjoining it was called in the allotments the "Hasseky Marsh." Farther east was usually an allotment of the same width of upland covered more or less with forest. Very early the "Hasseky Meadow" was crossed by a road or path about two rods wide running east and widening after passing the meadow. This road crossing the marsh was made passable by logs and was called a "corduroy" road. At its easterly end it was probably connected with the path leading to the Bay long known as the "old Bay Road."

Some of the early settlers came here from the Connecticut towns down the river. Windsor, Hartford and Wethersfield each had some representatives among Springfield's early inhabitants. Such settlers could avail themselves of the river as a way of travel. Boats, or as they were usually called canoes, were in frequent use for the carriage of goods and persons. Trees that were suitable for use in making boats were called "canoe" trees and the cutting of such trees was restricted by a vote of the plantation.

For the accommodation of persons who wished to pass to and from the town by the river there were three landing places, one at the foot of what is now Cypress Street, called the upper landing; another at the foot of Elm Street, called the middle landing; and the third at the foot of York Street, known as the lower landing. To each of these a street or lane led from the Main Street. The street leading to the middle landing was the same that conducted to the training-place, part of which was afterward used as a burial place. This street, the Elm Street of our day, was first one rod wide, but soon was widened to two rods. Later, wharves were built at all three landing places.

Probably most of the settlers who came early to Springfield came by land. Some of them brought their families and goods. The journey was a serious undertaking, but as an emigrating family went on they began to discover signs of civilized life; the smoke from the chimney of a rude cabin might catch their attention and they would begin to realize that they were near to old neighbors and friends. They might follow the course of a small brook, since called Garden Brook, and descend a slope into the valley. They sought to find first the one man whom they had known in England and with whom they had crossed the ocean. They found Mr. Pynchon's house, which had nothing striking or attractive about it to indicate that it was the house of the leader in this enterprise of founding a town in the wilderness. It was a one-story-and-a-half wooden structure, unpainted, with thatched roof. Mr. Pynchon gave the newcomers a cordial welcome to the hospitality of his house, and they were soon numbered among the settlers of the plantation. By such recruiting the population of the place was gradually increased.

The dress of the period expressed the honest simplicity of the Puritan religion. Most of the troopers and young men wore jerkins or waistcoats of green cotton, caught at the waist with either red tape or a leather band. Over this some would wear a sleeveless jacket held at the neck with hooks and eyes, and lined with cotton. As the migration to Springfield was through a wilderness at the time of a possible rainy spring, some of the party may have been clad in an uncomfortable warm doublet, and had hose of leather, lined with oiled skin. In such a case they would abandon their large, conical broadbrims for red-knit Puritan caps that were lighter. The half boot was worn freely, and Mr. Pynchon was likely to have on great boots that were a luxury limited by law to a person whose estate was at least £200. Broad, white collars of linen were much worn, but not on such an expedition.

The women had strong, simple gowns with hoods, capes, high necks and neckcloths. Gowns were homemade, and drooped primly to the stout boots. The law forbade short sleeves and bare arms, and bunches of green ribbon, but there is plenty of evidence in the pioneer life of New England that neither the ingenuity of man, nor the dangers of wild beasts or wilder men, kept the New England woman from reflecting in her attire something of the "grace and taste that Heaven sheds on her."

There must have been much of the picturesque in the journey from the Bay to the encampment at a hamlet of wigwams, and of marked contrast between the fair-faced matron and the leather-dressed squaw. No doubt, too, there was a mutual curiosity between the soft-voiced strangers in the psalm-singing circle around the campfire, and the wondering savages before their wigwams.

The emigration was one of families, and even children were not lacking. For instance, there were Mr. Pynchon's son, John, and his daughter, Mary, neither of whom had reached the age of twelve years, but they could at least walk some of the way, and at other times perch on horseback. Mr. Pynchon had secured an interpreter, through whom he could communicate with the Indians, and the great journey was accomplished without accident or serious delay.

Mr. Pynchon was no doubt too busy with the affairs of the plantation to travel about the valley to any extent during the first year. He wrote to John Winthrop, Jr.: "I will hasten to settle myself at Agawam as soon as I can, and then I shall see all the plantations." He was even then shipping goods to the younger Winthrop.

By the closing in of winter, Mr. Pynchon probably had his house far enough advanced to shelter his own family and possibly others. The pine forests on the great plain east and north of the new village were nearly free from underbrush owing to the Indians' annual autumn burnings. One purpose that these served was the greater ease of travel which was secured. Oak and chestnut trees, however, were carefully protected from fire. The time of the burnings coincided with the dreamy Indian summer, and with the fire climbing from tree to tree up the mountainsides, driving the game before it, the sight must have been very romantic, especially at night.

During the first year the settlers were unable to secure a minister and Mr. Pynchon collected the little flock at his house and conducted divine service. He wrote his sermons and his young son often took summaries of them.

It pleased the Agawam Indians in their fort on Long Hill to see the English settling near them, for they thus acquired powerful allies against warlike tribes to the south and west, and it increased the value of their planting grounds. The Indians' name for Springfield, including the Chicopee Plains, was Nayasset.

John Oldham was killed by the Indians near Block Island a few days after the Agawam deed was signed and a terrible struggle with the savages followed. In May, 1637, war was declared at Hartford against the Pequots. Mr. Pynchon was not present, but it was voted that his shallop should be taken for use in the warfare.

The new plantation now had quite a number of houses along the west side of the present Main Street, and these were tolerably well for-

ANCIENT SPRINGFIELD MILE-STONE
On the Boston Road, near the United
States Armory

tified. But the dwellers lived in constant fear, and if an attack had been made at that time they might easily have been exterminated. Their safety depended largely on the Agawam and Woronoco Indians, who showed no disposition to fight. In fact, they had looked on the whites from the start as allies. It was an exciting and trying year, for no one knew at what moment the entire Indian population might rise and join the Pequots in a war of extermination. Is it any wonder that house building and land clearing and the opening of Main Street were attended with an ever-present sense of insecurity?

Agawam Plantation

CHAPTER IV

Agawam Plantation

Not until over a year passed was the first article of the original town compact carried out and a minister secured. Reverend George Moxon, of Boston, arrived at Agawam, as Springfield was then called, in the autumn of 1637, bringing with him a wife and two daughters. He was a short, stout man, thirty-five years of age, and Mr. Pynchon was a personal friend. His coming was an occasion of great rejoicing, for which the allotment of land and clearing of forests were only preliminaries, because what the settlers had most in mind was to establish and spread the Kingdom of God in the New World. A belief was abroad in those times that America was a peculiar land favored by the Almighty, and many of the laws repugnant to modern ideas of freedom and justice were designed to hasten the day when their hopes would be realized.

The coming of Mr. Moxon was very timely because it occurred in a season of general thanksgiving throughout New England at the overthrow of the Pequots. Now, with all their trials and anxieties, there was more blue sky than clouds above them, and Agawam observed October 12, its first day of thanksgiving, with renewed confidence.

It is very difficult to form any adequate conception of Mr. Moxon's character, or the value of his ministerial labors, but from the declared purpose of the first settlers to get "some godly and faithful minister" and from the fact that he had been long and intimately known by Mr. Pynchon, it can fairly be inferred that he was a man of more than ordinary ability and character. The parishioners had confidence in him, else they would not have chosen him in 1638 to be a deputy representing them in the General Court at Hartford, within which jurisdiction Springfield was then supposed to fall. Another token of their regard is found in their assigning him a home-lot of nearly double the usual width, and in 1639, by a voluntary assessment, they built him a house that had the luxury of both a porch and a study. The house was to be thirty-five feet long and fifteen feet wide with stairs into cellar and chamber, and double chimneys at the sides of the cellar. This house was located on the westerly side of Main Street near what is now Vernon Street. John Alline was ready to undertake getting the thatch for the roof. There was careful consideration, too, for the daubing of the house and chimneys. Here the minister lived during the last thirteen years of his Springfield residence. In the spring of 1638, when there were at least fifteen men in Agawam, it had been voted that the expenses of fencing his home-lot on the Main Street, and of building his house, should fall in part on those who joined the plantation later.

Springfield's records of many early town meetings are unfortunately lost, and not until the spring of 1638 can we secure any definite idea of the course taken in local legislation. But actually every phase of it was more or less a reflection of English civilization. One of the important offices was that of church warden. Mr. Pynchon had been a warden of the parish at Springfield, England, and from the English conception of this office came the New England "Select Townsman." It may be said with some local pride that the hard rules of the Bay were materially modified from the beginning. There was little or no religious persecution, no clamping of the tongue with split sticks, no brandings of the forehead, and yet the scheme of parental supervision of men's movements was strictly adhered to. Nor is there any evidence for quite a number of years that "townsmen" were appointed with discretionary powers of governing. There was no need of selectmen, with the whole body of the freemen regularly in session once a month.

Wampum, as used by the Indians, served both for money and ornament. It was brought to Plymouth in 1627. Roger Williams wrote describing it a few years later. The Long Island Indians were the discoverers of its charms. In actual substance it was sea shells polished and shaped. Later the Block Island Indians and others became skillful in this money bead-making. The beads varied in color and value. There were black or dark purple beads, and there were the white beads which were the most numerous and the least valuable. Six of the white beads or three of the dark ones passed for a penny, and six feet of the white shell beads were worth five shillings. The dark beads were of double the value of the white, and they were entitled to the name wampumpeag. The wampum, because of its convenience, won the favor of the fur trade, and was largely used by the Indians themselves in the eastern colonies as far south as Virginia. There was even imitation wampum made of white porcelain for sale to the Indians. The various colored sea shell money was so plenty that the English, French and Dutch bought furs and other things with it for six hundred miles north and south from New England.

Meanwhile the prices for wampum continued nominally the same for many years; but as the supply exceeded the demand the value gradually became less and less. Massachusetts tried to provide remedies, but they were not a success. The white beads in some instances sold for money at twenty-four for a penny, and the black beads, too, felt the decline. The law had failed. It was repealed, and wampum was without a legal price. Silver coins were scarce and there was nothing satisfactory to take the place of wampum. Hence it continued to be much used in the towns along the Connecticut and in other parts of New England.

Wampum was often paid at ferries and inns instead of money. When a man settled a tavern bill on a journey he did not take out a purse of coins, but strings of wampum and loose beads. Innkeepers and ferrymen received so much of the shell currency that they complained of their losses, for there were large quantities that could not be disposed of as fast as received.

William Pynchon, and afterward his son John, were extensively engaged in trade with both Indians and whites, and they dealt more largely in wampum than any other traders, either above or below Springfield. They bought bushels at a time of the loose shell beads, and employed the women and children of the town to string them at home. The pay was three half pence for a fathom of six feet. Nearly 20,000 fathoms were strung at this rate. John Pynchon sold wampum to individuals he had licensed to trade with the Indians, and some of them bought to the value of one hundred and twenty-five pounds sterling at a time.

The Pynchons' accounts with the Indians were always kept in fathoms and hands, or fathoms, hands and pence; never in shillings and pence. They made use of compound addition and subtraction not found in arithmetics.

The Indians used some of their shell beads to make belts, girdles, scarfs, head-bands, bracelets, necklaces, and pendants for the ears. Besides, they contrived attractive bead caps, aprons and rich girdles. To make such a girdle, about 2,300 beads were required.

During the first three years of the Agawam plantation's existence, William Pynchon was a great traveler, both in the Connecticut Valley and the Bay country, and his impressive figure with its strange garb was a familiar sight to the Indians. Gradually, as acquaintance ripened with this stern horseman who haunted the bridle-path, he became to the Indians a personification of justice.

Farther down the river there rode in the valley another horseman, Captain John Mason, whose faith in the Indians was rooted to his sword-hilt, and the Indians feared him. The Pynchon and Mason policies toward the red men conflicted at all points. Neither had a high opinion of the Indian, but the founder of Springfield treated them with consideration and fairness, while the Connecticut man was continually crushing their sense of justice. A strange long-drawn-out controversy developed between Hartford and Springfield, full of bitter personalities. It even outlived the lives of those most warmly engaged.

Captain Mason was the popular hero of the Pequot War, although the methods he used were those of extermination. Nevertheless, his exploits were heralded abroad, and his reputation must have been a source of personal gratification. He had been an English soldier in the Netherlands, and may have known Pynchon at Dorchester, where both first settled in New England. Mason had from the start a contempt of the Indian as a fighting animal, while Pynchon was a student and lawyer, and believed that only through a primitive code of ethics could amicable relations exist between the English and the red men.

In March, 1638, Captain Mason called on William Pynchon at his Agawam home. It was a meeting of two notable men and was held in the first house that the settlers built. Mason was accompanied by some armed troopers, and a Nonotuck Indian. "I am come," he said to Mr. Pynchon, "to get corn from the Indians, and have already traded some at Woronoco, and I had purposed to meet you at Nonotuck. Instead I met this Indian here at Agawam, and would have

traded some corn with him yesterday night, but he says he dare not
without your leave. He said he was afraid of you, as are also the
Indians on the riverside, for they have stolen 13 coats that belong
to you, and some cloth, but whereas they say they stole only two
pieces of cloth, you say they stole six pieces. I told them I thought
you were not angry, and would not harm them, and now I pray that
you tell this Indian of Nonotock that you will not be angry with him
if he traded corn down the river."

Mr. Pynchon at once said, "I know of no reason why the Nonotuck Indian or any other should fear me. I believe they no more fear
me than they do their own shadow." Then he proposed that the
conference be carried on apart, as it would not do to let the Indians
know the extent of the English distress for food. "I care not who
knows," Mason said. But Mr. Pynchon ordered his trader to open
the trading-house door, and the party went in. There were four of
them—Captain Mason and an associate, and Mr. Pynchon with his
trader.

"This is what I will do," Mr. Pynchon said. "I will propose a
rate for carrying down the corn, and a lesser rate to bring it to my
house, and give them a choice."

At that the captain flew into a great passion and exclaimed:
"What hurt can it be to you? I pray, sir, let me know, for it is a
dark riddle to me."

Parson Moxon, who had been sent for, arrived at this juncture,
and Mr. Pynchon explained the situation, adding that Mason had
given the Woronoco Indians wampum in advance, and would have
done the same at Nonotuck if Pynchon had not objected. The
parties were testing Captain Mason's corn-bag when Henry Smith
came to the trading-house, and the discussion was renewed.

Then Mr. Moxon said, "An Indian promise is no more than to
have a pig by the tail."

This, by the way, is the only quotation in existence of anything
Moxon ever said.

It was agreed by Mr. Pynchon and his friends that advance payments in buying corn from the Indians were the worst way to get a
supply. He had been having a recent experience in connection with
a debt they owed him. What they did was to stay away and avoid
keeping to their promise, and Mr. Pynchon said, "Thus will they deal

with these Connecticut men, who will say afterward, by way of excuse, that they were fools, not knowing what they did."

Captain Mason at last began to harken to Mr. Pynchon, who agreed to aid him as best he could. Thereupon the Nonotuck Indian, who was loitering about, came at the call of Captain Mason, and Mr. Pynchon addressed this up-river Indian, telling him the captain was a sachem who wanted to trade corn. But the Indian protested that much of their corn was ruined by the snow, and that the river was too high for transporting any to Hartford. It was evident that the Indians knew the stress the English were under, and were trying to get more for their corn. There had been other similar occasions, and if corn went up, it did so on the issue of supply and demand, which holds good in most countries and times.

Mr. Pynchon now began making daily displays to the Indians of both cloth and wampum of the best, in exchange for corn if they would bring any, but still they put him off with excuses on purpose to make him raise the price. And he said, "Indeed it would weary any one to hear what crafty pleadings they have used for this purpose." The upshot of all this was a Pynchon-Mason interview from which they parted in anything but a cordial spirit. Captain Mason, in particular, was very much displeased, and made an abrupt departure.

Three days later the General Court of Connecticut issued an order for Mr. Pynchon's presence at the next session and a trial followed with very serious charges. Commissioners were assigned to hear the case, and the founder of Springfield with several witnesses, and with Reverend George Moxon as his counsel, put in a full defence. Mr. Pynchon was completely taken aback by the spirit and extent of the charges. He was represented as one who had traded on the misfortunes and privations of Connecticut towns that were less fortunate. For instance, he had raised the price of corn to Connecticut's disadvantage, and was holding the Indians to their bargains, all for his private gain. He refused to lend a canoe to a Woronoco Indian, who was under contract with Captain Mason to take corn down the river. He kept the local tribes in abject fear of him that he might be considered the great English sachem of the Connecticut Valley. Lastly, he induced certain Mohawk runners to sell him some beaver skins, which were sent by Mohawk chiefs to the Connecticut authorities as gifts and tokens of good will.

As to the charge of dishonorable speculation in corn, the condition of the Agawam Plantation in the spring of 1638 was such that the five hundred bushels Mr. Pynchon had contracted for with the Indians were not more than Agawam itself needed. Actually, the food situation was as acute up the river as it was down. Mr. Pynchon in his own testimony affirmed that the whole population had been in severe straits, both of persons and cattle, for two or three months together, and the wants of the plantation forced some to give malt to pigs in order to save the creatures' lives.

Three or four persons were in consultation planning to leave home for a while to earn their bread elsewhere until corn might be had at Agawam. Some women gave their poultry and swine English grain intended only for seed. Mr. Pynchon's wants were so great that he sometimes had no more than half a bushel of corn in the house for his family and cattle, and when a bushel or less was brought in to trade, he "as much prized God's mercy and Providence therein, and was as glad of it as at other times of twenty bushels."

All the while the Indians were willing enough to trade, if they might have their price. But that, Mr. Pynchon refused to give, and insisted refusal was for the public good. He said, "Though my family did urge me to raise the price, partly in mercy to my cattle, and partly to save their own lives, I held to my course." His family told him he had lost some cattle already and was sure to lose more if corn were not provided. "I found their word true," he said, "and my wife, walking more amongst the cattle than I did, professed it was her daily grief to see them in that poor, starving condition for want of corn, and did urge me to raise the price in pity for the cattle, whatever the cost. Yea, at that time I wrote a letter for advice with regard to raising the price of corn. My family and cattle, and neighbors had spent our former supply, and whereas before I had depended on the payment of five hundred bushels promised by the Indians, my hopes were like to a spider's web. Therefore, I wrote for counsel what course I should take with those Indians. I neglected mine own cattle and family, and suffered that loss which might have helped with God's blessing."

When the time came for a trial before the commissioners, Mr. Pynchon was surprised to find that the chief witnesses, besides Captain Mason, were the very Agawam Indians with whom he had negotiated for the five hundred bushels of corn, and he might well have felt serious concern, for they were only too anxious to do anything that would relieve them of their bargain with him. Their chief accusation was that he kept them in continual fear. The court sustained Mr. Pynchon's appeal, and after it had been explained to the Indians, that the five hundred bushels of corn must be paid, he expressed his good will and cordial feeling to the group of dusky savages.

The next point taken up that involved them was the charge that Mr. Pynchon bought of Mohawk runners beaver intended as presents to the authorities at Hartford. Mr. Pynchon said he could not imagine that it was come as a gift "because they spoke of no such thing, but called for trade. Besides, a large part of these skins were such as were not fit for a gift to great sachems. One of the Indians brought seven sachem scalps and he was first at my house.

"Neither in likelihood could they expect such a thing because these Pequot Sachems were killed two days' journey on this side of where the Mohawks lived. It was too far, therefore, and it is most probable the beaver promised, was to give the telling of some pleasing thing, as is their ordinary manner when they want a favor. They had an interpreter, and all they said was that the Mohawks did much love the English, and would be in friendship with them and destroy all Pequots that came in their way, but mentioned no such gift of beaver."

Mr. Pynchon's accusers not only made an assault on his general character, but used hearsay evidence picked up on Agawam streets. Finally, the commisisoners, after hearing Mason, the Indians and the rest, called in Reverend Thomas Hooker and Reverend Samuel Stone as experts on the ethical question of Mr. Pynchon's conduct. They both said emphatically that Pynchon had broken his oath. He then got up and explained his mode of bargaining with the Indians, which avoided any advance payment of wampum. But that only stirred the ministerial ire the more.

Mr. Hooker's comment was that such an offer to the Indians was as good as nothing, for Mr. Pynchon knew the Indians were afraid of him, and would not fetch corn to any one else. "He would have the trade to himself with the corn in his own hands, and could bring all that water to his own mill, and so wreck the country at his pleasure."

This extraordinary conclusion took Mr. Pynchon completely aback. To be condemned by the famous ministers, Hooker and Stone, grieved and silenced him. The commission found him guilty, and showed no little prejudice in arriving at the verdict, which was that he had not been so careful to promote the public good in the trade of corn as he should have been, and ordered "that the said Pynchon shall with all convenient speed pay as a fine for his so failing, forty bushels of Indian corn, said corn to be delivered to the treasurer." This was pretty severe, and while the court was gracious enough to continue giving Mr. Pynchon the monopoly of the beaver trade at Agawam, the fine was a crushing blow to his influence in Connecticut affairs. He was present when the General Court fined him the forty bushels of corn, but apparently never attended again.

After his conviction he hastily prepared an "Apology," which was circulated in the valley towns. It is a complete defense against the charges of dishonest speculation, written in strong English, and is an invaluable survival of seventeenth century composition. Pynchon was condemned because he was thought to have selfishly raised the price of corn, and yet Captain Mason was counted a hero two months later because he chartered an Indian canoe fleet laden with corn, for which he paid twelve shillings a bushel, and was compelled to ride in the canoes to make sure of its delivery.

The Captain Mason theory of dealing with the Indians—wampum in one hand and the sword in the other, inspired what follows: "It is ordered that there shall be six men sent to the Woronoco Indians to declare that we have a desire to speak with them and learn why they said they were afraid of us, and if they will not come to us willingly, then compel them to come by violence. They can have two of the English as pledges in the meantime. The messengers are to trade with them for corn if they can."

The court ought not to have been at such a loss to explain the fear of the Indians. It might readily have been traced to a previous commission given to Captain Mason to go to Agawam and treat with the Indians of Woronoco concerning tribute toward the charges of wars to the value of one fathom of wampum a man. As a matter of fact the English had no right to levy a war tribute on the native tribes.

The serious differences that developed between Agawam and the towns farther down the river, compelled the settlers to face the question of secession from Connecticut jurisdiction. The conditions at Hartford were intolerable to Agawam. Mr. Pynchon had been a trader from the start, and was so recognized at the Bay. His purse was always opened when prospecting expeditions were proposed, and prominent men, both at the Bay and in Connecticut, knew the generous extent of his personal loans. He was one of the few rich men of his time who embarked to New England, and he very naturally had been chosen treasurer of Massachusetts. When he settled in the Connecticut Valley with his little company of associates, there was the same fitness that he should handle the corn and beaver of the region. No one hitherto had accused him of failure to keep his promises, or of making money at the public expense. Such charges showed plainly the disposition at Hartford to limit Agawam's influence as much as possible; and as Captain Mason not only was privileged to pass up the river and trade, but had a troop of armed men at his back to coerce the Indians, and as he visited Agawam ten times a year to drill the training-band, is it any wonder that secession was the unanimous desire of the plantation? However, a formal withdrawal was too serious an enterprise to undertake lightly. Mr. Pynchon was no longer a member of either the Boston or Hartford General Court. The town was the most remote outpost in the colony with numerous Indian tribes in the widespread back country. Connecticut might refuse to allow Mr. Pynchon to keep the trading-houses which he had built at Enfield Falls. There is an ancient map placing these houses on the eastern bank of the Connecticut, opposite King's Island, which can be seen up the river from the car windows in crossing the railroad bridge at Windsor Locks. The name given on the old map is a Dutch equivalent for "Fresh River," and it was bestowed by Adrian Block, who, in 1614, cruised up the stream in his small yacht, the "Onrust," a name that means "Restless" in English. He went on until the Enfield Falls stopped him. Ten years later the Dutch had begun to make somewhat frequent trading voyages to the river.

Mr. Pynchon not only shipped freight in his own sailboats, but often sent goods to and from the valley in other vessels. It was out of the question to send beaver overland to the Bay.

No meetinghouse had as yet been built at Agawam, and the middle ferry lane, later known as Elm Street, was not yet opened. Tree stumps and fallen timber here and there obstructed Main Street, and what was more discouraging was the fact that the plantation was largely made up of men not destined to remain long. Fully half the settlers who arrived in 1638 only stayed a few years.

Unlike most towns of the period, Agawam was founded by a devout and well-read Christian, who could preach a sermon or debate theology with the ablest divines. He and his companions, after careful consideration, decided to separate from Connecticut, and trust to the future. No formal declaration was issued for a while, but that did not prevent the news of the revolt spreading through all New England before the year ended.

Reverend Mr. Hooker took a leading part in the controversy that followed, and he was especially bitter in dealing with Mr. Pynchon. For instance, he said: "If Mr. Pynchon can devise ways to make his oath bind him when he will, and loosen him when he desires—if he can tell how, in faithfulness to engage himself in a civil covenant, and yet can cast it away at his pleasure, before he give it sufficient warrant more than his own word and will, he must find a law in Agawam for it. It is written in no law nor gospel that I ever heard." A commission investigated and a long private conference took place between friends of the two colonies, but no agreement was reached.

Mr. Hooker's indictment of Agawam was very much in the spirit of his testimony in the Pynchon trial. He said that Connecticut would not trouble itself very much over the loss of Mr. Pynchon, because "we know him from the bottom to the brim, and follow him in all his proceedings, and trace him in his private footsteps; only, we would have him and all the world to understand he does not walk in the dark to us."

The alienation of Connecticut had the effect of postponing the project of a New England confederation for some years. Pending the settlement of Agawam's political condition, the little plantation did not allow local affairs to go by default.

In September there was granted to John Searle, by consent of the rest of the inhabitants, a house-lot eight rods broad, extending from the town brook to the great river which lies near the pine swamp with the meadow. Where there was need for the accommodation of other farmers a cartway was reserved.

The vote for a meetinghouse lot was passed January 16, 1639, and forty rods were reserved for it. Much of the land was as yet unapportioned, and a good deal of time had to be devoted to its regulation. The rich meadows on the west side of the Connecticut, from opposite the upper ferry to the present York Street, were at first used only for grass and planting. At that time the Agawam had only one outlet and joined the Connecticut near the South End Bridge.

Each inhabitant, after harvest time in November, was allowed to put horses, cows and young cattle on the west side of the Connecticut River.

Eleven months after the Pynchon trial, Agawam put forth a formal declaration of its allegiance. The people had met and decided, "Being now by God's providence fallen into the line of the Massachusetts jurisdiction, and it being far to go thither, in such cases of justice as may fall out among us, do therefore think it meet by a general consent and vote, to ordaine Mr. William Pynchon to execute the office of a magistrate in this our plantation until we receive further direction from the General Court convening in the Massachusetts Bay." The usual magistrate's powers were given to Mr. Pynchon, including authority to summon juries of six instead of twelve for small offences, pending any action that might be made at Boston. Meantime the boundaries of the plantation had been verified by a committee which reported that the bounds of the plantation up the river on the west side were at a brook above the great meadow which is opposite a point about a quarter of a mile above "the mouth of Chicopee river."

The first town meetings were probably held in Mr. Pynchon's house, for his was the largest, and nothing more like a democratic communism has had an extended trial in our history than the original Massachusetts plantations. The nature of this common proprietorship in land and local political procedure becomes apparent by glancing through the town acts. It was a genuine democracy and not even a selectman stood between its inhabitants and their desires. They met at least once a month, and with the simple election of a moderator and clerk the machinery of government was complete.

In October, 1638, the town voted that "no trees should be cut down or taken away by any man in the compass of ground from Mill river upward to John Readers Lot, which parsell of ground is appointed for house lots." No inhabitant was permitted to sell his canoe to outside parties. An infringement of this order brought down a reprimand on three young fellows, and they promised to redeem and bring the canoes to the plantation again within five months.

The town was laid out in a peculiar manner for New England, where a twenty-rod road was usual. This was incidentally of service to a community exposed to Indians. It could be stockaded, and cattle could be safely pastured on the broad street. The original Agawam seems to have had no such street, and the plantation was housed on the narrow plateau that stretched between the great river and the swamp at the foot of a sharp bluff. For time out of mind, until recent years, there was a brook running along Springfield's business street, and no doubt the planters found it there in 1636. It was on the east side of the street, and in the first records it is called a "ditch." It served as a drain for the marsh, and there are frequent references to work on it. Thus, in 1639, the town voted that all who have a ditch before their doors shall keep it "well scowred for the ready passage of the water, that it may not be pent up to overflow the meadow." Care of the ditch was insisted on, and two years later we find: "it is ordered that every inhabitant shall scower and make a ditch the breadth of his lot before his door, which to to be done by the last of next May, on the penalty of 5 shillings for every default." The inhabitants were often remiss in keeping the ditch open. Fines due in 1645 were suspended, and an extra month allowed in which to do the cleaning, "and if any are defective the penalty is to be paid to Goodman Prichard." It is doubtful whether the natural brook ran along the course of what has since been known as the Town Brook. The lowest ground was then nearer the bluff and probably the brook ran about where Dwight Street is now located. A fence was built in front of the houses, and no buildings were allowed between it and the ditch.

Once a month came Training Day. Henry Smith was the first "serjant," and he named the day of the meetings, and chose a corporal. Men who absented themselves forfeited twelve pence, and all above fifteen years of age were counted for soldiers. One thing not allowed was the selling or giving powder to Indians.

Community of interests failed to prevent friction between man and man, and the right to quarrel was exercised from the start.

HAMPDEN COUNTY COURT-HOUSE, ERECTED 1874.

William Pynchon, as magistrate, records in November, 1639, a meeting to try causes by jury. One suit was by Pynchon himself against Thomas Mirrick for "Not delivering back the boards lent him." The jury decided that the defendant should "make good 3 such like boards as we find not yet delivered with the rest."

William Pynchon was always the moderator of the town meeting, and thus the lines of his political and judicial activities were often blended. As moderator he would put a question proposed by the person being tried; while as magistrate he summoned the jury to try the case, administer oaths, and receive and record verdicts. Owing to the scanty number of men in the plantation the same blending of responsibility existed in the jury, and a person might be a witness and serve on the jury at the same time.

But there were also persons of another sort who made pests of themselves. Such was John Woodcock, who had a lawsuit at Hartford, in which Mr. Moxon was a witness against him. He was defeated in this Hartford suit, and being an unprincipled fellow, sought revenge by circulating a report that the minister had taken a false oath. This produced a decided sensation among the good people of Agawam Plantation, as Springfield was then called. Woodcock was summoned to appear before Mr. Pynchon, the magistrate, to answer for the slander, and as he was anxious to avoid a trial before a jury of the neighbors, to whom both were well known, he wanted this difference tried by a private hearing at Windsor or Hartford, which were the nearest settlements down the river.

Mr. Moxon "referred himself to the judgment of the plantation present whether it were fitter to be heard by a private reference down the river or tried here publicly by a jury." The general vote of the plantation was, "that, seeing the matter is public, it should be publicly heard and tried here by a jury."

Liberty was granted John Woodcock to produce his witnesses a fortnight later. Also, at that time, John Woodcock was warned to answer for his "laughing in sermon time this day at the lecture," and he was to answer for his misdemeanor of idleness. The jury returned a verdict in Mr. Moxon's favor for six pounds, thirteen shillings, four pence.

It may fairly be taken for granted that in the eleven years Mr. Moxon was still to spend in Springfield, he was engaged in the ordinary pastoral duties, and the routine, of course, included preaching Sabbath morning and afternoon, besides delivering the usual lecture every Thursday, at half-past ten in the forenoon.

Strangely enough, William Pynchon was subjected to a second trial on the old charge of speculation in trade to the detriment of the public. The charge was brought by certain members of the church at Windsor, Connecticut, with intent to withdraw from him the right hand of Christian fellowship. It seems likely that the summons to appear there was a manipulation of Captain Mason's friends. He was a member of the Windsor church, and to please him, they may have attempted a demonstration against the Agawam magistrate for its moral effect. There was a close affiliation between Agawam and Windsor during the first few years, and when Mr. Pynchon left Roxbury he took a letter from the church there to the one at Windsor.

September 6, 1640, the church assembled to determine whether Mr. William Pynchon's answers were satisfactory to the brethren's offense at his failings in the trust of trading corn for the supply of the country, contained in five articles presented to him by the said brethren. To the first charge Mr. Pynchon answered that he could not get any quantity at the price in the order. The response of the church was that he could not resolve so great a matter in one or two days' experience.

The church determined that Mr. Pynchon's judgment was not sound and that his answers were not satisfactory. At the same time Captain Mason's way of dealing with the situation was judged as "lawfull, though Mr. Pynchon thinks otherwise."

About a month was spent by Mr. Pynchon preparing a protest against the church decision. It was a good specimen of special pleading, and showed a keen, logical mind, and a sense of justice which even the ill will of a whole province could not shake.

Mr. Pynchon's first letter to Hartford informing the authorities of the unwillingness of the Indians to bring in corn, had given great offense, because it contained a recommendation as to what policy to pursue. And this also figured against Pynchon at Windsor, and he asks, "Can a church or anyone deny me liberty to expound my own thoughts by way of advice to the magistrates?" The case reduces itself to this: Agawam was on the border of the planting-grounds. Mr. Pynchon was the natural man to furnish Connecticut with corn. He made a contract with the river towns by which he could receive no commission or speculative gains, whatever the price might be, and he found the conditions difficult to fulfill. Captain Mason, the warrior, was then sent up with an armed force to trade and, of course, there was trouble.

After the Windsor church had condemned Mr. Pynchon, he appealed to Mr. Eliot and the church at Roxbury. An investigation followed, and presently the Roxbury church notified Mr. Pynchon's accusers, after a thorough examination, that Mr. Pynchon was completely vindicated. Thus the Connecticut General Court and the Windsor Church condemned Mr. Pynchon, and the Massachusetts General Court and the Roxbury church stood by him.

One of the early lacks was a blacksmith and for ten years Springfield was without any. Then it paid in wheat one of its citizens to build a blacksmith's shop twelve feet wide, sixteen feet long and "five foot stud betwixt joints" and equip it with a chimney and forge, one door and a window, with a beam "in the midst."

The next move was to get a blacksmith, and Mr. Pynchon bought one. That came about in this way: There had been war between Scotland and England, and the Scotch were defeated in the battle of Dunbar, and as a result many were taken to England as prisoners and sold for a certain period into slavery. So Mr. Pynchon, with the aid of an agent in London, bought a Scotch blacksmith, John Stewart, and soon he came across the sea to Springfield and was promptly put in charge of the new smithy, where from the start he was a great blessing. Time sped, and after a while his work had paid the expense of his voyage and for what Mr. Pynchon had spent, and then the town made him a present of the smithy.

Troubles of the Traders

CHAPTER V

Troubles of the Traders

At the April town meeting, in 1640, an important vote was passed changing the town's name from Agawam, which is the Indian name for meadow, and substituting Springfield, the name of Mr. Pynchon's old home in England.

Feelings of mutual distrust between Springfield and Connecticut continued to linger. The latter was disposed to lay claim to lands over the Massachusetts line, and a veritable tempest was roused by the Connecticut Court which passed an order that Governor Hopkins should have the benefit of free trade at Woronoco and any place thereabout on the river. All other persons were to be restrained for a period of seven years, and the land was to be bought for the Commonwealth. The region was the site of Westfield in the heart of the beaver grounds, and as soon as communication could be had with the Bay the situation was fully ventilated, and a letter was prepared by the General Court. This began with: "It is grevious to us to meet with any occasion that might cause differences to arise between your people and our standing in so near relation of friendship, neighborhood, and Christianity. Therefore our study is to remove the occasion of them on the first appearance. Now we have it certified that you have given leave to some of your people to set up a trading house at Woronoco which is known to be within our patent lying as much or more to the north than Springfield. We hear also, that you have granted to Mr. Robert Saltonstall a great quantity of land not far from Springfield which we conceive also belongs to us. We desire you to do us such right in redress hereof as you would expect from us in like case. We have thought meet on these occasions to intimate further that we intend, by God's help to know the certainty of our limits, to the end that we may neither intrench on the right of our neighbors, nor suffer ourselves and our posterity to be deprived of what rightfully belongs to us. Which we hope will be without offence to any."

Governor Hopkins and Mr. Saltonstall were becoming extensive traders, and under favor of the Connecticut Colony, were in a fair way to isolate Springfield. Hence the protest from the Bay did not arrive any too soon. With a warehouse built by Hopkins at Woronoco, and with Saltonstall enjoying grants of land near Enfield Falls, the plan to bring the trade of the valley to the door of Hartford was well under way. Considering the ill-feeling that was rife, we may well be impressed at the diplomacy which strove to loosen the tension of strained relations by way of the deference shown.

One result of all this was that, in 1638, William Pynchon was appointed by commissioners of the General Court "to have for this year full power and authority to govern the inhabitants at Springfield, and to hear and determine all causes and offenses, both civil and criminal, that reach not to life, limbs, or banishment according to the laws here established." This decree stood practically undisputed, but it left the question of river commerce open as a fruitful source of further contention.

During the two years after Springfield's declaration of independence from Connecticut, there was very little connection with the Bay. Its position had been unique, for it was not included in any tax rates levied at Boston, and was not represented at the General Court by deputies or the presence of a magistrate, nor is there any evidence that Mr. Pynchon attended court. Neither did Springfield appear in the official list of towns included in the four counties of Massachusetts. Mr. Pynchon was annually reëlected to his governing authority until the troublous times of 1650, and he was regularly chosen magistrate. He still continued the beaver trade, and he paid a license to the General Court for special trading privileges.

For some unexplained reason, it was not until 1647 that Springfield was included in any of the official lists of Massachusetts towns, and this inclusion was for brands on horses for each town, ordered to be set on one of the near quarters. There were five towns in the Colony then, beginning with "S," and the Springfield brand was a monogram composed of a "small s" and "p."

The influence of Mr. Pynchon over the local Indians was never lost, although his idea of their stability was far from flattering. In a letter to Governor Winthrop he advised dilatory means with the Indians, for he perceived it was their nature to be much provoked with the desire of revenge, but if means of delay were used, the edge of their revengeful desire was soon cooled. Thanks to Mr. Pynchon's sagacity, the Indian portion of this narrative is uneventful for some years. The relations of the Connecticut towns with the savages were not so assuring.

During the next few years a dozen or more new men arrived at Springfield, the most notable of whom were Deacon Samuel Chapin and Elizur Holyoke. Samuel Chapin became very prominent both in town and church. He was a man of affairs and a typical Puritan. Often he was made selectman, held positions of trust, and was the founder of a line of deacons who have been a credit to their ancestor. He was later immortalized by St. Gaudens' statue of a typical Puritan on his way to meeting, with a big Bible under one arm. This is perhaps Springfield's finest art treasure.

Thomas Cooper was another of the emigrating group—a useful man and a good fighter, whom the people of the valley held in high esteem. His personal influence with the natives was great, and it was his over-confidence in their fidelity to Springfield which finally cost him his life. Elizur Holyoke was a young man, who soon developed sterling qualities that have been transmitted to a family of great importance in New England.

The second immigration to Springfield in this period was the determining event of the plantation history. The first arrivals, aside from Mr. Pynchon's relatives and personal friends, were ignorant and adventurous. Typical ones were John Cable and John Burr, who soon gave up the struggle and drifted down the river. New blood was an imperative necessity. The period was full of the smaller complications of pioneer life, and was, on the whole, anything but promising.

It is recorded, in 1640, that Goody Gregory, the wife of Henry Gregory, who had only been connected with the settlement about a year, was accused by John Woodcock of "swearing before God I could break thy head!" She did not attempt any defense, and was fined twelve pence, in default of which she was to sit three hours in the stocks. The fine was much below the amount prescribed in colonial laws for this offense.

Another new arrival, Samuel Hubbard, was licensed to keep an ordinary. This was sanctioned by a vote in town meeting. The ordinary was a tavern or eating house which, in the seventeenth century, was often used for gambling after meals. It was very fashionable among the youth of that time. Hubbard was also commissioned to lay out all lots in the plantation.

John Leonard was appointed surveyor to see the highways cleared and kept in repair, and free from all stubs, sawpits or timber. Henry Smith and Thomas Mirrick were given power to restrain the Indians from breaking up any new ground, or from planting any that was broken up last year. Also they were "to pitch up stakes so the Indians might be limited from enlarging themselves in the swamp."

The importance of the marsh was further magnified by the opening of a highway in the spring of 1640 across the "hassakey" meadow. This was State Street. It had been voted, in 1638, that land for a highway be reserved out of the marshy ground of Thomas Woodford's lot.

The provision about canoes was broadened in 1640 by an order that none be sold to parties outside the plantation. In December leave was granted to Mr. Holyoke, William Warriner, and Henry Burt to seek out for their use each of them a canoe tree. Warriner made bad use of his permit and was afterward fined for selling his canoe.

In 1641 orders were passed requiring fire ladders with "15 rungs or steps at least." Each house was to have a ladder. One thing forbidden was the carrying of fire uncovered through the streets. Another progressive step was the ordering of a foot path and stiles to be built at every man's lot end next to the great river.

It was during this year that one of the town's irrepressibles, John Woodcock, scored a victory over Henry Gregory in two suits for slander about some hogs. The damages were forty shillings and costs. On hearing the award Gregory was very indignant and exclaimed: "I marvel with what conscience the jury can give such damages!"

Mr. Moxon interfered, charging Gregory to "Take heed! take heed!"

This case was tried before a jury with Mr. Pynchon as magistrate; and in a community where means of diversion were few, it probably called together a goodly number of absorbed spectators.

One of the first buildings put up after the pioneers had been housed was a sawmill on Mill River. At the same time a temporary bridge was made across the stream, and in the spring of 1643 a more substantial one was substituted. The order for it was passed at the March town meeting, and provision was made for both a bridge and highway to the mill for the passage of carts and cattle. Those men who failed to do their share of work on the former bridge were to make it up in the present bridge and the way over the meadow.

In January, 1642, a second division of planting-ground was decreed. The apportionment "provided that those who have broken up ground there, shall have allowance such as two indiferent men shall judge equal." Single persons were to have 8 rods in breadth, married persons 10 rods in breadth, "bigger families 12 rods, to begin upward at the edge of the hill," which is now Chestnut Street.

One year later, Elizur Holyoke, Samuel Chapin, and a few others were chosen "to lay out the lands, both of upland and meadow on the other side of the great river where the Indians lived over all the meadows on Agawam, so far as shall amount to a hundred and fifty acres." Present inhabitants were to be satisfied, including Mr. Pynchon. Mr. Moxon was to have first choice of the allotments by consent of the plantation.

This allotment was soon annulled. One cause of trouble may have been the taking into consideration the estates and importance of the inhabitants in apportioning these lands. The wonder is that the rule worked at all. There are certain expressions occurring later which lead to the belief that the planters resorted to something similar to drawing cuts, boy fashion. But in the first year the rule was "unto him that hath shall be given."

The year 1640 closed with Springfield's first recorded marriage. The new arrival, Elizur Holyoke, led to the altar Mary Pynchon, daughter of William Pynchon. Holyoke was a man of no ordinary force of character, and the event must have made an impression on the swains of the valley. Within a few months after his arrival he had won the most lovely maiden of her day, if tradition is accepted, and the match carried with it certain considerations of a worldly character. Holyoke was about twenty-two years of age. His birthplace was near Tamworth Tower in Warwickshire, England, and he had come to New England with his father. Marriage was followed by the assignment of a very desirable lot between Worthington and Bridge streets. His father-in-law's large lot bounded his land on the north, and Henry Smith, who had married Ann Pynchon before the settlement of Springfield, was close by on the south. According to custom, Holyoke received allotments of meadow and upland opposite his lot on the east side of Main Street, also land on the west side of the Connecticut and planting-grounds elsewhere. The marriage was a happy event, and hundreds of descendants in America hold in reverence Elizur and Mary Holyoke. One thing for which they are remembered is that in a dark hour of Springfield's history they refused to return to England and give up the struggle for mastery in this valley. Now they rest in the beautiful Springfield Cemetery. It is well written on Mary Holyoke's tombstone:

"She that lies here was while she stood,
A very glory of womanhood."

In September, 1644, the town meeting took the important step of intrusting the management of affairs to a committee. For eight years the town had been governed without selectmen. Now a board of five were elected and given power for one year to "prevent anything they shall judge to be to the damage of the town, or to order anything they shall judge good for the town." To these five or any three of them was given power to serve complaints, to arbitrate controversies, to lay out highways, make bridges and especially order the making of the way over the marshy meadow, and see "to scowering of the ditches, and to the killing of wolves, and to the training of the children in some good calling, or any other thing they shall judge to be for the profit of the town." The new selectmen were comparatively young and poor so far as having any estate independent of the lands voted them by the town was concerned.

Town rates in 1645 were based on house-lots only. The town met the last Thursday in each month, and notices of special meetings given on lecture day were considered legal warning. The penalty for absence, or for leaving town meetings during the session without a permit, was half a bushel of Indian corn.

Numberless instances of caution on the part of these primitive guardians of public policy abound in the record books. Every householder was required to carefully attend to the sweeping of his chimney once every month for the winter time, and once in two months in summer. If a man neglected this, the town swept the chimney for him at his expense.

Mr. Moxon's ministry had proved a great success, for he seemed to have just the elements to keep in check the uneasy spirits that were inevitably drawn into adventurous enterprises of this sort. He was educated in England at Cambridge University, and was at Dorchester for a while before coming to Springfield.

One of Mr. Pynchon's letters that have been preserved is particularly worth quoting because it reveals his religious attitude. Ordinarily we think of him as so absorbed in affairs of business and trade that one might fancy his grand motive in coming to New England was simply to pluck plums of gold. The letter was written to Governor Winthrop in 1644, and begins with:

"I praise God we are all in good health and in peace in our plantation; and the Lord has added to us lately three or four young men that are Godly. The Lord has greatly blessed Mr. Moxon's ministry to the conversion of many souls and hitherto the Lord has preserved us in peace from enemies."

Mr. Pynchon waited for the grace of God to have its perfect work on such of his associates as were not members of the church. The people at the Bay had the habit of continually giving the divine agency an impetus by way of punishments visited on those not disposed to hasten into the fold. But in their attempt to stamp out heresy by closing the mouth of Error, they had only invited an ill-feeling that often came out at the public meetings, and sometimes found expression in harsh words against the ministers themselves. For these offenses a fine was imposed, and if there was a repetition, the offender had to stand openly two hours on a block four feet high on a lecture day, with a paper fixed on his breast, labeling him: "A Wanton Gospeler, written in capital letters, that others may fear and be ashamed of breaking out into like wickedness." This law applied to Springfield as it did to all Massachusetts towns, but advantage was not taken of the privilege.

Of all events in the history of the plantation, probably none caused deeper satisfaction than the definite prospect of owning a house of worship—not thatched like many houses on the street, but a veritable framed and windowed temple in the wilderness. It was in February, 1645, that the contract was made in open town meeting for the building of the first Springfield meetinghouse. Each inhabitant was to furnish twenty-eight days' work, "when required by him who undertakes the building of it." No inhabitant could be forced to work more than six consecutive days. Thomas Cooper contracted for the work, and it was satisfactorily performed.

The building was forty by twenty-five feet in size, "9 feet betwixt joints," double studded, and had two large windows on either side, and a smaller window at each end. There was a large door on the south side, and two smaller doors elsewhere. Joists were laid for a gallery when it could be afforded. The roof was shingled, and there were two towers, one for a bell, and the other for a watch-house. The underpinning was stone "dawbed" in the old style. Cooper received four score pounds paid in quarterly instalments of wheat, peas, pork, wampum and labor above the twenty-eight days required of each mature male inhabitant.

Mr. Cooper had until September, 1645, to fulfill this contract, but the last stroke was done by the previous March. A place for the meetinghouse to stand on was bought by an exchange of several lots, some of them on the other side of the great river, and with no payments except in land. Evidently it was lots next to the river that were acquired for the meetinghouse, which faced south on a one-rod road leading to the training field and to the burial ground. This road has since been made wider and called Elm Street. Use of ground at the foot of Elm Street as a training field soon gave way to its use as a burial ground, and the lots thus occupied were on either side of Elm Street, extending from what is now Water Street to within a few feet of the margin of the river bank. The general control and care of these lots was in the hands of the old meetinghouse parish. Nearly all graves in this part of the town continued there undisturbed until the opening of a new cemetery in 1841. By an arrangement between the parish and the proprietors of the old cemetery, to which the consent of friends was obtained when possible, all the remains in the old burial grounds were removed to a new resting place, more remote from the rumble of the cars and the shriek of the locomotive.

The local scene when the pioneers assembled in their new meetinghouse must have been very interesting with Mr. Pynchon sitting under the pulpit and Mr. Moxon offering thanks, while the voice of praise rose from a full-hearted, though small congregation. In that gathering were at least sixteen men, founders of families. Their descendants have been noteworthy to a remarkable degree, and through each line has run the distinctive traits of mind and heart that were the making of Springfield.

It had been said at Boston and Hartford that the Agawam settlement would not survive, and indeed it did take nearly a decade of lonely but persistent toil to secure a footing.

Mr. Moxon's connection with the witch excitement in Springfield has led to the conclusion he was a weak and superstitious person. But those who have deciphered his sermons, and examined the meager traces of his teachings, come to a far different conclusion. He was what might be called an exhaustive preacher, for he always followed out an elaborate scheme of sermonizing covering about all that could be said on his subject, dividing and subdividing his topic with reckless prodigality of time; and if the sermon hour closed before the sermon did, he simply announced that the discourse would be continued on the Sabbath following.

It happened back in 1640, when William Pynchon was at loggerheads with the Windsor church, and the heavens hung low with clouds, spiritual and temporal, that he felt called on to fortify the position of his little congregation by the text: "Comfort your hearts, and 'stablish you in every good word and work." Here was a vast subject. It touched both the doctrine and deeds of men. Loyalty to the gospel, the fate of individual souls, and the future of the plantation itself seemed to hang on the voice from the pulpit. He began the sermon February 16 and finished it March 15, when the church probably felt refreshed in more senses than one. His exhortation to be "settled in well doing and to be stable in sound doctrine" was hammered into the metal of every soul present.

In 1645 we find that the settlement of disputes by the "arbitrament of two Indifferent Men" relieved the magistrate of much labor, but the town meeting continued to feel the burdens of its fence and land supervision. The appearance of a vote to force landholders in the southern part of the town to build fences was a reminder that the settlement was growing to the south, and this section finally developed into the town of Longmeadow. Several persons who had planting grounds there complained of others who refused to fence these grounds. They succeeded in getting an order through the town meeting forcing these to bear a share in a common fence against all cattle according to the several quantities of their allotments. Each man was also required to cut his fencing stuff on his own grounds, except he first have the consent of his neighbor to cut on his.

VIEW AT LUDLOW

The next move was for the inhabitants to join together in a general fence, each man bearing a share in proportion to his quantity of acres. This general fence was to be finished by the first of April, and the end next to the river was to be railed, leaving out a sufficient highway next to the river.

A few months before this the people had accepted the allotment made by seven men who were to divide the town in equal parts for estates and persons. Third and fourth allotments were provided in the long meadow, and on the other side of the river. The upper part of the town were to have their third and fourth allotments in the plain above the Three Corner Brook, and on the other side of the great river at the end of the five-acre lots.

In September of the same year it was voted that "whereas the planting of Indian corn in the meadow swamp on the other side of Agawam river has occasioned a long stay after mowing time before men can put over their cattle there, it is ordered that no more Indian corn shall be planted, either in the meadow or in the swamps, that the cattle of all that have allotments may be put over by the 15th of September, provided they keep their cattle from going over by having a keeper in the day time, and by having them in some fenced place in the night time. Only calves can be put over there by the 14th of August."

Complaint being made that various persons who kept teams on the other side of the river in the springtime to plough, "have much damaged other men by their cattle, in eating the green corn and the first sprouts of men's meadows: It is ordered therefore teams of cattle shall be kept in some house or yard until the first of May, and if anyone keep them longer there, they are to pasture them on their own ground, or on the common, or the three lots not improved for tillage."

Late in October, 1645, the Springfield community witnessed two marriages within three days. There had come to Springfield some time before, Mary Lewis, a married woman. Her husband was a Catholic, but she had not lived with him for seven years. It can be imagined that if Mrs. Lewis had lived in Boston, where a governor had taken his sword and cut out the cross from the British flag because it was a hated papal emblem, she must have had a very dismal time there, and may have sought Springfield as a place of refuge. Evidently she was a very sensitive person and was compelled either to work or marry. So she chose the latter.

There was a bricklayer in Springfield at that time, a man of rather voluble disposition, by the name of Hugh Parsons. One might say he was a queer stick, and unworthy to be matched with a woman of Mrs. Lewis' sensitive type. It was known in Springfield that Mr. Lewis was a Catholic, but she claimed there had been a seven years' abandonment by her husband, which gave her the privilege of marrying again under the laws of England.

Mr. Pynchon was in great doubt what to do, and he wrote to Boston for advice, explaining that Mrs. Lewis had fallen into "a league of amity with a brickmaker," and she was in great haste for an answer. The response was favorable, and on October 27 Hugh Parsons, the brickmaker, and Mary Lewis were married.

Three days later there was a wedding in Connecticut which delighted the heart of the founder of Springfield. His son, John Pynchon, destined to be an even more prominent leader than the father, had won the hand of Amy, daughter of Governor Wyllys, of Connecticut, and another Governor of the Colony performed the ceremony. John Pynchon was about twenty-three years of age, a quiet, thoughtful young man, who never had a boyhood, for the Puritan convulsions in Europe and the migration to the wilderness turned the spirit of youth into the prematurely serious disposition of the pioneer. The father was delighted with the alliance, and he wrote to the Governor of the Colony expressing his satisfaction that the young man had concluded to live at "my house where he may continue as long as he finds it for his comfort and benefit."

John Pynchon was well educated, and seems to have been under the influence of a lawyer. Possibly he formed his legal habits from his father, who trained him in the ways of the law; but John Pynchon was an entirely different kind of a man from the founder of Springfield.

During the five years beginning with 1645, Springfield and Hartford kept up a running sword-play over the custom duties on the Connecticut River. This was the first tariff war in New England, and finally involved all the colonies. Connecticut was nursing a commercial ambition and was bound to further its interests by all legitimate means. But it was evident in the temper of some of the charges formulated at Hartford that the bitterness was not lessened by a neighborly feeling toward Springfield.

Near the close of 1644 Connecticut had bargained for the fort at Saybrook, and Mr. Fenwick, the owner, agreed to accept certain duties, including two pence a bushel on exported grain passing the fort, and six pence a hundred on biscuits. Also, there was an annual tax put on hogs and cattle, to be paid to Fenwick, and all of these tributes were to continue ten years. Then the fort was to become the absolute property of Connecticut. Officers were to be stationed at Windsor, Hartford and Wethersfield, to give clearance papers to masters of outgoing vessels, and these papers were presented to Fenwick's agent at Saybrook. Springfield was doing a good business with Boston, and Connecticut at once concluded to bring its neighbor under the tariff. But the Hartford government had not secured the jurisdiction of the mouth of the river with the prospective ownership of the fort. The duty on exports was the purchase money for the fort, and thus Springfield was being forced to help secure for Connecticut a title for the very fort that might prove a menace to its own commerce.

When the Massachusetts General Court was informed of the Connecticut tariff, it voted that "none of ours" shall pay the tribute. Mr. Pynchon was threatened with utter ruin in a business way, and he promptly gave direction to his sailors to pay no attention to the orders, and to refuse to file invoices, or ask for clearance papers. His order was disobeyed by one of the crews for some unknown reason, and the cargo of corn was entered under the tariff provision, much to Mr. Pynchon's annoyance. His next ship passed the Saybrook fort in defiance of the Connecticut officer and the little cannon which was supposed to sweep the river under such circumstances. Fortunately the cannon did not open fire.

Pynchon wrote to Govenor Winthrop at Boston that "If we should be forced to do such a thing as pay duty, this plantation will be deserted. I think no man will dwell here to be brought under such payments. I desire your advice, whether we had better enter our goods or no."

The commissioners of the United Colonies, which had been in existence three years as a sort of itinerary congress, met at Hartford two months later to adjust this matter. They heard many arguments, and the most important one insisted that the maintenance of a fort at Saybrook was as valuable to Springfield as to Hartford. However, no definite action was taken until November, 1646, when the Massachusetts General Court held that Hartford had no legal right to force an outsider to buy a fort for the Connecticut Colony, and that the Saybrook fort was no protection to Springfield.

The next year there was a special session of the commission of the United Colonies in July at Boston, with Deputy Governor Hopkins and Captain Mason, who were the commissioners from Connecticut. Mason was thus confronted by his old antagonist of Springfield. A short time before, Mason had been given the military command at Saybrook—an act of no consequence, for owing to a recent fire the fort was little short of useless. The Massachusetts commissioners were Thomas Dudley and John Endicott. Much argument followed, and after considerable time Mr. Pynchon was called in, but he simply referred to the action of the Massachusetts General Court as reflecting fully his views. The commissioners, in spite of the fact that no duties were imposed on the Dutch trading vessels, passed a vote approving the river tariff. But as this decision failed to receive the signatures of all the commissioners, it only added to the difficulties of the situation.

Mr. Pynchon bluntly refused to pay two pence a bushel on grain, and about this time he wrote a long letter on the subject, addressed to "Goodman Johnson, my ancient and much esteemed friend." From it some of the most interesting parts are quoted. Mr. Pynchon wanted Johnson to get the General Court to take into serious consideration the jurisdiction of the river's mouth, and went on to say:

"Gov. Hopkins' letter to me, which I sent to you by my son, doth hold forth that we must pay certain rates for grain and corn transported, which will be our due share toward buying the fort down the river. I gather that Mr. Hopkins expects the rates as a custom, for when asked whether like rates would be expected of any other plantations that might be above us, he said, 'to the head of the river.' It seems they expect like rates of all other plantations that may in a few years be planted above us. Mr. Hopkins doth plead that we ought, in justice, to pay our share to buy the fort because we share in the benefit. I answer, no; except we had his consenting as purchasers, never like to be of any benefit, namely, to keep open the river against malignant ships or pinaces. For how can we have benefit by a fort which is a fort in name only, being no fort indeed.

"If the State were able to maintain them, which they are not able to do without utter undoing, yet there is no necessary use of a fort there to keep out malignant ships.

"We do not deny that the first intent of building the fort might be to secure the river against malignant ships and pinaces, but this must be remembered that it was made in haste, and therefore, it was only a palisade, which, when it was bought, was utterly ruined. Neither is there like to be any fort there of sufficient strength. Hence we judge such kind of fortification will rather be a dangerous snare to the river than a benefit, and it is a kind of fort that is an advantage to an enemy. Therefore, if ever we be forced to have any right or interest in the purchase of said fort we shall, in likelihood, give our votes to have it demolished, with all speed.

"There is no need of any fort here to secure the river against malignant ships or pinaces, for the river's mouth is naturally barred with a sand bank all over, which is sufficient to terrify all malignant ships from coming into the river, which is more than any fort there can do. Secondly, a fort there is needless against malignant pinnaces, for such as are of small burden and may easily pass in and out, either by day or night, without any great damage of a fort, the passage there is so broad.

"If malignant pinaces shall at any time attempt mischief against the river, we are fearless of danger, for no pinace can come nigh us by 15 or 16 miles. Therefore, the fort is not of a kind to secure us, as it is to secure you. So the combined jurisdiction should not expect us to pay an equal share with them of all that passes out at the River's mouth."

There was a meeting of the United Colony commissioners at Plymouth in 1648, and Massachusetts made another effort to win over the commissioners, but without avail. Consequently, when the General Court met at Boston in May, 1649, it was in no temper to rely longer on moral force alone. Solemn indignation characterized the speeches of the members, and a vote was passed rehearsing the facts of the situation—how Springfield was taxed to maintain a Connecticut fort, and how the Boston fortifications had never been a charge on the other colonies. Then, with equally solemn indignation they imposed tariff duties, both import and export, on all goods carried past "the castle" in Boston Bay by any inhabitant of Plymouth, Connecticut, or New Haven. A turbulent meeting of the commissioners at Boston two months later, and formal remonstrance against retaliatory duties on all the New England colony goods, had not the slightest effect on the Bay people.

The tariff war, thus begun, threatened to ruin Connecticut, and all New England would have been set back in its struggle for existence. There was a quick response to the retaliatory duties. Plymouth and

New Haven were grieved and Hartford irritated; but, they all gave way, nevertheless, and Mr. Pynchon's goods passed down the river unchallenged. Massachusetts, with equal promptness, gladly suspended the customs duties on the petition of the inhabitants of Boston, after being "credibly informed" that Connecticut had done likewise.

Springfield Around 1650

CHAPTER VI

Springfield Around 1650

In spite of local excitements, the minds of these remote pioneers continually turned to England, and even in the wilderness, they felt a kind of security to which England at that time was a stranger. Mr. Pynchon wrote, in 1646, after hearing of the struggle in the British Parliament over religion and the form of discipline to be adopted:

> "The Scotts say that their form of presbyterian government is the only way of Christ, and the Independents say that their form of government is the only way of Christ. But the Parliament say that neither of them is the only way of Christ, and therefore they have ordained commissioners to supervise the conclusions of the presbyterian courts. But truly where the zeal of God's glory and godly wisdom are joined together; a world of good hath been done by godly ministers that have held no certain form of discipline. On the contrary, where a cold spirit doth rule in ministers, though they may have a good form of government, they may yet be dead Christians."

This is a fair example of the spirit at the bottom of Mr. Pynchon's religious controversies. The attempts both in this country and England to secure an iron-bound form of religion as handmaid to the State had set him to philosophizing. On the other hand, the attempt to secure liberty of conscience had the effect of driving him into more conservative lines of thought, and even led him to say:

> "I perceive by some godly ministers that this is not a time of reformation, but of liberty of conscience, and I believe that when they have seen a little more of the lawlessness of liberty of conscience, they will change their judgment and say that it will give liberty to Satan to broach such horrid blasphemous opinions as were not the like in any age."

During the summer of 1646, there was a plague of caterpillars which came in such numbers as to greatly damage the wheat. Then an open winter was followed by terrible floods, and in the autumn there was an epidemic of sickness. The settlers had many natural enemies. Pigeons in overwhelming flocks assaulted the crops and the wolves made free with the sheep. A bounty of ten pence was paid for every wolf killed within five miles of the town.

The building of the meetinghouse added to the solemnity of the Lord's Day observances. John Matthews was ordered to beat "the drum for the meetings at 10 of the clock on the lecture days and at 9 o'clock on the Lord's days in the forenoon only, and he to beat it from Mr. Moxon's house to Mr. Stebbins' house, and the meetings were to begin within half an hour after, for which he is to have 6 pence in wampum of every family in the town or a peck of Indian corn, if they have not wampum." A bell was supplied a few years later, and Richard Sikes rang it and swept the house for one shilling a week. In March, 1646, the town voted money to complete the meetinghouse, but withholding ten pounds until an opportunity appeared for procuring glass, or until the house was finished.

The town meeting usually specified the kind of property to be taxed. Thus the wolf bounty was raised from a tax on "all sorts of cattle," which included horses. The tax for Mr. Moxon's maintenance, in 1647, had been raised "on all lands and goods." Cooper's meetinghouse debt was met by a tax on "uplands and live stock." Wheat was accepted for taxes, and so were Indian corn and peas.

Just when Miles Morgan came to Springfield is uncertain, but he probably had been a resident several years before he and George Colton were commissioned to get a smith for the town in 1646. Comparatively little is known of his early life. He was born in England, lived for a while at Bristol and, in 1636, came to this country when a young man, accompanied by two brothers. His house-lot was on the south side of Ferry Lane, now Cypress Street.

During the voyage to America, young Morgan made the acquaintance of a Miss Gilbert, and apparently won her heart. She settled with her family at Beverly, and he, after building a house in Springfield, pressed his courtship of the Beverly maid—but not by letter, for the simple reason that he could not write. Negotiations were carried on by mutual friends, and Morgan, after being accepted, made the eastern journey to his lady love about 1643, taking with him two neighbors and an Indian, duly armed. On the return journey, Miles and his three attendants walked all the way from Beverly to Springfield, while the bride and "some household stuff" were carried by the only horse at the disposal of this odd bridal party. For many years Morgan was a butcher when his farm work permitted.

In 1646, the first Tuesday in November was settled on for a regular annual town meeting. This was quite a change from the former habit of holding the meetings monthly. The fine for absence from town meeting, or for leaving the meeting before the blessing, was raised, in 1646, to one bushel of Indian corn. Centralization invited suspicions. Two months after the election of the second board of townsmen, it was voted that they should publish their orders "After Lecture, or at any training day or other public meeting." The townsmen began keeping a record in 1647. Some of the townsmen were chosen to act as surveyors. Their special instructions, besides keeping the highways in condition, were to "open a Horse-way over the meadow to the Bay path," and build a bridge over the Three Corner Brook into the plain. John Pynchon was made a townsman and elected town treasurer, in 1650, and began to be prominent in local affairs.

Much trouble was occasioned in those days by not obeying the town order as to swine, and it was specially decreed in 1646, that if a man let his hogs run abroad unyoked, and the swine broke in and trespassed, "the master of the swine should be liable to pay all damages as two indiferent men shall judge the damage to be."

The following year this matter was again taken up, and it was decreed that swine kept about a house or near any corn ground belonging to the plantation, and not under the custody of a keeper, "shall be sufficiently yoked according to the age and bigness of the swine. In case any swine that are above the age of six months shall be found in the street or about any of the common fences of the cornfields without wearing a yoke or having a ring in its nose—It shall be lawful for any person so finding them to drive the hogs to the pound, which may be any man's yard or outhouse in the present defect of no common pound." It was also provided that he give the owner of swine notice of his impounding them within twenty-four hours after it was so done.

Here are a number of items that give us interesting glimpses of the pioneers' daily life:

"Ordered by the town in September, 1647, that John Clarke or those that shall join him in the burning of tar shall have liberty to gather candlewood on the plain in the Bay path, provided they come not to gather any this side of the great pond and the swamps that point out from it to Chicopee river, and Mill river, which is judged to be about five miles from the town."

The candlewood which the men went to gather was knots of the fat pitch-pine. These were split fine for burning on a hearth in place of candles, and they were found everywhere in the pine woods. Governor Winthrop, the younger, records in 1662 that this candlewood was much used for domestic illumination in Virginia, New York, and New England. It was found in abundance in new settlements, and pine knots are still burned in the Southern States in humble households for lighting purposes. The light is bright compared to a candle, but a New England historian, writing in 1642, has said that "Candlewood may serve as a shift among poor folks, but I cannot commend it, because it drops a pitchy sort of substance where it stands."

That pitchy sort of substance was tar, one of the most valuable trade products of the colonists. So much tar was made by burning the pines on the banks of the Connecticut, that as early as 1650 the towns had to prohibit the using of candlewood for tar-making if gathered within six miles of the Connecticut River, though it could be gathered by families for illumination and fuel.

"The pine knots were such candles as the Indians commonly use, having no other," writes a colonial minister, "and they are nothing else but the wood of the pine tree which is so full of the moisture of turpentine and pitch that they burn as clear as a torch."

To avoid having smoke in the room, and on account of the pitchy droppings, candlewood was usually burned in a corner of the fireplace, on a flat stone.

At Springfield, in September, 1647, the town ordered that "no person shall gather any hops that grow in the swamps, or in the common until this present day yearly on pain of forfeiting what they shall so disorderly gather, and 2 shillings six pence for breach of order."

The forfeiture went to the informer and the penalty to the town treasury.

By order of the town, in January, 1646, if any trees were felled, "and had no other work bestowed on them for more than 6 months, from that day forward in the commons, it shall be lawfull for any man to take them, but any timber that is cross cut, or firewood that is cut out and set on heaps, or rails or clefts for poles, no man may take any of these until it has lain twelve months after it is cross-cut or cloven."

The townsmen then declared it unlawful to transport outside of the town limits any "building timbers, board logs or sawn boards or planks or shingle timber or pipe staves." Furthermore, the townsmen decreed that "Whereas it is judged offensive and noisome for flax and hemp to be watered or washed in the brook before men's doors, that is of ordinary use for dressing meat, therefore it is ordered that no person shall henceforth water any flax or hempe in the said brook on pain of a six shilling 8 pence fine."

William Pynchon held court four times a year, and all breaches of the peace were presented by a grand jury of two men. Mr. Moxon usually opened the court with prayer and the town meetings were now held in the meetinghouse. In later years taverns were sometimes used for that purpose.

Among the persons to whom Mr. Moxon ministered and whose confidence he enjoyed, there were some eminent, not only for their piety, but for their intelligence. Such were William and John Pynchon, Henry Smith, Elizur Holyoke, and Deacon Samuel Chapin.

Ministers who came as candidates after Mr. Moxon left were apt not to satisfy. Thus Mr. Hosford "was a disappointment," and Mr. Thompson "deserted this plantation." In 1657 services were conducted by Pynchon, Holyoke, Chapin and Burt, and Mr. Pynchon was authorized to read his "own meditations."

Several years passed, and then a young minister named Pelatiah Glover was settled over the Springfield church. He was something of a student and was well calculated to take up the line of theology approved in the valley. The people were not able to give Mr. Glover a liberal support in money, but they made free to supply him with valuable landed property.

Year after year the selectmen and deacons, or some committee chosen in town meeting, assigned the pews or "dignified" the meetinghouse, and their arbitrary duties often caused heartburnings quite as intent as those resulting from assignments of land, for the rule followed was worldly condition and social importance. The seating disturbance became so serious in 1666 that the selectmen were compelled to interfere. Many, indeed, refused to sit where assigned, and acted with a high hand.

THE OLD TAVERN AT NORTH WILBRAHAM

Some years later Miles Morgan and Jonathan Burt were stationed "up in the gallery to give a check to disorders in youth and young men in time of God's worship." Besides, Anthony Dorchester was to sit in the guard seat for the like purpose.

In addition to the family Mr. Moxon brought with him across the Atlantic, he had three children born here—all boys, and there were some of his children who never came over from England. Two daughters here in Springfield were Martha and Rebeckah, who won a strange notoriety in connection with witchcraft. They became early victims, if not the very first, of that delusion which for a time swept New England.

Super men and women of broad vision are uncommon in any age or race, and the Puritan settlers of New England were no exception. They varied as individuals through all the gamut of fit and unfit, and the path was inevitably thorny for the saints. It was an age of superstition. Nearly everyone was at least tinged with it. We can applaud the stalwart devotion of our forefathers, but their superstitions continually intrude, making it impossible to forget that they were the descendants of what in general was an ignorant and unreflecting age. They were self-assertive, brave, and Biblical rather than inspired. Until Jonathan Edwards' time one looks in vain for any serious attempt in New England to verify the teachings of the gospel in reason.

They were content to stop with close interpretations of texts. The grim terrors of witchcraft came within this interpretation, and formed a part of the belief on both sides of the ocean. However, it was not the Puritans who invented witches. The belief in a veritable devil was general in the seventeenth century, and the Bible accounts of devils dwelling in earthly habitations were its justification. Men and women accepted the idea that persons made a league with familiar spirits, entering into secret compacts with them, and for the price of their souls secured for a time a diabolical control over the laws of nature. These persons were called witches. Personal ugliness was a characteristic of the witch in the popular mind, and witchcraft was a statute crime in England, where no less than thirty thousand lives were sacrificed on the gibbet and at the stake to crush it out.

Nearly all the absurdities, superstitions and cruelties connected with the belief in witchcraft in America originated in Europe. Our courts in witchcraft trials had as guides the decisions of distinguished English judges, and the rules of eminent English lawyers. The vicar of Frome, chaplain of Charles II and a member of the Royal Society, was a distinguished writer in favor of the existence of witches, witchcraft and apparitions, and his books were read in New England.

Among the absurd protections against witchcraft was the horseshoe nailed against the threshold of the door, and yet there were New Englanders who had faith in its efficacy. The houses of two or three men in Northampton had a horseshoe fast ned to the threshold about one hundred and fifty years ago.

In 1648, the lower part of Springfi.ld's main street must have somewhat resembled a forest road, with clearings on the river side to make room for houses, barns and young orchards. Here lived Rice Bedortha and his wife Blanche. Their neighbors were Hugh Parsons, John Lombard, George Langton, and various others. In this remote part of the town the witch fever started. The houses were on the border of the wet meadows, and it is not unlikely that at times marsh lights were seen after dark. At any rate that was the assertion of Mrs. Bedortha. Besides, there were mysterious things happening in that part of the town which were enough to make the cold moisture stand on the brow of the bravest. Skulking lights at dead of night out on the marshes were not the worst. Blanche Bedortha told all along the street how Hugh Parsons, her neighbor, three doors below, had called at the house one day to see her husband about some bricks. While the men talked she joined in the conversation, whereat Parsons exclaimed sharply, "You needn't have said anything. I spoke not to you." At that Mr. Bedortha was offended and made a harsh comment.

However, the situation was not unusual. A woman says an unnecessary thing, a man retorts with feeling, and affairs get involved. The men probably soon forgot the incident, but Mrs. Bedortha treasured it and talked of it among her neighbors. One night, as she was retiring, three flashes of light startled her. They seemed to come from inside of her red cotton waistcoat, which she had just taken off and was about to hang on a peg. Quickly she held up the garment between her hands a second time, but there was no flash. The room had a fireplace, and in that a fire was burning, yet there was no possibility of seeing a flash from that because it had the protection of a double Indian mat through which no flash could be seen.

A month later a child was born to Mrs. Bedortha, and she was unwell for some time afterward in a strange, mysterious sort of way. She felt on her left side pains as if pierced with knives in three different places. "Suddenly after that," she said, "my thoughts were that this evil might come on me from what Hugh Parsons said. I do not think I was sick in any other part of my body except the three places, and by the extremity of these prickings only."

Any person familiar with Cotton Mather's elaborate accounts of how the little "gentleman in black" was in the habit of pinching and pricking people, will at once see the drift of such evidence. Mrs. Bedortha's nurse was a widow, Mrs. Marshfield, who had formerly lived at Windsor, where she herself had a character not entirely free from rumored connection with witchcraft. Possibly the widow went all over the neighborhood with her witchcraft chatter, and while the good matrons were carding or spinning, described the prickings, and told what Hugh Parsons had said.

It is still more likely that Mrs. Parsons heard the reflections on her husband's character with keen resentment. At any rate there was a falling-out between Widow Marshfield and Mrs. Parsons. By way of a home-thrust Mrs. Parsons went along the street and elaborated her case against the widow Marshfield. She said it was publicly known that the devil followed her at her house in Windsor, and added, "For aught I know follows her here."

This talking match culminated in a suit for slander, brought by Mrs. Bedortha's widowed nurse against Mrs. Parsons.

William Pynchon, after due deliberation, condemned Mrs. Parsons to twenty lashes, which were to be administered by the constable after lecture, or to pay Mrs. Marshfield "3 pounds damages toward the reparation of her good name."

The payment of this fine to the widow was in Indian corn, twenty-four bushels, and when it was offered, Hugh asked her to abate one-third; but she refused, because Hugh had said after the trial that her witnesses had given false testimony. Thereupon Parsons exclaimed in his usual reckless, mysterious way, "Take it!" and he added, "It will be as wildfire to this house and as a moth to your garment I'll warrant you, and make account it is but lent you!"

Mrs. Marshfield was continually on the watch. Presently her daughter was taken with fits. The threats and the fits ran hand in hand all over the excited plantation. They visited every household, and frightened the godly folk half out of their wits, but no one seemed called on to secure the arrest of Hugh Parsons. Martha Moxon and her sister, who were daughters of the minister, had been taken down with fits previous to this, and the reverend father at once recalled the fact that Parsons had grumbled because compelled to build his chimney according to contract, and had even made a mysterious remark that the bricks would do Moxon no good.

Public opinion now ran strong against the Parsons household. No deviation from the dull prose of life could take place without its being connected in some mysterious aspect with the quarrelsome family in the lower part of the street. Whenever the red coat of Hugh Parsons appeared, women trembled and clung to their children. The terrible fact was whispered in every kitchen—"Springfield has a witch!"

Five months after the Marshfield-Parsons slander case, a child was born to Mary Parsons that lived only a year. This made the home and village conditions worse than ever. Hugh was just the kind of person to annoy his wife, and when he was about the house disagreements were frequent. Besides, there were long unexplained absences of his that she considered heartless neglect of his family. The eye of suspicion and the finger of gossip were turned on them by the community, and finally, these and the death of the child, worked Mrs. Parsons' highly-strung nerves into a flighty hysterical condition, and she went down another step from vivacious maidenhood to the level of a social outcast.

Sarah, the wife of Alexander Edwards, added to the community fear of Hugh Parsons by telling how he called at their house for milk, and after she had refused to give him more than a pennyworth, the cow "almost dried up," and the next day the milk was as "yellow as saffron," and each day it turned to some other "strange odd color."

Neighbor Griffith Jones, not to be outdone in relating wonders that concerned the doings of the Parsons household, told the Bedorthas, who lived next door, that on the Lord's Day he had left his wife at a neighbor's after the first sermon, and gone home, where he proceeded to take up his dinner and to put it on a little table made on a cradle head. He then looked for a knife, of which he had two, but both of them were missing. So at dinner he was obliged to use an old rusty knife from a basket where he had things to mend shoes.

After clearing away his dinner dishes he laid the rusty knife on a corner of the table, intending to cut a pipe of tobacco with it when he had fed his pig, which had come up close to the door. After serving the pig, Jones returned to the house, where he was amazed to find *three knives* on his table. He was greatly disconcerted, but had presence of mind to cut his pipe of tobacco. And no sooner had he done that than in came Parsons at that very instant and asked if he was ready to go back to the meetinghouse. They smoked together, without either saying anything about the mysterious knives, but later in the day Jones told all through the neighborhood that Parsons had bewitched the knives.

Anthony Dorchester, who worked for Parsons, had a one-fourth interest in a cow, and a time came in the natural course of events when the cow was killed and divided with his employer, who also was part owner. Both wanted the tongue of the animal, and they drew lots for it, with the result that Dorchester got the tongue. However, when it came to cooking, the tongue mysteriously disappeared from the pot Of course, that was the work of a witch.

George Langton was another person with a story to tell. One day when his wife Hannah was indisposed, George slipped a pudding out of a bag after it was cooked, and the pudding parted from end to end as if cut with a knife. Langton had previously refused to sell Parsons some hay.

A bargain was made by Parsons with Thomas Miller for a piece of land, and immediately afterward he cut his leg while chopping. Men heard strange noises at night like the filing of saws. Blanche Bedortha's child, now two years old, cried out one day that it was afraid of Parsons' dog, yet Parsons had no dog. He was at Longmeadow working when he heard of the death of his second child. Several people were near him and heard him say, "I will cut a pipe of tobacco before I go home."

That was in everybody's mouth by the day's end, and when Parsons was appealed to for an explanation of this unfatherly remark, he replied, "I was very full of sorrow for the death of the child in private, though not in public."

He got no sympathy, and even the worthy Henry Smith could not withstand the infection. He had once refused to sell Parsons some peas, and in the summer of 1648 it was remembered that two of his children had died.

The effect on Mrs. Parsons was pitiable. She was already in a decline from consumption and her every movement was watched. Disgrace followed close on her heels, and her wavering mind invited suspicion. Was not her own husband a proven witch? The tragedy had begun, and Mrs. Parsons was becoming insane.

Gradually the suspicion that her husband was in league with the devil grew more pronounced. She watched him with cat-like tenacity, and when he lay asleep she searched for the little black marks that in those days the devil was supposed to put on persons making a covenant of witchcraft. She did not find the devil's sign-manual on Hugh, but he talked wildly in his sleep and had satanic dreams, which he told on waking.

The death of Mrs. Parsons' second child took place in March, 1651. She was now ready for the worst, and she went before Magistrate Pynchon and made oath that her husband was a witch, and the cause of her child's death. Parsons himself had been under legal examination some time before.

"Ah, witch! Ah, witch!" Goody Stebbins cried as Constable Merrick took Hugh Parsons past her door, and she fell down in a fit. Miles Morgan had been visiting Thomas Miller when the dreaded man approached a short time before, and he saw Miller's wife fly into a passion and cry, "Get thee gone, Hugh Parsons! Get thee gone! If thou will not, I will go to Mr. Pynchon, and he shall have thee away!" Then she too fell prostrate on the ground. The red coat of Hugh Parsons was the nightmare of the village.

Examination before Mr. Pynchon only added to the consternation of the community. Jonathan Taylor, after listening to Mrs. Parsons' evidence against her husband, saw in his dreams three snakes on the floor, and one of them, with black and yellow stripes, bit him on the forehead. Then he heard a solemn voice cry out, "Death!" and that voice was like the voice of Hugh Parsons.

After Mary Parsons had made oath to the witchcraft of her husband, she was placed in the hands of Thomas Cooper for safe keeping, and as Cooper watched the wretched, unnerved woman, he could not refrain from asking her questions, either from curiosity or pity, or a desire to extract new evidence. Here is his record:

"I said to her, 'Why do you speak so of your husband? Methinks; if he were a witch there would appear some sign of it on his body.' She answered, 'It is not always so. But why do I say that? I have no skill in witchery. It may be with him as it was with me that night I was at Goodman Ashley's. The Divill may come into his body only like a wind, and then go forth again, for so the Divill told me that night. I think I should have been a witch afore now, only I was afraid to see the Divill, lest he should fright me. But he told me that I should not fear, and so I consented. That night I was with my husband and Goodwife Merrick and Bessie Sewell in Goodman Stebbins' lot; and sometimes we were like cats and sometimes in our own shape, and plodding for some good cheer; and they made me go barefoot, and start the fires, because I had told so much at Mr. Pynchon's.'"

Poor woman! Her life had been a failure in all its relations, but especially in her second marriage which had tied her to a talkative, happy-go-lucky, pipe-smoking bricklayer, who had a way of appropriating other people's goods, and maliciously resenting all criticisms of his character. He had drawn her down to a level of life where even her good qualities only made fuel for the fires of persecution. This highly sensitive woman was forced to lose the respect of all who came in contact with her. Then her mind gave way.

Her husband had been carried to Boston, but more evidence was being taken against him in Springfield, to be forwarded to the Bay.

Madness and remorse wrought a change in the burden of Mrs. Parsons' talk, and she finally confessed that the blood of her child was on her own hands, and she also declared that she was under the influence of Satan. These wild words were accepted for sober truth, and she, too, was taken to Boston under arrest for both murder and witchcraft.

In May the jury that dealt with the case of Mrs. Parsons accepted her crazy confession of child-murder, but refused to believe she was a witch, and the General Court confirmed the verdict. She was sentenced to be hanged and the death watch was placed over her.

On the morning chosen for the execution, she was too feeble to be removed from her cell, and was respited. The second day of doom came, but then Mary lay on her couch dead, a martyr, to be held in commiserating memory.

Hugh Parsons' trial came in June and ended in conviction, but after he had been held in prison for nearly a year, the General Court refused to confirm the verdict, and he escaped the gallows. He left Boston and probably went on beyond the bounds of the State. At least Springfield saw him no more.

The Heresy of William Pynchon

CHAPTER VII

The Heresy of William Pynchon

What part Mr. Moxon took in the prosecution of Hugh Parsons is not known. That he believed in the reality of the demoniacal influence to which the common superstition of the times ascribed them can hardly be doubted. It was a weakness that infected some of the strongest minds of that period. Probably he was at least a promoter of the prosecution, and when that failed and the supposed witch was acquitted of the charge, there was left in his mind a discontent with his situation, which together with the troubles between his long time friend, Mr. Pynchon, and the General Court, induced Mr. Moxon to go with Pynchon to England in 1652, taking his family with him.

There is a tradition that the going of these men came near breaking up the settlement, but the shock though severe was not fatal, and there was no permanent check. The wise leadership that had been exercised by the elder Pynchon was shifted to his son John, then a young man of twenty-six, who all through the rest of that century and down to the time of his death maintained an influence, not only in Springfield, but in all this region, that made "The Worshipful" for his accepted title entirely fitting.

The religious interests of the people were ably cherished by the two deacons, Chapin and Wright, and others such as Elizur Holyoke. They were pious and capable men, and the people gathered in the sanctuary as they had been accustomed to in the past. Within five months after Mr. Moxon left, another minister was preaching for the supply, but did not stay long, and "it was agreed by joint consideration of the Plantation, that as the supply had deserted this plantation, and left us destitute in respect of any preaching, that Deacon Wright should dispense the word of God in this place until some other should be gotten for the work, and that he should have for his labor fifty shillings a month for such times as he attends the said work."

He did not continue long to "dispense the word" in Springfield. Soon after the passage of this vote, he emigrated with his family to Northampton, and there died in 1665 when asleep in his chair.

Mr. Holyoke and Henry Burt were chosen to carry on the work of the Sabbath, but in case, through any providence of God, either of them should be disabled, Deacon Chapin was to supply the vacancy. A little later Mr. Holyoke was chosen to carry on the work of the Sabbath once every Sabbath Day, and Mr. Pynchon was the choice for one part of the day once a fortnight.

However profitable from a spiritual point of view the labors of these intelligent laymen may have been, the church still aimed at securing the services of some godly, faithful minister, who would become its permanent pastor. But seven years had elapsed since the departure of Mr. Moxon when Mr. Pelatiah Glover preached his first Springfield sermon. He was the son of an early and prominent settler of Dorchester and received his education at Harvard College. In age he was about twenty-four when he came here, and was settled for life as was the habit of the times then and many years afterward. This was his home for more than thirty years.

The machinery of local government went steadily on, yet there were indications of an unsettled spirit in the community. Many of the inhabitants had shown a decided preference for the "long-meadow," and foreseeing that it was a part of the town destined to grow in importance, a request was lodged for a permit to surrender the planting-grounds on the river bank, and take lands back on the next plantation. This request was granted in 1648. Three years later lands were apportioned at Pecowsic and Mill River. The method of disposing of the meadows was by lot. Robert Ashley's section was given on condition that he keep an ordinary, but was to be surrendered if he failed in this respect.

John Pynchon was becoming an extensive trader and business man, probably due to the encouragement of his father. The son was pushed forward both in public and private affairs, and soon gained the confidence of the community. In the winter of 1630 we find: "It is agreed by the Town that if Mr. John Pynchon will make a chamber over the meeting-house and board it: he shall have the use of it entirely to himself for ten years." Then the town could secure it by paying the expense of building.

THE OLD FIRST CHURCH, SPRINGFIELD
Built in 1819

A year later a dispute arose between John Pynchon and the town concerning this chamber. The young man used the chamber for storing corn, and many thought the grain would come down on their heads. So the town limited him to four hundred bushels at a time, unless he underpropped the floor. Finally the town bought the chamber outright.

At about the end of the year 1649, John Pynchon headed a committee to bargain with Mr. Moxon for all his Springfield real estate and, after due deliberation and several meetings, it was agreed that his home-lot and buildings and all his meadow, wood and planting grounds should remain always for the use of the inhabitants.

Mr. Pynchon was much oppressed at this time by the trouble that had gathered around the town he had founded. Besides, a cloud hung over his head touching his theology, and the keenest minds in Boston had set to work to win him back to a belief that was considered orthodox. Pynchon had written a discussion in philosophic vein of the doctrine of atonement, and he had gradually come to the conclusion that Christ's mediatorial obedience was more important in securing man's redemption than His sufferings. When he finished his manuscript he sent it to England for publication. This was the now famous "Meritorious Price of Our Redemption." It reached Boston during the session of the October Court in 1650, and produced the most profound consternation.

How far the personal safety of Mr. Pynchon was imperiled is not clear. He was accused of heresy, and in those days the teaching of heresy was a grave offense which subjected the offender to trial and punishment. Thomas Dudley, one of the sternest Puritans of that period, was then Governor of the Colony, and not likely to relax any penalty which the law would demand.

Mr. Pynchon was peremptorily summoned to appear before the next General Court to answer whether he would acknowledge that this book printed in England under his name was his. If he did acknowledge it, the court declared their "purpose (God willing) was to proceed with him according to his demerits," unless he should sign a written retraction, which would be printed in England as well as here. Without any unnecessary ceremony the book was ordered to be burned by the common executioner in the marketplace, and the distinguished Mr. Norton, "one of the reverend elders of Ipswich," was chosen to prepare and publish a reply to Mr. Pynchon's book "with all convenient speed." This reply Mr. Pynchon was advised to take home "to consider thereof," and Mr. Norton was awarded twenty pounds by the General Court for his share in attempting to convince Mr. Pynchon of his error. The book was sent to England to be printed. The cautiously worded retraction which Mr. Pynchon expressed did not satisfy the authorities at the Bay, and they frigidly voted that he was in a hopeful way to give good satisfaction. Then they allowed him to go home, but bound him over to answer further at the next session. Henry Smith was promptly substituted as magistrate at Springfield—a bit of stern discipline that Mr. Pynchon felt deeply.

In regard to this theological controversy, Mr. Pynchon claimed that Christ's obedience was set over against Adam's disobedience, and if He had died unwillingly, the sacrifice would not have been sufficient. His death was miraculous, for though the devil and his agents had power to bruise Him, and to nail Him to the cross, they had no power to separate his soul from his body. So his death was not passive but active, and therefore a part of his mediatorial obedience. Those familiar with the long course of discussion over the philosophy of the atonement, will understand why Pynchon's book fed the flames on Boston Common, and why the General Court hastened to draw up a protest to send back to England in a vessel that was ready to weigh anchor. At the time the book had not even been read, and was condemned by the title page alone.

Sir Henry Vane, who had been a warm personal friend of Mr. Pynchon's, wrote the Massachusetts authorities from England and advised dealing with him gently. Sir Henry's letter brought this reply:

"We received your letter written in behalf of Mr. William Pynchon, who is one that we did all love and respect. But his book and the doctrine therein contained we cannot but abhor as pernicious, and are much grieved such an erroneous pamphlet was penned by any New England man, especially a Magistrate amongst us, wherein he takes upon him to condemn the judgment of most. Mr. Pynchon might have kept his judgment to himself, as it seems he did for more than thirty years, most of which time he has lived amongst us with honor, and much respect. But when God left him to himself in the publishing and spreading of his erroneous books to the endangering of the faith of such as might come to read them, we held it our duty, and believed we were called of God, to proceed against him accordingly. And we can further say that we had certain of our elders, such as he himself liked, to confer with him privately, lovingly and meekly, to see if they could prevail with arguments from the scriptures, and he was so far convinced thereby that he seemed to yield, and signed the case in controversy with his own hand. And for the better confirming of him in the truth of God, Mr. Norton left with him a copy of the book he wrote in answer to him; and the court gave him divers months to consider both, and what had been spoken to him by the elders. But meanwhile he received letters from England that encouraged him in his errors, to the great grief of us all."

After Mr. Pynchon had signed his retraction, and the General Court had decided it was not full enough to warrant their continuing him in the position of magistrate at Springfield, he returned home with his son-in-law, and as he rode for three or more days westward, what must have been his thoughts? He suffered from loss of public confidence. He was an object of hatred to the General Court, relieved of office, disgraced, and set upon by busy tongues!

The entire Commonwealth was shaken with a disturbed, unsettled feeling. Witchcraft and heresy, in the eyes of the Boston divines, seemed to be walking hand in hand. Springfield rested under a cloud, and the following solemn decree was recorded:

"This court taking into consideration how far Satan prevails amongst us in respect of witchcraft, as also by drawing away some from the truth to the profession and practise of strange opinions, think it necessary that there should be a day of humiliation throughout our jurisdiction in all the churches."

Mr. Pynchon did not appear at the October term, according to the direction of the court, and when it became known that he was not to be present during the session, the court voted that it "is willing all patience be exercised toward Mr. Pynchon, that, if it be possible, he may be reduced into the way of truth, and that he might renounce the errors and heresies, published in his book; and for that end, give him time to the next General Court in May." The penalty of non-appearance was one hundred pounds.

Springfield was much distressed over the strange events, and Mr. Pynchon determined to go back to England to live. Young John Pynchon decided to remain here, as his wife naturally objected to leaving her family in Connecticut. Those who accompanied Mr. Pynchon were his wife and Henry Smith, whose wife remained in Springfield, and Mr. Moxon. It was a melancholy fate for Mr. Pynchon, but only the usual one for the man who is ahead of his period. If he had chosen to remain in Massachusetts, he would have been banished as was Roger Williams a short time before. Pynchon's experiences were trying ones, for usually he was antagonizing the trend of government here. It was a broad spirit that moved him. But there is something to be said for the motives that dominated the earnest men of the Bay. They had fled to the forest from a corrupt civilization, and their loss of physical comfort, and the continued association with pioneer perils, was the price they were willing to pay.

Roger Williams watched the Pynchon controversy, and he wrote a letter to an acquaintance deploring the lack of liberality on the part of the Colony toward the Springfield man.

In July, 1652, Mr. Pynchon and his migrating companions were at Hartford on their way to England, and in May, 1653, he met at London his brother, who had come to greet him. Soon he had settled at Wraisburg on the river Thames, where he could see from his window Magna Charta Island and Windsor Castle. Whitelocke, the great Parliament lawyer of Cromwell's time, was a relative of Mr. Pynchon and some of the family lived near by.

William Pynchon founded Roxbury, the mother of fourteen New England towns; and he founded Springfield, the mother of thirteen New England towns, and godmother of quite as many more. Roxbury has a street named after him and so has Springfield.

Mr. Pynchon came to New England to avoid persecution, but now he left it to escape from intolerance. Yet it was evident that he was a man of affairs who operated successfully the financial concerns of the Colony, and so was made its treasurer. He managed wisely the judicial duties that were his lot as the only magistrate in western Massachusetts. He was a man of great enterprise and devoted his energies to building up the town he had founded, and that he intended should become a commercial center in the valley, from which should radiate an influence for the prosperity of all the region.

To accomplish this he gathered about him men of various trades and occupations with skill adapted to make the enterprise a success. He established a trade in furs and farm products that reached to Boston and the settlements on the Bay. But Mr. Pynchon never returned to America. He died in England at the age of seventy-two.

The town had touched low-water mark with the departure of its founder, its minister, and Henry Smith, its scribe. The young men left to take up the burdens and responsibilities thought seriously of abandoning the plantation and going down the river. They were poor, unprotected from the dangers of the great wilderness west and north and separated from the jurisdiction of the Bay by a one hundred mile forest, and they were unable for a long time to secure a minister. It was John Pynchon who saved the situation. He was methodical, and naturally given to the details of business and government, and he was a wiser man than his father in avoiding annoying complications, for he had a technical mind and was more of an executive officer, but less of a thinker. His handwriting was better and he was a natural student, but unlike William Pynchon, he could not take in with his eye the sweep of a new government and determine the principles that make for permanence in the State. John Pynchon was not the man to found a town, and William was not the man to perpetuate it.

John had come to Springfield at its first settlement and was familiar with its history and all its interests. The training received from his father was so thorough that he was prepared to enter at once on the management of all affairs which had been conducted by his father, and he immediately became the leading man of Springfield. His business was very extensive and included buying of his townsmen whatever products they had for sale. At Warehouse Point he had a storehouse where his goods were received from Hartford, transported to Springfield and sold to his neighbors. His dealing in furs were notably large, with beaver the most important. The beaver abounded in the Connecticut and Westfield rivers, and the collection of these furs gave employment to numerous men, both Indians and whites.

Young Pynchon was part owner of a vessel that transported beaver skins and other goods from Hartford to Boston for shipment to England. He was the owner, with his brother-in-law, of a corn-mill and a sawmill, at which the grain of the inhabitants was ground and their lumber sawed.

In his employ he had boats on the river and teams on the land. All this required the services of his townsmen of various trades and occupations, and brought to Springfield many persons who became useful citizens.

The public positions filled by young Pynchon and the public duties he performed exceeded in number and equalled in importance those of his father. When the military company here needed a captain to fill the place of Henry Smith, John Pynchon was appointed. From that he rose to be commander of the county regiment, which comprised all the State west of Middlesex, and in this capacity he acted during King Philip's War. In the records of that time he is commonly called the "Worshipful Major Pynchon." Often he was appointed to transact important business beyond the limits of the Colony.

In 1664 he was one of the commissioners who represented the English Government in receiving from the Dutch the surrender of New Amsterdam, which then took its present name of New York. A few years later he was sent as a commissioner by Massachusetts to Albany where, aided by the New York Governor, a treaty was made with the Mohawk Indians to secure the people of Massachusetts from the incursions of that powerful tribe. He succeeded, and the Indians addressed the major as "Brother Pynchon" and expressed their gladness at seeing him again at Albany and their resolution to keep the treaty they had just made with him.

John Pynchon and his young associates, Elizur Holyoke and Samuel Chapin, took the oath as magistrates in 1652, and this was the turning point in what makes Springfield a stronghold of regular government in local affairs. John Pynchon was only thirty-one years of age. The business of administration had closer attention, and the grand juryman was instructed to seek out offenses against the laws of the Colony.   Richard Sikes was fined for smoking on a hay-cock; Goody Griffith was punished for carrying fire uncovered in the streets; —and in a multitude of ways it became evident that a strong governing hand had taken hold of the helm.   Springfield had a training band, and John Pynchon was elected lieutenant and Elizur Holyoke ensign. Young Pynchon secured from the General Court the loan of a "great gun" for the protection of the town.

In 1653 the town appropriated a tract of land on Chicopee plain to support a schoolmaster, and at a later date Samuel Ely was released from duty on training days if he would agree to keep an ordinary.

A prison forty feet long, with a house for the prison keeper under the same roof, was begun at Springfield in 1661 and finished in 1668. Most of the boards, planks and timbers were sawed by hand.   The prison was burned by the Indians in 1675.

Daniel, a Scotch servant, got twenty lashes for profaning the Sabbath.   Jean Miller was summoned to answer the charge of calling her husband a "fool, toad, vermine," and threatening him.   Samuel Ely was fined for selling cider to the Indians.

An Indian named Aguossowump was flogged for theft.   Goodwife Hunter was gagged and made to stand half an hour in the stocks for sundry "exorbitancys of the tongue."

In May, 1653, John Pynchon's lot on Long Hill had been increased by the town on condition that he would buy a flock of forty sheep and sell them as he might to the inhabitants.

About 1659 John Pynchon planned to build the finest house in New England outside of Boston.   He made it a combination of garrison, residence and courthouse.   A Northampton man furnished the brick—in all 50,000—for which was paid over $2,000.   It stood where Fort Street is now and for many years was the most outstanding structure in the valley.

The death of William Pynchon, in 1664, caused John Pynchon to make a voyage to England, where he found his estate considerably enlarged by his father's will, but John Pynchon, himself, was rich for those times before this enlargement.   Previous to embarking for England he made a will of his own in America, and in that he speaks of his warehouses at Boston and of his wharf and lands adjoining.

Pynchon built a new mill in 1666, and later the town voted one-twelfth part of a bushel for all the grain ground in the new mill.

Shortly afterward he was voted some land if he would build a saw-mill. "Harry" and "Roco," Pynchon's slaves, worked on the first mill put up at Suffield in 1672. About that time the old road along the brow of Maple Street Hill, through the pines to the dingle was laid out, and on it the house of correction was built. It was found convenient, also, to build a pound on the west side, at the "hay place," which probably was not far from the old upper ferry, opposite Cypress Street.

In 1667, John Pynchon headed a committee appointed at the Bay to lay out lands, admit inhabitants, and complete the town organization at Quabaug. Thus it happened that the first records of Brook-field are in Major Pynchon's hand writing. His church, judicial, military, and political duties pressed heavily on him, but his business-like habits enabled him to carry a load which might have overcome a stronger man.

Pioneer Life in the New County

CHAPTER VIII

Pioneer Life in the New County

In 1662 Springfield appointed a committee "concerning settling the towns in this western part of the colony into the form of a county." As a result, the county of Hampshire was established in May of that year by the General Court, and it was proclaimed that:

> "For as much as the inhabitants of this jurisdiction are increased, so that now they are planted far into the country on the Connecticut River, and by reason of their remoteness they cannot conveniently be annexed to any of the counties already settled, and that public affairs may with more facility be transacted, it is ordered by this court that henceforth, Springfield, Northampton and Hadley shall be constituted a county, the limmits on the south to be the south line of the patent, the extent of other bounds to be full thirty miles distant from any of the other towns. The said county shall be called Hampshire, and shall enjoy the liberties and privileges of any other county. Springfield shall be the shire town, and the courts are to be kept one time at Springfield and another time at Northampton. It is further ordered that all the inhabitants of a shire shall pay their public rates to the county in fat cattle or young cattle, such as are fit for slaughter."

When Hampshire was incorporated it had only the three towns, Springfield, Northampton, and Hadley. Westfield was allowed to be a township in 1669. Brookfield, which originally was included in the Hampshire County area, became a town in 1673, but was destroyed by Indians in 1675. A few of the pioneers resettled it, and a garrison was kept there. Town privileges, however, were not restored until 1718.

After this new county of Hampshire was formed in 1662, the commissioner and selectmen of all the towns were summoned before the county court for not making out the tax assessment on time. Ensign Cooper, tax commissioner, who was specially summoned to appear, was fined six shillings, eight pence for not responding. The judges continued to have great difficulty in making the town and county officers do their duty for several years. The court found the burdens of administering justice no less severe.

A Hadley man who was to carry the votes for magistrates to Boston failed to do so and was fined, and Anthony Dorchester, of Springfield, constable, neglected to make returns of warrants for jurymen in 1666. Another Springfield delinquency was having a defective pound for stray cattle, and a five shilling fine was the consequence.

The fence question, which from the first settlement of the valley was a source of trouble, came under the eye of the county court, and it is interesting to note how the judges handled a matter that was the despair of local legislators. Here are some instances quoted from the records of the Hampshire County Court held at Springfield in 1664: John Dumbleton and Thomas Miller were presented to the court for not attending their office of viewing the fences on the west side of the river at Springfield, and the court freed Dumbleton on the plea that he would have attended to the fence viewing but could not get his partner to join with him. So Thomas Miller was fined the sum of two shillings for the use of the county.

Anthony Dorchester and Rice Bedortha, surveyors of the highways for Springfield, were presented to the court for neglecting their work in the season allotted by the town, "whereby the ways were very bad and dangerous"; therefore, they were fined five shillings.

The jury also presented Captain John Pynchon and John Scott for not maintaining their fences on the west side of the river. The court, after hearing the case and perusing the agreements between Captain Pynchon and John Scott, "did judge the blame of repairing the fences lies on Scott, because, though Captain Pynchon was to allow for making the fences, yet John Scott who improved the land was to repair the fence. Therefore we judge that John Scott shall pay his fine to the town."

The county court likewise had jurisdiction of the common lands, and were reported to for damages to crops by cattle. These disputes in the earlier years of the plantation were brought up in town meeting, and often put out to "two indifferent men." In 1664, John Leonard of Springfield, was fined five bushels of Indian corn to be paid Thomas Mirrick, for letting his cattle loose in the common cornfield.

In March, 1674, Anthony Dorchester was authorized to keep a ferry on the Connecticut, below the Agawam River, and to make these charges: Horse and man, eight pence; foot passengers, two pence; troopers on training days, three pence.

PYNCHON MEMORIAL MUSEUM, SPRINGFIELD

Mr. Glover was in court complaining against Robin, the Indian, for stealing three or four gold rings, two half crowns and some knives. When a search was made the rings were found in his wigwam, but he had sold the money to Goodman Ely. However, everything was restored to Mr. Glover. The Indian, after being caught and put in prison, made his escape from the jailor before any other punishment could be inflicted on him.

Both the court and the town authorities kept a strong grip on church members in matters of discipline. In 1665 the county court had Walter Lee before it for threshing corn on the Sabbath at Woronoco. We learn by the record that Lee was a hard case. When presented to the court "for passing the Lord's day last winter threshing corn on the Sabbath," he acknowledged it was so, and for calling Isaak Sheldon a member of Old Nick and a member of the Devil, he said that was so, and the court judged him to pay a fine of twenty shillings. It is sad to relate that this did not have a more salutary influence on him.

Pynchon, in 1672, was authorized to apportion land for a planta- tion at Squakheag, which the English called Northfield. A struggling community had been established at Brookfield some time before under the fostering care of Springfield.

The medium of trade in the British colonies was for a long time agricultural products, peltry, and other commodities, including the Indian shell-beads called wampum. Money was seldom seen except around commercial places. From 1640 to 1700 the Massachusetts farmers generally did their buying and paid their debts and taxes with the produce of their farms. Such persons as common laborers, sol- diers, schoolmasters, ministers and magistrates usually received for their services something that was not money. In the remote county of Hampshire, gold and silver were more scarce than in other parts. Church members sometimes found it necessary to pay the sacramental charges in wheat. The Northampton church voted, in 1666, that each member should contribute toward the charge of the sacrament three half pecks of wheat for a year.

The old custom among ministers, of staying at each other's houses in their journeyings, was necessary as well as convenient. They had plenty of eatables, and could easily entertain a minister and his wife, but many of them did not have money to pay innkeepers.

In March, 1673, George Filer, a Westfield Quaker, was pre- sented by the jury for various disorders. Firstly, he was examined "for entertaining Quakers last summer"; he owned that he enter- tained them, but claimed it was a necessity because no one else would do so. He said he would own before the world that he is "one of them whom the world calls Quakers"; also he was presented "for staying away from God's public worship on the Sabbath, and likewise he generally absented himself last winter. His speeches have been contemptuous of the ministers of the word and their work, and he seems to be a very seminary of corrupt and heretical opinions tending to poisoning the minds of those who listen to them."

In speaking of the religion of the Quakers, he speaks of it as distinct from that professed by our nation in this country and calls it *our religion,* that is—his own and such as he. Filer simply was reprimanded for his opinions, but a "five-pound fine, or be well whipped" was imposed for his "speaking against the ministry."

We find so often an unsympathetic hardness in the court dispensations of Puritan New England that we are prone to forget there is another side, yet right on the heels of these attempts in reforming and punishing offenders come some truly Spartan exhibitions of justice. We may not applaud the laws but must applaud their impartial application.

Three years later numerous ministers and judges alike shared the ill-will of unruly spirits. In 1668, for instance, John Matthews was led to the post and severely flogged for his exceeding contemptuous behavior toward Mr. Glover.

From evidence produced and read in this court, it appeared that his manner was odious to a very vile degree, and the court ordered that "John Mathews was to be well whipped on the naked body with fifteen stripes, and that he be bound in the sum of ten pounds for his good behavior in the court at Springfield in September, and that he pay the costs of court charges—twenty shillings."

One of the responsibilities of this John Mathews was the beating of the drum for divine service, and it is sad to relate that these duties did not have a more salutary influence on him. John Webb was before the same court for abusing the constables, saying of them "he would make it too hot for them if he lay there with his neck so streched." Also, he said he could afford to thumb both constable and his man that attended him. For his behavior toward the Northampton commissioners he was fined forty shillings.

The county court kept a sharp eye on the home and was quick to enforce parental authority. Samuel Ball was ordered to be flogged because he used abusive language to his father-in-law, Benjamin Munn, saying that he respected him no more than an old Indian, and exclaimed, "A father! There's a father indeed!"

In 1675 the county court lamented much "idle expence of Precious time," and prohibited tavern keepers from selling liquor to any but "Governors of families of sober carriage." Whenever a town showed signs of relaxation in family government the court would sharply reprimand the selectmen. By order of the court "Nine of the clock" at night was the time at which people were required to go to their lodgings or homes.

The inhabitants of the new towns were industrious and frugal, as a rule, and their lands were productive. They built good houses and barns, made additions to their furniture and implements, and multiplied their conveniences and enjoyments. The first emigrants to the Connecticut River were fully aware that their products must be sent to market by way of the river, and that their supplies would be received by the same channel. They simply selected a place that was safe. Mr. Pynchon and his associates made no attempt to plant themselves above boat navigation, and the great falls north of Springfield were an obstacle that prevented any settlement beyond their foaming waters for almost twenty years.

Nearly all the lands in towns bordering the Connecticut River were laid out unaided by any surveyor's compass, and the town measurers depended on a measuring-chain, and perhaps a square to form right angles. In general their calculations were sufficiently accurate, though not exact. The north star was sometimes regarded in establishing important lines. The first regular surveyor who had a compass and lived in a Connecticut River town was a Hartford man. He bought the compass a few years before 1700.

The early settlers owned fields in common, that were of necessity small, and surrounded by a common fence, except where a river, mountain or fence about other land served as a barrier against domestic animals. Each proprietor of a common field was to fence according to the number of acres he held in the field. The place of his fence, like that of his land, was fixed by lot. All fences had for their main object securing the meadows from domestic animals that roved in the woods outside. Some of the meadow fences, and most of the home-lot fences were made of posts and rails, but near the woods a ditch was often added. This type of fencing was taken from the English and was called "Ha! Ha!" Traces of these old "Ha! Ha's!" can still be found in the woods and brushland east of Longmeadow Street from Colony Hill down past the Longmeadow golf course to the Connecticut line. All fences were expected to be sufficient against horses, cattle, hogs and sheep. Gates were, of course, essential where fences crossed public highways, and these were rather troublesome to travelers. There were gates or bars that gave entrance from all highways into common fields, whether in a village or elsewhere. If a person left open the gate or bars of a meadow, he was to pay two shillings and six pence.

Complaints began to be made very early of dangerous places on the highways, and in March, 1664, the county court appointed a committee to lay out highways on both sides of the river between Hadley and Windsor. Of the six men on this committee, George Colton and Benjamin Cooley were from Springfield. In May a report was submitted which, much condensed, is as follows: "We agree that the highway from Hadley on the east side of the great river, to Fort Meadow gate, is in breadth six rods, and from there to the lower end of the meddow is ten rods." Then, omitting various measurements, we presently arrive where Mount Holyoke joins the Connecticut River. After that we go on with the cartway and come to Springfield at the upper end of the causeway going down into the town. Then we pass on through Springfield to Longmeadow gate, and from there to the bridge at the lower end by the river's bank, and to Freshwater River, so-called, and after that to Namerick, where John Bissell had a barn standing, then to Namerick Brook, which is the best place for a bridge, and then to the dividing line where the horseway is, and from the line on the west side of the river toward Waranoak and Two-mile Brook, and from there to Waranoak Hill where the trading house stood, and lastly to the passage of the river. Each town was to make its own landing places and provide for their "conveniency." One of the committee's stipulations for the several ways and bridges was that they should "be made and repaired sufficient for travel with carts." And lastly they added: "We determine that they be done by the towns, at or before the sixth day of June next." .

These were the first county roads in Hampshire, and Hampshire included Springfield at that time. They followed the ways previously used by the first settlers, and the three towns maintained for some years two roads that averaged nearly forty miles each, and that extended from Hadley and Northampton to the Connecticut line. The large streams, such as Chicopee, Manhan, and Waranoke, had no bridges and it was hard carting on the primitive roads. As for traveling in the forests, those were open and crossed with little difficulty. It was the streams, hills, and swamps that impeded the traveler. The Indian paths between their villages and tribes, which sometimes were followed by the English, were seldom broader than a cart's rut, for these red men of the forest traveled in "Indian file." There was a time when some of the Hampshire men had a project to lay out a way to the Bay for horses and carts, but it was not feasible, and runners did not pass from Hampshire to Boston for many years afterward.

Some of the millstones used in the valley in early days were of the red sandstone called pudding-stone. There were occasions when days would be spent looking for stones that were suitable. In 1666 John Pynchon gave John Webb, of Northampton, twenty pounds for a pair of millstones delivered in Springfield. These were probably sandstone from Mount Tom.

Boards had always been sawed by hand in England. There was no sawmill in Virginia when that colony had been settled forty years, and there were no sawmills in the old colony towns of Massachusetts for some years, so boards, plank and slit work were sawed by hand. Wages of sawyers were regulated by law in Springfield, Hartford and other towns. At New Haven, the "top-man," who was on top of the log and guided the work, had a little higher wages than the "pit man," who was in the saw-pit below. Two men were expected to saw about one hundred feet of boards in a day when the logs were squared and brought to the pit. The first sawmill in Springfield was built by John Pynchon, in 1667, after the town had been settled thirty-one years. He had previously paid to hand-sawyers two shillings a day for sawing many thousands of boards. The clapboards of those days, which were split out like staves, helped to supply the deficiency of sawn boards.

A Massachusetts law, passed in 1647, ordered that every town with fifty families should provide a school where children might be taught to read and write; and every town with a hundred families or householders should provide a grammar school and master able to instruct so far as to fit young men for college. There were previously many schools in the Colony, but this was the first law requiring them. By a somewhat earlier law selectmen were to look after the children of parents and masters who neglected to train them up "in learning and labor."

Long before this the Puritans meant that every child should be taught to read, at home or at school, and be able to read the Bible. New England grammar schools, with few exceptions, were Latin and English schools united. Some students were fitted for college, but about nine-tenths were confined to English studies. Before being sent to these schools, children were generally taught to read, at least, in the primer.

In the towns on the Connecticut River schools were commonly supported partly by the parents of the pupils and partly by the town. Schools were not maintained wholly by towns until after much discussion and agitation. Persons in moderate circumstances, with large families, wanted free schools. The wealthy, and those who had no children to send, were inclined to oppose them. Few towns would vote for schools entirely free until after 1700, and it was many years after that before free schools became general in Massachusetts.

The laws of the Colony and the votes of towns relating to schools used the word "children," and did not exclude females, yet it was plain that girls seldom attended the town schools. There was no controversy on the subject; it simply seems to have been considered unnecessary that girls should be taught as boys were.

There were many cheap private schools in Massachusetts during the seventeenth and eighteenth centuries. They were kept by "dames," and the teaching was done in their own rooms. Girls were instructed to read and sew, and in some of these schools small boys were taught to read. Children who did not attend school were taught to read at home. Writing was considered much less important, and it was not judged necessary that females in common life should learn to write. As a matter of fact the ability to write would have been of little use to them in former times. Probably, in the period when the War for Independence was being fought, very many of those wives and mothers whose patriotism we praise could not write, but they could read.

The early school books of New England were the same as those of Old England and were listed in 1690 as the Hornbook, Primer, Psalter, Testament and Bible. These were the only books used to engage the liking of children and tempt them to read. They were sold to the people of Springfield and its vicinity by John Pynchon, from 1656 to beyond 1672. Afterward, to 1680, he had customers for many catechisms, and paper books for writers, but he sold no spelling books and they were little used in the seventeenth century. Arithmetic was taught, though the books were rare. Hornbooks were not used in Hampshire County after 1700. They contained the alphabet, with a few rudiments on one page, covered, as Cowper says, "with thin, translucent horn," to keep them from being soiled. A book called a Primer has been used by children in schools for centuries. Our early Primers were imported from England, and probably were Puritan Primers. The New England Primer seems to have been published about 1660, and to have been intended for a child's school book.

One thing that required the town's attention was the management of the turpentine business. The inhabitants were prohibited from "boxing turpentine trees" on the inmost "common," and a committee was appointed to "regulate the drawing of turpentine." The region for operating in boxing pine trees was regulated by the proprietors of the commons, and no one was allowed to work more than one thousand new trees and for these there was a license fee.

When our forefathers crossed the Atlantic to establish homes in New England, they brought with them the habits of the Mother Country. The English of that time were addicted to malt liquors, the country was full of licensed alehouses, and an alewife was a woman and not a fish. Inns, taverns and ordinaries abounded. Wine and ale were the principal intoxicating beverages, but distilled liquors also were used. The English, as Shakespeare says, were most "potent in potting." "Drunkenness hath diffused itself over the nation," another authority tells us in 1617.

The first planters of New England were some of the best portion of this wine-bibbing, ale-guzzling nation. They abhorred drunkenness and intended to be temperate drinkers, and they followed the English custom of licensing men to sell intoxicating drinks. Alehouses in England were in bad repute, and the newcomers from across the sea

avoided using the unsavory name by substituting the word "ordinary," which in England signified an eating-house.

The planters of the Connecticut River Valley were conscious of
the evil effects of liquor houses, and in no haste to have these ordinaries. When the subject was agitated in 1663, they proceeded with
great caution, and the keepers and retailers in those days were very
respectable men. Selectmen would not approve, nor the court license,
any others. John Pynchon was licensed to sell wine and strong liquors
in 1671.

A while afterward the court that was sitting at Springfield in the
house of Nathaniel Ely, ordinary-keeper, fined him forty shillings for
selling beer that was not according to law—that is, with four bushels
of barley malt to the hogshead. In consequence of drunkenness
among the Indians, "the fruits whereof were murder and other outrages," the General Court, in 1647, forbade all persons to sell or give
to any Indian, rum, wine, brandy, cider, or any other strong liquors,
under penalty of forty shillings for every pint so sold or given. The
Hampshire courts were prompt to punish infractions of this law, and
were sustained by nearly all the people. But a few persons could not
resist the temptation of exchanging spirits for wampum and beaver
skins; and sometimes a farmer or his wife thought there was no great
harm in selling to the red man a few quarts of poor cider. The
Indians were sure to be drunk whenever they could get liquor enough
for the purpose.

The Indians in this valley were miserable, degraded beings when
these towns were settled, and it is evident that they did not become
any better. The great and crying sin of drunkenness reigned among
them. This was attributed by the courts to selling them cider and
strong beer. A very little strong drink would intoxicate their brains;
for being used to drinking water, they could not bear a fourth part of
what an Englishman could.

The early drinks in New England were wine of several sorts,
beer, ale, brandy and aquavitæ. Wine and beer were the principal
drinks until rum was brought from the West Indies. The General
Court of Connecticut termed it "Barbadoes liquor, commonly called
rum-kill-devil." One of the valley historians in a footnote comment
says, "This liquor was strangely misnamed. Instead of killing the

devil, it has greatly extended and strengthened his kingdom." Aqua-vitæ, which signifies water of life, also had a wrong name. Rum-kill-devil was much cheaper than aquavitæ from Europe, and the use became much more common. Cider was less in favor than beer until after 1700, and about that time New England rum, distilled from molasses, was added to the list of intoxicating drinks.

The county court in 1675 remarked, "it is found by experience that there is too much idle expence of precious time in drinking strong liquors by many of our youth and others." The court ordered that retailers should sell only to governors of families of sober carriage, the "intent being that such persons as have liberty to sell, should use their influence to prevent a trade of drinking and drunkenness."

John Pynchon did not commonly retail wine and spirits, but when he had rum for sale, there was no lack of customers. Reverend Pela-tiah Glover, the Springfield minister, bought of him two gallons of rum and six quarts of wine in a year. Mr. Pynchon, at the raising of his mill dam, in 1654, furnished wine and cakes to the amount of thirteen shillings, sixpence.

Every town was required to have a distinct mark for cattle and horses. What this should be was determined by the General Court. All those animals which fed in the open without constant keepers were to have a brand-mark on a horn, or left buttock or shoulder, so a per-son could tell in what town a stray creature belonged. The brand-marks used for the Hampshire towns in 1681 were: S.P. for Springfield, N.H. for Northampton, H.D. for Hadley, and W.F. for Westfield. The two letters for each town were united, as Hꓷ, for Hadley.

Sumptuary laws restraining excess of apparel in some classes were common in England and other countries for centuries. Massachusetts enacted such a law in 1651, ordering that persons whose estates did not exceed two hundred pounds, and those dependent on them, should not wear gold or silver lace, gold or silver buttons, bone lace above two shillings a yard, or silk hoods or scarves, on penalty of ten shill-ings for each offense. Any person wearing such articles might be assessed, as if they had estates of two hundred pounds.

The first attempt to have this law observed in our locality was made in 1673. At the March court, twenty-five wives and five maids belonging to Springfield, Northampton, Hadley, Hatfield and West-field, were presented by the jury as "persons of small estate, who wear silk contrary to law." Some were acquitted, some were fined, and others were admonished. Of the thirty, only three were fined, and the fines were remitted at the next court.

The jury of the March court in 1676 presented sixty-eight persons, of whom thirty-eight were wives and maids, and thirty young men, some for wearing silk, "and that in a flaunting manner," and others for long hair and other extravagances. Two were fined ten shillings and many others were ordered to pay the clerk's fees, two shillings, six pence each. Several of the sixty-eight were wives, daughters or sons of well-to-do men.

MEMORIAL BRIDGE, SPRINGFIELD

In those days the March courts were held at the house of a Northampton man who kept an ordinary, and most of the women and men of the five Hampshire towns of that period who were summoned to answer for their finery, came to the ordinary and appeared before the judges in the courtroom. They, and the spectators, attracted by the novelty of the proceedings, must have filled the house.

The men on the bench when the females appeared in court on a March day in 1673 were: John Pynchon and Elizur Holyoke, of Springfield; William Clark, of Northampton; and Henry Clarke, of Hadley. In September, a few years later, the selectmen of all the five towns were presented to the court for not assessing according to law their inhabitants that wore silk and were excessive in their apparel. The court endeavored to stir up the selectmen to assess those wearing unsuitable and excessive apparel, but it was too late; the women had already gained the victory and no longer feared fines or taxes for wearing silks; "yet many good men lamented the extravagance of the age, and the love of finery among the women."

The court sessions continued one, two or three days. There were commissioners or judges, jurors and a constable or marshal, making sixteen to eighteen persons who dined together, or dined at the same place, every court day at the ordinary where the court sat, and those from other towns had supper, lodging and breakfast. Some wine and considerable beer were drank. The judges and jurymen from these upper towns, in order to attend court one day at Springfield, had to be absent from home two nights. They lived well and the ordinary keeper charged much more than the common price for their meals. The food, drink and horse-keeping, which were paid for by the county, seemed to be the principal compensation they received. Twice the record mentions that most of the county rate was needed to pay the county reward for killing wolves. Nothing was received directly by the keepers of ordinaries for the room used by the court, or for fuel. Litigation was not cheap in Massachusetts, for every person who sued another in a county court was required to pay ten shillings for the privilege.

All the produce that went to Boston was carried down the river, and all the merchandise from that place, except a few light articles, was brought up the river. John Pynchon sometimes sent to Boston more than 2,000 bushels of wheat and peas in a year. At Springfield there were small boats carrying three or four tons, and in the accounts of William and John Pynchon these were called canoes. Each boat was managed by two men down and up the river and at Enfield Falls. Grain was carried to Hartford in the boats, and so were barrels of flour and pork and hogsheads of beaver. Sometimes the Springfield boats brought up the furniture of families moving.

The first settlers of New England knew nothing about sleds and sleighs, nor did they use them for some years. Heavy sleds came long before sleighs. Some wood was sledded before 1670, but in general it was carted many years after that date. Also, for a considerable period, logs were conveyed to saw-pits and sawmills on wheels; indeed, nearly everything was carted. Logs were carted to John Pynchon's sawmill some years after 1667, but in 1674 he bought a sled, and many logs were sledded. People did not keep sled roads open in winter even for fifteen or twenty miles, and there were no sleigh rides in the Hampshire towns until about 1740.

New England was far from being an unbroken wilderness when first settled by the English. In the vicinity of the Indian settlements there were not only plots of cleared land on which the squaws raised Indian corn, beans and squashes, but many openings that were covered with grass, and extensive tracts of woodland, where the trees were so scattered that green herbage and even strawberries flourished among them. The early settlers thought these thin forests resembled the English parks, and a Salem man wrote, in 1629, that the country was "very beautiful in open lands mixed with goodly woods, and with plains that in some places exceed five hundred acres, yet are not much troublesome to clear for the plow. The grass and weeds grow up to a man's face, and in the lowlands and by fresh rivers is abundance of grass, and large meadows without any tree or shrub."

The Indians burned the country that it might not be overgrown with underwood, and the burning made the region passable by destroying the brushwood. At the same time it scorched the older trees and hindered their growth. In many places the land was so free from obstruction that a person could ride when hunting.

The Indian custom was to burn the woods in November when the grass was withered and the leaves dry, for then the raging fire consumed all the underwood and rubbish, besides presenting a grand spectacle. That this Norwottuck Valley was wild, and its scenery to some degree gloomy, may be granted, but there must also have been much that was pleasant and full of natural charm.

The first planters of New England were entirely unaccustomed to the business of clearing woodlands, and they selected places for their homes where they could immediately begin to cultivate the earth. The rich alluvial lands that bordered the Connecticut and its tributaries attracted them at once. They found plenty of land ready for the plow and as soon as they could establish themselves, they began to raise Indian corn and other grain. Besides, there was grass to harvest and protect from the weather. The upland woods on each side of the river, above and below the towns, were passable for men on horseback, and with a little preparation, for carts.

After the Indians ceased to burn over a tract of land, bushes and brambles commonly began to grow in abundance on it, and this was considered very injurious by those who came to inhabit afterward.

Those bushes that sprang up so plentifully in the home-lots, highways, and elsewhere were indeed a great annoyance. There was so little travel within and between the towns with wheels and two animals abreast that the bushes choked up the ways, and it was difficult to keep an open path.

For a long time the woods were used by the English as pasture grounds, where all kinds of domestic animals grazed, and they fired the woods annually, as the Indians had before them. But there was no setting of fires near their habitations and fenced fields. That was reserved for the more distant parts of the township. Massachusetts enacted a law forbidding any person to set the common woodlands on fire, except between March 10 and April 30. According to tradition, there were some splendid burnings in the woods on the hills and mountains around this valley, especially in the night. The fires continued down to 1743, when a Massachusetts law was made to restrain such fires, arguing that the burning of the woods greatly impoverished the soil, prevented the growth of the wood, and destroyed much fence. Traditional accounts affirm that the woods used to be so free from underbrush, and the trees so thinly scattered, that a deer could be seen forty rods on the wooded hills. The burnings were as favorable to the white deer hunters as they were of old to the Indian hunters.

Valuable timber was not so plenty as some have imagined, and there were river towns that had fears of a scarcity very early. Springfield voted in 1647 that no timber, boards, planks nor shingle-timber should be carried out of the town from the east side of the river.

New England's first settlers knew the value of oak, but did not at first understand the importance of pine. In many places they not only used oak timber for the frames of buildings, but oak clapboards and oak shingles, and some used oak boards to wainscot rooms. Where pine was plenty, pine boards were perhaps sawed as early as oak boards, and everywhere the tendency was for pine shingles and clapboards to take the place of oak. Our forefathers had to learn how to split rails from logs after they came to this country.

When John Pynchon built his brick house in 1660 he put on shingles eighteen inches long and an inch thick at the thick end. In 1677 he used cedar shingles for one of his structures. He built saw-mills in Springfield, Suffield, and Enfield. After the first mill was completed he hired men to cut logs ready for the saw at eight pence each; and other men were engaged to cart them to the mill with their own teams at one shilling, eight pence each. The logs were to be from twelve to twenty-five feet in length, and from seventeen to twenty-four inches in diameter at the small end. Most of them were pine. White oak logs cost much more.

Lath for plastering are rarely mentioned in the writings of the seventeenth century. The wealthy plastered their rooms, but the farmers got along either with very little plaster, or none at all.

The first pastures in this and other British colonies were the woods that previously had been the hunting grounds of the Indians. These woodlands gave the inhabitants of the Norwottuck Valley a very wide range for their cattle during more than half a century.

Horses, horned cattle, sheep and hogs were pastured on the plains, hills and mountainsides. Cows were under a keeper, and so were sheep after they were numerous enough for a shepherd. In some towns there was an abundance of goats. Young horses and cattle commonly roved without restraint, and so did hogs. In many places the wages of a cowherd were twelve shillings a week, and very likely he was to drive out the herd every morning by the time the sun was an hour high, take them to good feed, and bring them home reasonably at night. A farmer who had only a few sheep would keep them on his home-lots and about the village, until the number had increased enough to afford paying a shepherd.

The owners of the herds and flocks usually took care of them on Sundays, so the keepers might attend public worship.

The common fields and private lots needed strong barriers to protect them against restless, rambling animals. Young cattle and horses often remained in the woods until winter, and some of them became wild and unruly and strayed to other towns. Many days were spent both in winter and other seasons looking for cattle and horses in the woodlands.

Swine were seldom killed by wolves or bears, for they defended themselves and their young with great vigor when attacked. By a law of the Colony, a dog that bit or killed sheep was to be hanged. The hanging of untrustworthy dogs sometimes gave a name to the vicinity where the execution took place. "Hang-dog Swamp" is an instance. The dog was taken to the woods, a leaning staddle bent down and a cord fastened to the dog's neck. Then the elastic staddle sprung back with the dog dangling in the air. There has been a time still more remote when cats and dogs were hanged at the heavy end of a well-sweep.

Settlers and Soldiers

CHAPTER IX

Settlers and Soldiers

The Indians of the Connecticut River Valley were eager to have the English settle among them, and they gladly sold their lands. No urging was necessary. Also, they knew perfectly well what use the English made of the lands they had bought in other places long before. Nor did they ever pretend they were ignorant of what was intended by a sale of land, and no quarrels resulted on that score. In the opinion of many intelligent men, the price the Indians received for land was all it was worth.

As one authority has said, "Whoever is conversant with the toils and privations attending a new settlement in the wilderness, and will take the trouble to compute what is expended and laid out to make the land produce anything, and how much its value depends on neighboring settlements, and on roads and the various improvements of civilized life, will come to the conclusion that wild land in a wilderness, remote from neighbors, can not be of much value." The Indians themselves manifestly were not conscious of giving up much that was useful or important to them. The Indian men were fond of fighting, hunting, and fishing, and they disdained other pursuits. Agricultural labor, and all kinds of drudgery were the lot of the women, who, with hoes of shells, wood or iron, cultivated small patches of land. Raising crops was a minor object with the Indians. Many of their deeds retained the liberty of hunting and fowling on the lands they sold, and of fishing in the streams. There are rare instances, too, of reserving the privilege of setting their wigwams on the commons, and getting firewood from there.

President Dwight, in his "Travels in New England" says, "the Indians were always considered as having a right to dwell and to hunt within the lands which they had sold." Such a right seems to have been practically enjoyed, though not expressly reserved, in all the deeds. When the women took land of the English for half the crop they may have obtained from well plowed land more corn than the same amount of labor produced when the land and all the crop were theirs.

The relations of the English with the Indians were far from tyrannical. In a land deal with John Pynchon that made a tract absolutely his, the Indians wanted sometimes to set their wigwams within the bounds of what they had sold. He agreed "he would be kind and neighborly to them," and besides he promised not to prohibit them from getting firewood out of the forest.

Pynchon was very careful in making deeds, as may be seen in this fragment wherein a chief, Umpanchala, "do give, grant, bargain, and sell to John Pynchon of Springfield, all the grounds, woods, ponds, waters, trees, stones, meadows and uplands lying at Norwotogg, on the west side of Quenecticut River."

Here follows a portion of another Indian deed written by John Pynchon, who now had reached a maturity and influence that entitled him to be called the Worshipful Major Pynchon:

"Be it known by these presents, that Wequagon and his wife Amonusk, and Squomp, their son, being the sole owners of the land at Norwotogg, on the east side of Quenicticutt River, southward toward Springfield, sell unto John Pynchon the neck or meadow which the English call Hoccanum, together with the uplands adjoining, and the brook or riverett called Cowachuck. Only a parcel of land upwards of sixty acres, being already mortgaged to Joseph Parsons of Northampton and bounded out to him by stakes and marks in the presence of two Northampton men, they exempt from this sale. The rest of the land, said John Pynchon, and his successors shall enjoy forever, absolutely, clearly and free from all molestation by Indians. We, the said Wequogon, Awonunske and Squomp will defend the will unto the said Pynchon against all lawful claims whatsoever. The intent is not to exclude the Indians from hunting deer, beaver or other wild creatures on the tract aforesaid, which liberty they yet reserve to themselves, and also to take fish, and sometime to set their wigwams on the commons, and to take wood and trees off the commons for their own use. In witness whereof the said Indians have hereunto set their hands and marks this eighth day of August, 1662."

Indian chiefs were inclined to get into debt. Wequagon and his wife and son, Squomp, owed Joseph Parsons eighty beaver skins for coats, wampum and goods, and they mortgaged to him a parcel of land in the meadow and upland called Hockanum. The debt was not paid when due, and Parsons sold the land for a considerable sum.

Indians, in signing deeds, commonly did something more than make a mark; most made a picture or representation of some object. In the old records at Springfield may be seen many of these Indian hieroglyphics, such as a beaver, a snake, a snow-shoe, a bow, a hand, and so on.

In John Pynchon's account book are charged all the wampum and other articles sold to Umpanchala, to pay him seventy-five pounds or three hundred fathoms of wampum for some land, including a fine for being drunk. Accounts with Indians were kept in fathoms and hands of wampum. Pynchon, in this account, estimated ten hands equal to a fathom, and made his hands more than seven inches, instead of the usual hand of four inches. Wampum was an article of traffic, and also the money of the Indians, the standard by which they measured the value of all other things. A fathom of wampum was a string of beads six feet long and made of shells.

Pynchon paid from his shop in wampum and merchandise, for nearly all the lands in the vicinity of the river that were bought of the Indians, from Suffield and Enfield, to Deerfield and Northfield, and received his pay from the settlers and proprietors of the new towns, to whom he assigned the Indian deeds.

From 1636, when Springfield was settled, until the Indian War of 1675, the Nipmucks inhabited the interior of Massachusetts, occupying many places in the present county of Worcester, and in the old county of Hampshire. They were not subject to a common sachem, but had many petty chiefs. Four small clans dwelt in the Connecticut Valley or within a few miles of it. These were the Agawams at Springfield and Westfield, the Waranokes at Westfield, the Norwottucks at Northampton, Hadley, and Hatfield, and the Pocomtucks at Deerfield. The four tribes of western Nipmucks may be reckoned at about eleven hundred when most numerous, and when they left this part of the country their numbers were much reduced. The Norwottuck chiefs had little authority, and were of slight importance. One writer makes the comment that the historians and novelists will not be able to make heroes of any river sachems, from Saybrook to Northfield.

At times our valley Indians had no acknowledged leader, and in 1668 they agreed that Chickwallop should be their chief, but there was nothing in Chickwallop to inspire the English or Indians with respect. The Norwottucks committed no great offenses, but there were times when they harbored evil-doers from other tribes, and there were some inclined to petty thefts. When they could get strong drink they became drunk, and brawls and tumults followed. At such a time they would insult and abuse the constable or anyone else. Yet when free from liquor they were generally peaceful and respectful toward the whites, who intended to treat them justly and humanely.

There is no reason to think that the Indians of the valley lacked food or that their supplies had been perceptibly diminished previous to their departure. The forests in every direction remained nearly as extensive as ever, and wild animals, fish and wild fruits were still abundant. The whites sometimes hunted and fowled, but they were too industrious to spend much time in such pursuits. There was land enough for corn, but without fences it was useless, and the squaws took meadow land on shares after the English had plowed it. They planted and hoed the corn, and picked and husked it without any aid from their lazy husbands.

The first settlers of the region lived in peace with the Indians until King Philip's War in 1675. There was constant intercourse between them, for the Indians came freely into the villages for traffic and other purposes, and the salutation, *Netop* (my friend) was often heard in the streets. Indian men, women, youths, maids and small children, in their scanty garments, were everyday sights, and roused no curiosity. The men sold furs and venison, and the women made and sold baskets, mats, and other things. Among these laborious Indian women were some who were mild and kind-hearted, but the western Nipmucks were pagans.

The Indians of the Norwottuck Valley had several forts which they erected to protect them from attacks of their enemies. A Dutch writer says: "They built their castles in places difficult of access, on or near the crown of a hill; the wall is made of palisades set in the ground, and within are their wigwams."

The Norwottuck forts seem generally to have been on top of a bluff or high bank, projecting into a valley near a stream. Some people have admired the taste of the Indians as shown in the picturesque situations they chose for forts and villages, but there is not much foundation for this admiration. The tribes were pugnacious, and it was owing to their wars that they selected elevated places for villages, where they could more easily secure and defend themselves and more readily see the approach of an enemy. The Indians did not all live in forts, and when our local Indians were fearful of an attack from the Mohawks or other enemies, many sought refuge near the houses and in the outbuildings of the English. This made living among them very troublesome.

The English and the Indians round about were alike in dreading the Mohawks more than any other Indians with whom they came in contact. The tribe lived about forty miles west of Albany. They were brave, but they were also ferocious, and carried on an exterminating warfare for more than a century after 1600, making a perfect desert of the country for five hundred miles west and south, and destroying more Indians than have been destroyed by Europeans in war since the country was settled. They were the worst of conquerors, and seemed to fight to gratify their thirst for blood.

They were extremely filthy and never washed either face or hands. It was their habit to cook fish from the water without any cleansing, and to devour the entrails of deer with as little ceremony. Actually, all savages are filthy, and our New England savages are no exception. For instance, by an agreement made with sachems at Concord in 1646, the Indians were not "to pick lice as formerly and eat them."

The early Dutch and New England writers were not long in discovering that the Mohawks were man-eaters. First they tortured their captives, and then prepared for a savage feast by roasting them before a slow fire.

About 1663, war was begun between the Mohawks and New England Indians, and while it was going on the Mohawks in small parties made raids into the region the white men had acquired. In September, 1665, the Mohawks came into Cambridge well armed. They were arrested and imprisoned at Boston. The English never had seen any Mohawks before and they attracted much attention. The local Indians flocked into Boston and wished to put the Mohawks to death, but the court dismissed them with a letter to their Kennebec sachem, and a convoy of horse to conduct them clear of the nearby Indians.

A couple of years later a number of hogs and cattle belonging to Springfield and neighboring places were killed in the woods, and the Mohawks shot and scalped the Indian servant of a Northampton man. Evidently scalping was something unknown to the English up to this time. Thereupon the General Court of Massachusetts wrote to the chief sachem of the Mohawks complaining that much damage had been suffered in the past summer from the Indians. Several cattle had been shot and wounded, and others had been killed, and the flesh cut from their bones and carried away. Speedy and full satisfaction was demanded, and emphasis was laid on the fact that an Indian youth who was servant to an Englishman was murdered in spite of the fact that "you told us your people would not meddle with any Indians that wore English clothes, or had their hair cut short." The letter ended with "hoping of your readiness to make satisfaction for what is past, and care for your continuance of friendship, your loving friends, the Governor and General Court of Massachusetts."

This letter had some effect, for the Mohawks wanted to be on good terms with New England, and they made reparation with leather that had a value of twenty pounds. This went to the hands of Simon Lobdell in Springfield, and by order of the court the town was to receive what was valued at five pounds for those persons who had lost swine and cattle. Northampton was to have seven pounds, of which half was for the killing of Nathaniel Clark's Indian servant. Hadley, which had lost more than any other town, received what was equivalent to eight pounds for those who had been damaged. Lastly, the court ordered Simon Lobdell to make the various payments with shoes at fair prices.

Militia companies were organized and armed in nearly the same manner as soldiers in England. For training purposes the favorite book was "The Compleat body of the Art Military," which many persons in New England owned. Major John Pynchon had one, and so did Captain Aaron Cooke, of Northampton. Cooke gave his in his will to his son. The manual furnished long lists to indicate the right manner of dealing with the matchlock musket and rest. It was a serious matter—those postures of the muskets, and you had to do such things as open your pan, cast off your loose corns and blow off your loose corns, but it fails to tell what to do with the corns that are not loose. You are asked to draw forth your scouring stick, and turn and shorten him to an inch. Later you are told in that same manner to "withdraw your scouring stick and turn and shorten him to a handful." Other curious orders are: "Blow your coal, cock your match, lay down your bandoliers. Here endeth the postures of the musket."

There were also funeral saluting and postures of lighter muskets which were used without rests, but fired with a match. "The Postures of the Pike" are given. Those of English make were sixteen feet long.

Muskets were generally large and heavy and required a forked staff or rest to support them when presented to fire They were handguns with matchlocks. The rests had a crotch or crescent at the top, and a sharp iron at the bottom to fasten them in the ground. The musketeer had a rest in his hand, or hung to it by a string, in nearly all his exercises. Musketeers carried their powder in little wooden, tin, or copper boxes, each containing one charge. Twelve of these boxes were fixed to a belt two inches wide worn over the left shoulder, and the boxes and belt were called bandoliers. Usually the primer containing the priming powder, the bullet-bag and priming were fastened to the leather bag. These, and the small, long boxes hung on the belt made much rattling. This belt with its dangling appendages had some resemblance to a string of sleigh bells. Each trooper was to have a good horse, saddle, bridle, holsters, pistols or carbine, and sword.

All males above sixteen years of age, if not exempt, were to attend military exercises and service. Companies were to be exercised six days every year, and there was to be a regimental training once in three years. It was the custom to have a prayer at the beginning and ending of a training and the captain was expected to make the prayers.

It was not until 1657 that the Springfield company had three commissioned officers. John Pynchon was captain, Elizur Holyoke lieutenant, and Thomas Cooper ensign. Northampton had a small train band in 1658. In March, 1663, certain persons of the soldiery met at Northampton and listed themselves into a troop with John Pynchon, of Springfield, for captain, and fifty-three members. The dress and equipment of the troopers were more costly and showy than those of the foot soldiers, and they may have deemed their service more honorable. The expensive trooping scarf of Captain Pynchon was embellished with gold lace, and silver glittered on his sword and belt

LONGMEADOW COMMON

and on various less important articles of military equipment. His companion officers wore silk scarfs or sashes. When this company met in a village for exercise, the day was one of great excitement, particularly for the young, who heard the shrill trumpet and admired the proud banner and prancing steeds and the gay appearance and quick motions of the men. Captain John Pynchon, of this Hampshire regiment, was the first regimental officer of the county.

After King Philip's war began men were soon aware that matchlocks and pikes, however efficient in European warfare, were of little avail against nimble, skulking Indians, who did not face their enemies in the open field. So flintlocks were used whenever they could be obtained. Many expeditions against the Indians were made on horseback by men who carried carbines, and much scouting was done on horses.

In November, 1675, Massachusetts ordered that every town should provide and have continuously six flints for each listed soldier in the town. Every trooper had, by order of the Colony, already furnished himself with carbines, and all pike men with firearms. By 1676 a revolution was effected, and pikes and matchlocks were for the most part laid aside. Pistols were considered useless against Indians. The Colony Committee of War estimated that two thousand flints were necessary for an expedition of five hundred men. New England discarded matchlocks, rests, and pikes many years before they were laid aside in Old England. In the new Colony law foot soldiers were to have a firelock musket or other good firearms; a knapsack, bandoliers, boots and spurs, powder, a sword or cutlass, three pounds of bullets, twenty flints, and more or less other articles.

Troopers were to have a horse worth five pounds, and not less than fourteen hands high, with a saddle, bit, bridle, holsters and crupper; a carbine with a barrel not less than two and one-half feet in length, and a case of pistols, a flask, and various things that were the same as those of the foot soldiers. Males from sixteen to sixty years of age were to train, except those exempt. Negroes and Indians were among the exempts. When soldiers were levied, a man impressed must go, or pay five pounds. A few years later he must pay ten pounds, or be imprisoned six months.

Militia companies, about the beginning of the seventeenth century, began indulging a fancy for flags of rich colors and costly fabrics. In 1660, John Pynchon sold to the Northampton company colors, staff, tassel and top for five pounds. The next year he sold to Hadley for the use of the soldiers, colors, staff, tassel and top for the same price. These flags were costly silk. Sumptuous flags seem to have continued down to the Revolution. When the wind blew, the ensign had much trouble, for it was necessary to gather the flag in folds, which he tried to grip firmly in his hands, but with a considerable degree of uncertainty.

The early laws insisted on having watchmen even in time of peace, from the first of May to the end of September. They were usually under the care of constables. There was always some distrust of the Indians. The watchmen began to examine night walkers after ten o'clock. Military watches were required in the several towns in time of war, and when danger seemed imminent military officers took charge. Every town was ordered to provide a watch-house, and candles and wood. Sometimes day watching was required. Watches were kept up in these river towns much of the time for a century. The people in those days bore without murmuring these and other burdens, which their descendants would deem intolerable.

Alarms in the night were made by firing three guns, followed by the beating of drums, and there were other ways of alarming the people. A hundred years later, in the Revolutionary War, the inhabitants of these towns were several times aroused from sleep by the firing of three guns, which was followed by the beating of drums.

"The Worshipful Major John Pynchon," son of the founder of Springfield, was for many years the town's leading citizen in wealth and influence. He carried on an extensive trade with both the whites and Indians. Sometimes he sent in a single ship to England five thousand dollars' worth of otter and beaver skins. Other skins that he bought were the gray and red fox, the muskrat, raccoon, martin, mink, wild cat and moose. Most of them were packed in hogsheads. Many of the skins were brought down the river from the distant north and west.

During Springfield's first forty years it was happily free from the usual experiences of pioneers attempting to occupy a savage wilderness, and the reason for it seems to have been that these first planters never took ground without paying for it. The Pynchon rule of even justice and fair play toward the Indian was known to the tribes hundreds of miles away, at least as far as the Mohawk country.

Often the Indians brought their disputes to Springfield for settlement. William Pynchon soon found, in dealing with the Indians, that they were lazy, unreliable, and quick to take offense. Their vengeful disposition and their secretive ways, and their long memory of slights, soon caused Pynchon to avoid employing them as much as possible. He even refused to use them as messengers and scouts when white troopers were in sight. Indians would loiter on the way, and were not above breaking their word. Nor did they come up to the English standard of personal tidiness, and if they had not been prodded with the white man's law, they would have been content to stroll about the streets and live off alms at the back doors. In 1669 the county court had occasion to admonish a constable for roughly handling some Indians found abroad on the Lord's Day. The Indians were caught at Woronoco carrying burdens of apples, which they said they got from Windsor, and they acknowledged shooting a gun when he came to the house. The constable seized four guns and called one of the Indians to appear at the court and answer for the offense.

"The which being proved, the court judges the constable striking the Indian, and the dog biting him, he should only be admonished." There was no end of trouble in keeping savage hands off portable property. The owners of the hands would dodge into kitchens and steal food, cider, and any articles in reach, and they would run off cattle and swine. The selling of liquor to the Indians was strictly forbidden, but the natives were continually securing it on the sly.

The Indians were not satisfied with their arrows after they had seen the blunderbuss, and though selling them firearms, like selling them firewater was prohibited, in one way or another they contrived to get them. They had not much thought for the morrow in their trading, and they often obtained blankets, food, and farm tools on credit. The result was that a mortgage system grew as naturally as weeds after a rain. One of the very early mortgages was to a group of Indians, and the person who became the holder of the mortgage was Samuel Marshfield, an active land speculator. However, the mortgage was duly approved by the selectmen, April 2, 1661.

The substance of it is that the Indians acknowledged their several debts for goods received, which they engaged to pay in beaver, "and we still engage to do the same if we can get it any time this summer, or else we engage to pay in corn or wampum, or if we can get moose-skins, or otter, or good deer skins, then to pay him at a reasonable rate, or guns which the said Samuel has in his hands, and if he lends to any of us we engage to return them to him when he shall call for them: and if we do not pay the aforesaid Samuel to his content by Michelmas, then we give full power to seize on all our lands and corn as his proper right."

Indian   Wars

CHAPTER X

Indian Wars

In the spring of 1675 the plantation entered on a terrible chapter of its history. It was about forty years old, and many of the first settlers had passed away. Others had grown up and taken on public responsibilities. Likewise there were scores of Agawam Indians who never had put on war paint nor remembered the time when the whites had not dwelt there. They had prattled in the dooryards of the white man, followed the deer and elk, and trapped beaver with them, had planted and harvested with them and come to look on their white companions as just, humane, and friendly. The feeling of trust among the whites was quite as deep-seated. One generation had grown up and another started, and no outbreak had disturbed the cordial relations of the two races. But a time came when King Philip undertook to stampede the New England tribes into a war of extermination. Still the local plantation had little fear that the Agawams and the Woronocos would listen to him.

Some squaws of Nonotuck revealed the secret that Springfield was to be attacked, but the whites could not believe it. The Indians up the river had assured Major Pynchon of their loyalty to the English and in general the Indians had been bettered by their contact with the whites, but the friendly Massasoit had died in 1660, and Philip became sachem not long after. King Philip was a natural leader and good fighter, in whom, however, was deep distrust of the English. In 1674 a praying Indian made definite charges of treason against King Philip, and in the following June the praying Indian was murdered and three Indians executed for the crime.

Philip kept himself constantly armed, and the forests were filled with his runners. When forced to leave his home at Mount Hope, he was able to send bands to plunder the Plymouth towns. Philip made a dash for the Nipmuck country, and on August 3, by the light of the moon, the Nipmucks set fire to a fortified house at Brookfield, the only settlement between the Connecticut River and Lancaster. This mode of attack the English had taught them in the Pequot War. Arrows with burning brands as well as fireballs were thrown on the roof, but quickly extinguished. The house was besieged for three days, when it was relieved by a company of troopers from the east. Philip arrived just as the Nipmucks had been driven back from Brookfield, and he refreshed their tired spirits by presenting the sagamores a peck of wampum. The Nonotuck Indians were connected with the Nipmucks by marriage, and when they heard of the Brookfield fight, they gave eleven "triumphant shouts" for the number of English killed. The Indians, in their fort a short way below Hatfield, held a pow-wow, and the young Indians were for war. An aged sachem opposed war and he was struck dead in his tracks. The entire party made a dash for the forests; then hastened north before daybreak, and the dreadful valley campaign opened.

The Agawam Indians remained for some time quietly in their wigwams on the river side, and in their fort that overlooked the bend of the river. This fort was on the old Long Hill Road below Mill River, where there was a little plateau on the spur of a hill that gave natural advantages for a fort. There is a deep ravine on the south side, which was probably the fortified approach to the fort. Many stone arrowheads and hatchets have been found in this ravine, and on the plateau pottery and pestles for bruising corn have been turned up by the plow. The capacity of the fort was sufficient to shelter at least four hundred Indians, and as it was the custom of this tribe to build a palisade large enough to permit putting up rows of little round wigwams covered with skins or bark, we may conclude that the entire brow of the hill was surrounded by a stockade. The neck joining it with the mainland was only a few rods wide, and a spring in the ravine furnished an abundant supply of water.

The inhabitants of this section were now thoroughly roused to a sense of danger. Major Pynchon wrote from Hadley about this time, "Our English are weak and fearful in scouting and spying." Not until the whole valley was aroused were any definite precautions taken against the Agawams in the shape of hostages. These were sent to Hartford for safe keeping.

At the beginning of the war there were communities of praying Indians who did not go on the warpath. John Eliot, known as "the Apostle to the Indians," in a letter dated December 10, 1675, says: "Another great company of our praying Indians of Nipmucks fled at the beginning of the war, first to Connecticut, offering themselves to Mr. Pynchon, one of our magistrates, but he, though willing, could not receive them, and they fled to Unkas, who was not in hostility to the English." Eliot translated the Bible into the Indian language and converted many by his preaching.

Our ancestors viewed Philip as the master spirit who influenced the councils and conduct of other tribes and contrived and directed most of the attacks, slaughters and desolations of the war, but he was no more inhuman and cruel than other Indians. He was not able to combine against the English in 1675, and he did not persuade a single tribe in Connecticut, Rhode Island or New Hampshire to unite with him, though Indians from those colonies may have aided him. Many of the Indians owed some kind of allegiance to Philip, yet not many were willing to engage in his quarrel. About one-third of his tribe, the Nipmucks, were in the vicinity of the Connecticut River. Not many of the Pawtucket and Massachusetts nations joined in the war. The hostile Indians were mostly Nipmucks. After he left the Pocasset Swamp in 1675 and fled toward the Nipmuck country many of his men withdrew from him, and the squaw sachem of Pocasset and her men drew off to the Narragansetts. It was believed that Philip had little above fifty fighting men left, but hundreds of old men, women and children. His warriors, exclusive of the Nipmucks, were not numerous at any time.

It is a little remarkable that the histories and other documents do not furnish any evidence that Philip, after he came among the Nipmucks, was present in a single fight with the English. No particular exploit or achievement performed by him is recorded. It is hardly to be doubted, however, that he was actively engaged in some of the furious attacks made on the English near the Connecticut River. But the Nipmucks showed they were capable of planning and executing daring enterprises without his assistance. They destroyed Brookfield and made numerous fierce assaults on the garrison house, and the river Nipmucks burned Springfield. When assaults were made by Indians it was impossible to know how many there were, but there is reason to believe that except in the Narragansett swamp fight not more than five hundred Indians were engaged in any battle during this war. The number of Indians which the English imagined they had killed in an engagement was usually much overrated. They did not find the dead bodies and could judge only by guess. The Indians often told a story to please those in whose power they were, and their admissions were seldom worthy of credit.

When King Philip's War began, the towns and plantations in Hampshire County were Springfield, including West Springfield and Longmeadow; Westfield, Northampton, Hadley, Hatfield, Deerfield, Northfield, Brookfield and, lastly, Suffield, whose people soon left and went elsewhere.

The war began near Mount Hope on Thursday, June 24, 1675, when the Wampanoags slew nine of the inhabitants of Swansey. Soldiers were sent from Boston and Plymouth and Philip and his followers fled to Pocasset. Houses were burned and people slain in the vicinity. On the fourteenth of July, while Philip was near Pocasset, the Nipmucks killed several persons.

The second attempt of the Nipmucks was in the county of Hampshire. The council ordered Captain Thomas Wheeler and a squad of horsemen to go to the Nipmucks near Quaboag and treat with them. They reached Brookfield with three Christian Indians on Sunday, the first of August. Captain Wheeler and his party and three of the principal men of Brookfield rode to the plain about three miles from the village and found no Indians. Captain Wheeler was persuaded by the Brookfield men to go farther and when they had proceeded four or five miles and were in a narrow passage, having a bushy, rocky hill on the right and a thick swamp on the left, a large body of Indians lying in ambush on both sides suddenly fired on them, killing eight and wounding five. The survivors were forced to go up the steep hill and by the guidance of the Christian Indians they escaped to the village. There they took possession of one of the largest and strongest houses and fortified themselves as well as they could in a short time. They selected a house used for an inn which stood on the road that passed from Springfield to Boston. There were about fifteen families, who on being informed of the disaster, all came in haste to the same house, bringing but little with them.

Soon the Indians flocked into the village and began to burn buildings. During two nights and days they continued to besiege the house and made various attempts to burn it without success. One man was mortally wounded at the garret window and another was killed outside the building. The house contained twenty-six men capable of doing service and fifty women and children. The twenty-six men, vigilant and brave, put out the fires on the building and repelled the assaults of the Indians until the evening of the third day, when Major Willard came to their relief with Captain Parker and forty-six men and five friendly Indians. Before the next morning the Indians left the place.

On the first night, Ephraim Curtis, to obtain help, crept out on his hands and knees and reached Marlborough on the morning of August 4. Some travelers toward the Connecticut River who saw the burning at Quaboag returned to Marlborough the same morning a little before Curtis arrived and a post had been sent to Major Willard, who was near Lancaster. The wounded left the house as soon as they were able to travel. The buildings were all burned excepting those of the innkeeper and another that was unfinished. The meeting-house was burned and a gristmill owned by John Pynchon.

One of the colonial majors records that when he came near Brookfield at the time of the Indian attack, the cattle had been frightened away by the yells and firing of the Indians, but fell into the rear of his company and followed them into the village. In this and later Indian wars, the people were alarmed when the cattle ran furiously out of the woods to the village.

The events at Brookfield produced much fear in the Colony and especially in Hampshire County. A company of river Indians and others from towns about Hartford came up and ranged the woods, but after the arrival of troops soon fled. Major Pynchon wrote, on August 22, that the various forces of soldiers had retired, and that nothing had been done except the burning of about fifty empty wigwams.

The Indian situation was so serious when autumn arrived that Captain Beers set forth from Hadley with about thirty-six men and some carts to bring away the garrison at Squakheag, later known as Northfield.

At the outbreak of King Philip's War, Northfield had been settled only three years, and its position was much exposed. Here were seventeen thatched cabins, a meetinghouse, a log fort, and a stockade of rough logs eight feet high pierced with loopholes. One day in early September, while some of the men were working in the meadows, a band of Indians under Sagamore Sam and another chief known as "One-Eyed John" assailed the town. They killed a number of people in the houses, shot down the workers who attempted to make their way from the meadows to the settlement, and burned several of the dwellings, but they could not capture the stockaded enclosure. The next morning when within three miles of Northfield, Captain Beers and his men were attacked from the side of a swamp by a great number of Indians, and for some time there was a hot dispute. But after losing their captain and some others, they resolved to hasten away across the swampy ravine to where they had left their horses. Nearly all those who escaped arrived in Hadley that evening. The next morning another came in and at night another that had been taken by the Indians and loosed from his bonds by a Natick Indian; he told that the Indians were all drunk, bemoaning the loss of a great captain and twenty-five of their men.

September 5, Major Treat set forth for Northfield with more than a hundred men. The next day, when they came near Northfield, his men were much daunted to see the heads of Captain Beers' soldiers on poles by the wayside. After getting to their destination they were fired on by about a dozen Indians, and Major Treat was wounded, but not seriously. He decided to lose no time in bringing away the garrison, and they did so that night, leaving the cattle there, and the dead bodies unburied. Afterward seventeen of the cattle came a great part of the way themselves and finally were fetched into Hadley.

On Sunday, the twelfth of the month, the Indians made an assault on two men of Pocomtuck, known now as Deerfield. They were going from one garrison to another to attend an afternoon meeting, when the Indians made a great volley of shot at them, but not a man was killed, and all escaped to the garrison, whither they were going, except one man, who was running to the other garrison and was captured. Afterward the Indians went to a hill in Deerfield meadow, which was a hiding and watching place of theirs, and burnt two more houses, killed many horses, and carried away horseloads of beef and pork to the hill.

After Major Treat left Northfield the Indians destroyed the village. This was the second place in Hampshire County that was laid
waste. It had been settled only two or three years, but contained
nearly as many families as Brookfield, most of them from Northampton. They had no minister nor meetinghouse, but a competent person
used to pray and exort in pleasant weather under a broad-spreading
tree.

The Nipmucks and Wampanoags, whom the English captains
had long sought in vain, did not show themselves in the Connecticut

A COVE NEAR THE SAW MILL, HOLYOKE

Valley until September. Then they came exulting in their successes,
and after Northfield was deserted lived on the good things which the
English had left.

A short distance below Northfield is Clark's Island, which has a
curious legend of Captain Kidd. We are told that the pirate sailed
up to this secluded spot, and he and his men brought on shore a heavy
iron chest full of gold and other precious loot. There they dug a

deep hole and lowered the chest into it, in what was considered the proper old-fashioned pirate way, and one of the crew was selected by lot, killed, and his body placed on top of the loose earth that had been thrown into the hole. His ghost was supposed to haunt the vicinity, and to forever guard the riches from audacious treasure-seekers.

From time to time, in the darkness of night when the gales howled, persons are said to have seen a phantom ship sailing up the stream, manned by a spectral crew, and commanded by a black-bearded ghost with the familiar features of Captain Kidd. Opposite the island an anchor was let go, and Kidd in a boat rowed by four sailors went ashore. After satisfying himself that the plunder was safe he returned to the ship and sailed down the river. Some people doubt the entire story, and ask how Captain Kidd ever navigated his ship up there past the rocky falls.

Most of the Indian attacks came from the north and were made by Indians friendly with the French in Canada. This meant that Springfield was spared many attacks because Northfield and Hadley were above on the same side of the Connecticut so they bore the brunt. Northfield was soon abandoned, but Springfield soldiers, under command of Major Pynchon, were often stationed at Hadley as protection to both settlements.

Soon after Northfield was abandoned it was decided that a large quantity of grain which had been thrashed at Deerfield should be conveyed to Hadley with some other things, and Captain Lothrop and his company were to be the guards. They began their march September 18, and meanwhile the Indians watched the movements of the English without being discovered.

Captain Lothrop is vouched for by Increase Mather as a godly and courageous commander. He had about seventy men provided with teams and drivers, but a multitude of Indians lurking in the swamps made a sudden and frightful assault, and seized the carts and goods. Many of the soldiers had been so foolish as to put their guns in the carts and step aside to gather grapes, which proved dear and deadly to them. Captain Lothrop was killed and more than three-score of his men. Presently friendly Indians and other help came and the enemy retreated. Night was coming on and there was no pursuing them.

This was a black and fatal day wherein there were eight persons made widows and twenty-six children made fatherless, all in one little plantation, and more than sixty persons buried in one dreadful grave. It has been said of Lothrop's men that they were "the very flower of the county of Essex."

The place of this assault was near Muddy Brook, a small stream which crosses the highway in the village of South Deerfield. It has since been named Bloody Brook. Two or three days after the Muddy Brook defeat, the garrison and inhabitants of Deerfield abandoned the place and a third village in Hampshire County was given up to desolation. The surviving inhabitants retired to Hatfield and other places. A petition was sent to the General Court in 1678 from "the remnant of Deerfield's poor inhabitants" scattered into several towns. They said "Our houses are burned, our estates wasted, and the ablest of our inhabitants killed, and their plantation become a wilderness, a dwelling place for owls."

Major Pynchon wrote from Hadley to the governors, September 30, "We are endeavoring to discover the enemy, and daily send out scouts. Our English are somewhat fearful in scouting and spying, and we have no Indian friends here to help us. We find the Indians have their scouts out." Soon afterward Major Pynchon's farmhouse and barns on the west side of the river were set on fire by a few Indians and consumed with all the grain and hay. The Council of Connecticut advised Major Pynchon not to disarm the Springfield Indians, but to take hostages of them. This was done and the hostages were kept at Hartford. The Indians continued to profess friendship for the English, but at length, roused by the victories of the Indians up the river, they concluded to help in destroying the English towns. Their principal fort on the east side of the river was at Long Hill toward Longmeadow. Pynchon, whose war headquarters for the county were at Hadley, learned that Indians had been in the vicinity of the town gristmill, and on the fourth of October he called off all the soldiers stationed at Springfield, intending to have his forces go against the enemy that night or the next day.

On an October morning in 1675, Major Pynchon, by order of commissioners who outranked him, rode at the head of a company of troopers to Hadley, where he, with others, were intent on arranging for a hot pursuit of the enemy. But King Philip was not seeking a pitched battle and meanwhile the Agawam Indians had been secretly persuaded to join in a war of extermination. That night a large number of warriors stole into the Agawam fort on Long Hill. Some of them had been down to Hartford, where they succeeded in freeing the hostages held there and on the way back they passed the word that Springfield was doomed. Toto, an Indian living with a Windsor family, became agitated, and the family with much effort learned his terrible secret. It was long after dark that the confession was made, and then, in frantic haste, a man was sent to carry the news to Springfield. When he rode into town at that late hour and roused the inhabitants, they were doubly terrified because the soldiers had gone off on the Hadley campaign.

The alarm was sounded at every door in the village. What few men were there seized their guns and ammunition, and with all haste escorted the women and children to the three garrisonhouses which had recently been repaired and fortified. It was a night of consternation. Among the men in the town at the time were the disabled Deacon Chapin, Reverend Mr. Glover, and Lieutenant Cooper. Messengers were at once dispatched to Mr. Pynchon at Hadley, and to Captain Treat at Westfield. Mr. Glover succeeded in transferring what he called his "brave library" to Mr. Pynchon's house, and Tuesday's sun rose on a common of homes almost empty except for the three garrison-houses, which were uncomfortably full. With the morning meal and possibly some religious services in the forts, courage returned, and Lieutenant Cooper went so far as to discredit Toto's testimony. Mr. Glover was of the same opinion and he carried his library back to his house.

Lieutenant Cooper had been a familiar figure among their Indian neighbors for over a quarter of a century, and he knew every Agawam Indian by name. Sometimes, as an officer of the law, he had to deal with one or two of them. Other times he aided them with loans and seeds or utensils. He had no fear of the Agawams, and he induced Thomas Miller, who always was ready for adventure, to go with him to the fort quite early in the morning. Less than a half hour later Cooper's horse returned on a full run up the village street from Mill River, and on his back was his bleeding master. The horse ran straight toward the Pynchon house, from which it had started, and when he stopped at the door Cooper fell to the ground dead. Miller was killed at the first volley from the Indians, just as they were entering the woods on the lower side of Mill River.

The Indians lost no time in making the air dismal with their yells. Some of Mr. Pynchon's mills at the south end were soon in ashes and the wife of John Mathews was killed in that vicinity. The excited savages applied the torch to the deserted houses and thronged through the streets in great numbers.

Soon the flames were leaping from thirty-three houses and from twenty barns, but the three garrison-houses were too well built and too well defended for the Indian mode of attack. One savage in his plundering became the proud possessor of a pewter platter. He held it before him and marched toward one of the houses, but it only served to guide the bullets that pierced his heart. This platter, with two bullet holes, was later sold by a servant and nothing more is known of its fate.

About noon some of Major Treat's soldiers arrived in great haste on the West Springfield bank, but the Indians had little trouble in keeping the reënforcements at bay. Three hours later Major Pynchon and Captain Appleton with two hundred troopers rode into Springfield, after coming all the way from Hadley on a dead run; but all that was left for them to do was to scare off the Indians who had no intention of fighting a pitched battle. They were heavily laden with plunder, and the ashes of the town showed what they had accomplished. For the time being they were content, and off they went into the forest. Their place of retirement was Indian Leap, otherwise known as Indian Orchard. There they built twenty-four fires on that naturally fortified spot overhanging the waters and slept in perfect security—yes! and woke the next morning in triumph; but Springfield slept in smoke and danger and woke in fear. The town never knew a darker day.

An Indian squaw captured by the English said there were two hundred and seventy warriors in the attack on Springfield. Other estimates vary, and some even claim there were six hundred. The squaw said that King Philip intended to burn three towns in one day and his divided army makes the smaller estimate seem the most probable.

According to Captain Mosely, this squaw had a terrible fate. He wrote that she was "ordered to be torn to pieces by dogs, and was so dealt with." Such a fate by order of the English seems incredible. If the squaw returned to her own people and suffered death for serving the English, that story might be accepted as plausible.

Springfield's plight seemed to most persons a death blow. Winter was approaching and the one thing that fate had in store was plainly abandonment. Mr. Pynchon so wrote to the Massachusetts authorities. Not a house nor a barn was standing between Round Hill and Mr. Pynchon's house, with one exception—the Pynchon garrison-house, but the Indians had leveled his barns and outbuildings. Many of his neighbors owed him money, and this with mills and property outside destroyed, almost bowed him down with sorrow, and the sight of the blackened districts was especially depressing. He had quite a property in grist and cornmills, and four tenements, all destroyed, and with them much corn.

"The Lord show us mercy," wrote the down-hearted magistrate. "I see not how it is possible for us to live here this winter, and if not, the sooner we are helped off the better."

There were left standing fifteen houses on the street, and with those on the outskirts and over the river there were forty-five. These forty-five occupied houses had to accommodate forty families more, as well as a garrison of two hundred soldiers. Besides, there was great need of medicine for the wounded, and provisions were scarce. Several whose houses were saved lost their goods in others' houses, whither they had carried them. Many of the soldiers complained that there was no bread to be had, but meat seemed to be plenty.

The loss of Lieutenant Cooper was severely felt. In town affairs his responsibilities were many. He was a practicing attorney before the county court; he was a farmer, a carpenter, a bone-setter and a surveyor, and among other things had been a deputy at the General Court and had been of great value in dealing with the Indians. In his way he had been as much a pillar of the town as Deacon Samuel Chapin.

With the disastrous beginning of the Indian War in October, 1675, Major Pynchon wanted to be spared further responsibility as commander-in-chief, and in making a formal request to withdraw, he said, "The distressed state of my affairs at home, the sorrows and afflictions my dear wife undergoes, her continual calls to me for relief, she being almost overwhelmed with grief and trouble, and in many straits and perplexities which would be somewhat helped by my presence there." Shortly afterward his request was granted.

Captain Appleton followed John Pynchon as military leader in the Valley. He said, "as to the state of poor desolate Springfield, to whose relief we came too late, though with a march that had put all our men into a most violent sweat, and was more than they could well bear, their condition is indeed most afflictive, but I am opposed to the idea of abandoning Springfield."

Immediately after the burning of Springfield the General Court issued a military manual for the government of the army in the field, and the first provision of the code was: "Let no man presume to blaspheme the holy and blessed Trinity, God the Father, God the Son, and God the Holy Ghost, on pain to have his Tongue bored with a hot iron."

The destruction of the Pynchon mills forced Springfield to go to Westfield for flour, and this was a very dangerous journey at that time. Scouts were sent in all directions to find some trace of the enemy, but the men were affected with "timorousness," as they had been when Major Pynchon was in command, and nothing came of it. On another occasion, when Appleton proposed to advance to Deerfield, Mosely did not want to get so far from the towns. Once a thunder storm played havoc with their plans and forced them back to Hatfield. Philip was nearby and his scouts were lurking here and there watching a chance for an attack.

Winter closed in early and the fighting season was over, but with many Springfield families living in closed cellars and dugouts.

Jonathan Burt, then or soon after deacon of the church, relates the facts of the burning of Springfield and entered them on a flyleaf of the records which is signed "Jonathan Burt, an eye witness of the same, recognizing devoutly the good providence of God in preserving the lives of the people."

An event of importance to the church that occurred a few days after the burning of the town, was the death of Deacon Samuel Chapin. From a very early period he had been one of the most useful and influential members of the church, a man of distinction, who was not only associated with Mr. Pynchon in the administration of the town, but was one whom the church often designated to carry on the work of the Sabbath. To lose such a man so soon after the great calamity must have been deeply felt.

The destruction of the town by the Indians was soon followed by taking down the old meetinghouse and building a larger one farther west, wholly or nearly within the limits of the present Court Square. Some of the Indians wintered above Northfield and for fear of skulking savages the whites lived in a state that was essentially imprisonment. In February the town met to elect a selectman, "God having taken away the aged Captain Holyoke."

The Longmeadow settlers were not able to visit the village on Sunday to attend service. In March a party escorted by guards to make the journey were attacked by eight Indians. Selectman Keep and his wife and child were killed and several wounded. There was a story told at Boston after this tragedy that the guards took to their heels the moment the Indians fired. John Pynchon with a company of horsemen pursued, but to no purpose.

The snow suddenly disappeared in the latter part of January and "a kind Providence gave the planters a mild winter and an early spring," and at the same time allowed the Indians to scatter into planting and fishing parties to provide against famine.

On the eighteenth of May, Captain Turner, of Boston, attacked the Indians while they were yet asleep at what is now called Turner's Falls. More than three hundred were killed, but another party of Indians hastened to the rescue and forced the whites to retire down the river. Captain Samuel Holyoke, of Springfield, was protecting the rear. He had seen some fighting and was gaining a name for Indian warfare. On the retreat Holyoke was brought into hand-to-hand contests with the savages, five of whom he killed with his sword in the morning fight. Holyoke's horse was shot from under him and as he fell numbers of Indians closed on him. The first was killed by Holyoke's pistol and the captain's men saved him from death. He was only twenty-eight years old. Turner had been shot in Greenfield Meadow, and young Holyoke, assuming command, succeeded so well in checking what was almost a panic, that he arrived at Hatfield with one hundred and forty men. He had taken charge of a rout and converted it into a military retreat, but it cost him his life. He never recovered from the exhaustion of those two days, and in October he sank into his grave and was buried beside his father, Elizur Holyoke.

On the thirtieth of May, Philip made a desperate attempt to overpower Hatfield, but he was repulsed with considerable loss, and his army was forced to scatter. In early August, when Philip was in a swamp near Mount Hope, an Englishman fired his gun at him and missed. Then an Indian friendly to the white men shot Philip, who fell on his face in mud and water with his gun beneath him. His hands were exhibited at Boston, his head at Plymouth, and the beasts of the forests fed on his mangled breast. He had been the terror of New England for fourteen months. Schemes were attributed to him which he did not contrive, and deeds that he did not do, and he was charged with the atrocities and cruelties of others, but Philip was a savage, and doubtless rejoiced in the havoc and bloodshed made by the fierce and furious Nipmucks and Narragansetts. The famous Indian was dead, the Connecticut Valley was at peace and Springfield was in ashes.

In May, when the fishing season arrived, the Indians established themselves at the falls north of Deerfield; and they planted corn at Northfield, and even as far south as Deerfield, without being disturbed.

The Nipmucks and other Indians assailed many places that had not suffered in the preceding year, and their success appalled for a time even the stoutest English hearts. In a March letter to Major Savage, the Council at Boston urged the necessity of bringing the people of the five towns into two places. "The lesser towns must gather to the greater ones," they said.

Some who knew the places best thought Springfield and Hadley the fittest places to fortify and plant. They said that to remain in such a scattered condition was to expose lives and estates to the merciless cruelty of the enemy. So they wrote that same day to Major Pynchon, assuring him there was no other way but for all Springfield and Westfield to come together—it was impossible to hold both towns. They said, "The like advice we have given to the other towns—come in to Hadley and fortify it well. Then, by united strength it may be kept, but otherwise all will be lost."

The people of Northampton decided to remain in their own town and boldly meet the dangers that menaced them. In a letter to the council, they said:

"We dare not entertain any thought of deserting this plantation. The Lord has wonderfully appeared of late for our preservation, and we fear it would be displeasing to him if we should give up into the hands of our enemies, that which the Lord has so eminently delivered out of their hands. If we should desert a town of such considerable strength it may so animate the enemy and discourage other plantations, as may prove no small prejudice to the country. Besides there seems to us a great necessity for holding this place, for the relief of those forces that may be improved in following the enemy. There can be no prosecuting of the war in these parts to advantage unless this and the two neighboring towns be maintained."

They thought Springfield was not the most convenient place for the refuge of others. "The bulk of the town is burnt," they argued, "and we fear you are incapable of maintaining yourselves or others. If the council will allow Northampton fifty soldiers besides those we have already, the town will feed them and pay their wages."

The people of Westfield felt much the same. They were resolutely against moving to Springfield, and they showed a disposition to go to Connecticut if they must move. It was their opinion that Westfield was much more secure from the Indians than Springfield, and much better for husbandry. A letter written by the Westfield minister was sent to the council, in which he presented the situation as follows:

"Springfield, on the east side, has but few habitations left. Those on the west side are scattered about a mile up and down, some of which are hid with bramble. Most of the tillage ground is a long distance from the town, and not clear from brush, and the danger from field employment is double ours. Springfield has been sorely under the blasting hand of God. To remove from habitations to none, from fortifications to none, from a compact place to a scattered one, from a place of less danger to one of more, seems to us such a strange thing, that we find not a man among us inclined thereto."

Mr. Russell, the Hadley minister, corresponded for himself and others with the Council of Connecticut in regard to the war. He particularly wanted to get opinions as to drawing the three upper towns into one. The Connecticut response was one of many reasons why Hampshire towns should not be deserted, and that same day they wrote to the Governor and Council of Massachusetts, giving similar reasons. They considered the towns up the river as the principal granary of the State. This seems to have brought the controversy to a close. What would have happened otherwise might have been a terrible tragedy.

In a Hadley letter from Captain William Turner to the Council of Massachusetts, he says:

"The soldiers here are in great distress for want of clothing, both linen and woolen. Some has been brought from Brookfield, but not an eighth of what we need. I beseech your honors that my wife may have the wages due me, to supply the needs of my family. I would be glad if some better person might be found for this employment, for my weakness of body, and other infirmities will hardly allow me to do my duty as I ought, and it would grieve me to neglect anything that might be for the good of the country in this time of their distress."

Turner's letter was dated April 25, 1676.

Springfield Street at this time must have presented a dismal aspect with the make-shift shelters, roofed cellars, fortified doorways, and barricades that extended into the street. Garrison soldiers were quartered in the town at times for some years, and prowling savages in the forests made every journey out to the commons for wood, or over the river, or to the region above the Three Corner Brook, a little military campaign. The appearance of Main Street can be imagined from this order:

"Henceforth no persons without liberty from the town shall dig or cumber the highway or street from the upper wharf to the bridge of Obadiah Cooley's, with firewood, clay, and timber. Also, no persons shall dig holes or pits in the streets without leave on penalty of five shillings."

The house of correction and jail, to supply the place of those burned in 1675, was located on a Main Street corner, and was built under the direction of Major Pynchon.

The eighth of June, 1676, was a day of much excitement in the river towns. An army of four hundred and fifty men from Connecticut was a novel and animating spectacle, and the local inhabitants gazed eagerly on the two hundred and fifty mounted men, with their red silk banners, and especially on the two hundred Indians as they marched past. The men on horses were nearly all from the towns on Long Island Sound. The Indians were of various tribes, but mostly Pequots and Mohegans from Hartford County. They formed a motley assembly. Their dress and weapons were various, and their decorations diversified and fantastic. Such a collection of friendly Indian warriors was a sight which the inhabitants of these towns never saw before.

It was an expedition into Hampshire County of forces from both Massachusetts and Connecticut, which were to scour the country. The Connecticut Indians under Major Talcott arrived first, supplied among other things with four thousand pounds of bread and twenty gallons of liquors. The Massachusetts troops were delayed and Talcott began the campaign without them. On June 5 in the Nipmuck country he reports "took fifty-two of the enemy," and two days later he says "took two of the enemy who were laden with as much fish as they could carry, and each had a gun, and their horns were full of powder. We sent twenty-seven women and children to Norwich under conduct of some of those we call honest Indians. The others are come to Hadley. We acknowledge the great goodness of God in saving and preserving us in the midst of all our difficulties. I have quartered our soldiers and am waiting for your further orders. Gentlemen, if you cause any bread to be made for this wilderness work it had need be well dried. A great part of our bread is full of blue mold. We need at this time a barrel of powder, and 300 pounds of bullets for carrying on the war. Please send powder and bullets with all possible speed. Remember flint stones."

Major Talcott soon wrote another letter, in which he said, "It is feared that you cannot suit us with bread sufficient for the field." So he sent forty or more horses and their riders in charge of a lieutenant to bring what bread they could from Deacon Moore, a baker in Windsor.

June 12 the Indians appeared at Hadley, ignorant that four hundred and fifty men had recently arrived in the river towns. The object of the Indians seems to have been plundering and destroying outside of the fortification. They were mostly river Indians and other Nipmucks, whose power was fast declining.

What happened that June day at Hadley, Increase Mather describes in the account that follows:

"When the morning sun was an hour high, three soldiers started to go from the town without their guns, and a sergeant who stood at the gate tried to dissuade them, but they alledged they were not going far, and were allowed to pass. Shortly afterward the sergeant thought he heard some men running, and when he looked over the fortification, he saw twenty Indians pursuing those three men, who were so terrified they could not cry out. Two of them were killed, and the other so wounded that he lived not more than two or three days.

"God, in great mercy to these western plantations, had so ordered by His providence, that the Connecticut army was come thither before the onset from the enemy. And besides the English there were nearly two hundred Indians in Hadley, who came to fight with and for the English, against the common enemy, who were quickly driven off at the south end of the town. Whilst our men were pursuing them here, a great swarm of Indians issued from the bushes and made their main assault at the north end of the town. They set fire to a barn which was outside of the fortification, and went into a house, where the inhabitants discharged a great gun. At that about fifty Indians came running out of the house terribly frightened with the noise and slaughter made amongst them. Our Indians followed them nearly two miles and would have pursued them farther if they had been ordered to do so."

On the fourteenth of June Captain Henchman came to Hampshire County with Massachusetts troops and a company of Christian Indians to make an expedition up the river. He went up on the east side and Major Talcott on the west side. There was a severe thunder storm that day, but they reached the falls, without, however, finding any Indians. There was a northeast rainstorm all the next day and night, which damaged their guns, ammunition and provisions. Scouts were sent up on the east side of the river as far as

Northfield, but they discovered no enemy. About thirty men went up toward the falls and burnt a hundred wigwams on an island, ruined the Indian fort, spoiled an abundance of fish which they found underground in Indian barns, and destroyed thirty canoes. The Indians were distressed and scattered and the people were fearful that they might return during the wheat harvest. But they were disunited and depressed, suffering from famine and disease, and hunted from place to place. Some were captured, some fled to distant places, and others gave themselves up.

Late in July a party passed through Westfield in their flight to the Hudson River. They seized some horses and cattle, and pulled up wheatstalks to suck for nourishment. Another party crossed the Connecticut between Hadley and Springfield. The next day they passed near Westfield, and Major Talcott pursued them. John Pynchon, in a letter to the Governor, said:

"August twelvth nearly two hundred Indians were discovered within three or four miles of Westfield. The people and soldiers then went out and made several shots at them and took a horse from them, but found them so many they sent word to me. Major Talcott, and sixty men and as many Indians have gone on. We find by our scouts that this parcel of Indians went over the great river on rafts at the foot of the great falls, and their track comes from the Nipmuck country."

The scouts found where the Indians slept within seven miles of Springfield, and had about twenty-five fires.

In September, 1677, a year after the war was apparently closed, an unexpected foray was made on Hatfield. About eleven o'clock in the forenoon, when the greater part of the men were dispersed in the meadows, and others were at work on the frame of a house outside of the palisades, a party of Indians suddenly assaulted the builders, shot down three and then dashed to other structures, where they killed nine more persons, wounded four others, took seventeen captives and burned seven buildings. This was a more calamitous assault than had been made on any town in Hampshire during the two preceding years. All the persons killed, wounded and made captive were women and children, except five, and they all lived in the northern part of the village that probably was outside of any palisade.

The Indians went north with their captives as far as Deerfield the same day and there captured four more of the English and killed one. They resumed their march up the Connecticut the next morning and stopped on the east side of the river about thirty miles above North-field, where they built a long wigwam and stayed about three weeks. They were pursued as far as Northfield, but not overtaken. During the three weeks above Northfield some of the Indians went to Wachu-set and brought back about eighty Indian women and children. Efforts were made to ransom the prisoners, but they were frustrated.

TOWN HOUSE AT HAMPDEN

Some time in October the captors and the captives again moved up the river. They crossed the country to Lake Champlain, and it was winter weather when they arrived in Canada. These sufferers from Hatfield and Deerfield were the first ever forced to leave their homes in New England and travel through the dreary wilderness to Canada. Hundreds were afterward forced to do the same. Two children of the captives were born in Canada. One was a daughter of Benjamin Wait and the other the daughter of Stephen Jennings. To commemorate their captivity, Wait's child was named Canada, and Jennings' child, Captivity. These names they retained ever after.

Wait and Jennings, who were men of energy and perseverance, undertook to redeem their wives and children and the other captives. They set out from Hatfield in October and went by way of Westfield to Albany. Discouragements were many, but they kept on and hired a Mohawk Indian to guide them to Lake George. This savage was humane and friendly, and as the lake was open, he fitted up a canoe for them, and drew a map of the lakes they were to pass. He was a great help, for they were the first New England men who ever passed down Lakes George and Champlain to Canada, and they were ignorant of the country. After going down Lake George, they carried their canoe two miles on their backs to Lake Champlain, where they were hindered by ice and headwinds many days. At Sorel and its vicinity they found the captives. From there they went down to Quebec, where they were civilly entertained by the French Governor, who granted them a guard of eleven persons to escort them toward Albany. They left Quebec on the nineteenth of April, and Sorel on the second of May, after redeeming all the captives. Late in the month they were in Albany, and from there a messenger was sent to Hatfield.

After staying five days in Albany they walked twenty-two miles to Kinderhook, where they found men and horses from the home town. They rode through the woods to Westfield, and soon all reached Hatfield in safety. The captives had been absent eight months, and Wait and Jennings seven months. The day of their arrival was the most joyful day Hatfield ever knew. The ransom of the captives cost more than two hundred pounds, which was gathered by contributions.

The fortifications around the Hampshire towns were repaired or rebuilt, and kept in order several years, and men went to their work and to public worship with their guns in their hands. In February, 1677, Hadley voted to fortify the meetinghouse, and the selectmen were to call out men and teams for the work. It was also voted that every male inhabitant above sixteen years of age should bring guns and ammunition to meeting on the Lord's days and at lectures, or forfeit a shilling for every neglect. The meetinghouse was surrounded by a palisade, to provide a place of refuge for the women and children which the men could defend. The guns were carried to meeting because it was important they should be near at hand in case of an attack on any part of the village.

In 1676 and 1677 the number of persons slain in different parts of Hampshire county, which then included the present Hampden, Hampshire and Franklin counties, were two hundred and twenty-two, and three more were slain in Canada. The number of dwelling houses burned during this period in Hampshire was at least one hundred and ten, but many of these were small and cheap. The number of barns burned was less.

In the three towns, Brookfield, Northfield, and Deerfield, which the Indians destroyed, it may be estimated that the number of houses burned were forty-five; Springfield, thirty-three; Westfield, three; Northampton, ten; Hatfield, sixteen; Hadley, none; Suffield, some; and Westfield, then called Swampfield, a few. Hatfield, in proportion to its population, suffered the greatest loss of life and property, but Springfield's loss in actual values was the greatest of all. Hadley lost the least property and Westfield the fewest lives. Hatfield, in a petition for aid, said they had lost the greater part of their cattle, sheep, and horses.

During the war the headquarters were at the house of John Russell, the Hadley minister, and he entertained the principal officers. Two petitions for pay were signed by his friends, and one of them by his wife, but not by him. The whole sum charged was then over seventy-eight pounds. It is said that the "chief gentlemen, improved in the affairs of the war," were entertained there, and called for the best provisions to be had. Mr. Russell was obliged to serve various "barrels of beer, and much wine, and fruit suitable to the company, yet had no more credit for such company by the week or meal than other men for ordinary entertainment." "The great trouble and burden on his wife were noticed," and presently the account was paid.

Matchlocks and flintlocks were both in use when the war began, but few matchlocks were used in 1676. Matchlocks and muskets with rests were unfit for Indian warfare. The Indians did not use them, and they were excellent marksmen. In Massachusetts a great prejudice was aroused among the people against all Christian Indians because a few had proved false, and their enmity knew no bounds. Honest and faithful praying Indians were falsely accused, insulted, robbed and imprisoned. Some were shot at and wounded, and others murdered. There was a savage hostility felt toward all Indians. But whenever the Christian Indians were employed in the army, they were brave and faithful, and gradually the hatred of the white race abated.

One curious item of the period, which concerns the Hampshire region, is furnished by the famous Boston minister, Increase Mather.

The subject is "Noises in the Air," and he says, "It is certain that before this war broke out there was heard in Northampton, Hadley, and other towns thereabouts, the report of a great piece of ordnance with a shaking of the earth, and a considerable echo, when there was no ordnance really discharged at or near any of those towns."

Hadley had a mill three miles north of the village, and it is remarkable that this lonely mill was not destroyed by the Indians in 1675 or 1676. The garrison kept there was very small—sometimes only two or three men, and at last the cornmill was burned by the enemy. During the war the Hadley ferrymen were kept exceedingly busy by the soldiers who were crossing the river sometimes by hundreds at the upper and lower ferries. Samuel Porter took care of most of the wounded soldiers at Hadley, and did much for their provision and comfort. Richard Montague baked for the soldiers and Timothy Nash repaired their weapons. Hadley was the headquarters during the Indian fighting for the soldiers from Springfield. The houses were often filled to overflowing, companies of soldiers were arriving and departing, and armed men appeared daily in the broad street.

More Indian Wars

CHAPTER XI

More Indian Wars

The next onset came October 19, at Hatfield, where first of all, the Indians made great fires north of the plantation to attract the English, and then came and lay in the bushes by the wayside, about two miles from the village. Toward noon ten horsemen were sent out to scout, and as they were passing the Indians in ambush, nine were shot down and one escaped to Hatfield. About four o'clock the Indians attempted to burn the village, and they came in fury, hoping to do again mischief such as they had newly done in Springfield. Seven or eight hundred of the enemy came on a sudden from all quarters, but they found it too hot for them where they attempted to break in on the town, and were beaten off. Captain Appleton's sergeant was mortally wounded by his side, and a bullet passed through his own hair, by that whisper telling him that death was very near. Night came on making knowledge of the enemy's losses uncertain. Some were seen to fall, some ran through a small river, others cast their guns into the water, it being their way to venture as much to recover the dead bodies of friends as to defend them when alive. At last, after burning a few barns and some other buildings, the enemy hastened away as fast as they had come, leaving the English to bless God who had so mercifully delivered them from their merciless foes.

After this defeat most of the Indians withdrew from this part of the country, and not long afterward the soldiers departed, except for a small garrison in each of the five old Hampshire towns, Springfield, Westfield, Northampton, Hadley, and Deerfield. It was against these towns that nearly the entire force of the enemy was directed that autumn, and men from most of the towns of Massachusetts moistened the soil with their blood.

In the following December and much of January the cold was severe and the snow deep. There seems to have been no direct communication between the Hampshire towns and Boston during that winter. The deep snow, the destruction of Brookfield, and especially the fear of the Indians, stopped all traveling in that direction. Sergeant Ayres no longer remained to greet the weary traveler at his rustic but comfortable ordinary on the hill in Brookfield.

The destruction by the Indians was widespread and every family had to entertain soldiers. During the latter part of autumn and the next winter the people built palisades about their plantations. These consisted of rows of poles, stakes or posts about ten feet in length with two feet in the ground and eight feet above the ground. The posts were made by splitting sticks of timber and hewing off the edges of the cleft pieces so that no part should be less than two or three inches thick. They were set close together in the ground and fastened to a piece of wood near the top. Many fence rails were used for the purpose. Such defenses, which would have been very inadequate against an attack by Europeans, were an effective barrier against the assaults of savages. A considerable body of Indians wintered near Ware River, north of Brookfield; others west of the Connecticut above Northfield, and some, including Philip, were in the vicinity of Hoosac River, northeast of Albany. The Dutch traders at Albany sold ammunition to the Hudson River Indians, who bought it for the New England Indians, and in that way got them a supply.

Early in March, 1675, a body of Indians were at Northfield, and with them was Mrs. Rowlandson, who won fame later by writing the story of her captivity. The Indians went up the river some miles, where were Philip and many others, of whom Mrs. Rowlandson records: "Now the Indians gathered their forces to go against Northampton. One went about yelling and hooting to give notice of the design. Whereupon they went to boiling ground nuts, and parching corn for their provision, and in the morning, away they went."

They assailed Northampton, but were defeated and returned without much booty. Evidently they did not know there were two or three companies of soldiers in the town.

Major Savage, of Boston, was now in chief command in Hampshire, where he had four companies. In a letter to Governor Leverett, he says:

"I have improved our time since we came hither in sending forth scouts, but as yet can make no certain discovery of any of the enemy's places of abode. This morning about two o'clock we were alarmed again from Northampton, which was occasioned by some Indians being seen on two sides of the town. The towns, both of Springfield and Westfield, are in great fear of the enemy, as well as those here. I humbly ask you whether this way of following the enemy up and down in the woods will best reach your end at this season of the year, in which they have no fixed station, but can take advantages against us, and avoid us when they please. As near as we can gather, their aim is at the towns on the river, to destroy them, so they can plant and fish with less molestation."

Above Deerfield a few miles was the great place of their fishing, and this was expected to furnish their provisions for the year. If an attempt were made to drive them from there it would rouse their utmost rage.

In the spring of 1677 Massachusetts sought a friendly league with the Mohawks against the Indians in Maine, and Connecticut joined in the project. Then John Pynchon, of Springfield, and a Hartford man were sent to Albany, where they treated with the Indians, and gave them presents of wampum, and of duffles, a coarse kind of cloth, and lastly added a present of powder and shot. The Mohawks boasted of what they had done for New England, and promised to use their endeavors against the Indians at Kennebec. But their pretensions and promises were deceptions, and the scheme of engaging them in our quarrel was a source of many calamities. Instead of going to Maine the savages raided the peaceable praying Indians of Massachusetts, first in September, 1677, and again the next June. Some they killed and some they made captives. They brought two squaws through Hadley and the people of that town tried to redeem them, but the Mohawks would not let them go. When persons were sent to Albany to demand the release of the captives, evasive answers were their only response.

In November, 1680, John Pynchon was again sent to Albany. He charged the Mohawks with "mistreating our friendly Indians," and with not releasing those who were captives. He accused them, too, of killing swine and cattle that belonged to the English and robbing houses and marching through villages in a hostile posture. He said such things must stop, and then he tried to win them by presenting gifts of duffles, shirts, blankets, and such things as rum and tobacco that had cost nearly three hundred dollars.

The Mohawks said he had spoken many hard things, but they were sweetened by the present. Nevertheless, they made an artful, dishonest reply and declined to give up the Christian Indians.

In October, 1683, the Mohawks sent a present of twenty beaver skins to Massachusetts, and the Colony sent in return a much more valuable present in wampum, shirts, duffles, stockings, rum, and tobacco. The expression "an Indian gift" was a byword in New England. It denoted a present made by a person who expected five or ten times as much value in return. After the war between England and France began in 1689, it was an object of importance to please the Mohawks and keep them faithful to England and her colonies. Thus it happened that three agents from Massachusetts and one from Connecticut left Westfield one August day and journeyed to Albany, escorted by ten troopers. They were gone more than four weeks, and during that time gave large presents to the Mohawks, small presents to the river Indians, and gifts to the sachems privately. Besides, there was considerable free feasting. Great Britain and New York, likewise, gave presents to the Mohawks. Robert Livingston, who lived in the vicinity, made the comment that he wished we needed not to court such heathen as the Mohawks for assistance, because they were a broken reed to depend on. They felt their importance, and at times were insolent enough to damage the houses they entered. Yet the people generally submitted to these abuses because it would not do to quarrel with the Mohawks. It was difficult to restrict any of the Indians. They must have what they desired. A great abundance of beef and other meats were furnished them, and also rum, wine, cider, beer, pipes and tobacco—all for their drunken revels.

John Sale, in 1733, charged the Colony one hundred and ninety-five pounds for keeping twenty-two Mohawks nineteen days, including breakage of windows, tables, chairs, knives, mugs, cups and glasses, and for daubing the walls. On another occasion, when Sale entertained nine Penobscot chiefs twenty-four days, he made charges for breaking furniture and for washing forty-nine of their greasy shirts, and his charge for "cleansing and whitewashing" two rooms after them was sixty shillings. It was no easy matter to cleanse a room that had been occupied by guests of that kind. Such scenes and transactions were familiar in other colonies when Indians assembled to make or renew treaties. European governments encouraged the Indians in their propensities. Both France and England courted a disgraceful alliance with savages, and both armed them against the defenseless inhabitants of the other party.

Some of the conditions at the Springfield plantations were distinctly barbaric. For instance, the spirit of the age made it possible for a court to order a man to flog his son on the bare back in the presence of the town officers and a gaping crowd! The county court kept a sharp eye on the home, and was quick to enforce parental authority. Samuel Ball was ordered to be flogged because he used abusive language to his father-in-law.

The children of the town were brought into very close relations to the tithing men, and at all times were made conscious that the eye of authority was on them. The court urged that the tithing men "diligently take care that the Sabbath be not profaned by youth or older persons sitting or standing out of their meeting-houses in time of public worship, whereby they are exposed to many temptations and diversions, but that they check all such persons, and so deal with them that they will go into their meeting-houses where they will be in sight to present their names in case they do not reform."

Also, "have a vigilant eye on persons who, without just cause, are unseasonably abroad in the evening from their parents or masters, all persons being required to go to their lodgings or homes by nine of the clock at night." Under the shadow of such supervision the youth of that period grew. One of the lads who was caught with others making a disturbance on a Sabbath Day, was the son of a member of the court that was to deal with him, but no parental consideration prevented his having to pay the regular fine. Eventually this boy grew up to be Samuel Holyoke, the noted Indian fighter.

When the first meetinghouse was built, there was a delay in getting glass for the windows, and when the glass did come there was more delay in setting it. This gave the children a chance to exercise their natural curiosity and some of the windows were broken. The selectmen had made a rule that a child caught at any sports about the meetinghouse should be fined, and in case those responsible for them refused to pay, the children should be whipped in the selectmen's presence.

For a long time there was great disorder in leaving the meeting-house at the end of a service. Many young people flocked out before the blessing was pronounced and most of these "could not be thought to have any necessity for so doing. This was a grief to serious minds," and the selectmen declared it must not be done excepting there be a necessary occasion. Increase Sikes was ordered to keep the east door and Isaac Gleason and Benjamin Thomas to look to the south door. It was also ordered that all persons under the age of twelve shall sit on the seat under the deacon's seat, and also on that seat against it, and on the stairs, only they must not block up the stairs when Mr. Glover, the minister, came.

The town voted, in 1677, that "Goodman Lamb, Sergeant Morgan, Joseph Crowfoot, and others be given a license to fish from the falls in the Chicopee River where the wading place is down to the mouth of that river." The prices fixed for them were, "Fresh salmon at the river, 6 pence, in the village, 8 pence. Fresh shad: half pence at the river, one pence in the village."

The meetinghouse was old and small, and not equal to the needs of the congregation even with benches in the aisles. The first meetinghouse was built in 1645, and stood on the southeast corner of Court Square, encroaching a little on Elm Street, which has since been widened. The second building stood slightly to the west of the first, and was erected in 1677. All of these were on Meetinghouse Lane, now Elm Street. When the first meetinghouse was superseded by the second, it sold for five pounds. The meetinghouse yard was inclosed by a five-rail fence, except in the rear, where a hedge was planted. A turret was installed, but a bell was not put in for nearly ten years. The deacons had a seat by themselves, and there are references to the great pillars, bannisters, posts, "benches in the alleys, and rods for the canopy."

They kept the children away from the windows in this building, but some dogs managed to break three shillings' worth of glass.

Among other expense items were two quarts of drink for John Gilbert when he made the glass. The meetinghouse was fortified against Indians by making a stockade of foot-logs, ten and a half feet long, and the same fortification was erected about Mr. Glover's house.

In 1677 William Madison, schoolmaster, was allowed to take three pence a week from those he taught to read English, and four pence a week from those he taught to both read and write; also, four pence of those whom he taught writing only. The town, for encouragement, this first year, agreed to allow him the rent of town land in Chicopee.

The following year Daniel Benton began teaching, and was paid twenty pounds. The "watchhouse of the new meeting-house" was set apart for his school room. In 1679 a schoolhouse twenty-two feet by seventeen feet, framed, clapboarded and shingled was ordered to be built "somewhere in the lane going to the upper wharf," now Cypress Street.

The watchhouse apparently disappointed expectation, and the schoolmaster gathered his flock of children in Goodman Mirrick's house. Mirrick's wife was somewhat of a teacher herself. When the frame for the schoolhouse was being put up, all the available young men helped at the work and afterward resorted to Ely's tavern. The town footed the bill.

Fines were imposed for neglect to send children to school, and all were urged to send both children and servants.

In January, 1694, the town authorized the selectmen to hire the schoolmaster. It was not unusual to have more or less selectmen who could not read or write. Miles Morgan was an example. His mark was a crudely drawn anchor.

About this time the town's county tax was often paid in corn, which was forwarded to the Bay in 1680 by water.

In 1691 a ferry was established over the Connecticut, and a Suffield man ran the ferry. He was allowed to charge four pence for each horse and two pence for each man as toll. The county court had now become the dispenser of liquor licenses and kept a sharp eye on these taverns, and it is sad to relate that Nathaniel Ely was convicted of selling cider to the Indians. Ten years later Springfield wanted another retailer of strong drink, and Luke Hitchcock was chosen on condition that he did not sell to children, servants, and extravagant persons, and insisting that he take care no person got tippling in his house.

One dubious family with whom the court had to deal consisted of Michael Towsley, Mary, his wife, and their daughter, all of whom

were presented to the court for varied disorders such as lying, stealing, killing some of their neighbors' creatures, and threatening these
neighbors until they were afraid of grievous mischief. The court bore
due witness against such spiteful, dangerous practices, and they found
the daughter, Mary, especially guilty of lying in that she charged her
father with stealing and teaching her to steal, which afterward she
denied. The court ordered the selectmen of Suffield to have Mary
put out to service to some person with whom she might be well educated, she herself saying that she could not reform while with her
father and mother. As to the wife of Towsley, the court found her
guilty of speeches threatening burning to her neighbors and sentenced
her to be well whipt with ten lashes. Towsley was sentenced to fifteen lashes, and he and his wife were bound in the sum of ten pounds
apiece for their good behavior.

In 1680 every inhabitant was required to keep at least three
sheep. No one could employ an Indian on his farm in 1686 without a
permit. For years there had been a premium on wolves, but in 1688 it
was taken from them and put on bears, which had been making serious
inroads among the swine.

Late in July, 1688, five friendly Indians were killed at Spectacle
Pond, about ten miles east of Springfield. John Pynchon was kept
quite busy sending aid to exposed points. Whether in time of peace
or war, he was the hardest worked man in western Massachusetts.
His disposition was placid, his bearing dignified. He was a town
organizer, an interpreter of laws. When he visited Boston, he took
his place among the assistants in the General Court, and when he
entered the county courtroom, either at Springfield or Northampton,
his seat was at the head of the bench of judges, and at town meeting
he was always moderator. Likewise, on training day he was captain
of the company and, in short, he was Springfield's most distinguished
citizen.

In 1680, when it became evident by repeated attacks of the
Mohawks on the peaceable Indians of Massachusetts that something
decided must be done, it was to John Pynchon the Massachusetts
authorities turned. He went to Albany to meet Sir Edmund Andros
and deal with the Macquas Indians, and he frankly rebuked them for
breaking treaty agreements, and then he made them presents of

blankets, shirts, rum and tobacco, which "sweetened the hard speech of the Major."

"Brother Pynchon," the savages said, "we are glad to see you here again, like as we did four years past." A cordial understanding was the result. Four years later these Indians, accompanied by an interpreter, went through an interesting ceremony, saying, "we do here plant a tree of peace, whose branches spread abroad as far as the Massachusetts Colony, and to Virginia, Maryland and all that are in friendship with us: and lie in peace, unity and tranquility under the shade of the tree of peace." In 1870 an ancient oak fell in Long-meadow, under which, tradition says, John Pynchon used to hold conferences with the local Indians.

EAST STREET. LUDLOW

Pynchon was seen at his best with reference to commerce and business. He made money for himself, but at the same time labored to build up the town. He was the village merchant, the beaver trader, land speculator, farmer, mining prospector, banker, and the importer and exporter of merchandise. He never relinquished the idea that the hills guarding the river were rich in minerals. His father was of the same opinion and spent much money prospecting.

John Pynchon thought he had found lead near Westfield, and was so confident he had discovered valuable ore near Miller's River that he and some associates secured a grant of a thousand acres. He had a warehouse in Springfield as early as 1660, where his goods were delivered on arrival from Hartford. It seems to have been near Mill River on the banks of the Connecticut. He also had a regular country store, and nearly everyone, from minister to hired hands, kept runnings accounts there. The farmers and merchants from Northampton to New Haven had the habit of paying off men by drawing orders on Pynchon for merchandise. Reverend Mr. Glover bought at one time ten bushels of barley malt, a firkin of soap, and nine and one-half yards of lace. Deacon Chapin paid for his merchandise in ox hides, meal, corn, hay, candles, peas, carting hay and stone. Thomas Cooper was continually delivering to Pynchon beaver, moose and deer skins, and he did miscellaneous carpentering, handed in wild honey, and drove hogs to market. Thomas Mirrick was often employed by Pynchon to cart goods from Hartford, and there are references to several voyages made by him on the river.

From time to time Miles Morgan bought calico, venison, razors, lace, raisins, sugar and gunpowder. A balance was struck by Morgan's carting and by his slaughtering cattle and selling produce. Miles killed as many as twenty hogs for Pynchon at one time. Anthony Dorchester carried lumber, and he transported hay and other things across the river. Griffith Jones tanned hides. Samuel Ferry could make ditches and fences, and his wife could weave. Francis Pepper was expert in tending sheep and in threshing.

Pynchon bought flour, wine, butter and other produce in New London and made up a cargo of wheat to offset it. Trade in pelts, both from domestic and forest animals formed the profitable basis for his business. He was continually letting out cattle to his neighbors for a share in the returns and increase. He rented, sold and bought lands, and took land and goods for debt, sometimes going as long as seventeen years before bringing suit on overdue accounts. He hired out his colored "maid Elizabeth" to Samuel Ely, for two years, and his oxen, "Collier" and "Russler" to Anthony Dorchester for one year. He owned cidermills, sawmills, gristmills, wharves and warehouses, canoes and boats, and he was also a ship owner. He had tenement houses on both sides of the river, and always was ready to sell, buy or rent.

Major Pynchon's sons, Joseph and John, were in Harvard at the same time, about 1664.

Joseph settled at Boston and, in 1678, his father deeded him one thousand acres of land on the west side of the Connecticut in Springfield, Hatfield, and Deerfield. For a time the major was accompanied to the General Court by Joseph. As the major grew old and infirm, the town was impressed that some special provision should be made for his safety on his long horseback journeys to and from Boston, and a man for his bodyguard was promptly provided. After a lingering illness, death came January 7, 1703, at the age of eighty-two years. There was an imposing funeral. A company of troopers were employed by the Pynchon family to do escort duty, and several hundred dollars were spent. One important item was five gallons of rum for the comfort of the mourners. The inventory of the estate included two negro slaves, a man and a maid. Tom, the man servant, lived to a good old age, and at his death the simple record of his outfit was— "A parcel of old clothing of black Tom, negro, ten shillings." The digging of Tom's grave cost three pence and, while there were no troopers to attend the last rites, the servants and slaves on the Pynchon estate were given one quart of rum to drink to old Tom's memory.

The Regicides

CHAPTER XII

The Regicides

One of the most famous Connecticut Valley traditions is concerned with two English regicides, and as the word regicide means king killer, it seems to have a very sinister significance. But in this instance the king killers involved are regarded as patriots, dealing with a lawless monarch. That monarch was Charles I, of England, and the fate that was his he brought on himself. The trial was conducted in an ordinary manner by the High Court of Justice, which was the forlorn hope of civil and religious liberty for the English race, and which so shattered with one desperate blow the battlements of unauthorized privilege, that its walls never can be fully built up again.

The High Court of Justice by which the King was tried consisted of sixty-seven judges, and they condemned him to death by beheading. Time passed and the Puritans' leader, the famous Cromwell, died. No one else seemed competent to take his place, and when it became apparent that Charles II was destined to be Britain's next King, the homeland was no longer safe for the regicides. They began to scatter and look for some quiet haven where they could live in peace. Two of these regicides regarded New England with favor. They were Edward Whalley and William Goffe. The former was a merchant in middle life when the contest began between King Charles and Parliament. It was then that he took up arms in defense of human rights, and he distinguished himself in many sieges and battles. That he should rise to such high offices in the State, and conduct himself with discretion in all of them, showed the soundness of his abilities. Oliver Cromwell was a cousin.

Goffe, the other regicide, was the son of a Puritan rector in Sussex. While still a young man he went into the Parliament Army, and his merit gradually raised him to the rank of general. Afterward he, too, became a member of Parliament. Goffe's wife, who was Whalley's daughter, was left in their English home, and as an exile he kept up a constant correspondence with her, under the assumed name of Walter Goldsmith.

There were plenty of discontented persons in England who had been sent back from Massachusetts Bay because the New World Puritans did not like their company. Some of them told their prospective King that all New Englanders were rebels at heart, and he was inclined to believe them. The probability that he would be the next King made Whalley and Goffe hasten to get away from their homeland while they could.

When they left London, Charles had not been proclaimed King, but the news of his crowning reached them while yet in the English Channel. They did not attempt to conceal their persons or characters when they reached the new country, except that Whalley assumed the name Richardson and Goffe that of Shepardson, for use if there ever seemed need of such disguise. Their first call was on Governor Endicott, who received them very courteously. They spent the day of their arrival in Boston, but the next day decided to reside at Cambridge, a village about four miles inland from Boston. Seclusion might be an advantage if they had to make a hasty escape from the region. They visited many of the principal towns, but it was Boston where they went most frequently.

The leading citizens of Boston returned the calls, and among the rest were "dyed-in-the-wool-royalists." The regicides went publicly to meetings on the Lord's Day, and to occasional lectures, fasts, and thanksgivings. Their appearance was in their favor. They were grave, serious and devout, and the rank they had sustained commanded respect. Goffe kept a diary from the day he left Westminster to embark for New England until the year 1667. On July 2, 1660, we find him writing in his diary: "It is the Lord's Day—heard the Cambridge minister preach."

On another occasion the two regicides attended an Indian lecture, probably by the apostle Eliot. Goffe made notes of the discussion that followed and was impressed by the searching questions of the natives.

The judges were making friends and things were moving smoothly. But after awhile there began to be disquieting rumors that made them feel anxious, and soon convinced them that staying in Cambridge was too hazardous, so they went into hiding. An English sea captain who had seen them in Boston gave information about them on his arrival in England. A few days after their removal there came by way of Barbados a "Hue-and-Cry" as Goffe called it in his diary, whereupon a warrant to secure them was issued from the Governor, and sent to Springfield and other towns in the western part of the Colony, but they were beyond the reach of it, as was doubtless expected by all except the royalists.

On August 16 the judges had supped with the president of Harvard College, who had said, "I am persuaded that the Lord has brought you to this country for good, both to us and yourselves." And now they were fugitives! About the same time the startling news came to Boston that ten of the other judges had been executed. Yes, and the Governor had received a royal mandate to have Whalley and Goffe secured. Such tidings greatly alarmed the public, for there was no doubt of the court's necessity to act. A crisis was at hand. However, the judges had friends who contrived to send them away from the Bay. An Indian guided them as far as Springfield, and there a local man named Simon Lobdell took them in charge and escorted them through Hartford to New Haven. There they arrived March 7, 1661, and were well received, as befitted their rank, by the leading men of both towns.

Forced by royal mandate, Governor Endicott, on the seventh of May, 1661, sent the captain of an English ship and a young Boston merchant, both zealous royalists, to search for the judges as far south as New York. On their return these agents reported to the Governor that their efforts had been ineffectual, because they could not induce the magistrates to give them authority to search for the judges. They had been put off chiefly by pretended difficulties. "And so," as they said, "finding the magistrates obstinate in their contempt of His Majesty, we came away the next day, after which we made our return by sea to give your honor an account."

The pretended efforts of Endicott did not blind observers in England, but although he had not wholly succeeded in saving his credit, the judges had fled beyond his jurisdiction, and he was spared further embarrassment.

For a while they seemed to be out of danger, yet the news of the King's proclamation made them doubtful. What they did for the sake of safety was to go to Milford, a few miles south of New Haven, and appear in the daytime making themselves freely known, but at night they returned privately and went to the house of the bold New Haven minister, Davenport, who openly aided and comforted them. There they stayed in hiding, but not for long.

The Colony of New Haven especially aroused the anger of King Charles because the two regicides were harbored there—judges who had sat in the court that condemned his father. So officers were sent across the ocean in pursuit of them, and if they had been caught and taken to London, their severed heads would have been set up on Temple Bar.

As things were, the judges had friends who kept informed of what was going on. One of these was William Jones, to whose house they moved from Mr. Davenport's. Jones cared for them until May 11 and then they found shelter in a mill. After a short sojourn there, they betook themselves to the woods, evidently by appointment with Jones, who came with two companions to meet them. Under the guidance of these friends the regicides went to a place called Hatchet Harbor, where they lay two nights until a cave, or hole in the side of a hill, was ready to conceal them. "Providence Hill" they called this resort and there they continued, from the fifteenth of May to the eleventh of June, but not always in the cave. Sometimes, when the weather was very tempestuous they took refuge in a nearby house. During this time the royalist messengers went through New Haven. They made diligent search and had full proof that the regicides had been seen at Mr. Davenport's, and they offered tempting rewards to English and Indians who would give information that would lead to their arrest, but by the fidelity of their friends the judges remained undiscovered. Mr. Davenport was threatened with being called to an account for concealing and comforting traitors, and might well be alarmed.

The judges had engaged to surrender rather than have the country, or any particular person, suffer on their account, and on intimation of the minister's danger, they generously resolved to go to New Haven and deliver themselves to the authorities there. After letting the Deputy Governor know where they were, they waited for developments, but he took no measures to secure them, and the next day persons came to advise them not to surrender.

So they contented themselves by appearing publicly at New Haven, thus clearing Mr. Davenport from the suspicion of still harboring them. Then they went into the woods again to their cave. There they continued, with little variation in routine, except an occasional venture to a house near the cave. Fortunately, there came a change in August. The search for them was about over, and they went to the home of a man named Tomkins, which was near Milford meeting-house, and there they remained two years, without so much as going into the orchard. Then they took a little more liberty, and made themselves known to several persons in whom it was safe to confide. Also they frequently prayed or preached at private meetings in their chamber.

Commissioners from King Charles arrived at Boston in 1664, and as soon as this news reached the regicides, they retired to their cave, where they tarried eight or ten days. Soon afterward some Indian hunters discovered the cave with the bed in it. The report was spread abroad, and then there was no safety for the regicides in that region.

On the thirteenth of October, they began a long night journey through the woods to Hadley, a little wilderness plantation only five years old and nearly a hundred miles distant. Some of their escapes on the way are said to have been quite exciting as, for instance, when hotly chased, they came to a small river and crawled under the wooden bridge, where they lurked, while their pursuers galloped overhead and away on a fruitless search. The Hadley minister had previously agreed to take them secretly into his home, and there he kept them concealed for more than fifteen years. Very few persons in the Colony knew of these regicides in hiding, but it seems likely that Major Pynchon must have known, as he was the most influential man in this section and used Hadley as his base in the Indian fighting.

During the period that the judges were harbored by Mr. Russell they did not burden him financially. He was no sufferer by reason of his boarders. They received more or less remittances every year from their wives in England, and those few persons who knew where they were hidden sent them frequent presents. Peter Tilton, at whose home the exiles sometimes resided, was often at Boston and donations could be safely made through him. Richard Saltonstall, who was in the secret, made them a present of fifty pounds when he was about to sail for England, and there were several other friends who made contributions. However, they were in constant terror, though after some years they had reason to hope that the search for them was over. One grim pleasure was reading the news of their being killed along with other judges in Switzerland. Goffe's diary, for six or seven years contained every little occurrence in the town, church, and certain families in the neighborhood.

There came a time when Governor Hutchinson was in possession of Goffe's diary, and his papers and letters. Unfortunately, a mob that disapproved of him because he was a Tory, rifled the house, and the regicides' material was gone forever.

In 1674 Goffe wrote to his wife that her father, General Whalley, was fast nearing his end, and went on to say: "He is scarce capable of any rational discourse, his understanding, memory, and speech do so much fail him, and he seems not to take much notice of anything that is either said or done, but patiently bears all things, and never complains. The common question is to ask how he does, and his answer, for the most part is, 'Very well, I praise God.' He has not been able for a long time to dress, undress, or feed himself without help. It is a great mercy to him that he has a friend who takes pleasure in being helpful to him." As time went on something brought Goffe's hitherto unfailing correspondence with his wife to an end. The letters he wrote received no response and he never succeeded during the rest of his waning life in getting any clue to why her letters stopped. They were almost his only comfort, and they had failed him. But no one knows when the day of rest for Whalley came. Neither have we any definite knowledge of Goffe's death. However, in 1685, we find Mr. Russell visiting Boston, and it seems probable that his "special work" had come to an end with a second burial in his cellar.

Rev. Ezra Stiles, president of Yale College, published "A History of Three of the Judges of King Charles I—Whalley, Goffe, and Dixwell," and dedicated it "to all the patrons of real, perfect, and unpolluted liberty." He collected a great abundance of traditionary information from the towns about New Haven and from Hadley. He found that the Providence Hill of Whalley and Goffe was West Rock, about two and a half miles northwest of New Haven, and that their cave was not in the side of the hill, but in a great mass of lava rock on its top. The judges were not out of danger while secreted in Hadley because public inquiry was made after them by men sent from England, and there was need of their always being on their guard.

Few persons in the town knew of their presence until long after their death and it was the surmise of some that the bodies were removed from Hadley to New Haven. Such removal seems incredible. The necessity of secrecy would have prevented, for they could only have been transported by oxen and carts.

The best known and most disputed tradition in connection with the Hadley regicides was published in 1764 by Governor Hutchinson in his history of Massachusetts. Here we have for the first time the full-fledged story of the "Hadley Angel":

> "September 1st, 1675, was a day of alarms and tragedies in that vicinity. For the Indians were making raids, and bloody warfare prevailed in the valley of the Connecticut. No doubt there was the utmost confusion, not only in Hadley, but in Northampton and Deerfield. The usual method of Indians in warfare is to watch chances for a surprise; then follows a swift attack and hasty retreat. In this instance the first shock was not a success, and the Indians lingered, and to some degree beseiged the garrisons, expecting to lay the whole town of Deerfield in ashes. Some were busy plundering and burning out of musket range from the stockades. Meanwhile this condition was discovered and reported by Indian scouts from farther down the river. Then followed the first attack ever made on any town in the valley. The main thought of the people was, 'What will be our fate after Deerfield is destroyed?'"

There is no doubt about the Hadley pioneers being in consternation by a most sudden and violent alarm. That can be taken for granted, and without doubt, a sleepless night followed.

In accord with habit in frontier towns, and even at Springfield in those Indian wars, a number of men of the various congregations were selected to go armed to worship. It was so in Hadley at this time, and when the Indians appeared on a fast day, September 1, while the whole village was gathered in the meetinghouse, the men who had guns immediately prepared to use them. Hitherto, there had been little or no need of firearms in connection with the Indians, and now, in time of stress, conditions became so panicky there was the utmost confusion among the people, and then there suddenly appeared in their midst a grave, elderly man who differed from the rest of them in manners and clothing. He encouraged them to defend themselves, and he put himself at their head, rallied them, and led them to encounter the enemy. By such means the Indians were repulsed, and as suddenly as the deliverer of Hadley came, so suddenly did he go, and the people were left in consternation, utterly unable to account for this strange phenomenon, except by considering that person an angel sent of God on this special occasion for their deliverance. Nor did they get any inkling otherwise until fifteen or twenty years later, when it became known that the two judges had been hidden in this region. The mystery was then unriddled, and as there had been a revolution in England, with a change of rulers, it was not very dangerous to have it known that the judges had been given an asylum here.

According to Governor Hutchinson the anecdote of Goffe in his history was handed down through Governor Leverett's family, who were at Hadley while the judges were there. Governor Hutchinson's father must have been well acquainted with the Leverett family.

It was the supposition of President Stiles that the people in the meetinghouse on that day in September were "suddenly surrounded and surprised by a body of Indians." This statement must be unfounded. The Indians, with a defenseless village a mile in length before them would not have surrounded a building which contained thirty or forty armed men. The attack was undoubtedly on the outskirts of the town, probably at the north end, and the approach of the Indians may have been observed by Goffe from his chamber, which had a window toward the east.

A time came when secrecy was no longer needed, but by then facts had grown hazy, and tradition had taken their place. Some effort began to be made in 1793 to gather from the oldest inhabitants their fading hearsays, with results such as follows:

One tradition they all had at Hadley was that Whalley and Goffe were secreted in the town, but that none knew it at the time except those in whose houses they found a haven. The general belief was that Whalley died in the town and that Goffe, after the death of

Whalley, went away. Tradition has it that Whalley was buried in Mr. Tilton's cellar. Most of those questioned said that while the regicides were here the Indians made an assault on the town, and that then a person unknown appeared, animating and leading on the inhabitants against the enemy, and successfully exciting them by his activity, to repel the Indians. "But when the Indians left, the stranger had disappeared—was gone! and no one knew where he went or who he was." If Hadley had been captured, discovery would have been inevitable. According to the tradition given by some, Whalley and Goffe were not concealed the whole time at Mr. Russell's and Peter Tilton's, but part of the time were at Lieutenant Samuel Smith's. "An old man among us says he remembers hearing the old people tell of a fruitless search by order of the government of all the houses in Hadley, but that they who searched did so as if they searched not."

He said, too, that after Whalley's death, Goffe went to Hartford, and later to New Haven, where he was suspected, because of his extraordinary dexterity with the sword shown on a particular occasion, and in fear of danger he left New Haven.

A still older man told of hearing his father and grandfather say that Whalley and Goffe were both secreted in Mr. Russell's house, and for their security in case of search, a hiding place was made for them between his chambers, and behind his chimney, and they said that one of them died at Mr. Tilton's, and was buried behind his barn. The tradition among some was that both men died in Hadley. One old man said it was a tradition that the one who died in the town was buried in Mr. Tilton's garden.

Stiles, in his "History of the Judges," tells of visiting Mr. Russell's house in 1792. It was a double house with two stories and a kitchen, and some repairing had been done, but the chamber of the judges remained in the same state as when these exiled worthies dwelt there.

One person who furnished the Yale president with information was Mrs. Porter, a sensible, judicious woman, who had reached the age of seventy-seven. She was born in Hadley in 1715, next door to Mr. Tilton's. In reply to his questions, she told him that before she left Hadley, "there were many flying stories, but so uncertain that nothing could be depended on." She knew of the tradition that one of the judges was buried in Mr. Russell's cellar, and another in Mr.

Tilton's lot.   In the course of the conversation, she said that when she was a girl it was a common belief among the neighbors, that for some reason or other, an old man had been buried in the fence, between Deacon Eastman's and her father's.   She also said the women and girls from their house and Deacon Eastman's used to meet at the dividing fence, and while chatting and talking together for amusement, one and another at times would say with a sort of skittish fear and laughing, "Who knows but what we are standing on the old man's grave?"   She and other girls used to be fearful, even in walking the street, when they came to the place of the supposed grave, though it was never known whereabouts in that line of fence it lay.   She thought all the excitement was only young folks' foolish notions.   Some were much concerned lest the old man's ghost should appear in their vicinity.   Stiles, in his history, tells us that he repeatedly visited Hadley for many years, and had often noticed in conversing with persons born and brought up in the town, but settled elsewhere, an impression that both the judges died in Hadley and were somewhere buried there in graves never known, except to a few, and now all definite knowledge was lost.   Yet at the time of Stiles' visits there was general agreement that one of the judges was buried at Russell's.

A portion of the house was erected as early as 1660, and the town aided Mr. Russell to build an addition in 1662.   The inventory of his estate thirty-one years later indicates that the house had a kitchen, lodging room, buttery and closet, with chambers over them, and a study.   Below was a small cellar divided by a partition.   The south side was the front, and had two large rooms underneath with an old-fashioned chimney, a front entry and stairs leading up between the rooms.   Above were two spacious chambers, and overhead appeared the whitewashed joists and garret floor.   The walls were boarded and not plastered.   Chester Gaylord, the owner of the house in 1858, was then in his seventy-sixth year.   In describing this house, which was torn down when he was thirteen years old, he said that north of the chimney was an inclosed place with two doors, used as a passage between the chambers.   The floor boards of this passage were laid from the chimney to the north side, and the ends went under the boards that inclosed the apartment.   One board, at least, was not fastened down, and it could be slipped two or three inches north or south, and then one end could be raised.   When Mr. Gaylord was a boy he had many times raised this board and let himself down into the space below, and restored the board to its place above him.   He was then in a dark hole, which had no opening into any of the lower rooms. There is a tradition that the judges were once concealed in this dark place behind the chimney when searchers went through the passage above.   They could easily lift the board and hide themselves in that under closet.   When the south side of the Russell house was pulled down in 1795 there was need of the stones in the old wall for use in the new cellar.   The building was supported by props, while the wall was being shifted.   During the shift the workmen discovered a place where the earth was loose about four feet below the top of the ground, and a little search revealed flat stones, a man's bones, and bits of wood.   Nearly all the bones were in pieces, but one thigh bone was whole, and there were two sound teeth.   The bones were laid on a shelf, where in a short time they all crumbled into small pieces. These bones may have been those of General Whalley, who was buried nearly one hundred and twenty years before.

A doctor, who examined the thigh bone, said it was that of a man of large size.   Modern expert opinion contends that the bones were too far gone in decay to be those of one of the judges.   It is more likely that this was the grave of an Indian buried long before Whalley came to Hadley.

George Sheldon, the historian of Deerfield, was one of the persons who did much research work connected with Hadley's angel story.   His interest was aroused one day when he was delving in Judd's "History of Hadley."   Some things caught his attention that made him start an investigation, and he arrived at the conclusion there had been no Indians, settlers, nor any regicides who took part in fighting at Hadley that September day in 1675.   Nothing of the kind had occurred then or later.   It was granted, however, that the regicides were real and that in Minister Russell's house there had been a secret passage to use in case of need.

For many long years Hadley's version had been the only one, and the challenge caused great consternation.   The people, from youth up to old age, had an affection for their deliverer.   Besides, an angel was something few towns can boast of.   It gave distinction.   To be without it would make the old town lonesome!

Mr. Sheldon luckily lived on the other side of the Connecticut at some distance, and so escaped most of the indignation. "What! Stealing Hadley's angel! It was a crime!" and mention was made of tar and feathers by a man whose father had been a general in the old-time militia. Things calmed down eventually and the consensus of opinion seemed to be that the angel should have the town backing, no matter what Sheldon said.

HOLYOKE DAM

Really, both Judd and Sheldon have argued effectively, and their views merit careful consideration.

The angel legend was a treasured heirloom in the Hadley annals, and it gave the natives a shock to have its genuineness not only doubted, but declared to be without any foundation. This was the more strange because it was stated that Judd, who wrote the history in the first place, was a person, always looked up to as a sound historical authority of the highest rank, and that the mistake he had made was simply a time when he was "found tripping." However, Sheldon accorded Hadley the consolation that as material for romantic fiction that myth would last for ages.

The attempted debunking of the alleged "angel" myth would have had the approval of Judd to a certain extent. He took for granted there was some sort of a fight with the Indians, but says, "we have no reason to believe there was any very large body of them, but because the people were entirely unaccustomed to war they needed Goffe to arrange and order them. The Indians appear to have fled after a short skirmish." No evidence exists, except in an artist's pictures, that anyone among Indians or settlers was killed or wounded, or that any buildings were burned.

Still another account of the Indian attack on Hadley is given by the famous Boston minister, Increase Mather: "On the first of September, 1675, one of the Boston churches was seeking the face of God by prayer before Him. Also, that very day, the church in Hadley was before the Lord in the same way, but were driven from the holy service they were attending by a most sudden and violent alarm, which routed them the whole day after." In a footnote we are told that Mather probably knew all the particulars, and it is conjectured in the text that "this was all Mather dared to publish in 1676." He does not mention either Indians or angel.

It is interesting to know that the Hadley angel roused more than local interest, and that among others it caught the attention of Sir Walter Scott, who made incidental use of it in his novel "Peveril of the Peak." Various artists of importance have found inspiration in it, and used its theme in their paintings and engravings.

The best history of early days in the Connecticut Valley was written by Sylvester Judd, whose fame grows brighter with the passing years. He was born at Westhampton in 1789, when Springfield was still in old Hampshire County. His grandfather, Jonathan Judd, was the first minister of Southampton, and after serving that rural community in the same meetinghouse for sixty years, he died in 1860.

Sylvester, at the age of thirteen, with only such education as the common school of those times afforded, was placed as a clerk in a store partly owned by his father. After two years of that, he tried being a merchant's clerk in Boston. The clerking was not much of a success, but he fell in with persons of intelligence, who stimulated him to cultivate his own mind. Presently he returned home to help his father, where he had been before in the village store, and any money he could get he spent for books. It was to their perusal he went between the intervening calls of customers. This by no means satisfied his thirst for knowledge, and during many succeeding years he was in the habit of sitting up until twelve, one and two o'clock engaged with his books. Here, in this little country town with no stimulus from libraries, reading rooms, or literary companionship, Judd mastered Latin enough to read "Virgil," learned enough Greek to understand the New Testament in the original; acquired a practical knowledge of French and gained some familiarity with Spanish. His activities were many, but as a matter of dollars and cents, not very gainful. Always his mind was more bent on the pursuit of enlightenment than the accumulation of property. One of his ventures was the acquiring of the "Hampshire Gazette," and he moved to Northampton to concentrate his energy in making the newspaper not only interesting, but instructive. To fill the paper with stories, anecdotes and other matter fitted only to amuse for the passing moment, was just the opposite of his ideal. He regarded a newspaper as an educator of the people, and he occupied his columns with matter calculated to enlarge the boundaries of knowledge, and promote aspirations for information concerning men and things. To enable him to do this he expended money freely in proportion to his means, buying books, including a ponderous encyclopedia, together with numerous volumes of travel and agriculture. He early enlisted his paper in behalf of temperance, and there is reason to think it was the first to exclude liquor advertising.

The "Gazette" in his hands won high esteem and doubled its subscribers. Nevertheless, he relinquished it. In regard to this he wrote, "The truth is that I have become too skeptical in politics to be the conductor of a public press, I have little confidence in politics and politicians." His resources were very limited, but he made up his mind to live on, in a humble way, on such means as he had, leaving himself free for whatever mental occupations appealed to him. At the age of seventeen he had begun filling manuscript volumes with summaries of biography, history and other things, including a private journal, which he kept up more or less continuously the rest of his life. As time went on he gave himself largely to antiquarian researches.

particularly with reference to the towns of Hampshire County, but extending to the whole state of Massachusetts. As the fruit of these labors he left about twenty manuscript volumes, entitled "Miscellanies," and filled with an immense variety of little known but curious matters gleaned from a wide range of varied reading. In his diary of eight or ten volumes, which was continued with regularity from 1833 to within a week of his death, are recorded his principles and opinions; the changes of wind and weather; the different stages of vegetation; the appearance and disappearance of birds and frogs, and of numerous kinds of insects and their habits. This native region of his had a great fascination for him, and he always kept account of its various aspects.

He was keenly interested, too, in his fellowmen and their ways, past and present, and he never hesitated to point out their failings and suggest reform. As an idealist he was perhaps too sensitive, for he often felt disheartened, there was so much that was sordid in the life round about. What seemed to disturb him most in local humanity was the propensity for alcoholic boozing.

Judd was not a successful business man. His mind was always more bent on the acquisition of knowledge than the accumulation of property. Dealing in dollars and cents was irksome to him. From the early period of his residence in Northampton Judd considered writing a history of the region, but deferred from year to year until 1857. Then, at the earnest request of persons interested, he began his history with a list of five hundred subscribers. Meanwhile his health had become impaired so that he was subject to many interruptions. Added to this, his extreme caution in trying to verify all his statements caused the work to progress very slowly. Yet he labored on with a diligence that was more than his strength could bear. Paralysis was the result, and his enfeebled system could not withstand it. In a few days the fatal disease had done its work. He died on April 18, 1860, leaving a wife and five children. His age was only slightly under seventy-one years, but though his body was weak his mind had retained its vigor. Fortunately, the history, in most essentials, had been completed. It was Hadley men who gave him most encouragement in his undertaking, and the book bears Hadley's name. In reality it covers territory for a score of miles up and down the valley of the Connecticut. Mr. Judd's last conscious efforts of a business kind were used in trying to send some directions to his printers.

He was eminently a self-made man, and had relied little on others for his knowledge or opinions. In business transactions he was very lenient to creditors, and lost much that was justly his due. His memory was clear and exact, and his eyesight continued unimpared long beyond the usual period. In temperament he was cheerful, and in social intercourse notably agreeable—a cherished companion of young and old.

Mr. Breck Disturbs the Town

CHAPTER XIII

Mr. Breck Disturbs the Town

John Pynchon survived the other magistrates of his time about twenty-seven years and died in 1703 when nearly eighty. Probably no man before or since ever had so great an influence in the affairs of western Massachusetts. War clouds darkened the outlook almost from the beginning of the eighteenth century, and yet the Springfield plantation prospered, even though there were from time to time garrison soldiers in the streets. The meetinghouse was fortified, and so were some of the dwelling houses and mills.

England declared war against France in 1702, and soon the Indians were raiding across the Canadian border. Then came the revel of death at Deerfield, which was so near a neighbor. The winter snows were stained with blood, and scores of men, women, and children made the long, slow wilderness journey to Canada as captives, most of whom were later redeemed.

Our forefathers were essentially a martial people and warlike virtues were to them a necessity. Military titles were in high repute among them, and were preferred above all others. A corporal was on the road to distinction; a sergeant had attained distinction and his title was never omitted. An ensign or a lieutenant was lifted quite above the heads of his fellows. A captain was beyond question a man of great influence.

Men in England below gentlemen, who owned or occupied land, might add "goodman" to their surnames. A husbandman was one that tilled the ground and the ancients called him a good man. Thus it came about that every tiller of the soil, when addressed in ordinary conversation, received the salutation, Goodman Such-a-one, a title of more honor and virtuous note than many that precede it in public places. It was much used among the husbandmen of the Connecticut Valley. The Goodman's wife was called Goodwife or Goody. Men with a middle name are rarely found previous to 1700.

A table monument in the Pine Street side of the Springfield Cemetery says: "Here lies interred the body of Mr. John Mallifield, a French gentleman who, passing through the town of Springfield, dying, bequeathed all his estate to the poor of this town. He died November 26, 1711. Psal. 41-1. Blessed is he that considereth the poor."

It seems likely that this epitaph refers to Jean Mellichamp, a French peddler, who came riding into Springfield a little before that date on an iron-gray horse and was there taken ill. His stock for sale included handkerchiefs, penknives, imported fans, laces, silks, jews-harps, books and 11,000 pins, and probably came up the river by boat. Realizing that he was dying he bequeathed all his worldly goods to the poor of the village and so became Springfield's first philanthropist.

"The Complete Soldier," a book of ninety-six pages, giving instruction in military exercises, was printed in Boston in 1701. This was undoubtedly the first military book published in the British colonies. It directs the soldiers to appear "with their hair or periwigs tied in bags, and their hats briskly cocked." This must have been an English direction. The Massachusetts General Court voted in 1700 to have "goose-necked bayonets with a socket, instead of swords or cutlasses." These were used only by the Boston regiment. Bayonets were of little use against Indians, and few were seen in Hampshire until the French wars. The powder horn continued to be used by many of the infantry, and the ear-piercing fife, after having been neglected more than a century in England and America, was restored in 1747.

It was not until the enemy made attacks in the winter, and could not be pursued, that snowshoes were deemed of importance. March 13, 1704, Massachusetts ordered five hundred pairs of snowshoes, and as many moccasins for the frontiers, one-fourth of them for Hampshire. The snowshoes or rackets were not used with common shoes, but with Indian shoes or moccasins. The province allowed only five shillings for a pair of each, for some years, though men in Hampshire and elsewhere affirmed that good ones cost ten shillings in money. Colonel Partridge sent the names of four hundred and sixty-three Hampshire soldiers who in 1712 had provided themselves with snowshoes and moccasins, and each was allowed seven shillings.

These Indian inventions for traveling on deep snow were noticed by Champlain in Canada in 1603. They were found, too, among the Indians of Maine. A few English hunters and soldiers in Massachusetts used them in the seventeenth century.

A Deerfield man, on April 11, 1709, was captured in the road above Hatfield. He thought he was in no danger because the leaves were not out. The Indians seldom appeared in the spring until they could be hidden by the leaves.

Early in January of 1712, after the rivers and Lake Champlain were frozen hard and the snow was deep, Colonel Partridge levied one hundred men from his regiment to strengthen Deerfield and other exposed towns. The men had snowshoes and made some excursions on them. In April, Thomas Baker, of Northampton, with thirty-two men, passed up the Connecticut and crossed it south of Cowasset. Then they proceeded to the Pemigewasset, where they found a party of Indians and killed one, and mortally wounded others, as they believed. They took as many beaver skins as they could carry and went down near the Merrimac to Boston. The General Court gave them thirty pounds beside their wages. Benjamin Wright, aged eighteen, of Skipmuck in Springfield, was captured and afterward killed. These are a few local events in the second ten years' war, called Queen Anne's War. The pay of soldiers in this war was generally six shillings a week. In 1704 the allowance to a man each day in a fort or garrison was one pound of bread, two-thirds of a pound of pork, or sometimes one pound and a third of beef, half a pint of peas, and two quarts of beer. Marching soldiers had a little more food. The first regular allowance of rum to soldiers seems to have been a gill a day. "This war, like all others, promoted idleness and vice, and had a pernicious influence on many of the people."

During Queen Anne's War, Massachusetts gave a reward of ten pounds for Indian scalps obtained by those who received wages and subsistence. Volunteers, who went out at their own expense, received one hundred pounds for a scalp after March, 1704. Not many Indians were destroyed. One authority said the charge of the war was so great, every Indian, killed or taken, cost one thousand pounds.

In November, 1706, the Colony passed an act for raising and increasing dogs for the better security of the frontiers, and presently forty-one pounds was paid for "trailing of dogs" on the frontiers of

Middlesex. Gideon Lyman, of Northampton was allowed various sums for buying dogs. Connecticut, about the same time spent fifty pounds to bring up and maintain dogs to hunt after Indians. New Jersey, in 1758, proposed getting fifty "large, strong, and fierce dogs" for the service. It is not known that any Indian was harmed by the dogs.

Springfield's courthouse was situated on the line of Sanford Street, back of Market Street. Land on both sides of the river was taken as part payment for the courthouse. Judge Sewall came to Springfield to hold the September court in 1718. He was met at Suffield by the sheriff and a company of horsemen, who saluted his honor with trumpets. It was quite dark when he rode through the Agawam River and he got his heels wet. He found Colonel Taylor and a number of friends eating supper at Ingersol's tavern and joined them. The next day Reverend Daniel Brewer offered prayer at the opening of court. On the Lord's Day he went to meeting with the associate judges, Colonel Pynchon, and the attorneys of the town, and Mr. Brewer preached very well from the text, "Salute one another with a holy kiss." The judge left Springfield, after giving Mr. Brewer twenty shillings for his prayers during the court session, and was accompanied the first five miles by the sheriff and troopers. He dined in the pine woods, and then went on toward Brookfield.

In 1723 another courthouse was built and the town contributed largely toward the expense. It was a plain two-story wooden building, the front of which projected some distance into Main Street. For years it was the only public building in the town. The lower floor was on a half dozen different levels in an attempt to indicate the rank and importance of the occupants, from judge and jury down to prisoner and public. In those times the judges appeared attired in robes and wigs according to the English custom.

In 1739 the selectmen placed orders for three or more "good Handsome Hewed stones to be placed before the front door of the town-house." One event of interest, in 1753, was a proposition to bridge the Agawam by a lottery scheme. This was voted down. In 1741 rewards were offered for the destruction of pests: Woodchucks, nine pence; old blackbirds, two pence; young blackbirds, one pence; crows, six pence; blackbird eggs, four pence a dozen.

"The Outward Commons," also known as "Springfield Mountain," were settled about 1731, and presently joined the family of Massachusetts towns. The Stony Hill people became the town of Ludlow in 1774.

In Massachusetts no persons were married by ministers for sixty-two years, except a very few in Boston and vicinity. In general, only magistrates and similar authorities were allowed to join persons together in marriage; but in 1692 the General Court directed that marriages should be solemnized by justices of the peace and settled ministers. In a few years after this law was enacted it had become the general custom for pastors to do the marrying. The marriages were occasions of joy and merriment. The groom had some new garments, and the bride had as rich a dress as in her circumstances could be afforded. It was expected that the newly married couple would appear as such at the meetinghouse after they were married and this was referred to by the young wife as "coming out bride." This custom continued more than a century. Stealing the bride was formerly done in some places, and there are many traditions about it. Some young men who had not been invited to the wedding would seize the bride in the street or house and carry her off and keep her until they were invited to join the party. Sometimes they took her to a public house and retained her until the groom ordered an entertainment for them. These affairs seem not to have produced any quarrels, but rather to have been an addition to the wedding frolic.

An old history tells of a two days' wedding in 1769. About eighteen couples attended the wedding and had a good dinner, and spent most of the following night in dancing and merrymaking. One of the party wrote in his diary: "We greeted the rising sun with fiddling and dancing."

The practice of partaking of wine, ardent spirits and cakes at funerals was brought from England to the American colonies, and also the custom of spending large sums for gloves, rings, scarfs and mourning garments. Men sometimes provided for their funerals in their wills.

In 1742 the General Court passed an act against giving scarfs, gloves, wine, rum and rings at funerals, except six pairs of gloves to the bearers, and one pair to the minister.

In May, 1734, the first parish invited the youthful minister, Robert Breck, to preach, with a view to settlement, and his impetuous oratory and originality made a deep impression on his worldly-minded congregation. Breck was a minister's son who had taken first honors in his class at Harvard when he had attained the age of seventeen. He was a deep thinker, fearless in controversy, and he took a young man's pleasure in debate and speculation. In his sermons he wandered continually from the beaten paths of exhortation and commentary. Previously he had preached for a short time at Windham, Connecticut, where rumors were now afloat that things were not all as they should be with him. Recently a letter had been received in Springfield from a Connecticut minister stating that the Reverend Thomas Clap of Windham, and Daniel Kirtland of Norwich, could furnish full particulars of Mr. Breck's unsound opinions. With this for a start, theology became a serious issue, reminiscent of William Pynchon's experience with his book that was burned in the Boston marketplace.

Mr. Breck, on being informed that Reverend Thomas Clap was industriously circulating reports about him, wrote a spirited letter, which began with saying: "I took you always to be a gentleman, and not only so, but a Christian." Soon after this Breck visited Springfield, at the request of the Hampshire ministers. The impression made by Mr. Clap's charges was detailed to him. He was told they expected he would bring a certificate of orthodox character from both Kirtland and Clap. About three weeks later Mr. Breck made the journey to Windham and met his accuser. The meeting was stormy and accomplished nothing. This put a serious aspect on the affair and a majority of the parish were much disappointed. It was still evident to the Hampshire ministers that the First Church of Springfield was determined to settle Breck, and they secured from Clap and others written statements as to what Breck had said in his sermons and conversations while in Connecticut. For instance, he had denied the authority of certain passages of Scripture like "the Father, the word, and the Holy Ghost"; he preached that the heathen who lived up to the light of nature should be saved; he said that Christ might be immediately revealed to them, or they might be saved some other way; that the contrary was harsh doctrine. But besides there were misdemeanors when he was in college that needed to be accounted for. On being confronted by the documents he told the Hampshire ministers that he would accept the call of the church if the people stood by him, and when he had to face a refusal of the ministers to ordain him, he provided the greatest consternation by promptly remarking: "I don't care for that; if one will not, another will."

THE OLD WOODEN BRIDGE ACROSS THE RIVER TO WEST SPRINGFIELD

The ministers then circulated the documentary evidence among the congregation, and the result was that the young man returned to the Bay intending to withdraw from the contest. Soon, however, there came a reaction that brought Breck again on the scene, and there was a renewal of the theological warfare. He did not mince matters when he wrote to William Pynchon that Mr. Clap had lied, and that the word of Huntington, selectman of Windham, could not be taken for a groat by his neighbors. The church was now thoroughly convinced they ought to settle Breck. A year or two later reports were handed about town that Clap was liable to a severe prosecution for what he had written.

When one story of this kind was worn out, another of the same sort was set on foot. Mr. Clap afterward became president of Yale College, where he was noted for his intense denunciations of theological error.

It has been mentioned that Mr. Breck was accused of stealing books when he was a college student, and in the exciting April meeting of the Hampshire association he was on hand and read the defense himself. According to rumor, expulsion followed stealing. He denied the expulsion, but told of saying to Mr. Clap, "with tears in his eyes," that he had nothing to say in justification of his conduct. But he added, "I went to college very young and fell into bad company, so that my conversation was not such as it ought to have been, and I hope that God has given me a light, and sense of my sins, and that I am truly humble on account of them." Mr. Breck was submitted to a sharp cross-examination. For one thing his critics tried to make him withdraw the charge that Clap had lied about him. He was willing to ask forgiveness for overheat in such discussions, but refused to yield an inch to Mr. Clap and his heresy charge. Another meeting was called for the twenty-fourth of April, and in spite of protests from the ministers, Mr. Breck was given a call, and the promise of a house within four years, and he accepted.

But the fires of dissent were still alive, and remained so for many years, sometimes smoldering and sometimes bursting into flames. In fact, within a few weeks the Hampshire ministers were on Breck's trail again, and as time went on many bitter things were said. When the call to be pastor of the First Church was accepted, arrangements at once began for the ordination, and the Springfield church succeeded in pledging four ministers from Boston to assist. The town was in a feverish state of uncertainty, and it was thought best to give up the preparations for the big dinner which was customary in those days. The Boston ministers all stopped at a public tavern. Most of the Hampshire ministers had arrived, and Mr. Clap had come up the river with a bag full of documentary evidence. The two parties in the parish maintained the strict lines of hostility. All business was suspended, and the whole community felt the unusual tension. The second day of the council opened, but not with the ordination as had been planned. After some negotiations it was stipulated that the evidence of the dissatisfied should be given with closed doors. Accordingly Mr. Clap and his witnesses were locked into a chamber in Widow Brewer's house with the council and the accused. Mr. Breck usually stayed at Mrs. Brewer's when visiting Springfield and in that way became acquainted with her daughter Eunice, a young woman with unusual gifts of mind.

Mr. Clap began a long address that soon brought Mr. Breck to his feet with protests, and the moderator had to protect Mr. Clap from interruptions. Another unusual feature was a commotion in the streets below, and once a minister attempted to enter the chamber. Also, a messenger rode up to Mrs. Brewer's in hot haste and called for Mr. Clap, who halted his speech long enough to carry on a private conversation. Then the messenger rode away, but in a few moments Mr. Clap's speech was again interrupted, and in came an officer with a sword at his belt, bearing a warrant for Mr. Breck's arrest. The cloud had burst, and the mysterious movements of strangers and judges and ministers were explained. The civil law had been invoked to prevent a Congregational Church ordination, and His Majesty's judges were asked to pass on the theology of a ministerial candidate.

When the council found they were left with no minister to ordain, great was their astonishment. But greater still was the consternation of the people, who ran through the streets as Breck was carried a prisoner to the town house, where four justices sat waiting. This was the hour of Mr. Clap's triumph. His face is said to have been radiant with satisfaction. At the same time those who were not satisfied were there in large numbers, including the indignant members of the church and other friends of Breck. Indeed, there was danger of an outbreak, but wiser and more dignified counsels prevailed.

Some of the ordination council appeared to defend the prisoner before the judges, and Mr. Clap was promptly put on the witness stand and was followed by others. That night Mr. Breck slept in custody of the law. The next morning the ordination council assembled again in Mistress Brewer's house and attempted to continue its investigation, while the whole town was at fever heat and many persons were present from the surrounding country. Someone in front of Mistress Brewer's house had gotten a copy of Breck's confession that morning and a young man mounted a white horse and proceeded to read it to a large crowd, consisting of both friends and foes of the young minister. Some of the crowd applauded and others showed disapproval.

Mr. Breck was ordered by the justices to be taken to Connecticut, where he had preached his heretical sermons, and many of the sorrowing and indignant congregation followed their youthful hero until well out of the town. That was an exciting night for Springfield. Some rejoiced, some feared evil results, and some were bowed down in anguish. The next day a public meeting of humiliation and prayer was held. The suspense was not long, and Breck was discharged and returned at once. The final decision was made by the Massachusetts House of Representatives. It was, that although the justices had the right to inquire into the facts charged against Mr. Breck, yet they "ought not by any means to have interrupted a church and Ecclesiastical Council while in the Exercise of their just Rights inquiring into the same."

Soon afterward the Springfield church set January 27, 1730, as the day of Mr. Breck's ordination, and a few days after that was past, Mr. Breck married Eunice Brewer. Their engagement probably took place in the dark days when the Hampshire association was trying to drive Breck out of the valley.

About this time the English Methodist preacher and revivalist, George Whitefield, made one of his visits to America, and it included the Connecticut Valley. He was a remarkable man in his way. Very early in his London career he preached in some of its principal churches, and in order to hear him, crowds assembled at the doors long before daybreak. His voice was so clear and powerful it could reach 20,000 listeners, and his fervor and dramatic action held them spellbound while his homely pathos soon broke down all resistance. For many years it was his habit in the compass of a single week to speak to thousands for forty or more hours. In the valley of the Connecticut opinion was divided. Mr. Breck, although no bigot, had little desire to see his people crying out hysterically over an eternity of anticipated bliss, but beyond question Mr. Whitefield's journeyings greatly stimulated the wonderful revivals in religion which were breaking over the valley. What Mr. Breck distrusted was the effect of special religious revivals, and later one of his congregation quoted him as saying: "I am opposed to the late stir in religion."

In Mr. Whitefield's first American journey he preached in Springfield in 1740 on his way with Jonathan Edwards from Northampton to East Windsor.

Just as Whitefield was leaving the village on horseback, the animal stumbled on a defective bridge and threw the revivalist over its head. Afterward Whitefield said, "My mouth was full of dust, but I fell on soft sand and got not much damage. When I recovered myself and mounted my horse, God so filled me with a sense of His love and my own unworthiness that my eyes gushed out with tears."

Some years later Whitefield returned to America, distinguished, portly, and richly dressed. In a Connecticut minister's diary of 1704 is this: "Mr. Whitefield came along; People seemed very fond of gazing at him. He rode in his chariot with a gentleman—had a waiter to attend him, and Sampson Occum, the preacher from India: There were three chariot horses and he rode one of them."

These were trying times for the First Church. Mr. Breck went into the pulpit just at the turning of the tide in New England. Men's speech was changing, and many old English words and phrases were falling into disuse. Moreover, the Puritan costume no longer satisfied, and was gradually being put away and instead the three-cornered hat and lace and ruffles were gaining in favor. William Pynchon died with a Puritan skull-cap hanging by his bedside. But his son John left a wig and garments covered with gold lace. John Pynchon's sons wore cocked hats. Whitefield noticed in the Boston congregations that "jewels and gay apparel" were commonly worn by the women, while little boys and girls were "dressed in the pride of life, and the little infants that were brought to baptism were wrapped in such fine things, and so much pains taken to dress them, that one would think they were brought to be initiated into the pomps and vanities of this wicked world." Moreover, the same elements were at work in Springfield.

There is no evidence that the visit of Whitefield had any effect on the Springfield church. But there were wonderful revivals of religion at Northampton, Hatfield, Longmeadow, and so on down the valley. There were the protracted meetings, the crying out of convicted souls and the falling in fits on the floor.

The Northampton revival of 1735 was the most remarkable, and the fame of it penetrated to England and Scotland. That there was no revival in the Springfield church is credited to Mr. Breck and, in fact, many in his time deplored the liberality that he encouraged, and they even separated from the parish.

Such a one was Joseph Ashley, who absented himself permanently. When he was asked why, he replied that he looked on Mr. Breck's church as no church of Christ, and the greater part of its members as carnal. He said that most of the discourse of most of the members was on worldly affairs, and that he believed such discourse was delightful to them. Also, he objected to the manner of admitting members because "a particular account of their experiences was not required, and instead, accepted a profession of dedicating themselves to God, and a life and conversation corresponding thereto." The increase of church membership during Mr. Breck's ministry was remarkable, and it continued even when a congregation gathering on Springfield Mountains drew heavily from the first parish. As a rule everyone went to church and the meetings on lecture day were largely attended.

Reverend Mr. Breck died in 1784, in his seventy-first year. In his early life the funeral costumes would have been severely righteous, but in these later times there were silk stockings, and silver buckles, and lace, and powder, bowed in grief. However, the old first parish meetinghouse was draped in black, Reverend Mr. Lathrop delivered the funeral sermon, and a solemn anthem was sung. The whole assembly followed the body to the grave. Mr. Breck had lived in the parsonage where his dignified manners, tie wig, shoe buckles, silk stockings and a slave attendant served to fill out the ancient notion of ministerial importance. The old Breck residence in its later years served as a laundry on Hillman Street. Mr. Breck left at his death a negro slave named Pompey, who probably was the last of Springfield's slaves. He died in 1813. The first wife of Mr. Breck passed away in 1767, and his second survived him.

Pompey, the slave, served her faithfully as long as she lived, and when the old darky was left alone in the world he now and then visited in the Springfield and Northampton region among "Massa George's folks and Massa Robert's folks."

An important event of 1749 was the building of a new meetinghouse. This, however, was not entirely finished until 1752. The length was sixty feet, the width forty-six feet, and the height between joints twenty-six feet. It was the third meetinghouse and the predecessor of the one used at present. It stood directly east of the one now occupied. There were two entrances, the principal one on the east side and the other through the tower. For a long time the imposing square pews were retained.

In the natural course of things a few cases of discipline disturbed the serenity. The most singular one first got active attention when complaint was made against a rather prominent but very eccentric member. He was charged with disturbing the devotions of his fellow Christians on the Lord's Day, and interrupting the public worship of God, by reading aloud while they were singing His praise.

After prayer for divine direction, the church found him guilty, and voted to debar him from Christian privileges until gospel satisfaction should be made.

Eighteen months afterward the offending member wanted a chance to confer with the church, and he asked whether his confession would be accepted, if made to the church in the absence of the congregation. The church voted to adhere to their ancient practice of receiving confessions of public offenses only before the congregation. Six more months passed and the member renewed his proposal to present his confession before the church only. After prayer and consultation, the church decided to comply with his request provided the confession should afterward be read to the congregation by the pastor. Another interval of six or eight months passed, and then the last course suggested was adopted, and the offender was "restored to charity."

In 1784 the church voted unanimously to choose Mr. Bezaleel Howard to be their minister. He came to Springfield an entire stranger to the village and its people, sent by the president of his college to supply the vacant pulpit for six Sabbaths. His journey was on horseback, the road was solitary, and the approach from the east far from attractive. As he rode down the hill to the Main Street, then the only settlement, he saw buildings mostly unpainted, and many of them dilapidated. The aspect was chilling to the young minister, and he said to himself, "The day when the six weeks of my engagement ends will be a happy one to me."

When he had that settled in his mind, he saw directly opposite the road by which he entered the village one white house that had a more cheerful aspect. He presented himself at the door of the house, and announced his name and errand to the man who lived there. "You have come to the right place," the man said, and there the six weeks were spent very pleasantly. The call to settle followed, and in that white house the young preacher found his future wife. He was ordained pastor of the church in 1785.

There are some things in the early parochial history of the church that appear strange from our modern outlook. One of these is a periodical assigning of seats to the congregation. The custom prevailed from the time the first meetinghouse was erected down to the present one. Thus, in 1664, when the town and parish were identical, it was ordered that "the select men and deacons shall from time to time seat persons in the meeting-house either higher, or lower, according as in their sound discretion they shall judge most meet."

What a strange jumble of officials! Selectmen and deacons, uniting in this difficult duty of seating persons higher, or lower, according to their discretion! A month later there is recorded an order of the selectmen which is a curious example of the way the parochial police work of those days was administered. It says, "Forasmuch as order is beautiful, especially in the house of God, and the want of it displeasing to God, and breeds disturbance among men—and whereas it doth appear that various young persons, and sometimes others, do yet neglect to attend to such order as is prescribed, either for their sitting in the meeting-house, or for their reforming of disorders in and about the meeting-house in time of God's publick worship—It is therefore ordered that whoever of this Township shall not submit themselves to the ordering of the Selectmen and deacons shall, He or She, forfeit three shillings, four pence, to the town's treasury." By the same authority, it was ordered "that the seat formerly called the guard seat, should be for smaller boys to sit in, that they may be more in sight of the congregation." In this seat none were permitted to sit above the age of fifteen years.

Care was taken in the earlier period of the town's parochial history that the men and women should be in separate seats. The first innovation connected with this practice came in 1751, when the parish voted to "seat the men and women promiscuously." Then, in order that those of tender sensibilities should not be shocked by so great a departure from long-established custom, the committee in charge were directed, on application being made to them by any person or persons desiring not to be seated promiscuously, to gratify them as near as they can. It is not surprising that the parish selected two of the wisest and most popular men of the town to perform this delicate duty.

At a parish meeting, in 1790, it was voted to choose a committee to seat the new meetinghouse. Twenty-two persons were chosen for the office, all of whom refused to serve. The meeting was then adjourned for two days. The seating had come to be attended with a good deal of difficulty, but after more meetings and adjournments a committee was provided, and "seating the meeting-house" continued until the erection of the present house of worship in 1819.

A record of a parish meeting held in 1737 indicates the rules by which the assignment of seats was regulated. The age of persons and the value of their estates, negroes excepted, are the principal considerations.

Few persons, if any, among the present inhabitants of the city are aware how largely the means for extinguishing fires used to be provided and controlled by the old first parish. The record shows that in November, 1792, the parish granted for the purpose of defraying the expense of building the enginehouse the sum of six pounds, eleven shillings, two pence and two farthings; and in March, 1794, voted to pay the expense for two firehooks and six leather buckets for the use of the fire engine. The same year Pitt Bliss was paid two pounds, twelve shillings and six pence for the six buckets and for "repairing the hose to the engine." Not content with repairing the old hose, the parish voted that Pitt Bliss and some others be a committee to examine the hose belonging to the engine, and if they judge it necessary, to procure a new one at the expense of the parish. All this makes the present-day reader wonder how the extinguishing of fires came to be regarded as a parochial duty. Be that as it may, the ancient church stands today on the spot where throughout three centuries it has always stood, and with vigor still unimpaired.

There were no means of warming the meetinghouse until 1826. Probably about that time winter Sabbath schools were introduced.

The Revolution and Its Aftermath

CHAPTER XIV

The Revolution and Its Aftermath

The first evidence of the spirit that led to national independence came to the surface in 1774. Alarming letters from Boston were read in open town meeting about public affairs and the aggression of England, and Massachusetts was thrown into a state of wild excitement. A notable Springfield Tory was John Worthington, who eventually was forced to make a statement in town meeting that satisfied the people. It had been said of him hitherto that he ruled the town with a rod of iron. The story has often been told beside Springfield firesides that the Whigs, who dominated the town at this exciting time, were so angered by his refusal to join them, that they led him out into a field, formed a ring, and compelled him to kneel, and swear before God that he would renounce his Tory views. Later, we find him advancing money for arming soldiers, nor was this money reimbursed until after the surrender at Yorktown.

Toryism had taken a deep hold on several leading Springfield families, and there are in New Brunswick many tombstones bearing old Springfield names. Such relics give us a curious testimony to the tenacity of the Tory spirit. Among those who went to New Brunswick was Jonathan Bliss, who became Attorney-General of the Province and also Chief Justice. His wife was the daughter of John Worthington.

The Springfield Pynchons, during the Revolution, were notably patriotic.

Merchant Jonathan Dwight, at the first echo of war, closed his store and made his plans to leave Springfield. Then he heard a rumor that a decree had gone forth from Boston to seize his goods, and he directed his slave, Andrew, to drive his cattle across the Connecticut line. He modified his political sentiments later, due to the influence of his wife, and reopened his store.

Means were taken in Springfield to aid the poor at Boston, and the town stock of ammunition was increased. An association had been formed pledging the members not to wear or use any clothing or produce imported from Great Britain. This self-imposed embargo was a severe test of patriotism. The subsequent exclusion of tea from the table was accepted in good part by the community, although tradition infers that some worthy dames of Springfield were not above steeping tea at the hour of midnight and drinking it in the seclusion of their closets.

OLD DAY HOUSE, PRESERVED AS A MUSEUM, WEST SPRINGFIELD

On the day that the battle of Lexington was fought, the British soldiers left Boston before daybreak on the tenth of April, 1775, and on the next day Captain Kent, within an hour's notice, was at the head of a Suffield company of fifty-nine men and a provision wagon, rushing for Springfield, where they ate supper, and then hurried on. Each Springfield soldier was given a half pound of powder and a supply of flints. The Springfield taverns and the streets were in a perfect uproar, and during the next two days soldiers were constantly forwarded. The British troops had left Boston to the tune of "Yankee Doodle." In twenty-four hours it was the other army which was playing that tune.

George Washington was in Springfield in 1775 and stopped at the old Parsons' Tavern on Elm Street. He was on his way to Boston to take command of the Continental Army. A company of horsemen went with him and his party to Brookfield.

A company of Highlanders was billeted in Springfield from June, 1776, to the following March; and in July, 1777, Colonel Cheever had charge of the transfer of army supplies to Springfield, where it had been decided to establish an arsenal and supply depot. Large use was made of local horses and wagons in this business. Town committees of safety met and arrangements were made for sending supplies to the army. A Northampton convention called attention to the conduct of persons in the county who were unsuitable persons and declared the selectmen of the various towns "dare as well be damned as to draught them for the army, and that, if they were draughted, they would rather fight against our own men than against our enemies."

The year 1777 brought an alarming spread of smallpox and led to measures for building a "cleansing house" near the pesthouse and for the complete isolation of these buildings. At the same time provision was made that the "Physicians of the Town be desired not to inoculate any persons for small-pox or give them any preparatory medicine without the allowance of the larger part of the Selectmen." But the inoculation party again captured the town.

During the following year sentiment gradually changed and we find the town appointing a committee to draw up regulations for inoculation. Then came another setback. Several deaths from inoculation among soldiers increased the popular distrust of that remedy.

The following notice of General Washington's reception in Springfield was published in the "Hampshire Chronicle" of October 28, 1789:

"Last Wednesday about 3 o'clock in the afternoon this town was honored with the presence of the President General of the United States accompanied by his two private secretaries. He was met at the 'Great Ferry' (now Cypress Street, but formerly Ferry Lane) and a number of gentlemen on horseback escorted him to Landlord Parsons'. There he was received by the Independent Cadets who saluted with three volleys, and paid him every other respect which the dignity of his character merited. They were politely noticed by the President, who soon after visited the arsenal on Federal Hill, where he spent considerable time viewing the public stores deposited there, and was well pleased with the good order in which he found them. Early on Thursday morning he proceeded on his way to Boston."

In his diary Washington mentioned that "Colonel Worthington and many other gentlemen sat an hour or two with me in the evening at Parsons' Tavern where I lodged."

The Continental soldiers at the end of the war were poor, and a fierce conflict followed between debtors who had borne arms and creditors who had not. It was a time that tried at least every poor man's soul, and fully half the State's citizens were in debt. The excursions of sheriffs searching for property to levy on embittered the people against the courts of law. There was a spirit of discord even before the end of the Revolution. Reverend Samuel Ely, a Connecticut minister of unsavory character, interfered with the courts at Northampton in 1782. He was convicted and imprisoned in the Springfield jail, from which he was released by a mob. It was the twelfth of June, and Springfield was in great commotion. About one hundred and fifty men, mostly strangers from up the river, and from the Berkshire Hills, with swords, guns, and bayonets, demanded the keys of the jail. When refused, they broke open the doors, released Ely, and a debtor, and a negro. Some citizens returning from a funeral pursued the party and caught and locked up three men as hostages for the return of Ely. Northampton and other towns joined in the chase, and no less than one thousand armed men took part in the episode. On Sunday word came from Northampton that the hostages were to be liberated by a mob, and two hundred armed men marched in short order from Springfield to the rescue. General Porter, of Hadley, called out the militia, and it was by his firmness that the law was sustained when six hundred determined men confronted the five hundred and fifty who guarded the Northampton jail. It is not to be inferred that the spirit among the Massachusetts people of that time was exceptional. They simply became poverty-stricken and distressed.

Daniel Shays, at the beginning of the Revolution was a hired man at Brookfield. He entered the army as sergeant under Washington near New York, and he received one of the swords that Lafayette distributed to American officers. It is said that he was ostracized for a time by his associate officers because he sold this sword and continued to use the old one. Eventually he became captain in a Massachusetts regiment, and his record at Bunker Hill, Stony Point and Saratoga was creditable.

At his home in Pelham after the war he was sued for debt, and as he did not appear judgment and costs were recorded against him. He was naturally a reckless character and liked nothing better than to spend his evenings in the taverns criticizing the government. The sale of a sick woman's bedding gave him a good text for tavern harangues. The Conkey Tavern at Pelham was made vocal, and so was the Clapp Tavern at East Amherst, and likewise the West Springfield tavern, where Luke Day, legislator-at-large, talked by the hour.

Daniel Shays and Luke Day took a bold step at Springfield by interfering with the session of the Supreme Court, but General Shepard, of Westfield, prevented a collision with the forces of Shays, as they marched and countermarched before the Springfield Courthouse, or gathered at Stebbins' tavern, in North Main Street. After the court had adjourned he withdrew his militia companies to the arsenal, and the Shays men returned to their homes. Three weeks later, Shays issued an order from Pelham requiring all his men to arm, and furnish themselves with sixty rounds. He went to Rutland and supervised the interruption of the courts of Worcester and elsewhere. Then he hurried to Springfield and found the judges of the Court of Common Pleas an easy prey to the clubs, drums, muskets, and threats of his men.

While these sorry affairs divided brother and brother in the village of Springfield, and set friend against friend, the Springfield town meeting voted that the increase of paper money at a time when it was already a burden was preposterous.

The insurgents found hearing in the papers, and loud-mouthed men declaimed in the taverns of Springfield and elsewhere against the riot act. These agitators sported the hemlock twig that was their banner and emblem. When it had been decided to call out the troops, the commissary-general reported that he could get no supplies without cash, and the treasury was empty. At once General Lincoln visited a prominent Boston club and laid the case before them. A subscription was started the following morning with the Governor heading the list, and the money was raised before sunset. An army of four thousand and five hundred collected in short order, and General Lincoln prepared for his long march. He arrived in Worcester January 22 and protected the courts with little difficulty. Daniel Shays, after sending to the Governor a message intended to mislead, tried the difficult feat of capturing the Federal arsenal at Springfield. He made a dash from Rutland with over one thousand men armed with a motley array of guns, but thoroughly equipped with an incendiary vocabulary. On the twenty-fourth they reached Wilbraham and the women and children of that terrified community were transferred to Longmeadow. General Lincoln was two days' march in the rear of Shays, and the plan was to overpower General Shepard before the eastern troops arrived. Eli Parsons, with four hundred Berkshire insurgents, was at Chicopee. Luke Day was the only man among the rebels who made any pretense at military discipline. He was resting at West Springfield with a company of four hundred whom he kept in good temper by occasional orations on the oppressions of the government. Thus, Shepard was confronted by about two thousand rebels, twice his number.

Shays ordered Day to attack on the twenty-fifth, but Day said he would not be ready until the twenty-sixth. This answer miscarried and Shays advanced on the twenty-fifth. Meanwhile General Shepard was doing his best to keep an exasperated people in hand. Public sentiment was against him. In speaking of supplies, he said of rum and other liquors, "They must be forwarded from Boston as there is little to be had in Hampshire County," and he added, "the men cannot be kept together, especially at this season, without a daily allowance of spirituous liquors."

There was pressing need of money at Springfield for the support of the soldiers. Not one cent of the money subscribed at Boston had been forwarded. As neither Congress nor General Knox had given permission to take arms from the arsenal, General Shepard's men were poorly equipped and he felt more and more concerned. He was cut off from Berkshire by the vigilance of Luke Day and he was unable to communicate with Northampton. Caleb Strong, of that town, wrote Lincoln that insurgents had taken possession of Chicopee Bridge, and had captured a provision train on its way to Springfield for the militia. The weather was bitterly cold and Shepard called on Lincoln for at least four hundred men to be forwarded in sleighs. His food was limited to a five days' stock and the loss of his provision train was a serious handicap. Besides, his men were unpaid, and he was obliged to be personally responsible for the fuel and forage he needed. Evidently he could not continue in the field much longer unless money was sent to him.

Shepard had learned that three hundred insurgents had lodged at Northampton on the night of the twenty-second. Shays, Day, and Parsons had completely cut Springfield off from all approaches, and the insurgents were enjoying the contents of Shepard's provision train. Luke Day had scoured the country on the west side, and his sentries and reconnoitering parties were very annoying. He even deployed troops in the Longmeadow direction and secured many prisoners. He captured General Parks and Doctor Whitney in sleighs, and took a loyal Longmeadow man out of his bed and shut him up with other prisoners of war at West Springfield. Shays was at Palmer on the twenty-third with eleven hundred noisy men. The insurgent officers held a council of war there, and a friend of the government overheard the proceedings. It was decided to join Day's forces in an attack on the arsenal before Lincoln could come to Shepard's relief. This information was taken to Lincoln, and a deputy sheriff rode through the crusted snow across fields from Wilbraham to the Stony Hill Road on the twenty-fifth, drawing blood from the legs of his horse.

Within an hour General Shepard was warned, but Shays did not appear on the Boston Road in view of the armory until late in the afternoon. Shepard sent several messages of warning to Shays not to advance, but received only insolence and defiance for his pains. At a hundred yards a howitzer was discharged each side of the advancing forces; and a few minutes later a shot at short range was leveled directly at the column and three men were killed and one mortally wounded. A scene of ridiculous confusion followed. Not a return shot was fired at the militia, and about twelve hundred very much frightened men raced toward Ludlow. The killed and wounded were taken to a house near by.

General Lincoln, with the main body of his troops, reached Springfield on the twenty-seventh and at nine o'clock of the twenty-fifth the news of Shays' defeat reached Palmer. After getting to Springfield, Lincoln, with part of his army, moved up the river on the ice, intending to prevent a junction of Shays and Day and, if that were not attempted, to cut off Day's retreat. The other part of the troops he moved across the river. Soon the insurgents turned out and retreated about half a mile to the main body, where they showed some disposition to attack. But they changed their minds and went to a high piece of ground in their rear, where they were met by Lincoln's horsemen, and then they fled in every direction. Most of them reached Northampton about twenty miles distant. This left Shays' men exposed to attack and induced him to move on the same night to Amherst. At three o'clock next morning Lincoln went toward Amherst, where Shays had been joined by Day. On his arrival in the borders of the town, the rear of Shays' force left it, and some fell into his hands. Then Shays went east from Amherst and Lincoln's men went to Hadley and Hatfield on the river.

When the insurgents in western Massachusetts had scattered, Lincoln said at Pittsfield that he found "the people in general had been in arms, or had encouraged those who were." Governor Bowdoin offered one hundred and fifty pounds for the arrest of Shays and one hundred pounds each for the arrest of Luke Day and Eli Parsons. Day was eventually brought to Springfield a prisoner, but Shays made good his escape. This region for some weeks was made lively with martial anecdotes. At Hadley, seven soldiers were court martialed for stealing property from private citizens, and were condemned to march before the army on parade, with papers pinned to their breasts on which was written in capital letters, "FOR PLUNDERING."

Long after the events that have been recorded we find General Shepard complaining that he had not been repaid by the State for his services in defending Springfield, and he added:

"As to private injuries and insults which I have received, some have been by burning my fences and injuring my woodlands by fire beyond recovery for many years; others by wantonly as well as cruelly destroying two of my horses by cutting off their ears and digging out their eyes before they were killed; also by insulting me with the vile epithet 'a murderer of brethren,' and through anonymous letters threatening me with the destruction of my dwelling-house and family by fire."

After the Revolution it was a common custom to paint houses bright red or yellow and wearing apparel was likewise gaudy. Scarlet cloaks or richly flowered blue silk coats were worn by the women, and also the calash, the furbelow scarf, camlet riding-hood, or white hoods trimmed with lace.

Girls in families of moderate means had hoods of coarser material and calico gowns. Woolen petticoats with calico borders were common. It was a rare daughter who could not ride horseback either single or on a pillion, and tourists from abroad spoke of the charm of these rosy-faced girls racing down country roads in white aprons and calico dresses. Both men and women patronized the hair dresser. William Doyle kept a fashionable place after the Revolution opposite Zenas Parsons' tavern and a little north of the courthouse. He made wigs, "attended the call of ladies," and kept "a stock of cushions and curls, and for gentlemen full-bottomed wigs, periwigs and scratches," which were wigs that partially covered the head.

On Fridays, in 1783, the Hartford "Stage wagon" left David Bull's inn for Parsons' tavern in Springfield, and returned Saturdays. A few years later Reuben Sikes ran a line of stages from New York to Boston through Springfield three times weekly in summer, and the fare was three shillings a mile. The arrival and departure of such ladies and gentlemen as were equal to the expense of travel was an event of no small account. On the south side of Ferry Lane, which later was known as Cypress Street, dwelt Dr. Charles Pynchon, who had a wide practice all through the valley. There had been a time when Ferry Lane seemed destined to be the business center of the town. Opposite the doctor's office Zebina Stebbins had his residence as well as his dry goods store, but finally he moved one of his buildings to the east side of Main Street. It contained a printing establishment, and there his son, Dr. Cad Stebbins, had an apothecary shop, and among other things sold tea, coffee, needles and Bibles. Mr. Stebbins was overseer of the poor and he was thrifty in business; hence his proposal to make up a job lot of coffins for a group of aged unfortunates who plainly would need such receptacles soon.

A conspicuous merchant of this period was Jonathan Dwight, whose "old red house" lives in storied memory, and here used to gather for converse, and to smoke and to trade, people of all classes and conditions. The red house was removed in 1799, and the old store was drawn by long lines of oxen up Main Street to Mr. Dwight's meadow, an event which greatly impressed the school children of that day. Jonathan Dwight and others joined forces and started a gin distillery on Main Street near Cross Street, connecting with a malthouse in a rear meadow.

Joel Marble kept a drug store one door south of the courthouse, and he had a counter devoted to books. William Warland, chaise-maker, was located near the Great Ferry. The best known tavern of the period was the old stand of Zenas Parsons.

Formerly a magnificent elm stood in the southeast corner of the present Court Square, and there was just room for the "stage waggon" between it and the hotel veranda. In the rear were extensive barns and sheds, and auctions were frequently held there. In that part of the premises, too, the young men on training day often tried their powers in wrestling. Over the shed was a long dance hall, much used by the young people and interest in the tavern was further increased by the fact that George Washington had put up there either when going to take command of the Continental Army at Cambridge, or when he visited the armory after the war.

The first Springfield newspaper was "The Massachusetts Gazette and General Advertiser," in 1782. It was a dingy affair containing some foreign matter and very little local information. The printing office was a few rods south of the courthouse, where was kept an extensive stock of books, writing paper, and maps, to be exchanged for rags and country produce or money. Goldsmith's "Deserted Village" and other books were sold by the several post riders from the printing office. These post riders furnished a lively feature of the day, riding up and down the valley on both sides of the river. One post rider covered a route from Northfield to Hartford.

In 1784 the publishers moved to the Great Ferry and changed the paper's name to the "Hampshire Herald." In general the existence of the early papers was precarious. They changed names and owners, and were prone to disappear altogether.

By 1790, the floating of timber down the river was a busy industry, and about that time the Legislature incorporated a company to build locks and canals on the stream. John Worthington, of Springfield, headed the list of stockholders and Northampton was strongly represented.

Work was soon begun. This was the pioneer project of canaling in New England, and there were numerous engineering difficulties. Besides, the scarcity of money was a serious handicap. Finally an agent was sent to Holland, and there a Dutch loan was secured. Soon a canal was built in the rocks, and a dam started to raise the river level at the upper end of the canal. But the consequence of that was an overflow of the Northampton meadows. The company was prosecuted and a portion of the dam was torn down. Next, the Dutch capitalists became alarmed and wanted their money back, and the faith of the American investors enabled the Dutch to cash in at a considerable profit.

When more money was needed in 1802, the company was authorized to raise it by means of a lottery and they used this source of income to deepen the canal several feet.

Demoralization attending the wars was plain. Burglary and horse-stealing from 1787 was very common and deserters and bounty-jumpers flourished. About this time two young men of the town were induced to enlist at Worcester under false names to secure the sixty dollar bounty. They were detected, but were let off with a published card full of humble contrition, and the payment of twenty dollars "smart money," to be used advertising for deserters.

A great sensation was caused in May, 1782, when a woman dressed as a man enlisted in Springfield as Samuel Smith. She failed to get mustered in or to receive the bounty, and was locked up. Lack of a beard roused the suspicions of the authorities. Another person dealt with was William Jones, passer of counterfeit State money, who broke jail. In fact, there were many crimes against property. In 1782 thieves made a descent on Zenas Parsons, and much plate and other valuables were secured.

By an act of the Legislature in 1794, all the courts of Hampshire County were directed to be held at Northampton, which was made the shiretown of the county. The reason assigned for making the change was that Northampton, on account of its central situation, was the most suitable place for holding the courts of the county and most likely to give general satisfaction. Later years, however, showed that the center of business and population was nearer Springfield, but no further change was made until the creation of the new county of Hampden in 1812, with Springfield the shire town.

When the proposal was made to establish a Federal arsenal near here public opinion was divided. If West Springfield had made an effort the armory would probably have been located there; but the majority on the west side like the minority on the east, feared the moral effect of drawing in the soldier element which would make up the bulk of the armorers. Brookfield and Hartford had been thought of as suitable places for a government storehouse. Stores could be

CRAFTS TAVERN, HOLYOKE
On Springfield and Northampton Highway

sent down the river from here, but the town could not be reached by a hostile flotilla, and the final decision made by George Washington and General Knox six months later was in favor of the Springfield training ground.

There was quite a flutter in 1792, caused by a colony of laborers with their families who settled here. But a meeting of the selectmen and a few visits of the two town constables, with writs of warning to depart in fifteen days, restored the equilibrium. It was this kind of invasion that the community feared.

Congress passed a bill establishing a United States Armory here in 1794. The appearance of the hill at that time was not very formidable. There was a powder magazine made of brick with an arched roof three feet thick. This magazine was blown up in 1846. There were two red wooden storehouses, some soldiers' barracks, and an old dwellinghouse where the storekeeper lived. Other buildings had been put up at the lower watershops. The upper watershops were built in 1809 on the site of a powder mill which had exploded that year, and it was possible then to abandon hand work for waterpower in forging, boring and grinding. The first musket was made by the United States here, in 1795. Forty men were employed at first, and during that year they turned out two hundred and forty-five muskets, less than one for each working day.

Armorers were exempted from jury and military duty after 1800. Colonel Roswell Lee became superintendent of the armory in 1815. He was a six-footer, dignified and placid. Old armorers showed great respect and affection for him. Among his numerous improvements was the rebuilding of the north shop, burned in 1824. It was a source of anxiety to him that the armorers spent so much of their earnings for rum, and he tried with a good deal of zeal to check the practice. The "Old Toddy Road" to Japhet Chapin's tavern did not reduce the travel along this route. He discharged two workmen who were found wrestling in the midst of a ring of armorers. There was a liberty pole in the center of the ground that had been erected by the subscription of the workmen, and here the friends of the discharged men gathered and passed around the bottles. "If we can't have any liberty," they said, "we won't have any liberty-pole," and an axe was brought ready to wield. The colonel and others hastened to the scene. They saved the pole, and the little "rum rebellion" was at an end, but "Toddy Road" did not lose its name for some years.

The first guns made at the armory were the French model, but afterward English models were favored. These were heavy, long-barreled, large fore-guns that were favorites with the Indians, one of whom, according to legend, declared his liking was for "big gun, big noise, big bullet." The first American model was made with flintlock, in 1822. This was abandoned in 1842 and the percussion lock adopted.

This seemed so perfect that a proud historian declared in the "Springfield Directory" of 1848 that it was "confidently believed the arms made at this armory since the percussion lock was used had no equal anywhere else in the world." The new model was used in the Mexican War. When the great war of the North and South began only a few up-to-date guns were available and until the 1862 model could be made and put in the field the Union volunteers had to take such guns as they could—Enfields, Austrians, Belgians, flintlocks, rifles, fowling pieces—anything in the shape of a gun. A large increase in the armory force and the addition of new buildings followed the outbreak of war. At the time Fort Sumter was fired on one thousand guns a month were made, but production continued to increase until that quantity was finished every twenty-four hours, with the works running day and night. The payroll at this time was more than $200,000 a month, and the foundation of many a thrifty Springfield mechanic's home was begun in those years of turmoil.

In Field and Forest

CHAPTER XV

In Field and Forest

The floating of timber down the Connecticut River did not begin until after peace with the Indians in 1726. The first notice found of floating states that several persons assembled on the bank of the river, August 31, to see twenty-five masts float down Enfield Falls, and that one struck a rock, which turned it from its course in a manner that killed a boy of Windsor. A company was formed, about 1730, of several men who belonged in Suffield, Westfield and Deerfield, for the purpose of cutting and floating down the river white pine logs suitable for masts, booms, yards and bowsprits, for the British Navy, in accord with an agreement approved by the King's contractor in Boston. By October, 1733, they had gotten to New London a shipload of timber, and they had in the woods, seventy miles above Fort Dummer, a considerable number of men preparing another shipload. Two logs that lodged on the river bank at Saybrook were three feet in diameter at the large end and eighty feet in length.

After the conquest of Canada and the settlement of towns far up the river, great numbers of logs were floated down in freshets, and many lodged on the lowlands in various towns. After the Revolution, pine trees were cut and sent to market without restriction. When there was a big freshet a great number of logs and trees lodged on the flats of Hampshire. It is said that in the high flood of 1801 a man could walk one hundred rods on logs in Northampton meadow. In some places they were heaped up one above another, and there were amazing piles in many of the coves. When the freshet was not high, the river sometimes was so full of logs that it seemed as if a person could walk on logs across the stream. Some of the logs on the meadows were drawn to the river in the spring, and others in the fall. The owners of the land were entitled to compensation from the owners of the timber for any damage incurred. Some of the logs were sold to owners of sawmills, and some to men who wanted them to use in building houses. They were glad to buy a few logs for clear boards and for shingles. Such pine did not grow in this part of the Connecticut Valley.

It was common knowledge that some men stole logs, and others ingeniously obliterated marks; if a log had not been marked, the logmen could not claim it.

THE OLD PYNCHON FORT

A few rafts of boards were floated down the Connecticut from the upper settlements, before 1755, and these gradually became numerous. Such rafts were safely guided down the falls and rapids of Willimansett and Enfield. John Pynchon sent small rafts of boards, sawed at his sawmills, down Enfield Falls to Hartford and other places, but all sawed lumber and shingles were carted past the falls at South Hadley and Montague. In April, 1765, a road was laid from the head of the falls at South Hadley to a landing place below the foot of the falls, about two and a half miles. The landing was twenty-five rods on the river and ten rods wide. This was named the "Lumber Road." When it was finished, in 1765, there was no house near the river or falls. Titus Pomeroy, from Northampton, was the first innkeeper there, beginning in 1767, and after his death his widow kept an inn many years. There were two sawmills in 1771, and a third one in Fallsfield, near the lumber road. After 1765, the transportation of lumber and the taking to pieces and putting together rafts, made considerable stir about the falls.

Some rafts and boats stopped at the mouth of Stony Brook and boards, produce, and other things were carted from there either to the landing at the foot of the falls, or to the landing below Willimansett rapids. Much merchandise was carried up past the falls to Stony Brook from this lower landing, and some was taken at the foot of the falls. The farmers of Falls Woods changed their employment, in part, and were the carriers of lumber and goods by the falls for more than thirty years. They could not cart lumber and cultivate their farms, and the land and fences had a neglected appearance. Sometimes farmers from other parts of the town were transporters of lumber.

The mouth of Stony Brook, where everything is now so quiet, was a bustling place at times more than half a century ago. It was a harbor for rafts and boats, and in freshets great numbers of logs lodged on the adjoining lands. Immense piles of boards were sometimes on the south bank, and numerous men and teams. Elijah Alvord had a warehouse near the brook. He sold goods and kept a public house, more than a mile below. When the canal was in operation, and boats and rafts were daily passing through it, the rafts above waiting their turns were sometimes so numerous they lined the shore from the head of the canal to Stony Brook, a distance of more than two miles.

In 1770, Elias Lyman was licensed to keep a ferry between Northampton and South Hadley, not far from his inn, where Smiths Ferry is now. No one had been licensed before, though people had long crossed the river in boats at this place. Northampton had boats and boatmen on the river below the falls when needed for one hundred and twenty years, before the first canal of 1795. They carried freight between "Hampton landing," in West Springfield, and Hartford and other places below. There was a Hadley boat on the river in 1668. Boats continued to navigate the river until they were superseded by the freight cars of the railroad.

When the English established themselves on the banks of the Connecticut, there was in the river and its tributary streams, during the proper seasons, a great abundance of shad, salmon, bass, and other fish such as the Indians had used for food from time immemorial.

The shad, which were very numerous, were despised and neglected by a large portion of the English for nearly one hundred years in the old Connecticut towns, and for about seventy-five years in the Hampshire towns above the falls. It was discreditable for those who had a competency to eat shad, and it was disreputable to be destitute of salt pork. Eating shad implied a deficiency of pork. The story has been handed down that in former days the fishermen took the salmon from the net, but often restored the shad to the stream as not worth saving. It has been related that when a family about to dine on shad, heard a knock at the door, the platter of shad was hastily hidden under a bed. There was a prejudice against shad because they were so generally used by the Indians.

The first purchase of shad found in any account book of the valley towns was made by Joseph Hawley, of Northampton, in 1733. He gave for thirty shad one penny each—which was not equal to half a penny in good money. Ebenezer Hunt gave two pence for "good fat shad" in 1737, and he bought bass, suckers, pickerels and eels. For forty years after 1733 the price of shad did not exceed a lawful penny. The dams across the river and other impediments diminished the number of shad, and gradually the price advanced to six pence, nine pence, one shilling and even higher prices, so that men ceased to buy shad to barrel for family use.

Shad-eating became reputable thirty years before the Revolution. They were carried away on horses, and some thousands of barrels were put up in Connecticut for the troops from 1778 to 1781. Shad never ascended Bellows Falls at Walpole, nor could they ascend the falls of Chicopee River. Salmon passed up both. In 1639 Brookfield petitioned the General Court for liberty to make a passage for shad through the bars of rocks across Chicopee River in Springfield, so they might come up the river into their ponds. Springfield opposed, and liberty was not granted. Salmon nets began to appear by 1700, and some salmon were salted in casks by families. They were seldom sold, and the price in Hartford was less than a penny a pound. Fish were so abundant in the Connecticut and its branches that laws were not necessary to regulate fishing for a long time. There was a law in Massachusetts against weirs or fish-dams in rivers without permission. Petitions for liberty to erect weirs to catch fish in the Hampshire streams began in 1729, and these were chiefly for catching salmon. In Northampton, salmon were sold from 1730 to 1740 at a price equal to one penny a pound in lawful money. The first dam at South Hadley, about 1795, impeded the salmon, and the dam at Montague was a much greater obstruction. The salmon soon ceased to ascend the river. Few were caught after 1800. Northampton had two fishing places opposite each other, and there was a time when as many as forty salmon were caught in a day, the largest of which weighed between thirty and forty pounds. The fishermen often were near each other, and they bantered and joked abundantly, and sometimes played tricks and encroached on each other. These things did not proceed from ill nature, but from a desire to indulge in fun and sport, but there were many coarse jokes and some harsh tricks.

In South Hadley was a noted fishing place near the mouth of Stony Brook, and another above Bachelor's Brook. Many salmon were taken at those places; twenty-four are said to have been caught at one haul near Stony Brook. The falls of rivers were great fishing places in New England for the Indians and the English. At South Hadley, the falls, known as Patucket by the red men, were one of the most favorable places on the river for taking fish, and it cannot be doubted that the Indians caught fish there in early days, and the English before 1700.

Fishing at the falls generally began sometime between April 15 and May 1. It was at its best in May. Shad were caught in seines below the falls, and in scoop-nets on the falls. Where the falls were rocky, boats were drawn to them, fastened, and filled with shad by scoop-nets; then taken ashore, emptied, and returned. In this manner a man could take from two thousand to three thousand shad in a day, and sometimes more with the aid of a boatman. The movements required men of some dexterity. Below the falls other large hauls of fish were made and brought to wharves. The greatest haul was about 3,300. However, it was not often that even 1,200 were taken at one sweep of the net. There were as many as fourteen fishing wharves at the foot of the falls in 1801. Salmon were taken on the falls in dip-nets, and below in seines with shad. At times, and in some places, the river seemed to be full of shad, and in crossing the oars often struck them. Old time fishermen at the falls used to say that it was much more difficult to sell salmon than shad.

After shad time some bass were caught with hooks. Sturgeon were taken on the falls with spears. Lampreys, commonly called lamprey eels, had long been plentiful on the falls, and many were taken at night by hand, with the aid of torchlights. Some were eaten in a few old Hampshire towns, but most were carried to towns in Connecticut. These lampreys came above the falls in great numbers, and entered the streams that run into the river. They were caught by the light of torches, sometimes several hundred in a night. Men waded into the stream, grasped them with a mittened hand, and placed them in a bag. At night, the lampreys sometimes crawled into and about the flutter-wheel of the mill and into the throat of the gate, in such numbers that the wheel could not be turned in the morning until they were cleared away. In Northampton Mill River, down the stream beyond the lower mills, lampreys were caught as in Hadley. On a dark night men might be seen in the river clasping with one hand, now and then, a squirming lamprey, and holding in the other a birch-bark torch, which threw light on the river and on everything along its borders. Very few lampreys were cooked, but many were given to hogs. None are now caught above the Holyoke dam.

During shad seasons multitudes of people came to the falls on both sides of the river from various quarters. Some came from Berkshire, and all came on horses with bags to carry shad, except a very few, who had carts. Some, with intention to buy two loads of shad, led a horse. For some years the only licensed innkeepers at the falls were Daniel Lamb and Widow Mary Pomeroy. But in shad time every house on both sides of the river was full of men and some lodged in shelters and outhouses. Horses filled the stables and many other places. On one occasion it was estimated there were 1,500 horses that day on both sides of the river. Often the men brought food with them; many cooked shad and others bought food at the houses. There were numerous instances where persons were detained one day or longer. Another element consisted of those who indulged in plays and trials of skill.

Where men were so numerous and rum was plenty, there naturally was much noise, bustle and confusion. But the greater part of the men were industrious farmers, and after leaving the falls they went off over the hills and plains with their bags of shad in every direction. There was another class at these gatherings composed of the idle, the intemperate, and the dissipated. They came to drink and frolic, and some to buy shad if their money held out.

Many thousands of shad were still taken annually at South Hadley Falls after the Holyoke Dam was built in 1849, but none could ascend the river, and instead of a penny each, which was paid in early times, the price for shad at retail was from twenty-five to forty cents, and sometimes fifty cents. Gradually the waning of the shad industry at the falls continued until there was an end to it. Yet even now, in some seasons, a few stray shad find their way up the river to the spawn waters of their ancestors, and fishermen on the rocks may hook two or three.

Wolves were very common and destructive in the New England and other colonies, and they long tried the patience of the settlers. They were considered "the greatest inconveniency in the country." The nocturnal howlings of these ravenous animals have been heard by the inhabitants of almost every township. Wolves continued to annoy the people more than a hundred years after the settlement of Springfield.

The reward for destroying wolves in 1643 was thirty shillings. In 1693 the bounty for grown wolves was twenty shillings, and for whelps five shillings. The Colony paid for one hundred and forty-seven wolves killed from 1650 to 1655. Wolf killing was at its height in the latter part of the seventeenth century. In twenty-eight years, between 1700 and 1737, a bounty was paid for killing 2,852 old wolves and one hundred and ninety-one whelps, averaging a few more than a hundred a year. Wolves were killed in many of the Hampshire towns down to about 1775. Some wolves were caught in traps and some were shot. Many were taken in wolf-pits, which were fitted to entrap them. They were seldom killed by dogs. To get a bounty the heads were carried to the constable or selectmen, who were to cut off the ears. A famous wolf killer on one occasion sent a wolf's head by his daughter. Wolves killed sheep, goats, calves, swine and deer. When the county reward was twenty shillings, it required most of the Hampshire county tax some years to pay for wolves. In the winter of 1660 a man killed a wolf on the ice of the Connecticut, and the county court decided that each abutting town should pay half of the town bounty.

A reward for destroying wildcats was first offered in 1727. Twenty shillings were paid for those over a year old, and ten shillings for those younger. In the next seven years two hundred and eighteen old wildcats were killed and eighty-eight young ones. After this havoc they did not become so numerous. The common wildcats of New England were a species of lynx.

In 1742 a bounty was offered to persons who killed bears—ten shillings for old ones and five for cubs, from the first of April to the first of September. The small reward, and the delay in giving it, indicate that bears were much less harmful than wolves and wildcats. Yet in some seasons, especially when acorns and and nuts were scarce, bears destroyed pigs and sheep, and devoured soft corn. About 1788, John Montague, of Hadley, shot a bear which his dog had treed in Hadley meadow, and carried it to the broad town street on the top of his load of corn. This was long after bears had disappeared from the valley. Bear meat was eaten in the river towns, and was accounted about as good as venison. The price of bear meat from 1721 to 1759 averaged about two pence a pound in lawful money.

There were a few catamounts formerly near the west border of New England. In 1742 the State offered a reward of forty shillings, which was gradually increased to four pounds. The killing of a catamount must have been a rare occurrence. There are stories of the creatures being killed in Hampshire, but some of the tales relating to the catamount are not credible. The creature has a terrific scream, yet rarely, if ever, attacks man, woman, or child. The stories about lions in early writings of New England came from the reports of Indians who had seen the catamount and heard its scream.

Towns often gave premiums to encourage the destroying of crows and blackbirds. At first it was the blackbirds that were the more mischievous, and most towns offered rewards for them before they made war on the crows. A premium of one penny each for blackbirds was first offered and the heads were to be cut off in the presence of one of the selectmen. For woodchucks eight pence apiece was paid, and their ears were to be cut off in the presence of a selectman. A one shilling premium for crows was paid in 1727. The shrewd and cautious crow has maintained himself against all the arts and efforts of men and still abounds. He does much harm by pulling up the corn that is planted, but is useful as a scavenger, devouring reptiles, worms, insects and all sorts of dead carcasses.

Woodchucks and skunks were very rare in New England when first settled by the English. These and some other quadrupeds, and many species of birds greatly increased in the neighborhood of civilized men, whose farms yielded much more food for them than the forests and Indian towns.

Long ago woodchucks were caught and their skins tanned for whiplashes. Many boys in the Hampshire towns trapped them at the mouths of their holes, and afterward, with the aid of lime or ashes, the skins were freed from hair and then tanned—many of them in the common soap barrels. The whiplashes were a means for the boys to get spending money.

Beavers, which were once numerous in the region, were nearly all caught by the Indians before King Philip's War in 1675. For some years the beaver trade with the Indians was in the hands of John Pynchon and those appointed by him. He packed for England in six years forty-seven hogsheads containing nearly a thousand beaver skins, and sent many more in bundles. He packed six hundred and ninety-nine otter skins, about nine hundred skins of muskrats, and many of the gray and red fox, raccoon, marten, mink and wildcat; also four hundred and twenty-six moose skins weighing from twelve to twenty-five pounds each. Many of the beaver and other skins were brought from the north and west, and most were bought of Indians.

For a long time the mild and nimble deer were very numerous. The early planters of Hampshire, though they occasionally hunted deer, turkeys and other game, were too industrious to spend much time in such pursuits. The Indians were the principal hunters in this region while they remained. Many persons of the succeeding generations sometimes diverted themselves by hunting, but few let this recreation interfere with their regular business. Harmful animals were hunted from necessity. Deer were more useful to men than all else that was hunted, and as they were lean in winter, and the females produced their young in the spring, the Colony enacted in 1698 that deer should not be killed between January 1 and August 1. Other colonies had similar laws. In 1739 each town of the province was required to choose men annually to prosecute or inform against any persons who killed deer out of season. Two men called "Deer Reeves" or "Informers of Deer," were chosen yearly from 1758 to 1780. Only a few deer were killed in the river towns after 1780.

The county records note the prosecution of many persons in Hampshire for killing deer unlawfully. The fine was ten pounds, half going to the informer.

Long ago a number of men in the valley towns were known as the "old hunters." They had chased deer and other wild game before the Revolution, and sometimes a social party and a venison feast came after a hunt. Many of their hunting stories were in circulation, and some of these were so wild as to be scarcely credible. Occasionally such men were trappers as well as hunters. Those who spent a large portion of their time in hunting were poor. The habits of such were not consistent with regular industry. "Hunting does not increase property nor improve morals."

Levi Moody, of Granby, born in 1784, used to say that deer continued on the extensive pine plains in the eastern part of Springfield, and were killed by hunters from South Hadley and Granby until after 1800. When pursued by hounds they often crossed Chicopee River. Mr. Moody shot deer on these plains—the last one in 1820. Heath hens, similar to prairie hens, were formerly on the Springfield plains.

William Pynchon and John Pynchon bought much venison from the Indians and sold it to the inhabitants of the town. Many quarters of the venison weighed from fourteen to thirty pounds each. Venison was sometimes salted in a cask, and deer tallow was sometimes made into candles.

Leather garments were common in England and a vast number of deer skins were prepared in New England for use as apparel. Dressing deer skins, moose skins and beaver skins was a regular trade. Breeches were the most common garment made of deer leather, but jackets and waistcoats were numerous, and there were leather doublets and coats, and some had a leather suit. A few had wash-leather stockings and many had deerskin gloves. Moccasins were made of deer leather and moose leather. Many of the men in this region wore leather breeches, and some had other leather garments. Even the clergy had their leather breeches and waistcoats to some degree, and there were military men who did not disdain leather breeches. When sheepskins were scarce, leather aprons were, on occasion, made of dressed beaver skins. The only fur made into hats was that of beavers, raccoons, and muskrats. Beaver hats, after 1750, were sold for from twenty to forty-two shillings each, and raccoon and muskrat hats brought from twelve to twenty shillings. Raccoons have been hunted for hundreds of years, for both pleasure and profit. They have commonly been hunted in the night with the aid of a good dog which trees them. A raccoon on a climbable tree would be shaken off by a man and caught by the dog. Sometimes one was shot by moonlight. The hunters often kindled a fire and waited until morning. Then they perhaps shot one or two more; if a raccoon was in a hollow tree, the tree was cut down and the dog seized the 'coon. Sometimes a boy was allowed the privilege of going along and carrying a lantern for the hunters. The raccoons still devour green corn and are still hunted in many of our towns. The meat used to be esteemed by some nearly as good as venison.

Muskrats are still plenty in some regions of Hampshire, and they continue to be hunted, though perhaps more for sport than for the pelt. When a flood covers most of the meadows and lowlands, and the muskrats are driven from their habitations, boats may be seen carrying men with guns and a dog, and now and then is heard the peculiar clicking noise made by the discharge of a gun near the water; then the dog leaps out and brings to the boat a muskrat, if one has been killed.

That big, formidable animal, the moose, sometimes strayed into Hampshire. One was killed at Brookfield in 1765, and another, six feet high, was killed there two years later. Wild turkeys were abundant in the Colony. They naturally frequented the oak, chestnut and beech forests, rather than the pine lands. Wild turkeys sold about 1720 at one shilling four pence each. They weighed from five to fifteen pounds. Turkeys were hunted on Mount Tom and other places in the region. Deer hunters were also turkey hunters. Many years ago the initials of several turkey hunters might be seen in the bark of a white birch tree, near the path over the mountain called by the hunters "Turkey Pass." Turkeys were killed in this vicinity after 1800, but they were not so plenty on the east side of the river. Sylvester Judd said that when he was a boy in Westhampton, about 1800, he often saw small flocks of wild turkeys in the woods near his father's home. He observed their tracks in the winter snows, and heard their gobbling in the spring. Wild turkeys continued on Mount Tom longer than elsewhere. There was a flock on Mount Tom in 1842, a few in 1845, and a single turkey in 1851. The old writers tell large stories about the weight of wild turkeys, even reporting it to be from forty to fifty pounds each, and in two instances sixty pounds. A more moderate authority said fat ones weighed from twenty to thirty pounds. In Northampton a man who weighed many of them found only two or three that went as high as twenty-four pounds. These weights were before the turkeys were dressed. Pigeons passed over the eastern part of the Colony in countless multitudes in early days. Onlookers could see neither beginning nor ending of these millions of millions. In 1741 they had a breeding place near the line between Hampshire and Vermont, and their nests on the beech and hemlock trees extended for miles. Pigeons were taken in nets around Boston as early as 1700, and in Hampshire many were shot before 1740. They were sometimes decoyed by a flutterer or stool pigeon, but more often were taken without such a lure. In former days they were caught so abundantly that at Granby they could neither be sold nor eaten, and the bodies of many were given to the hogs after the feathers were plucked from them. Pigeon feathers were much used for beds. In August, 1736, pigeons were only two pence a dozen and many could not be sold at that. In 1850 they sold from seventy-five cents to fifty cents a dozen. Since then their interminable multitudes have rapidly melted away. Why, remains a mystery.

Partridges are greatly lessened in numbers, and their spring drumming is much less frequent. Quails, which were sometimes caught in box traps, are rare and their prediction of "more wet" is seldom heard. Wild ducks were formerly abundant, but now seldom are seen and wild geese are still more uncommon. The old hunters did not shoot singing birds, nor did the Indians. That barbarous practice belongs to later times. Squirrel hunts with two sides and shooting at tame turkeys about the time of Thanksgiving are sports introduced into this part of the country since the Revolution.

The rattlesnake excited the curiosity of many Europeans who came to this country. It was correctly reported to be ''a most sleepy and unnimble creature, never offering to bite unless trodden on.''

Rattlesnakes inhabited Mount Tom when the region was settled, and they continue to be there. Now the section in the county most thickly populated with rattlesnakes is Mount Tekoa, just north of the Westfield River from Woronoco. After a while several men were bitten, and it is alleged they were cured by snake weed. It is believed that for more than two hundred years no person in the valley towns has lost a life by them. Two young men named Smith, south of Holyoke, were bitten by a rattlesnake in the eighteenth century, but were cured. A few cases were fatal elsewhere. Several of the snakes are killed almost every summer on the sides and near the foot of the mountains.

Physicians formerly supposed there was much medicinal virtue in the flesh and gall of the poisonous viper of Europe, and of the rattlesnake of America. Rattlesnake flesh was eaten by some infirm persons in this vicinity a century or more ago and the gall was mixed with chalk and made into balls. Even physicians bought these precious balls and gave eight shillings a dozen for them. Traders bought them also, and country stores.

About 1775 a Southampton man killed five rattlesnakes at the same time near the foot of Pomeroy Mountain. Then he cut off their heads, fastened the bodies to the saddle and carried them home, dangling from his saddle. It has long been believed by some that rattlesnakes have the power of fascination. The stories told of blacksnakes, or any others winding themselves around the bodies of persons in New England are fabulous.

How The People Lived

CHAPTER XVI

How The People Lived

Massachusetts settlers for want of oxen at first tilled their land mainly with the spade and hoe for some years. But when the valley of the Connecticut was settled, men had cattle and plows. No part of New England was more productive of wheat and other grain than this valley. In the three towns above the falls every farmer raised wheat, and wheaten bread was common, though much Indian corn was also prepared for food. But the alluvial lands became less productive as early as 1680, and the crops of wheat had seriously diminished by 1700. In the next sixty years the crop became so uncertain and so often failed, that most men ceased to sow wheat on the lowlands, and during the next sixty or seventy years the greater part of the wheat consumed in Hampshire was raised on uplands newly cleared. Wheat was sparingly used. Many families had only enough for the entertainment of friends and the annual Thanksgiving. The blasting of wheat began in eastern Massachusetts and Plymouth in 1664, and it was deemed a judgment. Pies were sometimes made with rye paste for the bottom and top, and some had rye below and a wheaten upper crust. Most of the people in the Hampshire towns, though they consumed much corn, commonly had bread made of bolted rye flour for nearly a century. Rye bread was long used in considerable quantities. In the counties east of Hampshire the common bread of the inhabitants was made of sifted rye flour mixed with corn meal, and it was dark, glutinous and heavy.

A few years after 1800 barrels of flour began to be brought up the river into Hampshire. For some years the quantity was not large, but no sooner were the Erie Canal and railroads ready to furnish transportation, than the quantity of wheat flour consumed in New England was greatly increased.

The people of New England could hardly have been sustained without the American grain, Indian corn. It has furnished them with much of their food for generations. The average length of an ear in 1676 was nine inches, and the colors of the corn were yellow, white, red, blue, olive, greenish, black, speckled, striped and some other tints, but yellow and white were the most common. The stalks grew to the height of six or eight feet. The planting was in rows several

Gul Pynchon Armg Effigies
Delin Anno Dom 1657
Ætat 67

WILLIAM PYNCHON

feet apart each way, and four or five grains in a hill. The corn was hoed three times, and at the third hoeing a hill was made. Some English, following the example of the Indians, planted beans in corn hills, and pumpkins and squashes in vacant places between the hills.

Farmers who had a cornhouse husked their corn in it. Others husked in the barn, or in the great kitchen. The evening husking party was generally composed of the family, but sometimes a few neighbors were present. They were lively and cheerful, but not very noisy. At the close there was a simple serving of food. The boisterous husking frolics and the kissings connected with red ears, which took place in some parts of New England, were not known in this vicinity.

Hasty pudding was made in Great Britain of flour and milk, and of oatmeal and water, before New England was settled. This name was improperly given to our puddings of Indian meal and water, for everything made of Indian meal requires thorough boiling or baking. It was formerly the custom in the local towns to make hasty pudding once a week. That usually meant making it on Saturday and eating it with milk at night and the next morning. The New England hard pudding, boiled many hours in a linen bag, was long a part of the dinner in most families in farming towns. It was reported that some Hampshire families had three hundred and sixty-five such puddings in a year.

The culture of potatoes was introduced in New England by the Scotch-Irish who came over in 1718. Few were raised in Hampshire until these people settled in Palmer, Pelham and Blandford. The inhabitants were indebted to the new settlers for their knowledge of potatoes, and of the manner of cultivation. Most were satisfied with raising a few bushels. A Spanish potato, fit only for the hogs, was raised, and a red potato used for the table. A good white potato followed.

Pumpkins ripened under the suns of New England were much more dry and sweet than those grown in England. One authority praised stewed pumpkin with a little butter, spice and vinegar. Another called it a "fruit which the Lord fed his people until corn and cattle increased." Pumpkin bread—made of half Indian meal, was one way of serving it. The Indians dried pumpkins and strung them for winter use, and the colonists followed the Indian custom.

Some boiled beans, peas, corn and pumpkins together and liked the combination. Pumpkins have been raised to feed animals in the river towns from very early times. Stewed pumpkins and pumpkin bread were common ways of using the fruit for food.

Pumpkin pies were early made in New England, and the delicious pumpkin pie at the annual Thanksgiving may well remind us of the hardships of our forefathers. A hundred years ago most of the kitchens of Hampden County farmers, late in autumn, had poles suspended from the joists loaded with pumpkins cut into circular slices, and these slices were dried for pies and sauce. A pumpkin-paring sometimes made a merry evening, as well as an apple-paring.

Flax was an absolute necessity to past generations. Nearly all the linen and tow cloth used for garments, sheets and other bed furnishing, tablecloths, napkins, towels and bags, was made in families. The industrious females also made linsey-woolsey of flax and wool, and other cloth of flax and cotton. Tow cloth made of tow and flax was an article of traffic more than half a century. Traders bought it, and it was sent to Hartford, New Haven and other places. The wives and daughters of farmers exchanged tow cloth, checked linen, woolen, and other cloths with the traders, receiving instead stuff for gowns and other articles.

Some of the farmers sowed small fields to hemp, and both hemp and flax were used for ropes and cords. There were men who made cart-ropes, bed-cords, leading lines, and halters. The wild hemp from which the Indians made lines and nets still grows in the region.

Flax was cultivated by the early settlers, and by succeeding generations, until the establishment of cotton factories. It used to be an important crop in old Hampshire, and was made into cloth in most families, but so complete has been the change that few persons have ever seen a woman hatchel flax, or card tow, or heard the buzzing of the foot wheel, or seen bunches of flaxen yarn hanging in the kitchen, or linen cloth whitening on the grass. The flax dresser, with the shives, fibers and dirt of flax covering his garments, and his face begrimed with dust, has disappeared; the noise of his brake and swingling-knife has ended, and the boys no longer make bonfires of his swingling-tow. The sound of the spinning wheel, the song of the spinster and the snapping of the clock-reel have all ceased; the warping-bars and quill-wheel are gone, and the thwack of the loom is heard only in the factory. This revolution, and a similar later one in the household manufacture of wool, have made a great change in domestic life.

Broom corn, a native of India, has long been cultivated in Southern Europe, chiefly for the seed, but brooms and brushes were made
of it in Italy for some centuries since. Various minor experiments
were made with it here in America by Benjamin Franklin and others,
but to Levi Dickinson, of Hadley, belongs the credit of finding a way
to raise broom corn abundantly, and of supplying the country with
brooms. He introduced an important industry, and women have
been furnished with better sweeping tools than they ever had before.
He succeeded in getting a little broom seed and planted some hills in
his garden at the upper part of the old back street of Hadley. That
was in 1797. When harvest came he had enough seed for a half
acre, and the next spring he planted the first half acre ever cultivated
for brooms in America. He continued to plant more in the following
years. Strangers who were passing, after it had put forth its tufted
panicles, were puzzled to know what that strange thing was and often
they stopped to make inquiries.

Mr. Dickinson made twenty or thirty brooms in 1797, and between
one hundred and two hundred the next year. Heber, a colored man,
began to tie on brooms for him, but he, himself, contrived a better
way. He sat in his chair, with the string round a roll under his feet
and wound it round the brush in his lap. The seed at first was scraped
from the brush by a knife, and afterward by the edge of a hoe with a
short handle, fastened to a bench. Upright teeth were used later.

Mr. Dickinson peddled in a horse-cart in Williamsburg, Ashfield
and Conway, in 1798. He used to say that the day when he first sold
a few brooms was the happiest day in his life. He had made certain
that some women liked his brooms and would buy them. In 1799 he
went to Pittsfield with brooms, and about 1800 to as far as New London. From the beginning, most people in Hadley thought he was
visionary and his projects fanciful, and sneers and sarcasms were
frequent. These things were very unpleasant and he found obstacles
and up-hill work, but he was not diverted from his course. He was a
man of energy and persistence, though of small estate and infirm
health, and he boldly predicted that the broom business would be the
greatest in the county. At length his neighbors began to think he was
prospering, and some of the most influential began to raise broom
corn and make brooms. That was about 1800, and it was not far
from that date when Cato, a negro, planted the first broom corn in

the meadow. Three or four years later Dickinson carried brooms to Boston and Albany. He and others at first made their own handles and the twine was spun from their own flax. A real boom developed and other towns joined the broom corn ranks.

Levi Dickinson died at the age of eighty-eight, but long before his death the broom business had been widely extended.

The brooms of New England in early days resembled those of Old England and the best were made of hair or bristles and imported. Most of those prepared here were made of birch and hemlock and of various materials such as rushes and husks. Later, what was called Indian brooms became the common brooms of the country. They were made of sticks of birch, ash or other sturdy material, long enough for the broom and handle. The broom was formed of two lengths of thin, tough splints or filaments, the upper doubling over the lower, and both at one end adhering to the handle. They were called splinter brooms. People were supplied with Indian brooms until after 1800. In 1762 a merchant had seven hundred and sixty-one of these brooms, valued at six pence each, and retailed at eight or nine pence. Indian men and squaws peddled brooms and baskets and begged for cider. In many country families the fathers or boys made the brooms. Oven brooms were made of husks.

There were sixty-five distilleries of cider and grain in old Hampshire in 1810 and every distillery made drunkards.

The inhabitants of the valley always have had gardens and cultivated some common garden vegetables, the women often aiding. Among other things our foremothers had medicinal herbs in the garden, and many of the women had a small plat of flowers. Garden seeds from London were advertised in Boston in 1719, and in most years down to 1800.

Horses, oxen and cows were not plenty in the river towns until some years after settlement. When they became numerous prices were reduced. The horses, which obtained most of their living on the commons, were cheaply raised, and often much neglected, yet there always were some good horses in Hampden County. In the eighteenth century horses received more attention, and between 1750 and 1775 they were worth from seven to thirty-two dollars each, and a few, at least, forty dollars. They were chiefly saddled when in use.

Down to 1750 there were very few sleighs, and no wheel vehicles for horses to draw. They were used in some farming operations before oxen, and a horse drew the plow and harrow, and kept the wheel of the cider mill going. The harness was very simple. Often the horses were tethered and could feed only to the extent of the rope, and many were restrained by fetters. Oxen were the principal animals used in farm operations for a long time, and they conveyed loads on the highways a few miles or many miles.

John Pynchon sent cattle in the fall from Springfield to Boston before 1655, and he sent winter-fattened cattle in the spring for many years after. There was some horse stealing in New England, though less than in other colonies. Horse thieves were hanged in several colonies, but not in New England. Grass-fed cattle were driven to Boston from Hampshire in the seventeenth and eighteenth centuries, and great numbers after the grazing towns were settled. Many were barreled for market. Colonel Moses Porter went to Boston with fat cattle every year for fifty-one years, beginning in 1791.

Children, and many adults, commonly had milk with bread or hasty pudding for breakfast and supper. However, care was not taken by some to have a supply of milk one or two months in the winter. That short allowance of boiled winter skim milk was long remembered. Other things that helped out the milk supply were combinations of pumpkin and milk, berries and milk, and roasted and baked apples and milk, often with bread. Many children were fond of bread and cider. The cider was not very sour, and it was diluted with water that was sweetened with molasses and warmed in a basin, and the bread was toasted. People often made use of cider with bread for want of porridge, milk and tea. Much pork was smoked in the great kitchen chimney, and these big smoked sides were the "flitches of bacon" about which we read in the old records. Long ago hogs were driven from the Connecticut River to Boston. The ancient laws of the Colony ordered that hogs going at large should wear a yoke as long up and down as two and a half times the depth of his neck, with a bottom piece three times as long as the thickness of the neck. Salt pork kept in brine was the principal meat of New England farmers during most of the year for a long time.

John Pynchon and others bought sheep at Rhode Island and elsewhere about 1656, and there were sheep above the falls soon after-

ward that gradually increased. For three-fourths of a century, beginning about 1700, some families in these Norwottuck towns occasionally sent to the "Island," as Newport, Rhode Island was called, for
wool and other things. The diligent housewives made woolen cloth
for garments and bed coverings, and they knit stockings. They
"sought wool, and flax, and cotton and worked willingly with their
hands." They and their daughters were manufacturers, and a part
of almost every house in our country towns was a factory at times.

STAGE ADVERTISEMENT

Those who went to the Island did business for all who wished—often
for twenty or thirty. They carried for themselves and neighbors
much tow cloth, some whitened cloth, many bags and a little cash.
They returned with wool, molasses, sugar, indigo, tea and other
things. The heavy articles were sent home by way of a Hartford
boat, and when these arrived the buyer went from house to house and
distributed the wool, molasses and other miscellany.

Hogs often ran in the streets until 1790, and meanwhile they shared their pasture with a small army of noisy geese and, as if that were not enough, there was added many sheep fattening during the winter.

A few years after 1802 carding machines were built in many towns, and this relieved women who carded wool. In those days before there were one-horse wagons, girls sometimes carried behind them on a horse a bundle of wool almost as high as their heads. Some of the best wool was combed and not carded, and worsted was spun from it. The household manufacture of wool in this vicinity ceased before 1822.

Apparently the early settlers brought the common domestic fowls across the sea about as soon as they came themselves. At any rate they were in Springfield before 1645, and it is safe to conclude that the crowing cocks at daybreak, and the cra-ing and cackling of hens were heard in the towns above Springfield soon after settlement. In early years these fowls were sold for from four pence to six pence each, and eggs were three pence a dozen. Their feathers were used for beds. Geese began to be plentiful in the towns by 1740, and most families had a flock. The loud noise they made was called "squawking" in this part of the country. In the olden time bees were kept, and many of the keepers were ministers. Hives were made of straw and the bees were suffocated with fire and brimstone, as in England. Swarms of bees sometimes flew to the woods, and the racket made by beating pans and kettles did not check them. Bees have inhabited hollow trees in the woods from time immemorial. Many persons have hunted for bee trees which, when found, were marked, and afterward cut down and the honey taken out.

Tobacco is described by one old-time writer as: "This nauseous and noxious weed first used by the American Indians." It was cultivated in Europe before 1570 and smoked by men and women, and in after years was assailed in vain by European sovereigns and the general courts of New England. Smoking was so common in New England in 1676 that Mrs. Rowlandson, celebrated as a captive of the Indians, said "an invitation to smoke is a usual compliment nowadays among saints and sinners." She smoked before she was captured and found the use of tobacco "bewitching." Soldiers in England and America loved liquor and tobacco, and in King Philip's War it was necessary many times to send tobacco to soldiers, who were to pay for it from their wages. In the seventeenth and eighteenth centuries merchants sold pipes in abundance, as well as tobacco boxes and tobacco tongs for lighting the pipes with a coal from the fireplace.

The "Boston Courant" complained, in 1724, of the enormous use of tobacco in smoking, chewing, and snuff-taking. The accounts of traders in Hampshire show that they sold many pipes as well as spices, a few days before Thanksgiving, and that innkeepers sometimes bought a gross or more of pipes at once. Many of the clergy were smokers. Numerous elderly men and women smoked, and some chewed. When the women came together they seemed to have a pleasant time with their pipes. The plastering of some rooms was tarnished with tobacco smoke. Young people, however, did not smoke. Men were apt to have little yards or patches of tobacco, and part of this was sold. Some smokers had a little wooden box hanging against the wall with pipes in the upper open part and tobacco in a drawer at the bottom.

Snuff was first advertised at Boston in 1712, and there were silver snuff-boxes. To take snuff was considered genteel. Farmers' families seldom took snuff and it was not kept for sale in Hampden County until nearly 1760. It was first sold here in bottles. After yellow snuff was supplied in bladders, about 1786, snuff taking was much extended. Taverns, especially those frequented by soldiers in the French and Revolutionary wars, were, as Macaulay said of the old London coffee houses, full of the eternal "fog and stench of tobacco." Two brands of high grade leaf tobacco that won favor were Twist and Pigtail. Fields of tobacco were cultivated some years before 1800, and the culture presently became extensive.

For a long time the river towns made their own butter and cheese. In other words, they made all they ate, and no more. There was not much demand for oil in those days. A man who passed through the valley, in 1762, said that most of the buildings were old and dark colored, and few dwellinghouses were painted on the outside.

The open woods of New England were full of strawberries. Huckleberries were formerly plenty and were used in milk, pies and puddings. Small parties went huckleberrying more than a century ago. The berries grew on the mountains and plains, and in some highways. For a long time many of the town streets were covered with these

bushes.   Children picked the scarlet checkerberries, and all the spicy
leaves of wintergreen when tender.   Chestnuts and shagbark "walnuts" were sold in Springfield at two coppers a quart in 1760.   The
chestnut blight of recent years has all but destroyed the lordly chestnut forests.

Hampshire families made soap from their own ashes and grease.
Some did not have a supply of grease, and John Pynchon bought in
Connecticut and sold mostly to Springfield people more than one hundred firkins of soft soap between 1658 and 1676.   Soap was usually
made in the spring.   Madam Porter records in 1752—"made soap
three days, the first week in April."   Soapmaking was tedious and
sometimes vexatious, and a woman who had good luck was congratu-
lated by her neighbors.   Most families still made their soap in 1860.

Memories of Springfield

CHAPTER XVII

Memories of Springfield

A visitor to Springfield village in 1776, standing at the corner of Main Street and Ferry Lane, which at that time was the business center, would have in sight, down the west side of the street, most of its one hundred and seventy-five houses and the solitary church spire, with pasture land running back to the river. On the east side were a mountain brook and a narrow strip of wet grassland known as the "hasseky marsh," though often a pond or a meadow. Close at hand, too, was a forest of pine fringed with elm and oak and rising into a broad plateau. To the right on a narrow vista of river could be seen the ferryman's flat scow that was pushed across the stream with poles, either bringing grain and hay from West Springfield or taking back groceries. Up and down the street walked the old-time merchants in knee-breeches, and the younger and gayer in scarlet coats, with perchance a passing slave or wigged magistrate or plain housewife carrying water from the brook across the way. There was a chance, too, that you might hear the sound of a rifle on the plain where a venturesome deer had browsed, or perhaps a stage-horn from the Bay Path, before the coach entered from Boston over the marsh by a narrow corduroy causeway, known later as State Street.

The early appearance of the houses of Springfield was unprepossessing, though soon after the Revolution travelers described it as a neat and orderly place. There were but two brick houses and the others were shabby and unpainted. As the armory grew, red, yellow and brown-colored buildings multiplied, and in the village red was a favorite color, as it was at Longmeadow, where nearly the whole street was lined with bright red homesteads. There were no porticos, piazzas or columns. Timothy Dwight says that it was customary in early times for people to turn in and rebuild men's houses when they were burned, and at Springfield, as elsewhere in New England, most of the people slept with unbolted doors.

In 1759 inspectors from Northampton visited Springfield and found that over thirty of the best families had encroached on the road. In some cases the fence had been advanced, in others the pig pen or shop. Among those fined were Rev. Mr. Breck, Colonel Worthington and Edward Pynchon.

Down toward the big elm the most important and uninviting building was the courthouse, built fifty-five years before. It stood out into the road at the head of Sanford Street and near the brook was a whipping-post. Executions used to be in public and on high gallows that could be seen at a distance. The whipping-post was likewise prominently situated. A little to the south was an elm used also for a whipping-post. To some persons, at least, it was a pitiful sight to see the unfortunates stripped and publicly flogged.

Across the way, eighteen feet north of the large elm on the corner, rose the famous tavern of Zenas Parsons, which had a fearfully high wing on Main Street, and when detached later this wing was called the "lighthouse."

Beyond the barns and sheds along Meetinghouse Lane, standing partly on Elm Street and partly on the southwest corner of the present Court Square, stood the church holding on the finger of its steeple the same golden rooster that today wags his tail in all weathers. The ground back to the river was open pasture and meadowland. There was a pair of bars across Meetinghouse Lane by the church, and at a later day passers leaving the bars down were fined. This lane led through the burying ground and adjoining training field to the Middle Landing.

It was not an accident that the other field was so near the gravestones. Training was a sacred duty, always opened with prayer and continued to the beat of the same drum that called all to Sabbath service. Along the river bank was a fenced path protected by a town law. Each fence had a gate with a post set in the middle to check the cattle. The church at this time was about twenty-five years old with the main entrance toward the east. The pews were square and the pulpit high, extending over the "deacon seats" which faced the congregation. Above was a ponderous sounding board and nervous people used to fear during sermon time that it might fall on the deacons below. The old box pews and high pulpits have their origin in the English churches. The broad galleries held as many as did the floor of the church, and in a back and high corner nearest the shingles the colored people took their religion. The meetinghouse was not warmed in those days and the preacher often pointed to the ceiling with his big, worsted mitten while the women used footstones and everybody else knocked heel against heel.

The familiar picture of a solemn Sabbath begun at sundown on Saturday night, continued on Sunday morning when "the rooster crowed psalm tunes," and ending at the next sundown, when the children played blind-man's-buff in the streets and the young men drank flip at the taverns, was a true one.

Judge Bliss, one of the deacons, was not less distinguished for his sterling parts and godliness than for his eccentricities. He wore a powdered wig, knee breeches, low shoes and shining buckles. They say that he first heard of the Declaration of Independence as he touched the wharf from West Springfield with a load of hay, and not being able to elevate his continental heels and cocked hat high enough, he at once set fire to the hay amid the unlimited enthusiasm of everybody. This sort of originality ran in the family, and probably came from his father, Jedediah. They were called "Jedites" and to be odd was to be "jeddy."

Jonathan Dwight came to Springfield in 1753 and was an old-time gentleman. He was a great smoker, lighting his pipe in summer with a burning glass and often crossing the street in such a cloud of smoke as to be nearly invisible. He was almost the last representative of the silk stocking, short breeches, and silver shoe-buckle gentry—rather scant clothing the boys thought who knew of his practice of going out to fodder the cows before daylight or breakfast on cold winter mornings with stockings down about his heels and rubbing his legs when he came in to get up a circulation. As the fashion changed to pantaloons there was much discussion as to whether they were as durable as knee breeches. The stockings were thick and wore for a long time, especially the silk ones. Mr. Dwight was a slaveholder to the extent of one African, and lived in one of the very few painted houses of the village.

On Maple Street was a house occupied by Lizzie and Martha Ferre. When the road by the house was straightened the outbuildings were complimented with a position in the front yard. These two white-haired women were the terror of the third and fourth generation, thereabouts, for sweet flag and mint grew in abundance near by. The children would watch until the old maids were away before starting to gather the wild edibles, but often, to their grief, the owners would suddenly put in an appearance.

Zenas Parsons was born in 1740, and in manhood became the proprietor of a great, widespreading tavern which stood on Court Square. He kept the inn before and after the Revolutionary War and it was known as "Parsons' Tavern." It stood near the southeast corner of the Square, by "Meetinghouse Lane," that later was known as Elm Street.

OLD VIEW OF COURT SQUARE, SPRINGFIELD

General Washington arrived in Springfield on a visit to New England and lodged in this five-story house in October, 1789. John Adams, on his return to Massachusetts from the sittings of Congress at Philadelphia, in 1775, passed through Springfield in November and dined at this tavern, where Captain Pynchon and others came to see him.

It is related that on Sundays in the winter the folks who went to the old First Church brought their foot stoves with them, and before entering used to go to the bar room of the old tavern and replenish them with live hickory coals from the blazing fire always kept ready for their use. Mr. Parsons died in a fit at the age of seventy-eight.

Springfield village had its crop of strong, noble men, who could legislate or hold the plow with equal excellence. One of these was Colonel John Worthington. He was born at Springfield in 1719, entered Yale College and graduated in 1740. He received his military title by commanding a regiment of Massachusetts Militia in Hampshire County, and he was one of a company chartered in 1792 to build locks and canals on the Connecticut River. For his loyalty to the cause of the British Crown in the Revolutionary War, the Whigs forced him to kneel and ask forgiveness for his "Toryism." President Dwight, of Yale College, said of Colonel Worthington, "He was a lawyer of the first eminence and a man who would have done honor to any town and any country."

Boston authorities were very anxious to have him for Attorney-General. In a letter sanctioned by the Governor the salary was discussed, but without much hope. Among other things the letter says:

"It is necessary that you should live at or near Boston and I know your attachment to that foggy, unhealthy air from the Connecticut River which, if you do not remove, will shorten your days."

Colonel Worthington had an attending halo of touch-me-not. Children held their breath when he talked and the irreverent called him "don." He made heroic efforts to impress his name and character on a male heir, but he merely contributed three little tombstones to three infant "John Worthingtons." It was the other side of the house that was to hand down the high breeding of his family. This breeding took a peculiar form sometimes. He once snatched a "Butler's Analogy" from the hands of a daughter whom he caught reading and sweeping the room at the same time, and said: "This is not a book for a girl to read." To be sure, she was only twenty-four!

He allowed no bed in the house to be made until after dark on Sundays. Abler men than he have lost the hair on their heads for interfering in such matters. There was a secret closet in his house, not an uncommon thing in those days, but he put it to the uncommon use of concealing tories, and it became a noted retreat for refugees. While the afterward distinguished Fisher Ames was paying attention to the colonel's daughter, Frances, it was his misfortune once to be asked to carve a turkey. He squeezed, and sliced, and twisted the bird into such forbidding ligaments, right before the girl's family, that he vowed to himself the "don" would never give him a chance to carve for a family of his own. In deep chagrin he posted to Boston, took carving lessons, and on his return found a goose on the platter which he served most beautifully. "Mr. Ames," observed the "don," "you find a tough goose easier to carve than a tender turkey."

Once Worthington's barn was struck by lightning and Phillis, a negro slave woman of his, proceeded immediately to put on her best, including a bright red petticoat. She said: "De barn am struck. I think de day ob judgement am about to cum, and I want to 'pear's well's I can before de Lord."

Rev. Mr. Howard was as prominent in a progressive way as the colonel in his conservatism, and his home rule was as rigid. At five in the afternoon, at all seasons, every door in the house was "opened and swung," which let in lots of pure air and hard colds. When coal was first introduced, he gave it a trial before the assembled family. It was placed on the embers, and as it did not burn, it was solemnly and once for all pronounced stone.

One of the out-of-the-way stories told of Moses Bliss is that one day he heard that a deer was browsing in "hasseky marsh." Taking a flintlock, he insinuated his knee-breeches among the bushes, a little back of the present Market Street, where, sure enough, there was a veritable stag. As cool as a cucumber, he took aim, and yelled "bang" at the top of his voice. There was no bullet in his voice and he forgot to shoot, so the game escaped.

Charles Brewer, who lived on Maple Street not far from the dingle, had a huge pear tree on which he did the grafting and mulching and sundry boys the harvesting. One day, seeing the little thieves approach, he thought of a hogshead near by where he could hide. The idea seemed good and he agilely crawled in. The boys saw him disappear and had to stuff their elbows in their mouths to keep from laughing. They crept up to the hogshead and set it rolling down the hill. For weeks Mr. Brewer wore on his knees and elbows the biggest knobs he ever had.

The father of Daniel Lombard, while at work on his Long Hill farm, once noticed through the corn a skulking Indian with drawn bow. He at once cocked his rifle and both watched a chance to shoot, and neither dared uncover. After an excited passage at this deadly game of peek-a-boo, the Indian backed out until he found shelter in the forest. It was a common amusement of the friendly Indians to take little children off in the morning and return them at night to the frightened but non-resistant parents.

In Springfield it was an early custom to have one drinking mug on the table for water and to pass it around. It was a royal source of merriment among the young people of one of Springfield's first families, when the head of the family brought home a second wife and she insisted on having a mug by herself. She was a New York Dutch bred lady and could not come down to the one-mugged habits of the village.

The staple bread was made of rye flour. Sometimes a man would buy a bushel or two of wheat and have it ground. This was used for pastry and would generally last through the year. The story is told of how an innkeeper's wife economized in her pie crust, but she was shown up in a couplet recited by one of her guests:

"Upper crust wheat, under crust rye;
Please, Mrs. Smith, may I have some more pie?"

"Pop-robbin," a sort of milk porridge, was a great local dish and, at the time of the Boston tea excitement, people substituted it in a lighter form for tea. A lady used to tell that just after the war she was invited out to breakfast, where she, for the first time in years, enjoyed a cup of tea; but it didn't satisfy, and on going home, she filled up with hot porridge. In the early part of this century coffee was a luxury which few families enjoyed more than once a week. Burnt rye was used as a substitute and was a common article of sale as late as 1822.

The river was early filled with salmon, so that in seining for shad it was necessary also to take the salmon, strange as it may seem. At one time the shad became a drug. A man was "pretty hard run who would eat shad." Foolishly enough few people would admit that they ever lowered themselves to such depths. Indeed, they have even been known to snatch a shad from the frying pan, if a neighbor dropped in on them at odd times. A little later one of the conditions in hiring a man was that he should eat shad so many times a week. Salmon, at the time of the Revolution, was called "Agawam pork," and it was a condition in buying shad that a certain amount of this Agawam pork should be taken with it.

Jonathan Dwight is authority for the statement that there was but one clock in the village in 1753, and that people used to call at Josiah Dwight's to see it and wait a long time to hear it strike. There were then but two chaises in town, horseback riding being the common mode of traveling. Springfield was a three days' journey from Boston.

The aristocratic snuff-box had penetrated numerously to the Connecticut, and by the time this century began snuff taking was a very prevalent evil.

The only piano in the village, in 1810, was owned by David Ames, and James Dwight had one in 1822. At the church the leader of the choir would start the tune by a preliminary toot on the square music box, the size of a common hand Bible, with an aperture in one corner for a mouthpiece and a slide below to regulate the key. Colonel Solomon Warriner was leader for forty-two years, beginning in 1801, except for a break of five years. He sat in the gallery back of the congregation. The "second treble" was on his right and the tenor on his left; the "first treble" were scattered all along the north gallery, and the bass were opposite.

The first rocker skates were sold by Ely, of West Springfield, where the boys on this side of the river went with their spare change to buy them. Doctor Chauncey Brewer, when young, was a fine skater, and once when at Yale College, while darting over the ice, he came to a broad opening, and is said to have saved his life by making a thirty-foot jump.

Colonel Thomas Dwight once discovered a leak in his stock of butter. Suspecting a certain gardener, he invited him into the office and heated up the room. Soon sweat, then butter, came running down the fellow's face, and on lifting his hat, Mr. Dwight found the butter.

Jonathan Dwight once sharply told a clerk not to say "no" bluntly, when a customer asked for something not in the store, but to suggest another article. Shortly afterward a lady inquired for some cheese, and the clerk replied, "No ma'm, we haven't any, but we have an excellent grindstone."

There were many queer looking things to be seen on the public roads in early days; for instance, on a Sunday morning, a man on horseback, with his wife sitting on a cushion or pillion behind him, having one arm about her Bible and the other about her master, clinging close to both. If a fellow happened to be riding in the opposite direction from the meetinghouse, he was very liable, especially if he had something handsome on the pillion, to find a tithingman's long pole across the road. One Sunday a Lombard was carrying a sick child in a shay to the doctor, and the infallible tithingman, deciding that religion was suffering more than the child, compelled him to turn back toward home.

Tippling was more common at the beginning of the nineteenth century than now. There was not a dealer in the village who did not keep distilled spirits, and every hired man took his "constitutional" both forenoon and afternoon. Sometimes eleven hogsheads of liquor were sold at the old Dwight store on the corner of State Street before breakfast. Not a social gathering, not a marriage feast of parson's or deacon's daughter, but there was a goodly show of wine or flip.

It was customary for the parishioner when the minister called to set out a bottle of rum, and nothing less than this, except among the poor. It is told of an up-river minister that he was once highly incensed because one brother on whom he called offered him a mug of cider instead of the rum bottle. It was accepted as an insult and was doubtless intended for one.

Flip drinking was not confined to a few. The children and all would warm their noses after church with it. It is made of much beer, a little rum and sugar, and some hot poker. Most families had a "brewin" each week, and flip irons were "amazin' plenty." In 1825 temperance societies were first formed and the elder and more moral names of Springfield were quoted against the movement, just as they were when the young folks wanted to warm the meetinghouse. But when they found it wasn't a sin to hear the word of God with warm ears, and that moral force is better for the drinking community than a police force, both religion and temperance went up.

Pretty much everything was kept at these early country stores— Turk's Island salt, steel knitting needles, Jamaica spirits, hum-hums, jeans and fustians, bake-pans, plane-irons, japanned waiters and mugs, pigtail tobacco, cherry rum and so on.

The Dwights ran a four-horse team to Boston the year round to do the smaller freighting. Teamster Bliss, who lived at Ten Mile Brook, presided over this four-in-hand, and when the Dwight boys went down to Harvard College, he took a turn by Cambridge, so as to leave their bedding for them.

Many fine cattle in the early part of the century were driven from Chicopee to the Boston market.

James Dwight was forever doing astonishing things, and always winning in the end. He once came back from New York with the enormous quantity for those days of *"six* mortal barrels" of wheat flour. Father Jonathan embraced his paste knee-buckles in horror, clerks thought he was mad, and the next Sunday people who had often sung "All my bones are made of Indian corn," with considerable rye porridge mixed in, talked the matter over after sermon. "Master Jim," however, took it coolly. He said: "I will take a barrel, father one, John and Colonel Dwight each one, and John Hooker another."

Honorable John Worthington inherited his father's estate and became one of the old "River Gods." Among his many distinctions is that of being the first Springfielder who carried an umbrella, for the sun, however, instead of for the rain.

A line of coasting boats brought goods from Boston around the cape to Hartford for all the up-river towns, the rest of the way flat-boats with sails being used. A line of boats which ran to White River took a fortnight to make the round trip. When the wind was contrary the loaded scows either had to be poled or rowed all the way up from Hartford. Three trips a week were often made. At one time there were ten of these boats, carrying twelve to fifteen tons, and worked by four men each, with long oars and twelve to fifteen-foot poles and one sail. Liquor was a large item of freight and often a boat would have nothing else, the boatmen preferring this cargo as they could draw it freely for their own use. Sometimes as many as twenty-five flat-bottomed boats would start out from Hartford on a single morning. The captains usually let their freight bills go until winter, when they would take a turn among the valley towns "to settle up." The journey of the old sea and river captains up the valley was a royal sight. The Dwights were the largest importers in the region, and it was a common thing to see there a dozen or more of the buck-skin-faced captains with freight bills as good as gold in their pockets.

For years the ground in front of the meetinghouse was a tavern site, plentifully shedded and barnyarded, and back of the tavern somewhat marshy, though dry enough in spots to allow room for trials of muscle. Many a well-oated filly or pillion horse has stood over his time in the stable while a wrestling match was in progress on 'lection day, or as an accessory to an out-of-town gander party. The spirit born of the War of 1812 led to the opening of a common. Church and business sentiment grew into a strong opposition to the monopoly of so fine a site for a tavern. The new meetinghouse was finished in 1819, and as the tavern sheds which extended back to the church, and right in front of it, were a growing nuisance, it was proposed to buy that property and lay out a common. Prominent citizens clubbed together, the land was bought, and the common given to the county.

In connection with the old tavern is remembered the time when a couple of Springfield boys slept together in the attic, on a bed made on the floor, as their twelve dollars a month wages would not allow better accommodations. They drove ox-carts from the Middle Landing, where the flatboats delivered merchandise to the various stores, and their names were Willis Phelps and Chester W. Chapin.

There was a time when the aged as they walked our Springfield streets, meeting a crowd of school children, would be honored by a short curtsy from all the girls, while the boys would take off their hats. Even a person passing in a shay was curtsied and bowed to. Children "did their manners" as it was termed, as soon as they arrived home, and also on entering and leaving the schoolroom. No child was allowed to answer back when spoken to, and in some cases babies were instructed, like Susanna Wesley's nineteen children, not to cry after they arrived at the age of one year. It was an early custom, too, in the prominent families of such country places as Springfield, for all the family, wife, children and guests to rise and stand when the man of the house entered the room. This was the habit in the Reverend Jonathan Edwards' household at Northampton, and it may have originated because of the great respect paid to the profession. On a Sabbath morning, after the families were assembled in their high-backed pews, the minister in his black gown would lead his family up the aisle, and at the first notice of his appearing the whole congregation would rise. When he had seated his family and mounted his pulpit throne, the people would sit amid the creaking of boots and thumping of foot-stoves when the weather was cold, with perhaps a rap of the tithingman's pole for the boys who sat together and apart from their families.

Obedience of children was pushed to a doubtful extreme and child life was not particularly enviable. School kept every week day but Saturday afternoon and the only school holiday was the day of the April elections. The common English branches and the Westminster catechism were taught, and one of the qualifications of the "master" was the ability of mending quill pens. The minister sometimes visited the schools on Saturday mornings and heard the children recite on "sanctification, justification and election," and gave them, in turn, a few words on insubordination.

The illustrations in their textbooks were aimed more at religion than æsthetics. One edition of catechism had a woodcut of the martyr Rogers with the flames well advanced. Among the religious rhymes are:

> In Adam's fall
> We sinned all.
>
> Thy life to mend
> This book attend.
>
> Young Obadias,
> David and Josias
> All were pious.
>
> Xerxes the Great did die,
> And so must you and I.

The zealous teacher often prayed and exhorted when he should have been hearing lessons. He would talk to the pupils about the devil, who went around from house to house with a red hot pitchfork to carry off naughty children, and that hell was a place where the wicked were burned in "fire and brimstone." The first thing in school every morning was Bible reading, each one old enough reading a verse. It occasionally happened that some disturbance would interrupt the reading, but it would be calmly resumed after the birch rod was put away.

The ordinary housewife, living in Springfield in the early days, had a low-raftered kitchen, with perhaps no floor but the hard clay. There her husband might bring her a shad on a deerskin string, which would furnish the dinner in place of the ham which had lasted over from the previous winter and was still swinging from the rafters. A pot of beans hanging on the crane and simmering in the fireplace would make another meal with the brown bread and pies taken from the big brick oven with the long-handled "slice" or "peel." A "fire broom" of coarse husks bound to a handle was used to sweep out the oven before baking, and a "birch broom" of twigs from that tree kept the hearth tidy. A handy man might furnish his wife with a more durable "splinter broom," which he had carefully whittled out in the long winter evenings. The shad would be cooked on the turn-spit or in the skillet, and served on a pewter platter scoured like the silver moon. The housewife stepped about her work in calfskin shoes of her husband's raising, butchering, tanning, and making, and her caps and aprons were large and abundant. She could never sit down in idleness as there was always homegrown wool to be spun into yarn, a width of blanket or checkered flannel on the loom to be woven, or an unfinished stocking on the needles to keep her hands busy. Two pieces of woolen cloth sewed into a narrow strip were pinned to the side of her dress to keep her knitting needles in place.

Fashions, as ever, continued to change. The courtly styles of the colonial period are familiar to us. Then a lady's coiffure was elaborate and striking, involving curls and pompadours. The Empire period brought in very narrow satin slips with diamond-shaped necks and the waist coming close up under the bust. There were also satin shoes with tiny high heels, rich trains of great length and sleeves of great brevity. Voluminous "pumpkin-hoods" covered the elaborate head-dress in winter and a calash could be worn in summer. Calashes were made of rattan and silk. By pulling a cord or ribbon called the "bridle," it could be brought clear over the face in case of storm or modesty.

Once a little boy was lost in the cemetery dingle, where he had gone to get chestnuts. At night the church bell was rung and nearly every man in the village turned out with a lantern to search. Parties were organized to go in different directions, and one of these took the Chicopee Road along which were seen little footprints which soon led to the bank of the Chicopee River and there stopped. The searchers, however, worked up the river some distance and finally under some boards they found the sleeping wanderer. He had become tired and pulling the boards over him for a shelter had fallen asleep from exhaustion. It had been arranged that if the child were found notice of it should be given by firing a cannon. So the men hastened back with the good news, and at four o'clock on that weary Sunday morning the booming of a cannon on Armory Hill announced that the search had been successful and there was great rejoicing.

George Colton, an honest and devoted churchgoer, always made the same long prayer whether at meeting or at home. His last sentence was: "And to thee we give never-ending praises. Amen." One Fourth of July morning his little son was very impatient during the lengthy devotions. Outside, crackers were popping, boys were shouting and cannon being fired. As the paternal prayer drew its long length to a close, the excited boy, not being able to wait, sang out "and to thee we give never-ending praises. Amen. Heard it a thousand times," and ran out of the door before he could be caught.

Among the early customs that hung on was that of posting public notices of intention of marriage for three weeks. In Springfield the public place was the church vestibule. The notices were deposited for three Sundays in a mahogany box, covered with a wire screen, from which it was dubbed the "squirrel-box." After sermon time people often said: "Let's see who is in the squirrel-box this morning."

The Early Eighteen Hundreds

CHAPTER XVIII

The Early Eighteen Hundreds

It was said about 1820 that the Dwights ruled Springfield. The firm adopted the policy of setting up its clerks in business in surrounding towns, but retaining an interest in the various stores. They had a store at Chester Village, one at Northampton, and one in Enfield, Connecticut, that included a gin distillery, in which Longmeadow citizens and others were interested. At South Hadley Canal the Dwights had a store, a gristmill and sawmills. There was also a Boston branch, the manager of which lost his life in the wreck of the "Albion," in May, 1822, on his way to England. The Dwights owned several coasting vessels between Hartford and Boston and New York, and were interested in a line of boats between Hartford and Springfield. They were also interested in banking as far west as Detroit.

The last appearance of pounds, shillings and pence in the town records is November, 1795.

In 1800 the town brook, also known as Garden Brook, had become filled with rubbish. This overflowed the eastern meadows, and caused sickness. As a remedy the stream was deepened.

The first proposals for a bridge over the great river were received with ridicule. "Parson Howard talks like a fool," Colonel Worthington said in 1786, when that gentleman predicted such an engineering event. But late in October of 1805 the bridge was opened. The fact that financially it was the child of a lottery did not prevent the famous preacher, Joseph Lathrop, of West Springfield, from delivering a dedication sermon and offering prayer in the presence of about three thousand people gathered on the bridge; the church bells were rung, cannon fired, and the public made themselves hoarse with shouting. The bridge was a creditable piece of engineering for the times, and was considered equal to anything in America. However, a succession of floods weakened it, and it gave way under a heavy load of army supplies nine years later. The bridge was an open one, painted red, was 1,234 feet long, 30 feet wide and stretched 40 feet above low water mark. The six spans were supported by two abutments and five piers, each pier and abutment containing about 2,000 tons of stone. Two guard-piers to check the force of the ice were built 80 rods above the bridge. It was a clumsy structure, so arranged that the traveler was compelled to go up and down with the curves of each span. It was pulled down soon after the freshets of 1814.

The tolls were: Foot passengers, 3 cents; horse and rider, 7 cents; horse and chaise, chair or sulky, 10 cents; chariot, phæton, or other four-wheeled carriage for passengers, 33 cents; curricle, 25 cents; horse and sleigh, 10 cents; neat cattle, 3 cents; sheep or swine, 1 cent. The tolls were abolished in 1872.

ENTRANCE TO THE OLD TOLL BRIDGE

The second toll bridge was opened to the public October 1, 1816, and the newspaper advertising announced: "Springfield bridge lottery is a fine tide of riches. Improve it, set every sail. Soon it will be too late." The tickets were six dollars each. There were several drawings in the town, and at least one local tavern scene where little girls in white frocks drew the numbers. The Harvard College lottery, which was running at that time, was well patronized in Springfield.

For a considerable period Springfield was outranked by West Springfield in the number of inhabitants, but in 1820 it took the lead. In 1814, the Springfield bank was organized. It kept a deposit in a Boston bank, and often a cashier would bring back by stage $50,000 or $100,000 in bills in his valise. 1820 was memorable in Springfield as the year when Thomas Blanchard invented at the armory a machine for turning irregular forms that revolutionized manufacture and is ranked among the greatest of the world's inventions.

Slavery in this region gradually faded away, yet ended with a dramatic climax. The Springfield citizens in 1808 bought and freed a fugitive slave. This was in February, and later a bill of sale was given by a Schenectady man of Dutch descent to the selectmen of Springfield whereby a negro woman "Jenny" was given her freedom. She had become favorably known in Springfield, and the subscription of $100 was easily raised. She and her husband, "Jack," lived for many years near Goose Pond, and they added to their fame by selling a fine quality of spruce beer.

Easterly of the stores on Main Street was a dilapidated two-story brick schoolhouse that stood near the north line of the school ground, with the play ground about eighty feet wide between the schoolhouse and the causeway. On the front of this ground and near the causeway stood an old engine-house and the gunhouse for the two artillery cannon. At an early date the old brick schoolhouse was taken down and a one-story wooden building with two rooms erected. This was later burned and a two-story brick house built in its stead. About 1826 these schools were discontinued and the front part of the lot was sold to the town for a town hall and the rest to private parties.

The Baptists wanted to hold meetings in the town house in 1809, but were refused. However, the time for broader religious toleration was fast coming, and this was true also of medicine. "Inoculation of the kinepock," for example, was regularly practiced under the supervision of a town committee.

The appearance of the village had improved since the shabby Revolutionary days. There was a raised sidewalk in 1810 on the west side of Main Street, from the gate that led to Zebina Stebbins' place to the Bridge Lane, then to Meetinghouse Lane, and from there to the home-lot of Samuel Burt. Also, there was a sidewalk on the south side of Meetinghouse Lane.

This was a period rich in philanthropic and public spirit. The Hampden County Colonization Society issued a circular in November, 1826, closing with these words: "Our country has been verily guilty of despoiling Africa of her children. Who can say that this will not be overruled by a righteous Providence as the principal means of diffusing the knowledge of salvation by a crucified Saviour to millions of our fellow-beings who are now buried in the thick darkness of the grossest superstition and idolatry?"

The Fourth of July celebration of the first half century of the Republic was planned at a meeting of "all parties, religious or political," and Hampden Guards marched from the Hampden Coffee-house to Dr. Osgood's church, where William B. Calhoun delivered an oration. From the meetinghouse the mounted guards and others marched with a great crowd and band music, firing cannon and ringings bells, to the new armory storehouse on State Street, opposite the Olivet Church, where a banquet for four hundred was spread. Samuel Lathrop and Colonel Lee offered the toasts, and the speaking continued until dusk.

In 1826 a new line of stages was advertised, which left Springfield daily at 5 A. M. for Hartford, taking the west side, and returning at 7 P. M., for one dollar. This line stopped at a Springfield hotel. The following year there was started a stage line from Springfield to Belchertown by the Factory Village. In 1828 still another line was started between Norwich and Springfield, and the distance between the two places was covered in eleven hours.

At Chicopee, about 1823, the cotton factories on the Chicopee River belonging to the Boston and Springfield Manufacturing Company were begun. In 1826 there were two brick five-story factories, with seven thousand spindles and two hundred and forty looms, and there were about twenty tenement houses for operatives with accommodations for fifty-four families.

The poorhouse, which was built in 1802, was situated on the west side of North Main Street. Up to 1824 the inmates had numbered one hundred and fifty males and sixty-five females, besides a number of children. In August, 1802, Calvin Stebbins was made master of the workhouse. He promulgated a rule that no inmate should have any rum or ardent spirits not furnished by him, on pain of being put in the stocks, not exceeding three hours at a time. When a committee was appointed to consider the condition of the poor, it deplored the fact that the inmates were given so small an allowance of liquor.

In January, 1825, a committee of the Connecticut River Association addressed circulars to all towns interested in river navigation to meet at Windsor, February 16.

It was proposed to open river traffic to Lake Memphremagog. National aid was expected in continuing trade communication with Canada. A shipment of lumber which had to be carted forty miles to the Erie Canal, and thence carried two hundred miles to Troy, go by sloop down the Hudson to the Sound, up the Connecticut to Hartford, and then be transferred to furniture manufactories, troubled the visions of local students of commerce. The project of connecting the river at Bellows Falls with Boston by a canal was also talked of, but engineers preferred to strike the river at Springfield. The Windsor convention memorialized Congress and took steps to form a navigation company. A largely-attended meeting of the citizens was held at the Hampden Coffee-house in May to consider canals and river traffic. It was resolved that a Boston and Springfield canal was practicable and desirable, and that the river could be improved so as to admit sloops to Springfield. George Bliss was in the chair and delegates were chosen to attend a meeting at Brookfield.

A writer in a Boston paper declared that "a canal from Springfield to Boston will render our harbor the mouth of the Connecticut River." The papers of the State were filled with arguments pro and con, and every step of the engineers commissioned to survey the Connecticut and a canal route across the State was followed with lively interest.

Among other things, Thomas Blanchard, the inventor, was very much interested in steamboat navigation, and he built a little stern-wheel boat which he named after himself and launched in the autumn of 1828.

Not long afterward he invited a party of citizens to go with him on a trial trip. The "Blanchard" had a sixty-foot keel and twelve-foot beam, and a cabin ten by twenty-four, divided into two compartments.

The river was very high and a few days before the "Blanchard" had cruised around the swollen river, steamed up the Agawam to the bridge, and ventured across the flooded meadows to the Connecticut River again, about a mile above the mouth of the Agawam.

The first trip to Hartford was made in two hours and fifty minutes, carrying fifty passengers, and the arrival at Hartford was greeted with a cannon salute. Much attention was given to Mr. Blanchard as an inventive genius. The "Blanchard" soon became very popular as an excursion boat. During a single week it took no less than six hundred school children on various pleasure trips. The steamer "Vermont," also built by Captain Blanchard, was completed in July, 1829, for a Brattleboro company. The hull was brought to completion on Hubbard Avenue and drawn on wheels through Main Street, then down Elm Street to the river, and thence floated to the wharf at the foot of Howard Street. It was seventy-five feet long and fifteen feet beam, and had a large promenade deck. Ascending the Enfield rapids was done with ease and the boat could pass through the Willimansett Canal. The Hartford "Mirror" noted in July, 1829, as evidence of business conditions, that four boats arrived there from Springfield in one day loaded with produce and merchandise valued at $100,000.

The steamer "Vermont" was able to run the Enfield Falls without the aid of poles. In April, 1830, the townsfolk saw for the first time a schooner under full sail. It was "The Eagle" on the river, and had come up through the Enfield Canal. The "Blanchard" and the "Vermont" both happened to be lying at the wharf, and the excited people at once dreamed of a metropolis.

A convention of the river towns at Windsor, Vermont, in October, 1830, recommended forming a company for a steam tow-boat navigation of the river. Arrangements were soon made to superintend the building of a number of boats. Three boats were already plying between Springfield and Hartford. Captain Blanchard's new boat, the "Massachusetts," was ninety-six feet long and considered a beauty. Some people called these Connecticut boats "sauce-pans," and had their smile when the "Massachusetts" was not small enough to go through the Enfield Canal, and had to wait for high water before it could run up the falls. One boat took down to Hartford sixty passengers, most of them tourists, and the steamboat "William Hall" would arrive at the wharf with six or eight boats in tow. The Valley Company at this time owned some thirty freight boats and charged $2,000 for the season.

The "Agawam" made its trial trip down the river July 20, 1837, and ran the falls on the return trip easily, with no pole men employed. The steamboat "Barnet" was three days running the Enfield Falls, even with the assistance of no less than fifty men, so that the "Agawam's" trip of six miles of rapids in an hour's time was considered a great triumph.

After the decline of training day and the multiplying of feast days, there sprang up a number of special military organizations that graced many a festal occasion and covered the town with glory. The old artillery company, organized before the War of 1812, was the admiration and wonder of this vicinity. It had a couple of six-pounders which were kept at the foot of Elm Street, near the gate of the old cemetery. The dark blue coats and belts with big brass buckles lingered fondly in the memory. But it was the Hampden Guards that took the lasting honors for military prowess. This organization included most of the flower of Springfield. They wore white trousers, tall leather caps, blue dress coats with bell skirts and standing collars. The local organizations often participated in the May trainings, and always in the fall muster when the militia of the county gathered for inspection and parade and sham battles. The fields adjoining North Main Street, the "rye field" on the hill, and West Springfield have been the scenes of these martial displays.

In 1824 the Governor's Foot Guards of Hartford made a return visit to Springfield in the "Blanchard." They were welcomed by the selectmen, a company of sixty horsemen, the Hampden Guards, the Springfield Artillery and a large crowd. They went to the Ordnance Yard and a banquet followed, and there was a reception in the town hall in the evening. The next day there was much marching and plenty of speeches.

The 1st and 2d Regiments of Infantry with the local artillery company were reviewed October 7, 1830, in Springfield, by Major-General Sheldon. They made a fine appearance and drew a big crowd, which improved the day by "stowing away oysters, gingerbread and other food well peppered with dust, and seemed as much fatigued with the labors of the day as the military."

By 1828, much attention was being paid to village improvements. New streets were laid out and Charles Stearns was appointed to widen and deepen a part of the town brook, for which he used 1,500 feet of block stone, over 10,000 bricks and 9,000 feet of planking. There was a bit of what now seems vandalism attending these improvements. In May, 1829, Charles Stearns proposed to cut down an ancient elm standing on Main Street, near the land of George Bliss, in order to carry out the work of draining the meadow by enlarging the brook. The elm was in the way and much feeling was caused by the plan to cut it down. The Blisses applied to Chief Justice Parker for an injunction, which, after a learned argument, was denied, and the elm fell. Another handsome elm stood in the yard of James Bliss and it was cut down in 1853. A West Springfield farmer is said to have gathered some seeds under this tree, sowed them, and in due time traded elm saplings for a cemetery lot, whence came the avenue of elms leading to the beautiful Maple Street entrance of the cemetery. The old elm that stood on Court Square was planted by the Pynchon family, according to tradition, and was a large tree at the time of the Revolution.

A tree which figures in "The Autocrat of the Breakfast Table" stood on Barnes' lot on the old line between the Dwight pasture and the Pynchon lot. It was called the largest tree in New England. At its most slender girth, which was about two and a half feet from the ground, it measured twenty-eight feet in circumference. It stood only a few feet from the brook which flowed through the lot and there joined the town brook along the side of Main Street. One could almost sit under its great branches and catch the trout which abounded in the stream. The rails of the fence for which the old tree was the post had been placed against it so long that the tree had grown around them.

One of the town's famous trees was in front of the Elm Street schoolhouse. Attempts were made at various times to have it cut down, but it continued to stand long after it was a hundred years old.

There was another elm opposite Worthington Street, on the east side of Main, which was cut down when that street was laid out in 1841. This tree was often called the "offering tree," as the dense shade of the tree and the unfrequented neighborhood made a favorite resort. The roots of the tree protruded in a snarl on the south path. The trees on North Main Street which were set out in 1770 by Major Joseph Stebbins were brought by him from West Springfield on his back and in a boat. The row formerly extended from Carew Street to Cypress Street.

Evidence of lawless men abounded in those days, and the authorities had their hands full for a time. In 1828 a number of bold burglaries took place, and the people began to know the value of lock and key. Up to the War of 1812 no one bolted the door of his residence in the town and this was true of most New England villages. In 1828 John Kinder, employed by Coolidge and Sanderson, stole one hundred and sixteen muskrat skins from them and was arrested while attempting to dispose of them at Worcester.

A gang of thieves had spread their operations through all this region. They had made raids on stores in Chicopee, West Springfield, Winslow's Clock Shop, and the residence of Jonathan Blake in Springfield. Elijah Blake distinguished himself by organizing a party to scour the woods, and on a Sunday morning in May, Russell Stephenson and George Ball were cornered in a hovel where booty was concealed. Stephenson drew a pistol on Blake, but he was not quick enough. Ball was seized and it was said at the time that some of the party were too busy looking out for their own safety in the event of stray bullets to be of service. Judge George Bliss committed the men for trial. At the trial of Stephenson and Ball a humorous court scene developed. The prisoners had entered the Blake house through the buttery window by pulling away a twine net, and the lawyer for the defense asked the judge to charge that burglary implied a breaking of the house, and "that tearing down a net made of double twine nailed to keep out cats is not such a breaking as to constitute the offence charged." The judge declined to so charge; the case went up on appeal, and the offenders were sent to prison for life. William L. Loring was convicted this same year for receiving and concealing a body taken from the Springfield burying ground on Elm Street.

In the autumn of 1832 the post-office was moved from its "uncomfortable little coop" to a building opposite Court Square, on Elm Street, where there was a reading room above.

Among the industries of the town at this time were seventy-three mechanic shops, six cotton factories, three paper mills, four printing offices, thirteen warehouses, a rifle factory, six sawmills, four gristmills, a powder mill, three tanneries, two forges, a sword factory and a spool factory.

The Springfield brewery was known to store liquors in the cellar of the present Congregational Church. Besides there was the Hampden brewery and the Sixteen Acre distillery, and for variety, a book store opposite Court Square.

The main armory building burned in March, 1824. Fire fighting was still very primitive, but there had been some improvement since the early plantation days. Then, many of the houses were thatched with straw, and great pains had to be taken lest a spark should get into the straw. The town voted that no one should carry uncovered fire along the street and that every man should sweep out his chimney every month in winter and every two months in summer. Also he was to keep a ladder of sixteen rungs to use in getting at the roof, and if a man smoked on a haystack he might be fined. To make certain that water would always be on hand, the brook in front of the houses was ordered to be kept well scoured, and a good stream running. Then, in case a roof caught on fire, some of the men went up the ladder, and others passed up water from the brook. There was no other way of getting a fire under control until after the Revolution.

When improvement came, it was a little fire engine provided by some of the citizens who donated it to the church for the use of the town. What it amounted to was simply a pump on wheels. There was a receptacle for water, called a tub, and the pump handles were long wooden rods at each side known as brakes. Whoever discovered a fire shouted an alarm, and all who heard it joined in the shouting. The cry would keep spreading until there was an uproar from Mill River to Round Hill. "Fire! Fire!" And then the bell on the old meetinghouse was rung. Every man had a fire bucket and some had bags in which to carry things to safety. The little fire engine was kept at a place near Market and State streets and it was pulled out and hauled on the run to the burning building. Men arrived from all directions and took their places in a double line which extended from the house to the town brook. The buckets were passed full of water up one line and emptied into the tub. Then back they came to be filled. One of the men stood on the engine directing the stream on the fire through hose only five feet in length. It had to be gotten very close to the building, and at best was not very effective in reaching the roof.

Some years later a longer hose was acquired which was capable of suction, and the engine, standing by the brook, got its own water, and with that hose the firemen could reach the Main Street houses.

The old engine was presently replaced by others named "The Lion," "The Tiger," "The Niagara" and "The Cataract"; and then came "The Eagle" and "The Ocean." In those times "Firemen's Muster" was favorite holiday, and the procession was gay with red coats, shining black hats and blue trousers as the men pulled at the ropes attached to their engines and hose carts. Later came a great trial of strength to decide whose engine was best, and who could attain the dizziest height. In October, 1837, there was a grand muster with five engines, one hundred and sixty men and over a thousand feet of hose. By the use of two engines, hose was run to the balustrade at the foot of the spire of Dr. Osgood's Church, and a stream of water thrown ten feet above the old rooster. The annual festival of the fire department took place January 2, with one hundred and seventy-five sitting down at the Hampden Coffee-house table, and Samuel Bowles acting as one of the vice-presidents.

The old rooster on the First Church is perched one hundred and sixty-nine feet above the pavement and the bird himself is five feet high. London is his native home, but he left there about 1750, and has looked down on generations of firemen and on soldiers going off to wars. Tradition maintains that an eagle once alighted on him and was shot from below.

The celebration of Washington's Birthday in 1832 was another of those days that the town may well remember. Fully three thousand people took part, and politics was forgotten. Cannon on Armory Hill and Court Square were thundering at daybreak, and every church bell was ringing. Just before noon a procession formed at the town house, and the column proceeded to Dr. Osgood's meetinghouse, where hundreds and hundreds were unable to get in. There was music and prayer, and passages quoted from Washington's Farewell Address, and there was an oration and later in the day the town hall banquet. When evening came there was dancing at Factory Village, where "300 fair spinsters" skipped over the floor of the new factory building.

The Springfield Temperance Society was making fair progress in its crusade. Its membership after a three years' existence was two thousand five hundred, and in 1835 one thousand six hundred legal voters petitioned the county commissioners to refuse liquor licenses.

What was perhaps the most unusual of Presidential elections was at hand and now the old-timers gathered at Springfield in February, 1840, to give the Whig candidate for President, William Henry Harrison, a good send-off.

In April the famous campaign of "Tippecanoe and Tyler, Too," was underway with all its picturesque features. One day some Longmeadow boys rigged up a log cabin drawn by six horses. A fifteen-gallon keg served as a chimney. The hard cider candidate was well toasted, and both parties were ready for the fray. October 9 there was a grand Harrison demonstration in Springfield, and on the evening of the eighth the town hall was occupied by the Whigs. A triumphal arch spanned Main Street, put there by the merchants of "Fountain row."

Early Friday morning a cavalcade with a band rode in from Monson and some wagons and horsemen poured in from Wilbraham. Besides they arrived from numerous other places. The Westfield delegation came in a huge wagon drawn by twelve horses, and on its banners was inscribed "Old Tip's Buggy." Over half a dozen bands were tuning up the party patriotism and Revolutionary soldiers were at the head of the column, six feet deep, proceeding to Worthington Grove.

All the afternoon was spent in speechmaking and singing Whig songs. The American eagle, in all sizes and conditions, perched on the decorated floats about the grove. Whig mottoes fluttered in the breezes on familiar terms with the stars and stripes, broken Democratic arches lay in ruins and lampoons furnished food for the merry. Stuffed roosters stood proudly on log cabins, and General Harrison was located in drinking booths on the edges of the grove. It was a great day, and there were many great days before the strife was over. Harrison won, but the time of triumph was short and then there was deep mourning for the death of their standard bearer.

On the twenty-first of December, 1841, the railroad from Albany to Chatham Four Corners, New York, was so far completed that trains passed through to Worcester, thus joining Boston and Albany with a continuous rail. The project of a canal over this route had collapsed. By October, 1839, trains were running between Worcester and Springfield. There was a grand celebration on the arrival of the first train. A procession was formed and after marching up and down Main Street a stop was made at the roundhouse, where a dinner was waiting with tables arranged like the spokes of a wheel.

One local man who early became interested in railroads was George Bliss, and eventually he was chosen president of the Michigan Southern Road, a position he held until the project was completed to Chicago. Afterwards he was affiliated with various other lines.

One local man ventured to prophesy in a public meeting that they would be able to go from Springfield to Boston between "sun and sun, and back again." The audience were inclined to shake their heads.

The new railroad's chief engineer was Major Whistler, and he brought his young son James to live in Springfield with him. James entertained his schoolmates with his clever drawings and when he was older he went to England, where he became one of the world's famous artists.

The word armory, as used in the United States, indicates a place for the manufacture of arms, and an arsenal is the place where they are stored. It was decided that the heavy work of forging should be done at the Water-shops, where the trip hammer could be run by waterpower, and on "Armory Hill" should be done the lighter work. The hill began to be almost a village by itself, where the homes were largely those of armorers. Indeed, the communities were so individual that rivalry prevailed between the boys of the hill and those of the street, so that snowballing and other fights were common between "Hillers" and "Streeters." If a boy of either clan passed the line of School and Spring streets he was open to attack from the enemy.

The tower of the arsenal is a trifle more than eighty-eight feet high. One of those who ascended it for the pleasure of overlooking the widespread valley was Longfellow, the poet. At that time one of the floors was stacked with guns in frames, and Mrs. Longfellow mentioned that these resembled the pipes of an organ. As a result, he was inspired to compose one of the finest poems ever written in the cause of universal peace.

When the English novelist, Charles Dickens, was making one of his American tours he passed through Springfield in the winter of 1842. A noted river pilot named Allen had charge of the steamer "Massachusetts," which was about to make the first trip of the season, and the suggestion was made to Mr. Dickens that as the roads were bad he had better go by steamer. Accordingly "Kit" Stebbins was asked to captain the "Massachusetts" and Allen to pilot it. This was the largest of the steamers then built and it could not go through the Canal because that was filled with ice and it would not have done to send any other craft. The steamer had a high ladies' cabin built up on the rear of the deck and there the steersman stood on top of this cabin, thus giving the famous novelist an impression of insecurity. Mr. Allen was stationed at the bow while shooting the rapids, and the rest of the time was in the cabin. When they reached Hartford

Mr. Dickens asked Pilot Allen if he chewed tobacco, and a few days later Allen received a package from Dickens inclosing a tobacco-box. In writing of the boat, Dickens said:

"I should think it must have been about half a pony power. The cabin was fitted with common sash windows like an ordinary dwellinghouse. These windows had bright red curtains, too, hung on slack strings across the lower panes, so that it looked like the parlor of a Lilliputian public house which had gotten afloat in a flood or some other water accident, and was drifting, nobody knew where. But even in this chamber there was a rocking chair. It would be impossible to get on anywhere in America without a rocking chair."

One of the active boatmen of that period said of the famous author:

"The light weight Englishman wore a swallow-tail, snuff-colored coat and a red and white figured vest that was not long enough to reach his pantaloons, which were of the true Yankee check, and looked as if they had been bought from a North-street Jew shop in Boston."

Two years before the visit of Dickens the steamboat "Greenfield" had exploded near South Hadley Falls, killing two men and wounding several others. The boilers of the "Greenfield" and the "Agawam" were made on Mill River by a man who was killed at South Hadley Falls when the former boat exploded. Another boat was built at the foot of State Street, and in making a return trip from Hartford, hit a rock at the head of the fall. Help came from Thompsonville, and Dr. Osgood and others waded into the water and worked the boat off with levers. Samuel Bowles was on board with a new font of type for the "Republican."

Springfield Newspapers

CHAPTER XIX

Springfield Newspapers

The first Springfield newspaper was the "Massachusetts Gazette and General Advertiser."

For a time Springfield had a newspaper known as the "Hampden Patriot and Liberal Recorder." It was published weekly, and I have before me three issues, the oldest dated October 3, 1821, and the others April 3, 1822, and September 11, 1822. Each issue has four pages, twenty-four by twenty-two. There are three crude illustrations in the oldest paper, another had one, and the third none. The most attractive illustration is a little woodcut of a stagecoach drawn by four horses.

One of the papers starts with a scriptural slogan, and continues wholly religious for more than three columns. Much of the space was taken by a lecture on Unitarianism. Next comes a half column featuring a new Massachusetts mortgage law, and after that is a two-column article that is caged under the heading Miscellany, although wholly devoted to an article that has for its subject "Facts respecting the first establishment of stagecoaches in New England." It was in 1783 that the first line of these coaches was put on the road, and the original projector was Levi Pease, who, in consequence has been called "The Father" of the stages. This old gentleman, who told the experiences related here in his eighty-third year, survived to see every part of the United States traversed by stages that were running with a celerity unequalled in any country excepting Great Britain. For some time previous, Captain Pease, then residing in Somers, Connecticut, had been revolving the scheme in his mind, and at length cautiously imparted it to those he thought might assist him, but his plan met with the most disheartening reception. Some ridiculed his folly, and his friends talked of the ruin he would bring on himself. Among those to whom he appealed in vain was an enterprising Boston man, yet stubbornly convinced that the country was not old enough or prosperous enough to maintain a line of stages. He remarked to Captain Pease, that a century hence, or at the shortest, in fifty years, people might begin to think of such a thing, but it was idle to talk of it before.

Captain Pease became discouraged and was about to renounce all hope of success when he happened to bewail his disappointment in the presence of his townsman, Reuben Sikes, a young man twenty-seven years of age, who made an offer to embark with him in the undertaking. They united their small resources, and on the fifteenth of October, 1783, they began running a line of stages between Hartford and Boston. The coach went from Somers to Hartford on Monday morning of every week. There it took in passengers, and on Tuesday morning started for Boston. The coach from Boston set out on Monday, came as far as Northborough on Monday night, and on Tuesday morning proceeded to Brookfield, where it met the stage from Hartford. Both stages stopped over night at Brookfield, and next morning continued to Hartford and Boston. The running of the stages was altered the next summer, and the coach from Hartford started on Monday morning for Springfield and Palmer up the Connecticut River, and in another two years the line was continued to New York. For quite a while Pease and Sikes drove their own teams. They lacked money to hire drivers, and the line was constantly running them in debt. About four years after the line was established they took measures for getting the chance to transport the mail in the coaches. They believed this would be a great accommodation to the public, and without it the proprietors despaired of being able to support their line, which as yet had not yielded any profit. Captain Pease was appointed agent to appeal to the Postmaster-General. The appeal was made, but was met by a peremptory refusal. The Postmaster-General stated in emphatic language that it was not yet time to entertain such a project. The state of the roads, particularly in winter and spring, was such that the mails could not be carried with so much safety and dispatch in carriages, as on horseback, and he therefore declined the proposition.

The next move of the proprietors was to get a petition presented to Congress, and as a result a resolution was passed directing the employment of the stagecoaches on the line from New York to Boston in the transportation of the mail. The wisdom of the measure was soon proved, and Captain Pease became contractor with the government for the whole route. At that time there were only five post-offices on the main road between Boston and New York. These were Worcester, Springfield, Hartford, Middletown, and New Haven. Not many years later, on this same route, there was a post-office in nearly every village.

For some time after the mail began to be carried in the coaches, the proprietors employed persons in addition to the drivers. They were called conductors, and they had to take care of the mails. Besides they acted as agents for the transaction of such business as might be committed to their care on the route, and in the different towns and cities. But it was the proprietors who were responsible for all goods and money entrusted to these conductors. The fare for passengers was six and one-fourth cents per mile. When arriving in Boston, the first stagehouse was at the Sign of the Lamb, in Newbury Street, and the house was kept by Widow Moore.

One curious Congressional contribution in the newspaper consists of sarcastic comments on "The flying man." He had come to the House of Representatives to plead for an invention he had made. Congressman Milnor introduced him as James Bennet, of Philadelphia, and Mr. Bennet then stated that he had invented a machine by which a man could fly through the air, could soar to any height, steer in any direction, start from any place, and alight without risk or injury, and prays that an Act of Congress may be passed, securing to him and his heirs for the term of forty years "the right of steering flying machines through that portion of the earth's atmosphere which presses on the United States, or so far as their jurisdiction may extend; by which act the honor of the invention will be conferred on the United States." The motion was made that the petition be referred to a committee. Mr. Sergeant opposed, saying that the committee did not undertake to soar into regions so high, their duty being nearer the earth. Besides they had so much business of a terrestrial nature before them that they could not devote their time to philosophical and aerial investigation. There was more discussion, but in the end the motion was laid on the table.

One of the thrills that the old papers gave their readers was "More Pirates Captured," and these were nearby, right down in Cuba.

Captain Seabury of the brig "Joseph" had arrived at Falmouth and reported that while off Cape Antonio he was boarded from the United States brig "Enterprise" and informed she had captured that morning eight piratical vessels, with their crews, amounting in all to one hundred and sixty men, who were now prisoners on board. Captain Kearney's success against the Cuban pirates in breaking up their lurking place and destroying their vessels, and finally capturing one hundred and sixty of the pirates, "is unexampled."

Shipwrecks are chronicled, and wars and conspiracies; also agricultural distress in England, coupled with increased taxation.

Locally, persons who have died or married get attention, and a shoemaker advertises that he is in his usual place, and that he has lately been furnished with as good an assortment of the most fashionable stuffs for ladies' and gentlemen's shoes as can be procured in the City of New York. The "subscriber also wishes to employ a LAD between the age of 14 and 16, as apprentice to the business."

Other advertising includes "Cough drops, the most valuable medicine in use for coughs and consumptions. Many certificates of its efficacy accompany each bottle." This advertisement takes up most of a column.

A large stove is offered for sale or exchange. It has an open fireplace and a large oven—a very suitable piece of furniture for a family who wish to live snug in one room by one fire.

A tavern stand, toll bridge, blacksmith and wheelwright establishment, farm and sawmill are advertised for sale, on the main road from Hartford to Northampton and Westfield, six miles from the flourishing town of Springfield.

In 1822 Springfield had a circulating library, and some of the late publications received were Schoolcraft's "Journal," "Life of Wesley," "Hundred Wonders of the World," "Pirate," by Scott, Byron's "Tragedies," and "Views of Society and Manners in America." The fact was advertised that some books were missing from the library. For instance, 2d Vol. of Irving's "Sketch Book," 1st Vol. of "Ivanhoe," and so on, ending with "whoever has any of the abovementioned books belonging to the Library, are requested to return them immediately!"

Besides the circulating library, the town had at least one book store carried on by T. Dickman. He sold law books, but he also had school books and stationery, and he emphasized the fact that he had for sale "Martin's Life," 3d edition, and that it was about Michael Martin, the notorious highway robber.

In this issue of the paper was one solitary illustration, a small picture of a stagecoach. This was for advertising the firm of Clark and Crocker, "who would inform the public that they had taken a stand a few rods west of the new courthouse, where they intend carrying on the business of coachmaking and repairing."

Poetry was accepted rather freely, but the type used in printing it was distressingly small. This was a period when William Cullen Bryant had recently become a star among the American poets, and the lesser poets copied his style. One of these had a long poem in the Hampden paper that in a weak way was plainly inspired by the famous Hampshire poet. It was of considerable length and was entitled "Stream of Time." Besides, the editor tells us he was informed that the poem was written by an aged man, author of the "Gloom of Autumn."

The largest and most eye-catching of the newspapers' features was the advertising of alcoholic liquors.

Humor in the old newspaper is perhaps best sampled in what follows:

"Proof that a man can be his own grandfather. There was a widow and her daughter-in-law, and a man and his son. The widow married the son, and the daughter married the old man. The widow was, therefore, mother to her husband's father and consequently grandmother to her own husband. They had a son to whom she was grandmother; now as the son of a great-grandmother must be either a grandfather or great-uncle, this boy was therefore his own grandfather. N. B.—This was actually the case with a boy in a school at Norwich."

The terms of the "Hampden Patriot and Liberal Recorder" were two dollars a year, payable at the year's end. "Advertisements inserted at prices usual in the country. No paper will be discontinued until arrearages are paid." Other advertisements were: "Henry Sterns, directly opposite Court Square, has just received a very extensive assortment of choice groceries and liquors—wines, brandy, Holland gin, cordials, Irish and Columbia whiskey, London porter, Spanish segars, raisins per box, very low, superior quality sugars, teas, nuts of all kinds, lemons, coffee, chocolate, and every article of West India goods. Mackerel, in half barrels, for family use, very fine."

"Just published and for sale at this office, sermons on the unity of God and on the character of Jesus Christ. By Winthrop Bailey, minister of the gospel, in Pelham, Massachusetts. Price, 37½ cents."

"Canal—At a numerous and respectable meeting from several towns in the counties of Hampshire and Hampden, convened at South-ampton, on the subject of a proposed canal from the north line of the State of Connecticut, at the town of Southwick on the river above Northampton. After several remarks by different gentlemen a committee of nine was appointed to take the whole subject into consideration."

"Clay's ointment for the itch" is advertised, and we are told that "for pleasantness, safety, ease, and certainty, it is infinitely superior to any other medicine known for the cure of that most tormenting disorder. Price 33 cents a box."

One short column of varying length in the paper has for its heading "Patriot." A good example of the messages it carried is this: "We are requested to state that the Rev. John Bisbee, Pastor of the Universalist Society in Western (now Warren), will preach next Sabbath at the chapel near the United States Armory in Springfield."

"Suicide—A coroner's inquest was held in this town on Saturday, over the body of Mr. Shubael Cleveland, aged 34. The verdict of the inquest was that 'he came to his death by taking opium.'"

"For Sale—Copper stills, containing from 30 to 1,000 gallons. Pewter and copper worms. Dyer's kettles and brewer's kettles of varying sizes. Sheet and pig lead. Church bells, 300 to 2,700 pounds; school, ship, clock, door, cow, and sheep bells."

"David Bryant has for sale black, blue, snuff and drab cloths; printed cassimere shawls, very low; twilled bombazetts; red, white and yellow flannels; merino handkerchiefs, merino fringe and trimmings, silk and tabby velvets, Italian crapes, damask table linen, fine thread laces, with a variety of other articles making a general assortment of dry goods. Also groceries and crockery ware, ground rice; cheap for cash or approved credit, four good muskets, which will be sold low."

"Dancing School—Mr. Stebbins returns his most sincere thanks to the gentlemen and ladies of Springfield for past favors, and most respectfully informs them that he is wishing for their continued favors another quarter. Mr. Stebbins is wishing to open another quarter in September, the present month. All favors will be most gratefully accepted. N. B.—Mr. Stebbins will open his school on Thursday, the 12th, at two o'clock P. M., in the hall of the Hampden Coffee-house."

A druggist whose stock included paints, groceries, wines, and choice liquors, "solicits a share of patronage," and offers to receive all sorts of country produce in payment at cash prices. Another druggist features confectionery along with his wines and choice liquors, "and a complete assortment of all the nostrums and other articles usually kept in a druggist store."

The proprietor of a Springfield bakery "Respectfully informs the public that he has established his business a few rods north of Court Square, where he will constantly keep on hand large and small Crackers; Butter Biscuit; Gingerbread, Cookies and Rusk—warranted of as good quality and as cheap as can be bought in Hartford or New York."

The newspaper from time to time advertised "For sale at this office." Usually that meant some book or pamphlet. One such pamphlet was entitled "A Reply to a letter from a Trinitarian to a Unitarian," price 12½ cents. It was a very warm subject at that time.

"Water! Water! Water! I am a well digger, and would respectfully inform the citizens of this and adjacent towns that I continue to sink wells, and perform all other business connected with my profession—such as taking up old wells, sinking those deeper which have become dry, blasting rocks, and laying down aqueducts."

"A volatile aromatic snuff—prepared by a doctor," is advertised and we are informed that it has been selling for ten years in almost every part of the United States. It is very fragrant to the smell and stimulating to the spirits and is put up in elegant bottles, that retail at fifty cents each in Dickman's Bookstore.

POETRY

THE INSENSIBLE FAIR

William unsheathed his shining blade,
        Then fixed the point against his breast
And gazed upon the wondering maid,
        And thus his dire distress expressed:

"Since cruel fair! with cold disdain,
    You still return my raging love;
Thought is but madness—life is pain.
    And thus at once I'll both remove!"
"O stop one moment," Celia said;
    Then trembling hastened to the door;
"Haste, Sally!—quick!—a pail, dear maid!
    This madman else will stain the floor!"

"Lake serpent, an animal more than thirty-seven feet in length, and resembling the Cape Ann sea serpent, has been seen on Lake Ontario. When first discovered he lay asleep on the water; but when approached nearer, he raised his head several feet, and with incredible velocity darted through the water in a serpentine direction, creating a foam as he passed along."

"Olympic Theatre, for a few evenings. Mr. Blanchard respectfully informs the public that he has erected a suitable building where he will begin his performance with mathematical and philosophical experiments, too numerous to mention. Master George, the young Hercules, will perform his Olympic feats of balancing. Miss Elizabeth, the flying phenomenon, only seven years of age, will go through pleasing equilibriums on the slack wire, and conclude her performance with a fashionable song. The whole to conclude with Mrs. Blanchard's grand performance on the tight rope, in a style far superior to anything of the kind that has been seen in this town. Performances begin at seven o'clock in the evening. Admittance, fifty cents front seat, back seat twenty-five cents."

On September 8, 1824, appeared the first issue of the "Springfield Republican." Its founder, Samuel Bowles, at this time twenty-seven years old, was a Hartford printer. He came from a Roxbury family of quality, and one of his ancestors was John Eliot, the famous missionary to the Indians.

Editor Bowles' father, the first Samuel in the line, was a boy of thirteen in Boston when the Revolution broke out. Toward the end of the war the family moved to Hartford, and there young Bowles set up as a grocer, and is said to have prospered "in a small way," so small, in fact, that when he died, all he left to Samuel, his youngest son working in the grocery shop, was a watch and the family Bible.

The next year the boy was apprenticed as a printer, having an older brother as his guardian, and continuing to live with his mother, who took boarders to make ends meet. When the apprenticeship ended he tried various things in the printing and newspaper field, and then came an offer from the Springfield Federalists, which he accepted. What they wanted was a newspaper medium that would express their viewpoint on public affairs, and they loaned him $250 which he returned in due time with interest at six per cent. Mr. Bowles borrowed $150 more and bought type and other printing equipment.

He hired a crude hand-lever press, and not until some years later was he able to buy it. With such slender resources, but with a habit of economy and perseverance, and not least, with the encouragement of a wife never afraid of putting her shoulder to the wheel, the "Springfield Republican" was founded.

Mr. Bowles began by doing nearly all his own work and attempting nothing beyond his ability. He was proprietor, publisher, editor and devil; he set his own type and ran his own press. Without delay he advertised for a boy to serve as apprentice, but seemed to have some difficulty in finding one.

The press, and the things that went with it, and his household goods and family were poled up the Connecticut River from Hartford to Springfield on a flatboat, and there the press was hauled from the river bank by oxen.

In that straggling town of 4,500 inhabitants, scattered in widely separated hamlets, he started a paper which is still controlled by Bowles' descendants.

The year 1824 in the Connecticut Valley was a time of simple ways and small beginnings.

When the young printer from Hartford began publishing his newspaper, the town's leading institutions were the arsenal overlooking the region from the east and the First Church on lower land beside the river near the spot where the original settlers had built their first meetinghouse. The town was growing slowly; two hundred hands were employed at the arsenal and, in 1826, 15,500 muskets were made.

The first issue of the "Republican" contained no local news. It was painstakingly made up of articles and items selected from the latest available editions of papers printed in New York and Boston, and possibly Philadelphia.

Events that took place in Washington were not reported in print at Springfield until eight days afterward. When the roads were heavy with winter snows or deep with spring mud, the delay was sometimes greater. It is a curious fact that in the early issues of the "Republican" there was news about nearly everything but the life of Springfield itself. However, the newcomer gradually found time

THE FIRST HOME OF THE "SPRINGFIELD REPUBLICAN"

to look around, and probably the apprentices who began to be taken into the editor's home broadened his outlook. An account of work being done to enlarge the plant of the United States Arsenal was the first piece of local reporting. According to the newspaper, the celebration on July 4 was "a respectable gathering of gentlemen" met to hold the patriotic exercises which were then customary. After much speechmaking and the reading of an ode, they went to the arsenal and there a banquet was held, while "toasts" were announced from the ends of the tables, and drunk to the music of discharging cannons. A good deal of gunpowder was burned that day, and those who drank all the innumerable toasts which were offered with the formality of the time, we can imagine grew as tired as the gunners. The toast Editor Bowles offered was "The Connecticut River—a natural canal—may it be made navigable without the aid of locks."

The founder of the "Republican" has often been described as solemn, earnest and undemonstrative. That he lacked humor has been taken for granted. And yet, in November, 1825, we find the publisher giving warning that "we shall publish no marriage unless the writing is accompanied by a piece of wedding cake and a little wine, if convenient,—but we are not particular as to that."

In the next issue he says, "We must apologize to the ladies this week for not being able to supply them with a few marriages to read, but we expect a supply after Thanksgiving."

The founding of the "Daily Republican" marked the entrance on the stage of an eighteen-year-old youth, who was destined to become one of the great figures of American journalism. The announcement of the Daily began: "We have resolved to try the experiment of a daily paper in Springfield. Two years since, we proposed the matter to the public, and consulted some of our friends who dissuaded us from it as an unprofitable undertaking. We commence now without a single subscriber or advertiser promised. After continuing the publication six months, or a year, if we find it too much of a loss, we shall stop." There were five weekly newspapers in the town, and they found it difficult to make ends meet.

The third Samuel Bowles was born in Springfield in 1826. He was brought up in a frugal household, where, as a small boy, he shared his bed with the youngest of his father's apprentices, while two others had their bed in the same room. The day in that household began with breakfast at six o'clock the year around, and at seven the master and apprentices were at work, doing a general printing business in addition to producing the newspaper.

It was the father's intent that his oldest son should learn the printer's trade just as he had himself, but the boy had little skill with his hands. If a kite was to be made, or so much as a nail driven, his younger sister was apt to be called to his help. All through life his hands were long, pale, and delicate, and had an air of helplessness. Some lack of physical vigor seems to have kept the boy out of hardy sports, and in manhood his health was never robust. His favorite occupation was reading.

When he left school at the age of seventeen he went into the "Republican" as office boy. One of the employees was Chauncey White. There was a time when he contracted to print both daily and weekly, and the printing included all the work of production—even to folding, packing and directing papers. It was further agreed that

White, in accord with the methods of the period in paying for sub-scriptions, was to accept in part settlement orders for such things as "groceries, dry goods, clothing, and farmers' produce for the supply of his family and apprentices, so far as he may want such supplies." In this way the farm products that often were turned into the

SAMUEL BOWLES

"Republican" as payment for subscriptions were then transferred to a local grocery.

At the end of a year the "Daily Republican," which hitherto had been an evening paper, began to appear in the morning. Soon, it was the routine custom to set up the type of the entire paper, advertise-ments, news and editorials before nine o'clock in the evening, at which time all hands went home to bed. White would lock up all the forms but one, in which space was left to the extent of half a column for "late news." "Young Sam" filled that space with neighborhood items which he gathered about the town in the evening. After all the others had gone home to sleep, he was at work. He would leave his copy on the composing stone, where Chauncey White would find it when he returned to the office about three o'clock in the morning to get out the paper.

With the arrival of winter, and the end of 1844, the younger Bowles suffered the first of what were destined to be many failures of health. So serious did the situation become that he sought a warmer climate and spent several months in the South, mostly in Louisiana. That climate agreed with him, and he wrote a series of fifteen letters for the paper. They were in a clear and direct style, and showed something of his capacity to boil down the news and the views of others, for which he later became famous. The letters combined observation with vivid comment in such proportion as to make them readable and informing. They dealt with the climate, the productions and the business of the places visited; they told something of manners and morals, gave an occasional bit of picturesque description, touched on local politics, and drew the inference that slavery was worse for masters than for slaves.

The part taken by Samuel Bowles at the Know Nothing convention in Philadelphia, in 1855, did much to gain national fame for him and his newspaper. Not long afterward Horace Greeley said in the New York "Tribune" that the "Republican" was "the best and ablest country journal ever published on this continent." With the advent of the Civil War, the files of the "Republican" from 1861 to 1865 reflect the growing determination of the North to preserve the Union, and then to free the slaves. The war stimulated the reading of newspapers throughout the country, and to Springfield it brought a considerable increase in population. Here were made the weapons that won the war. The employees of the United States Arsenal in its war-time manufacture rose rapidly from a few hundred to a force of nearly three thousand. The circulation of the "Daily Republican" doubled during the war, and so did its price, which was first raised from two cents to three and then to four. The cause of the increased price was the mounting cost of white paper, which continued to rise until it reached thirty cents a pound. Wood pulp for the manufacture of paper was not then used and there was a shortage of rags, due in part to the greatly increased use of rags for bandaging the wounded.

On November 15, 1861, the paper declared that if South Carolina sought to withdraw from the Union by peaceful negotiations, her withdrawal should be permitted. It added, "A Union that must be maintained by force is not desirable." This was very different from the stand the paper took a few months later, and maintained to the end of the war with unsparing vigor. The demand was for preserving the Union, and for a persistent use of force until the rebellion was put down and the Union restored.

Lincoln's Gettysburg speech occupied in the "Republican" of the morning after about a "stick full" of type under a small sub-heading, where it followed immediately after Everett's polished but forgotten oration. On the second day the "Republican" printed a separate editorial on Lincoln's speech. It declared that, "surpassingly fine as Mr. Everett's oration was," the honors of the occasion were won by President Lincoln, whose "little speech was a perfect gem, deep in feeling, compact in thought and expression."

The most famous editorial adventure of Mr. Bowles was that of being jailed in New York. It was the result of a conspiracy between a corrupt judge and a celebrated speculator who gave Samuel Bowles and the "Republican" the most valuable advertising they ever received. The newspaper took a special interest in James Fisk, Junior, who was Jay Gould's notorious partner in the fraudulent operations of the Erie Railroad. His birthplace was in Vermont in territory served by the paper. He began as a peddler on a glorified scale, with many traveling wagons. His later career in New York made him a national figure through his corrupt manipulation of railroads and courts.

In November, 1808, the "Republican" described Fisk as the "New Hero of Wall Street" and told the story of his recent operations and his previous history with biting and daring truthfulness. The "Republican" carried its attack to a climax in the statement that many of Fisk's friends predicted he would end his days in State prison or a madhouse. Fisk's response was a libel suit for $50,000. This was not pressed, but gave Fisk an opportunity to attempt personal revenge. The next month, when Mr. Bowles was in New York with his wife, who was not well, he was suddenly seized in the old Fifth Avenue

Hotel on a writ issued by one of the most notorious of Fisk's corrupted judges. Without being given a chance to see Mrs. Bowles, he was hurried off to the Ludlow Street Jail and held there through the night. A friend succeeded in locating the sheriff at a carousal, and applied for an order of release, whereat the sheriff shuffled out of the way.

In the morning a host of friends came to the support of Mr. Bowles, and his release was secured on bail. Nothing more was done in the case against him. The episode made a national sensation and was widely discussed in the newspapers. Its chief significance was in the illustration it gave of how far the judicial and administrative machinery of the metropolis was at the service of a set of gamblers, and could be used by them to gratify a freak of personal malice.

Less than four years later, Fisk's career was cut short before he had reached prison, madhouse, or his fortieth year. He was shot by the pistol of his rival for the favors of a dissolute woman. In editorial comment on the crime, the "Republican" mentioned the character of the man, who in three or four years had made himself notorious the world over for reckless financing, the corrupting of courts and the pillaging of railroads. The public saw the worst side of him, and it was a very bad one; but there were traits in his character that enabled the preacher of his funeral sermon to speak the kind word that charity to the dead demands.

No man ever strove harder to keep mistakes out of his newspaper than the second Bowles. One of his friends who saw him coming away from his office late in the night, made the comment to a companion, "There goes Sam Bowles after killing himself trying to find a misplaced comma." When a mistake had been made it was not easy to admit the error. Indeed, the story has been told of a man who complained to Mr. Bowles that the "Republican" had mistakenly reported his death, and he wanted the mistake corrected. In response Mr. Bowles expressed his regret that the paper could not make a correction, but offered reparation by putting his name in the birth notices.

Samuel Bowles, the second, traveled more than any other of the great journalists of his time. Within a period of fifteen years he crossed the continent twice, one of the times covering two thousand miles by stagecoach.   Another western trip took him to Colorado and four times he crossed the Atlantic.

He went wherever else the search for news or health called him, and wherever he went he was making notes and writing to the paper or filling his mind with facts and impressions to be drawn on later. He tells in one instance of working forty-two hours at a stretch without sleep.   On a trip to Colorado at a time when the Indians were making trouble, his party was in the mountains and they had the thrill of an Indian scare, and of being forced to hurry back to Denver for safety.   Mr. Bowles died in 1878.   He had made his paper a national influence, and he had shown the qualities of a statesman. Many of his characteristics had a likeness to those of Horace Greeley, but were without Mr. Greeley's oddities.   There was no class of editorial work that he did not do well, but above all he was a born leader of opinions.

On a Sunday morning in September, 1878, a well-known Springfield citizen appeared on his front porch, clad in dressing gown and carpet slippers.   In his hands were the family tongs.   With these he carefully picked up a tainted object which lay before him.   Then, marching around the house as if to avoid possible contagion to holy precincts, he deposited the object in the garbage can by the kitchen door.   With the crisis met and duty done, he resumed the day's meditations.   The cause of the offense which had been dealt with so sternly was a copy of the first issue of the "Sunday Republican," laid before the good man's door in hope of getting his patronage—and in the course of time the old gentleman yielded to temptation.   Before he was summoned to final judgment on his sins, he became a subscriber.

During the Civil War the "Republican" sometimes issued extras on the receipt of great news, and distributed them on Sunday through the Massachusetts hill towns.   They were received with mixed emotions.   Good church members were torn between troubled thoughts at the desecration of the day and desire to get the news from the front.   The desire to get the news seems to have been the stronger.

No head of a newspaper ever exercised closer control over every department than did the third Bowles.   He first joined the paper as a regular in 1873, but his father's waning strength compelled him to take charge of the business management, and it was in looking after minute details, and in "telling others how and what to write," that his life was spent. His day began with a painstaking, methodical reading of the paper in his library at home. A clipping was made of each mistake, and when he had walked to the office the clippings went to those responsible. It used to be a by-word in the office that it was not possible for a mistake to escape him. He was appreciative of work well done, and for a member of the staff to receive a clipping from a page with one's initials on it, and the added words "Good!" or "Fine!" in Mr. Bowles' familiar script, carried a message more precious than words.

Until 1914, the "Republican," in common with most other newspapers, printed liquor advertising, particularly of the local brewery products, which at times inserted copy occupying full pages. Early in 1914 a Massachusetts State commission issued a report showing that drunkenness was increasing alarmingly with a host of attendant evils.

The "Republican," in commenting editorially, declared: "It is the duty of every citizen to consider carefully what he personally may do to aid in turning the rising tide of inebriety into a tide of sobriety, which must mean better lives among the people of Massachusetts."

When Mr. Bowles reached the office that day he sent for two members of the editorial staff. One of these was Waldo Cook, author of the editorial. The other was a director of the company. He turned to the latter, saying, "Do you think the 'Republican' should eliminate liquor advertising?" The answer was "Yes." His next, and only other question was: "Will you back that up as a director?" That question was answered likewise, and he abruptly terminated the interview with a terse "Good-bye." Nothing more was said, but before the end of the week every liquor advertisement was thrown out of the "Republican" with intent that it should be forever, although advertising amounting to thousands of dollars a year was sacrificed.

In August came the outbreak of the World War, and financial advertising, in which the "Republican" always had been a leader, nearly ceased to exist. Newspaper revenues were gravely reduced, yet Mr. Bowles, in his annual report to the stockholders of the Republican Company, made a few weeks before he died, told with undaunted pride of eliminating liquor advertising, as a step which was the only one the "Republican" could have taken in the situation it faced.

The Springfield "Union" dates from 1864, when it was founded by Edmund Anthony to "expound Republican principles." It changed hands a number of times, and in 1872 was bought by C. W. Bryan. In 1890 the paper was taken over by the Springfield Union Publishing Company, and shortly afterward a morning edition and a Sunday issue were started. In 1926 "The Republican" acquired control of the "Union."

In 1880 the "Penny News," or the Springfield "Daily News" appeared, published by Edward and Charles Bellamy. This paper has the distinction of being the first penny journal in New England, which attracted considerable attention to it. Edward Bellamy, who wrote "Looking Backward," retired, and Charles carried on with the "News" until 1915, when it was sold to "The Republican."

The daily and Sunday newspapers, through these events, came under one ownership, that of Sherman Bowles, descendant of the famous Samuels of that line. The editorial policies differ, however, and on any question the Springfield reader can gain three separate views and thus draw his conclusions. The Springfield "Union" is strongly Republican in politics, both morning and evening; the "Daily News" expounds the Democratic side, and "The Springfield Republican," with its tradition as an independent newspaper coming down over a century, takes definite stands wherever it sees fit. A few years ago the Springfield "Union and "The Springfield Republican" combined to form a single Sunday paper. The Springfield papers are a power in the State, and "The Republican" is read all over the country.

People and Events

CHAPTER XX

People and Events

A distinguished member of the bar was George Ashmun, and great intimacy existed between him and Daniel Webster. Mr. Ashmun was chairman of the Republican convention at Chicago in 1860, which nominated Abraham Lincoln for President.

In the chair, as in the private councils attending the progress of the convention, he shone out with all his power; his voice rang clear through the great wigwam, and stilled the passions of its excited thousands. His manner and his presence commanded order throughout all the proceedings, and his political sagacity and quick-witted instincts early prophesied and contributed to the final result.

Growing out of this relation to the nomination, he had a pleasant intimacy with President Lincoln, and his counsel was sought and accepted by the administration. For years he occupied an influential and useful position at Washington. Probably the most notable instance of his influence was the result of his interview with Stephen A. Douglas directly after the Confederates fired on Fort Sumter. Such were his appeals, and the strong force of the arguments addressed to Douglas, that the Senator rose superior to partisanship and to rivalry, and took his stand with his country.

Although very late at night, Mr. Ashmun said, "Now let us go to the White House and talk with Mr. Lincoln. I want you to say to him what you have said to me, and then I want the result of this night's deliberations telegraphed to the country." Then and there Mr. Douglas took down the map, planned the campaign, and gave most eloquently and vehemently his strong support to the administration. Mr. Ashmun, himself, briefly abridged the story, and it went by telegraph that night all over the country.

Springfield never made to its public the gift of a character about which is associated more good humor, genial humanity or more dignified eloquence than that of George Ashmun. Whoever had a liking for the olden times took a lifelong delight in telling how he would drop in of an afternoon, "rub his nose, take some snuff," and awake to the pleasantries of cordial conversation. The more serious read

GEORGE ASHMUN,
A Leader of the Old Hampden Bar

his political addresses, pitched in lofty sentiment, while the gossips treasure a fund of anecdote concerning him. He had the rare faculty of hospitality which is spontaneous without being familiar. If the tradition of the town is authority, one of the most brilliant occasions in our local annals was the dinner given by Mr. Ashmun to Thackeray, the English novelist. We have the word of the "Springfield Republican," long since recorded, that "the company floated out for hours on a tide of humor, of brilliant gossip and suggestive criticism, so that even Thackeray, accustomed to the finest society of England as well as America, often laid down his knife and fork—a thing he would not have done without occasion—and listened or applauded with wonder."

Edmund Allen was born in Belchertown in 1786. He learned the trade of carpenter and cabinetmaker in his native town, and being a superior mechanic, he applied for a position at the United States Armory in Springfield. He was given a place in April, 1809. When he received notice that he could have the position, he started and by running and walking reached the armory grounds, a distance of nearly fourteen miles, in about two hours.

Colonel David Ames, Senior, was the son of one of the first iron workers in New England. Early in life he engaged in the manufacture of shovels and guns, and supplied the American Army with those articles. During the Revolutionary War, he held a commission in the militia, and was occasionally called into service. In 1794, on account of his knowledge of the making of arms, he was appointed by President Washington to establish and superintend a national armory at Springfield, and under his supervision and direction the armory was first begun and was managed by him from 1794 to 1802. After leaving the service of the government he gave his attention to the manufacture of paper. In this business he was successful and became, in 1838, the owner of the most extensive paper manufactory in the United States. Mr. Ames was known as a man of sound judgment and great business activity, and was generously disposed to give both publicly and privately for the benefit and improvement of the town. In 1810 Mr. Ames was the owner of the first piano brought into Springfield. It attracted much attention, and people would stop and listen to its sounds.

For a long time Springfield's most imposing home was the "spacious" Maple Street mansion of David Ames, Junior. The house was built in 1826-27 and was charmingly situated on one of Springfield's bold, rising hills. In early life Mr. Ames engaged in the manufacture of paper and was the active manager in the firm which did a prosperous and extensive business, and had mills in Chicopee Falls, South Hadley Falls, Northampton, Suffield, Connecticut, and Springfield. After a period of nearly thirty years of remarkable prosperity the firm was induced to make investments in Canadian lumber and sawmills, and coal lands in Pennsylvania. The crisis of 1853 came and they were obliged to suspend payment. It is related that when the firm was at the height of their prosperity Ames' father remonstrated with him because of the lavish way in which they were spending money. His reply was: "Why, father, the money comes in faster than we can spend it; a thousand dollars a day. Why, father!" The warning was not heeded and suspension followed.

Colonel Galen Ames, son of David Ames, Senior, entered Yale College in 1814, where he remained two years, and afterward, as a sailor, made a voyage to the eastern quarter of the world. On his return home he began business as a dry goods merchant, and for a while had a store next north of the Corner Book Store on Main Street, where he had various partners at different times. In 1826 he was chosen lieutenant-colonel of artillery.

John Ames, "a natural inventor," was also the son of David Ames, Senior. While in New York, in 1822, he heard of a machine for making paper that had been invented at Brandywine, Delaware, but had failed to be a success. He became interested in it, went to work, and on the fourteenth of May, 1822, received his patent for the cylinder paper machine. Other paper industry inventions of his followed, and he did his utmost to prevent his inventions and methods from being stolen. The mill was guarded with great secrecy and the workmen were sworn not to reveal his ideas and plans for the manufacture of paper. Mill owners throughout the country were watching the marvelous inventions made at the Ames Paper Mill, and workmen sought employment in order to steal the inventions. Mr. Ames died in January, 1890, in the ninetieth year of his age.

Another of the talented Ames family was James T., born in Lowell, Massachusetts, in 1810. He spent his boyhood days with his father, learning the cutlery business, but presently went to Chicopee Falls with his father and brother, where they engaged in the manufacture of edge tools, and there remained until 1833. The final move brought them to Chicopee Center where the pilgrimage ended, and the Ames Manufacturing Company was established with James T. Ames, superintendent.

Ames had a rare genius for inventions. In company with General James, of Rhode Island, he invented a ball, afterward patented, out of which grew the necessity of rifled cannon. During the War of the Rebellion, Ames had large contracts with the government for the making of swords and cannon, and for military accouterments. Besides a contract was secured for government mail bags.

Mr. Ames was one of the original owners of the Chester emery mine. He was also first to introduce bronze statuary work in the United States. His first work was the construction of the Washington statue in Union Square, New York. The bronze doors of the Senate extension of the National Capitol at Washington were made under his supervision, and "were masterly specimens of his genius, and famous as triumphs of art." Mr. Ames died at the age of seventy-two.

Nathan P. Ames was another of the clan that aroused more than ordinary interest. He was born in 1803 and as a young man came to Chicopee Falls, where he established the cutlery business with nine workmen. In 1833, about thirty men were employed. A little later the business removed to Cabotville and located in a new shop. The company had a foundry for the casting of bells and cannon in connection with the manufacture of swords. In 1838 they made a bell for the city hall in New York, which weighed seven thousand pounds. Mr. Ames died at the age of forty-four.

One other Ames notable was William, born in the Massachusetts town of Dedham, in 1801. His mother was a daughter of Colonel John Worthington, who was one of the "river gods." When a lad of eleven William came to Springfield to live with an aunt, and there he remained a number of years. For one period he served as a clerk in a Springfield store, and he tried other things, finally settling down to devote himself to literary culture and historical research. For more than forty years he made his home in Dedham, but came to Springfield every year for visits to his relatives. His personal appearance on the streets attracted attention "by his measured tread, moving along in the summer days bearing his hat in his hand, and a kind expression of satisfaction with all mankind." He was a cultured Christian gentleman of patriotic nature.

When asked one day his opinion of the Yankee soldier, he replied: "The Yankee soldier is active and rough, wiry and tough." On another occasion during the Rebellion he remarked very gravely: "I wish I had command of an earthquake for five minutes. I would place it under Charleston, South Carolina." He died in 1880 at the age of seventy-nine years.

George Bancroft, famed as a historian, was a resident of Springfield for a three-year period, during which his home was a large house at 49 Chestnut Street. The house was a gift from Jonathan Dwight, Junior, to his daughter Sarah, whom Mr. Bancroft married. In 1834 he published the first volume of his history of the United States.

On the Fourth of July, 1836, he delivered an oration before the democracy of Springfield. While in Springfield he completed the second volume of his history. At this time he had his office on Elm Street in a block the second floor of which was used for lawyers' offices, and to that place he moved his library from Northampton. In January, 1838, he was appointed Collector of the Port of Boston by President Van Buren, and was later appointed Secretary of the Navy by President Polk, in whose term of office the War with Mexico was carried on, resulting in the conquest of California.

He devised and founded the Naval Academy at Annapolis, Maryland, and alone set at work this institution. For one month in 1846 he was Secretary of War and gave the order to General Zachary Taylor to march to the Rio Grande and into Texas, which was the first occupation of that soil by the United States.

Toward the end of 1846 Mr. Bancroft was transferred to the post of Minister to Great Britain. Later President Andrew Johnson appointed him Minister to Prussia, and he filled other posts in the German Empire. He rendered important service to his country in the settlement of the northwestern boundary between the United States and the British Dominions. After his return to America he delivered a memorial address on the life and character of Abraham Lincoln at the request of both Houses of Congress, speaking before them in the House of Representatives in February, 1866. The last revised edition of his six-volume history appeared in 1884 and 1885. He had been engaged for more than fifty years in writing his history, which he began when a young man. The immense amount of labor bestowed on it was so colossal in its purpose that for years he carried it on at great expense and with a large number of assistants. At one time there were twenty clerks employed. When he died he had attained an age above ninety.

Captain David Barber, a native of West Springfield, was born in September, 1789, on the Kirtland place, just below the South End Bridge. Among the incidents of his early life was the great freshet of 1801, known as "Jefferson's Flood." The water rose higher than ever before and one night it swept off the western bank near the Barber place, tearing away the entire front part of the house and leaving a roaring flood where the cellar had been. The floating front was finally towed ashore far down the river, while the back part of the house, which the flood left standing, was torn down and another dwelling was erected farther back from the river. This was a famous shad-fishing place at that time, but shad, now so much prized, were then lightly regarded. The old inhabitants used to say that people were ashamed to have it known they made shad a regular article of food; more highly esteemed were the noble salmon, which began running up the streams early in April, and were taken in a seine net like shad and often along with them. Twenty-nine salmon, weighing from twenty to thirty pounds apiece, were taken in one day at the old fishing place near Barber's home. When he was five years old his father, who was one of the famous river boatmen of the past, was engaged in boating stone for the old toll bridge across the Connecticut from the quarry at Enfield Falls. The boats were hauled up the river by horse-power, with the horses walking on the beach of the western shore. Often they went far out in the water toward the center of the river to avoid shallows, and sometimes swam the deep holes or the mouth of tributary streams.

Two boatloads of stones were hauled by a single horse, and on one of these horses young Barber, then twelve years old, was perched day after day until the bridge was completed. To go down to the falls and back was a regular day's work. When the bridge was completed Mr. Barber's father resumed his former business and the boy went with him. Before long, however, young David began to be known as Captain Barber, a title which he retained as long as he lived.

When navigation opened he was constantly employed transporting freight from Hartford to Springfield and towns above in the old boats so common on the Connecticut River. These boats were flat-bottomed, about twenty-five or thirty feet long, eight or ten wide, and usually carried one mast, which could be taken down going under bridges. Two men were the ordinary crew and fourteen tons was considered a full load. In the early part of the century the boats had no cabins and the captain was accustomed to cast anchor opposite one of the old river taverns that abounded all along the Connecticut in those days, and go ashore for the night with his crew of *one*.

Sometimes, if the wind was fair, the trip from Springfield to Hartford and return would be made in two days, and Mr. Barber used to tell the story that on one occasion when the south wind blew strong, he made the run from Hartford to the foot of Elm Street in Springfield within three hours. It was high water at the time so he ran straight over the Enfield Falls. Running the falls, especially going down stream, was by no means safe, and often boats were swamped in the raging waters. Three boats were wrecked on the falls one spring, and when one of them, which was laden with grain in bulk, went down, Mr. Barber's boat was so close on the wreck that the crew of the sinking craft sprang on board at a single bound.

Of course, everyone who worked on a boat held himself ready for a ducking at any minute, and one day young Barber came near taking his final plunge. He, with two other boys, had come down the river with a horse, to haul up an empty boat from the uppermost part of Enfield Falls. The horse was hitched to the boat by a long rope in the usual manner, and one boy remained on shore while the other two went on board to make the boat ready. Suddenly the old boat swung into the current and in an instant was making down stream, dragging the poor horse backward through the water in a decidedly lively manner. The boys saw at once there was no chance of stopping the boat and they hastily released the horse by cutting the rope. Then they hurried to lower the mast before they reached Enfield Bridge. They barely succeeded and shot under the bridge like an arrow. They passed the upper falls in safety, but when the boat lunged along to the lower falls it was caught by an eddy and sank in an instant. Young Barber and his comrade barely escaped with their lives. However, they did not give up the sunken boat, but when the flood subsided they worked like beavers to raise their craft and bring it to Springfield.

When Mr. Barber reached the age of twenty-two he gave up his boating life and went to live in Springfield, where he found work in the armory. This was in 1811, and the War with Great Britain loomed in the near future. Mr. Barber presently married and lived on what was then called Factory Road, from the fact of its leading to "Skipmuck," where the first cotton factories were built on the Chicopee River. Later, Mr. Barber bought a lot on Walnut Street and built a new house. The street at that time had a thick pine woods border, but otherwise was just a sandy road leading to the Watershops and some other trails.

Mrs. Barber often told of picking huckleberries on both sides of the street close to the house, and spoke of the time when only two houses were in sight, for the woods shut out all view of the little clump of buildings on the hill. Yet, curiously enough, the front windows of their house commanded a full view of the Connecticut River from the bend below the South End Bridge to a point near Thompsonville. Mr. Barber often sat by his front window and counted as many as six sailboats from Hartford laden with freight for Springfield and towns above.

Moses Beach, when a boy, was a fifer in the War of 1812, and served the garrison at New Haven Harbor. When he arrived at the age of fourteen he was an apprentice to a cabinetmaker at Hartford, but soon bought a release with money saved by investing his earnings in candles, and doing work on his own account in the evenings. He moved to Northampton in 1820, and in 1822 established a branch business in Springfield on Main Street. Mr. Beach's work was celebrated. He had the secret of veneering with mahogany, and his competitors could not do it nor find out how he did it. For a long time considerable of his fine cabinet work was to be found in the old residences of Springfield.

He was among the first to spend money establishing stern-wheel steamboating on the Connecticut River, between Springfield and Hartford, and devised a plan for taking a steamboat over the falls at Enfield. Mr. Beach invented a rag cutting machine to be used in paper mills, and patented it. This machine was used in all paper mills, and the Ames Company in Chicopee were constantly calling on Mr. Beach for improved devices.

In 1835 he removed to New York City, where he bought from his brother-in-law the New York "Daily Sun" for $40,000. It was then two years old and the first penny paper. From then on it was the main business of his life and to him it owed its early reputation. By his energy and enterprise he made a success for his newspaper, and a fortune for himself. In those days "pony express" was used, and his advice to his sons was "get the news always, and always get it first if you can." He, with Mr. Hallock, established "The Associated Press," and on his lines the great American News Company came into existence.

In 1846 he was sent by President Polk as a special agent to Mexico for the purpose of arranging a treaty of peace, and he was

THE OLD TOWN HOUSE, STATE STREET

eminently successful in negotiating a basis on which the war was finally ended. Sam Houston always declared that Texas owed much to the advocacy of Moses Beach.

In 1849 he retired from the management of the "Sun" and during the "gold fever" he equipped and sent a vessel to California which was a profitable venture. The next year he built a costly residence in his native town of Wallingford, Connecticut, where he spent the remainder of his life, leaving his home only once to spend a year in Europe for the benefit of his health. He had five sons and three daughters.

Springfield's most notable inventor was Thomas Blanchard, born at Sutton, Massachusetts, in 1788. When he was eighteen he showed much mechanical genius and was associated with his brother Stephen in the manufacture of tacks by hand. In 1806 he invented a machine whereby tacks could be made more perfect than the handmade, and he sold it for $5,000 to a company that made a business of their manufacture. Afterward he invented a machine for turning and finishing gun barrels by a single operation. This invention he extended to the turning of all kinds of irregular forms. It was one of the most remarkable inventions made in that century. While employed at the United States Armory he received nine cents from the government for each musket made by his machines, and this was his only pay during the first term of his patent originally granted in 1820. In 1831 he received a patent for an improved form of steamboat stern-wheel, which was used on the Connecticut River between Springfield and Hartford and on some of the western rivers.

He built the steamboat "Blanchard" and launched it in 1828; then followed the steamer "Vermont," built on a lot at a corner of Springfield's Main Street and launched in 1829. Other vessels he built were the steamer "Massachusetts" and the steamboat "Agawam."

He introduced many improvements in the construction of railroads and locomotives, and about 1826 he made a steam wagon, which was the first vehicle of the kind made in this country. It was brought to such perfection that it was pronounced a success and he patented it. It was exhibited on the Springfield streets and created the greatest excitement. The boiler held three gallons of water and the carriage weighed half a ton. A bevel-geared wheel running parallel with the carriage wheels was attached to the hind axle-tree. Pinion wheels plied into the cogs of this wheel and the engine had a two-inch cylinder.

In 1851 he devised a process for bending timber by steaming it to use for knees of vessels, arm-chairs, thills and handles of shovels. He constructed machines that would cut and fold envelopes at a single operation. Mr. Blanchard was awarded more than twenty-five patents for his inventions, and from some of them he received ample compensation.

A Springfield newspaper editorial notice that appeared in May, 1829, stated that:

> "The new steamboat 'Vermont,' built by our ingenious and enterprising townsman, Thomas Blanchard, was on Friday last carted from his shop through Main Street to the middle landing, and in the afternoon was launched into her destined element in gallant style, accompanied by an excellent band of music and the loud huzzas of a large concourse of spectators.
>
> "The 'Vermont' was a Falls boat of handsome model, 75 feet in length, 15 feet breadth of beam with a promenade deck that had two cabins forward, with the engine after and the wheel at the stern.
>
> "This is the first steamboat with engine complete ever built in this town, and is intended to ply in the river between Hartford and Bellows Falls."

One of the noteworthy deacons of his time was Moses Bliss. He graduated from Yale College in 1755, studied for the ministry, preached for a while and then retired from the profession, read law and became an eminent lawyer. He was a judge in the old county of Hampshire, a deacon in the First Church, and greatly respected for his learning and devotion to the church of which he was a member. One of his habits that made him conspicuous was his being one of the last of those who wore a cocked hat, powdered wig, knee breeches, low shoes and shining buckles.

Others of the same name helped to make the family an outstanding one. When Governor Caleb Strong, of Northampton, and the Legislature were looking over the field of western Massachusetts for the best men to represent this section at the important Hartford convention, George Bliss, of Springfield, was immediately selected. In August, 1814, when a British fleet was discovered off the New England coast, and a call for troops had immediately followed, General Jacob Bliss, of Springfield, started with the Old Hampshire Militia Brigade, and on his staff was Master George's son George, who served with the rank of captain. Governor Strong and Lawyer Bliss had often been pitted against each other in the courts, and both were stalwart Federalists. "Master George's" son, after returning from

Boston with the troops, took his father from Springfield down to Hartford in a chaise to the convention.

There he served on several important committees, and in a volume printed some years later, the secretary of the convention took occasion to refer to George Bliss as a lawyer of extensive learning and unshaken independence, both of principle and conduct, and he added, "no man ever passed through life with a fairer reputation for integrity or in a more entire possession of the confidence of the community in which he lived." Mr. Bliss' knowledge of the law was profound, and the zeal with which he conducted the studies of young men and engaged in examinations for their benefit, might easily have led to establishing a law school in Springfield if there had been a college to which it could be attached. He was considered a great oracle on all knotty questions.

George Bliss, in an account of his own life, says:

"I attended the district school kept by a female until I was eight years old, which was in 1801. Then I was transferred to the school kept by a man. Out of school I wandered about the streets, or engaged in play with every boy I could find. My father, when at home, was very rigid in his family government, controlling me more by fear than by affection, as was the habit in those days. Afterward I went to the district school, where my most serious recollections are of the master's ferule or rod, with which I made close acquaintance almost daily, yet I fail to recall that anyone at home inquired about my progress at school or aided in my instruction, except occasionally an examination into my ability to repeat the Assembly's catechism, which in those days was taught us by Reverend Bezaleel Howard."

George Bliss lived at a time when his profession, and society at large, was undergoing a change. He saw it and recognized its force, but he still lived in constant protest to many innovations. One of his griefs was having a favorite son join the Unitarian Church, and he looked with doubt at the number of young men admitted to the bar who were strangers to its traditions. Indeed, New England's revolutions in society from 1700 to 1776, or during George Bliss' lifetime (1764-1830), were more marked than anything we have witnessed since. Mr. Bliss had heard his father deliver a plea dressed in a gown, wig, silk stockings, and shining shoe buckles, and he lived to see his son confront an array of judges in a gray business suit.

George Bliss, the younger, aided in the support of the Unitarian Church; he gave the site of the city library, besides $10,000 in cash; and the Home for the Friendless and other local charities knew the extent of his substantial interest. He was president of the Springfield Cemetery, and active in organizations like the Hampden Park Association. His death at the advanced age of eighty was full of honors.

Joseph Carew, Junior, was born in Springfield in 1807. The early part of his life he worked in his father's tannery, which was near his residence at the corner of Main and Carew streets. He also worked near at hand on the Carew farm, and there was a two-year period when he attended the Monson Academy. Then, at the age of seventeen he entered the employ of a Springfield firm on Main Street, where he displayed such energy and thoroughness in the business that the next year he was promoted to the position of bookkeeper. Incidentally, he changed his home in the spring of 1825 to South Hadley Falls. His employers supplied the United States Government at Washington with paper, and as the firm deemed it necessary to be represented by some one at the capital, Mr. Carew was offered the position. He declined, but finally was induced to serve as a representative of the company. Thus it happened that he spent the winter at the capital, and had the good fortune to hear the debate in the Senate between Daniel Webster and Robert Y. Hayne, of South Carolina.

While in Washington Mr. Carew secured orders for paper from that veteran printer and publisher of the "Globe," Duff Green, and through him was introduced to many of the celebrated men of those times. In 1830 Mr. Carew went into the paper mill as clerk, and eventually was put in charge of the manufacturing. About 1845 he retired from the paper mill for a time and engaged in a general milling business and the grinding of grain and rock salt, the latter of which came from the island of Nantucket. It so happened that his former employers went bankrupt, and the mill passed into the hands of some New York men, who put Mr. Carew in charge of the property. He and others organized the Carew Manufacturing Company, which carried on with great success, and he and his family gradually acquired a controlling interest.

In 1852 the Carew Company was awarded the first premium by the World's Fair in New York. This was a great surprise to the English manufacturers, and caused a commission of Englishmen to visit the mills for the purpose of seeing the process of making paper by a machine that had triumphed over theirs made by hand.

Mr. Carew was generous in making public gifts, and among others he gave Amherst College the money for a scholarship, to which was added the condition that no one who used tobacco should receive its benefit, he being decidedly opposed to its use in any form, as well as to the drinking of intoxicating liquors. In May, 1881, Mr. Carew died in his seventy-fourth year.

His son Frank, who was treasurer of the Hadley Falls Paper Company, died in 1877, at the age of thirty-nine, from injuries caused by a frightened horse.

In many ways Chester W. Chapin was the leading citizen in the Springfield region. His birthplace was Ludlow and the date of his birth 1798. While still a boy his father moved with his family to Chicopee Street, but died soon afterward, leaving a farm for Chester and his brothers to carry on. He attended school at the Westfield Academy for some time, but when the foundations for the cotton mills were being prepared, he was employed by the superintendent at a dollar and a half a day. In 1822 he was collector of taxes, a service for which he was paid $80. About the year 1826 he bought an interest in the stage line from Brattleboro, Vermont, to Hartford, Connecticut, and the firm of Sargeant and Chapin soon became widely known as stage proprietors and large mail contractors. In 1831, when the first steamboats began to run between Springfield and Hartford, Mr. Chapin engaged in the steamboating business, and made his first venture by acquiring the property of Thomas Blanchard, the pioneer of the line. He soon was sole proprietor of the steamboats, and for fifteen years controlled the passenger traffic between Hartford and Springfield. Besides, he was the principal owner of the steamboat line between New York and New Haven, and had a large interest in the line from New York to Hartford.

In 1843 Mr. Chapin was one of the selectmen of the town and was often chosen moderator at the town meetings held in the old Town

Hall on State Street. He was early interested in the Hartford and New Haven Railroad, and was the principal mover in having the line extended to Springfield. When the extension was opened in 1844, he sold his steamboats running to Hartford and, in 1850, he was chosen president of the Connecticut River Railroad Company, and that same year a director of the Western Railroad, now the Boston and Albany. In January, 1854, he was elected president of the corporation, and soon after began the reconstruction of the road, which needed repair-

PARSONS' TAVERN, 1776

ing. The rails had become much worn, new bridges were essential, and new rolling stock was required for the increasing business of the road.

In May, 1855, the Legislature authorized the corporation to raise money by an issue of bonds, and within a short time Mr. Chapin went to London and negotiated a loan of a half million dollars, which was used to buy iron for renewing the track. He was an early advocate for a bridge across the Hudson at Albany, and a charter was obtained for one in 1856, but the erection was delayed for several years. Finally, however, with Chapin's accustomed energy and perseverance, and the aid of "Commodore" Vanderbilt, the bridge was built. From 1875 to 1877, Mr. Chapin was a representative in Congress from the Tenth Massachusetts District and served on the important Committee of Ways and Means.

One of his gifts locally was $50,000 to Amherst College. Another was $26,000 to the building fund of the Church of the Unity.

Lieutenant Elisha Chapin was born at West Springfield in 1774, and at the age of twenty-four we find him entering the service of the United States as a marine. He was then six feet and one inch in height, had dark eyes, dark hair and dark complexion. He sailed to the East Indies, where he remained most of the time in the vicinity of Sumatra, Java and adjacent islands for the protection of American commerce in that region. After about three years' service, he was honorably promoted and went home. There he married, and in the course of time he and his wife had a family of one son and six daughters.

In the War of 1812 he enlisted again and was put on recruiting service, but later joined the army at Sackett's Harbor, where he remained most of the time while in the service. At the close of the war he was ordered to report at Washington and received an honorable discharge. After the war, owing to ill health, he did not engage in active business. Instead, he spent his time in his garden and with his books. As a result he became very well informed in astronomy and botany.

Captain Erastus Chapin, son of Captain Ephraim Chapin, was born at Chicopee in 1783. While living in Willimansett, about 1820, he decided he would shift his home to Springfield, and in 1821 built the Hampden House, which was opened to the public in June, 1822, in accord with the following notice:

"Hampden Coffee House

"North side of Court Square, Springfield, Mass. The subscriber furnished the new and elegant brick house erected last season on the corner of Court Square for the reception of company. It is deemed by competent judges to be the most commodious building of the kind in the State, west of Boston, and its situation is peculiarly pleasant and attractive. Travelers and parties of business or pleasure will find every accommodation usual in such establishments and can at all times have access to a room regularly provided with the leading newspapers and journals in the United States. The choicest liquors will at all times be kept, and during the summer months a soda fountain will be attached to the establishment.

"Horses and carriages will be furnished at the shortest notice. The subscriber will be assiduous and devoted in his attention to all who may honor him with their company.

"ERASTUS CHAPIN."

Lieutenant John Dale was born in Springfield in 1813, and in due time he entered the naval service of the United States. He became a midshipman in February, 1829, and a lieutenant in 1845. Next he served on the United States brig "Porpoise," which sailed from Norfolk, Virginia, in 1838, in an exploring expedition under the command of Charles Wilkes, of the United States Navy sloop of war "Vincennes." This expedition was ordered by an Act of Congress "for the purpose of exploring and surveying the sea of the great Southern Ocean, and to determine the existence of all doubtful islands and shoals and accurately fix the position of those which lie in or near the track of our vessels interested in the whale fisheries and other commercial adventures in that sea." This expedition was completed and Lieutenant Dale served in another to the River Jordan and the Dead Sea, sailing in the United States storeship "Supply" from New York.

Lieutenant Dale died at a village near Beirut, Syria, at the age of thirty-five. He had been attacked by a disease of that country and became speedily worse. So in hope of being invigorated by the mountain air he rode about twelve miles up a mountain, arriving at the summit thoroughly exhausted, but he was much better the next day and then a sirocco set in that lasted three days and completely prostrated him. He became delirious and labored under a low, nervous fever, lingered a few days, and then gently expired. He was buried in the neighborhood of Beirut and his body laid beneath a Pride of India tree. Now he sleeps on the slopes of Mount Lebanon on the borders of the beautiful Mediterranean, which he had so long wished to visit

Frederick Dwight was born in Springfield in 1815. He graduated at Harvard College in 1834 and was in the law school for two years. After that came the study of medicine, but he never practiced it. His means were ample, and as he had a desire for travel, he went to California, and thence to Australia, Japan, and China, living for some time in the Orient. He passed through nearly all the countries of Europe before returning to the United States in 1847.

A few years after the Black Hawk War, Mr. Dwight went to the Rock River Valley and was so pleased with the country he bought a tract of land in Prophetstown, Illinois, and on it built a two-story dwelling and large barn, which in those days was considered an expensive outlay. Prophetstown is situated on a high bluff of Rock River, and is about one hundred and forty miles west of Chicago.

Mr. Dwight was one of the few survivors of the terrible explosion of the steamboat "Moselle" on the Ohio River near Cincinnati, who escaped unharmed. He was a member of Frémont's second expedition which set out to cross the Rocky Mountains in 1843. The party numbered thirty-six white men, one colored man and two Delaware Indians. They traveled 3,500 miles in eight months, and the journey was accomplished through much privation, danger and suffering. During the expedition no word had come back to the East, and there were doubts of their safe return. After many years' absence from his native town, Mr. Dwight returned, and in 1853 bought a farm in Agawam, on the bluff overlooking the Agawam River, where he quietly spent the remainder of his life.

It is related that when he wanted to make his European trip he asked his father for money to meet the necessary expense, which the old gentleman declined. Frederick went, nevertheless, and when he was in need he drew on his father who paid the drafts.

Captain Henry Dwight was born in 1796. Early in life he followed the sea and afterward he engaged in mercantile business. In 1829 he came to Springfield and opened a grocery store under the old Town Hall at the corner of State and Market streets. For a while he was interested in a distillery at the south part of the town. Later he retired and went to New Bedford where, by aid of family connections, he bought an interest in a whaling vessel and sailed in it as master. After an absence of about two years he made the homeward voyage, with a fair cargo of oil and whalebone. He died in West Springfield in his fifty-second year.

James Sanford Dwight was born in 1799. He entered Harvard College, where he remained two years, and then retired from his studies on account of poor health. When he recovered he presently became his father's successor to a large and lucrative business, with branches in various towns up and down the valley. These branch stores were managed by young men who had been clerks in the Dwight store at the corner of Main and State streets. The business was started by Josiah Dwight, and mostly continued by other members of the Dwight clan. They filled their stores with goods of their own importation and kept a line of sloops and boats plying between Springfield, Hartford and New York, and were members of a transportation line to Hartford. James Sanford Dwight went abroad in the latter part of 1830. It was a pleasure trip, but at Florence, Italy, he was seized with malarial fever and died at the early age of thirty-one years.

Jonathan Dwight, son of Captain Edmund Dwight, was born in Boston in 1743. At the age of ten he came to Springfield and soon entered business with his cousin, Colonel Josiah Dwight, first as clerk, and then as partner, with a store on the corner of Main and State streets. He took great interest in the formation of the Unitarian Society and built the church edifice at the cost of $20,000. Mr. Dwight was almost the last representative of the silk stockings, short breeches, and silver shoe buckle gentry, of small stature, active habits, and a great smoker, lighting his pipe in summer with a burning glass, and often crossing the street from his house to the store in such a cloud of smoke as hardly to be discerned.

Springfield's last survivor of the Revolution died in April, 1857. He was familiarly known to the children as "Grandpa Edwards." He had long been a feature in Fourth of July processions, riding in a carriage and returning salutations. His funeral was made an occasion of military display with martial music, and the City guards wore blue frock coats and looked very formidable in their bear skin hats. The Horse Guards were gay in red coats and white trousers, while at the same time they appeared dangerous, for they carried sabers and had pistol holders on each side of the saddle.

Captain Robert Emery was born in Newburyport in 1773. In his early manhood he resided in Salem and followed the seas. He was master at various times of vessels engaged in the East India trade, but retired from maritime life while still youthful and moved to Springfield. He married for a second wife, Mary Lyman, who died, aged forty years, and from her he inherited the estate she had received from her father. That continued to be known as the "Emery farm," and consisted of about one hundred and thirty acres, later covered by the Boston and Albany Railroad and various streets and adjacent lands. Captain Emery was known as a gentleman farmer. The cultivated portion of his estate produced large crops of hay, grain and fruits, and during the summer pasturage was had for cows, the owners of which, on payment of ten dollars, could turn them in for the season.

Thaddeus Ferry, a soldier of the Revolution, was born in Springfield in 1777. When sixteen years old he volunteered for six months under Captain Gideon Burt, of Longmeadow, as a fifer, and was stationed in Springfield for garrison duty and the guarding of public property. In May, 1778, he enlisted as a fifer for eight months, marched to Fishkill, New York, and joined his regiment at White Plains.

Then he was detailed in scouting parties and in foraging or guarding the transfer of provisions, until ordered to Danbury, Connecticut, which was an important depot of military supplies. In that vicinity he remained a number of weeks, finally leaving for Peekskill, where he was discharged. From the spring of 1779 he was three months a guard to the public property in Springfield, and then he served three months under Captain Keep, of Monson. Late in the fall of 1779 we find him aiding Captain John Carpenter as guard in Springfield, and he experienced the extraordinarily cold winter of 1779-80 while on duty. Later, when Ferry had volunteered for six months and marched to West Point, he was ordered down the Hudson, and while at Haverstraw the treason of Arnold occurred, and at Tarrytown Major André was executed as a spy.

Mr. Ferry was outstanding as a fifer, and his reputation as such was so high that when Baron Steuben called for volunteers in a special service, and Ferry had offered himself, a field officer of the regiment objected to having the best fifer in the service taken. He died in

January, 1847, and on his headstone in the Peabody Cemetery at Springfield is the following inscription:

"Our aged sire now sleeps in dust,
    And from his grassy tomb
A warning voice speaks to us,
    Prepare to meet thy doom."

John Goodrich was born in West Springfield in 1802, and on reaching mature years he went into the livery business on State Street about opposite "the old Gaol." In 1839 he opened a tavern on Main Street in the gambrel roof house which stood where Hampden Street now is. After he had kept the house as a hotel about two years it was moved to the east side of Main Street, and he opened Hampden Street to Water Street, now named Columbus Avenue.

Mr. Goodrich was well known as a successful trainer of horses for speed and endurance. In the spring of 1831, he, with three others, bought for sixty dollars each, the famous trotter, "Ned Forrest," and kept him until the spring of 1833, when, after beating all the horses in this region at scrub races, he trotted with the noted "Sally Miller" and made his mile in 2.31½, which was a very remarkable performance at that time.

Chester Harding, widely famed as an artist, was born in Conway in 1792. At the age of twelve he hired out to a Hatfield farmer at six dollars a month and lived with him two years. He went to school in the winter and learned enough to read the Bible. When he was fourteen the family migrated to Madison County in York State, and at nineteen he worked one winter with his brother, who was a chairmaker. When war was declared between the United States and Great Britain in 1812, his brother enlisted in the service for one year. After six months he returned home and Chester offered himself as a substitute and was accepted by filling the position as a drummer. About the close of the war he married Caroline Woodruff, a woman of much amiability of character. Then for a time he engaged in tavern keeping, and after that tried his fortune in the then "Far West" by going to Pittsburgh, where he took up the art of sign painting. While thus engaged he met a portrait painter named Nelson, in whose studio he caught the idea of painting heads. His first effort was the portrait of an Englishman, for which he received five dollars. Afterward he went to Paris, Kentucky, and in six months he had painted one hundred portraits at twenty-five dollars each. He spent two months in Philadelphia, devoting his time to drawing in the academy and studying the best pictures.

After returning to Kentucky he decided to try new fields and went to Cincinnati, but met with no success until he moved on to Saint Louis. There Governor Clark assisted him in securing a studio and then offered himself as a sitter. For fifteen months Mr. Harding was engaged at his work. One of his portraits was of Daniel Boone at the age of ninety years. When he came East it was with his family to western New York, where his parents were living. Thence he went to Washington and spent six months, and he painted many portraits in Pittsfield, Northampton and Springfield. On August 1, 1823, he sailed from New York for Liverpool and was absent from the United States three years. On his return he stayed a while in Boston and afterward moved to Springfield, where he lived in the Trask mansion on State Street. Later, he made a second visit to England and spent nine months there with profit and pleasure. As a portrait painter he was one of the first in excellence that America produced. Many of the old families of Boston have choice specimens of his skill, and many of our public men were painted by him. Among these were Presidents Madison, Monroe and John Quincy Adams. Mr. Harding was an intimate friend of Daniel Webster and painted many portraits of him, which are among the best.

Reverend Bezaleel Howard was born in November, 1753. He was a graduate of Harvard College, who came from there to Springfield on horseback in November, 1784, and rode up to the Five-mile House, then kept as a tavern. He learned the distance into town, and was further informed there was a good bridle path with marked trees through the woods, but he still felt anxious because he had heard something about a robbery in the vicinity, and he hurried rapidly to the hill. The day had been chilly and now a cold night was at hand. Peace had been declared with Great Britain a year previous, but the few dwellings in the town had a dilapidated and forlorn appearance, and the loosened clapboards were flapping in such a dismal manner that the young minister, in spite of being a Harvard graduate, began to feel terribly homesick. He reined up at the only white house, rapped at the door, and soon found himself in the presence of the owner of the house, Jonathan Dwight. He stated that he had been engaged to preach for six weeks, meanwhile feeling conscious that he wished the time was over, so he could get back to the civilization he had left behind. Mr. Dwight encouraged him by saying he had come to the right place and should stop with him over Sunday. At the end of six weeks he received a unanimous call to settle, and as a mutual interest had sprung up between him and Mr. Dwight's daughter, Lucinda, he chose to remain and was ordained pastor of the First Church, in 1785. There he remained until 1803, when he resigned on account of failing health. He died in January, 1837, after reaching his eighty-fourth year.

COCK ON OLD FIRST CHURCH, COURT SQUARE,

Used as a Weather Vane, a Symbol of Vigilance. Brought from England 150 Years Ago; 4 Feet Tail to Beak, Weight 41 Pounds

Major Edward Ingersoll was born in Westfield in 1812, and his father moved to Springfield when Edward was a boy. His first employment was as a Main Street clerk. In 1830, at the age of eighteen, he went to Michigan and with an associate established a trade with pioneer settlers. Later, he returned East, and was employed for a time in a Northampton dry goods store. In 1837 we find him in Savannah, Georgia, where he formed a partnership with his brother, John, in the dry goods trade. There he remained about two years and then returned to Springfield and became connected with the armory. A notable soldiers' fair was held in 1864 in the City Hall and realized nearly $25,000 for the "Soldiers' Rest." Major Ingersoll was the leading spirit and gave his time without stint to its formation, and the success of the fair was largely attributed to his unwearied attention and counsel and his executive ability.

He took great interest in the Moody and Sankey meetings held in the City Hall during 1878, and did much to promote their usefulness. He was a zealous prohibitionist and should be credited with the success he made in breaking up the custom of the armorers in pledging their wages to saloonkeepers. An effort was made to transfer him to another post, but failed. He went to Washington and had an interview with the Secretary of War, who asked if the charges against him were true. Major Ingersoll replied they were. "Then," said the Secretary sternly, "go back to your work. You are just the man I want in that place." Major Ingersoll possessed sterling qualities and great sincerity of purpose in the performance of his duties. He was a conscientious Christian gentleman, believing in example as a test of profession.

Colonel Roswell Lee came to Springfield in 1815 and was appointed Superintendent of the United States Armory. When he attempted to correct certain abuses allowed by his predecessors, and forbade having intoxicating liquors brought into the shops, the workmen were not disposed to have their liberties curtailed and, in taking such a step, a rebellion was raised. Colonel Lee, going into one of the shops in March, 1816, found two men wrestling in the middle of the room while the rest of the men stood around. He promptly discharged the two offenders and, as was the custom, they got some rum and invited all hands out to the "liberty pole" in the center of the grounds to drink. There the men resolved that if they couldn't have any liberty, they wouldn't have any "liberty pole" and went to work to cut it down. Colonel Lee sent out his clerk to remonstrate, but they paid no attention, and then the master armorer went out for the same purpose. He was told by one man, swinging an ax, to look out for his legs, for he couldn't tell where the ax would strike next.

Finally the colonel himself went out, and by threatening prosecution before the United States Court, with some concession in the way of explanation, they desisted. Colonel Lee admitted afterward that he was hasty in the matter though, on the whole, he thought it resulted in good to all concerned.

Daniel Lombard, quartermaster and postmaster, was born in 1764. Shays' Rebellion came to an issue in his time, and he was active on the side of the government in quelling the insurrection. It was while Thomas Jefferson was in office that Lombard was appointed postmaster of Springfield and he held the office until June, 1829.

Mr. Lombard kept a store and had the post office in a wooden building which stood on the corner of Main and Elm streets. He became largely interested in the turnpike corporations of western Massachusetts, and was the owner of one turnpike that had its toll gate in Wilbraham. The pike extended eastward to Palmer and was known as the "Lombard Turnpike." It was finally bought by the Western Railroad, now the Boston and Albany.

Mr. Lombard married Sylvia Burt, of Longmeadow, who died at the age of eighty-six years, and he died at the age of ninety-two. They had lived a married life of sixty-eight years—a remarkable duration. Their children were three sons and six daughters.

Charles Merriam, son of Dan and Thirza Merriam, of West Brookfield, was born in that town in 1806. He became an apprentice in a printing office in Hartford, but in 1820 returned to West Brookfield and worked for his uncle and brother, who were in partnership.

He attended school at Monson Academy and at Hadley taught school for a short time. Then he worked at printing in Philadelphia and Boston. In 1831 he came to Springfield, and in company with his brother George, started a printing office and book store in a building on State Street.

In 1832 the firm of G. and C. Merriam began its business career. The great amount of labor attending the revision of Webster's Dictionary in 1864, in which he read every word of proof, had greatly impaired his health, but he continued in business until 1877 and then, after forty-five years of service in the firm, he retired. Mr. Merriam was noted for his liberal charities. He gave $5,000 for the erection of the library building and often made donations of money to buy books, and many other gifts came from him. At the South Church he taught a large Bible class of young men, who afterward ranked among the city's most valued population.

Deacon George Merriam, oldest son of Dan and Thirza, was born in Worcester in 1803. His father owned a farm in West Brookfield and in connection with his brother Ebenezer carried on a small printing business. George worked on the farm until he was fifteen years old and then went into the country store of the town as clerk.

After three months of service there he told his father he did not like the business. So he was put as an apprentice into the printing office of which his Uncle Ebenezer had charge, while his father carried on the farm. George became so efficient in the office that at the age of twenty his father offered to give him the rest of his time until he was twenty-one, but he declined, saying: "Time enough to be my own master when I *am* twenty-one." Before the son became of age the father died, leaving a widow, four sons and three daughters, and weighty responsibilities fell on him.

In August, 1831, he came to Springfield and went into business with his brother Charles under the firm name of G. and C. Merriam. They first located on State Street as retail book sellers and printers, but removed in 1835 to the corner of Main and State streets.

In 1847 they bought the plates and copyrights of Noah Webster's large dictionary, which had not then gained a strong hold on the public. The Merriams, however, put new life into the work and by their energy, Webster's Dictionary has won rare standing and appreciation in the civilized world. The firm were publishers of a famous spelling book of which millions have been sold. Homer Merriam, a younger brother, was admitted to the firm in 1856. Mr. Merriam was a generous giver to schools and colleges, but most unusual was his gift to the Confederate home at Charleston, South Carolina. It was established in November, 1867, "for the care of widows and orphans of Confederate soldiers." He gave $2,000 and equipped it with a library and furniture.

Judge Oliver Morris holds a distinct place in local annals as lawyer, citizen and lover of Springfield village. He sometimes remarked, "In my youth I saw an aged man who remembered seeing persons who came over in the 'Mayflower.'" And the judge was quite as proud of this as if he had led a victorious army to battle.

He knew everybody and everybody knew him. All the ways of rural New England life were pleasing to him; he enjoyed its shady walks, its humble thrift, its simple democracy, its deference to the village fathers, its solemn Sabbaths, and its old nine o'clock bell. However, such satisfaction as Judge Morris felt for his own local prominence was not simply a personal pride. It came to him by the study of local history. He thought much of the past and delighted in talking of the Springfield plantation to reproduce the pioneer scenes when every yeoman was a defender of the gospel, a tiller of the soil, and at times a fighter of Indians.

Morris never wanted to live to see the time when the town meeting would adjourn forever; when the stages would be taken from the old turnpikes and the town brook buried in the Main Street sewer. But he did, and he lived also to be the oldest inhabitant and to see the city wards spring up where once were open fields. "I do not like to see so many strangers," he once remarked to a minister here, "I used to know every voter." This lament was not the result of a natural desire to oppose progress, but a deep affection for the quiet, quaint, old days of Springfield. He had been looked on for nearly two generations as the antiquarian of Springfield. He was familiar with more genealogies than anyone else, could give more facts about old buildings, historic spots, traditions, stories, anecdotes and lore of the place. Law was his profession, but Springfield village was his life.

When distinguished men visited Springfield, the judge was quite apt to be selected to give the speech of welcome. He introduced John Quincy Adams to the people in the First Church, and he welcomed Henry Clay at the ovation given him in the old Town Hall.

It has been related by a citizen who was a schoolboy when the Adams reception took place, that Morris had several times begun public addresses by saying, "When I look about me and behold the sea of upturned faces," and so on. This lingo with more of the same sort the boys memorized, and when the eloquent judge rose to introduce John Quincy Adams and had gotten as far as "When I look about," the boys shouted in chorus the familiar words, "and behold the sea of upturned faces."

When age began to tell its story of lessening powers and ambition, the venerable judge was in the habit of dropping in at the "Old Corner Bookstore," where he chatted and argued with both old and young. One of his Sunday school scholars entered the bookstore and found the judge discoursing on old-fashioned morals. The Sunday school scholar was encouraged to dispute with the judge about the degeneracy that so distressed him and he asked: "Do you remember the ordination of Reverend Dr. Osgood?" And the judge said: "I do." "And do you remember whether there were any refreshments?" "Yes, a feast and a ball also." "Do you remember where you were, judge, after the ordination?" The judge was greatly taken aback, for he did not know it was common talk that he with three other church members repaired to a chamber over Elijah Blake's shop and played euchre—and it was not a dry game either.

One of the later ministers, destined to be long remembered, was Samuel Osgood, commonly known as Dr. Osgood. He was born at Fryeburg, Maine, in 1784, and completed his studies preparatory to entering college under the instruction of Daniel Webster. In after years, whenever Webster was in Springfield on the Sabbath, he was accustomed to attend the old church on Court Street and listen to the preaching of his former pupil and lifelong friend.

Dr. Osgood graduated at Dartmouth in 1805, and he preached his second sermon in Quincy, where he had for hearers Ex-President John Adams and his son, who afterward was President John Quincy Adams.

Mr. Osgood's ministry began under very auspicious circumstances. He was in the vigor of youthful manhood, with a constitution that gave promise of uniform health, a promise that was remarkably fulfilled for more than half a century of his after life. His parish included the population of the town from Chicopee River on the north to Longmeadow on the south, and from Wilbraham line on the east to the Connecticut River, and it included over 2,000 persons.

Many of the ministers and churches in this Commonwealth at the time of Mr. Osgood's settlement were drifting away from Trinitarian orthodoxy toward Unitarian views. Mr. Osgood, although adhering in the main to the Trinitarian doctrine, was at first regarded in his own fold as too liberal, but as time went on, and the breach between the two faiths widened, he had no hesitation in ranging himself with those who adhered to the tenets of John Calvin. In fact, he was one of the first ministers in this region who refused ministerial exchanges with the disciples of a laxer faith. It was a measure which at once alienated him from many who had been his warm friends, and brought him into collision with much of the wealth and influence of his church and parish. The storm had been gathering for some time, and now about twenty-five members, including "some of the most respectable and influential," prepared to form a separate church. The result was a secession, formidable, not in numbers, but in the standing and influence of those concerned. However, the era of ill-feeling gradually passed away and forbearance and courtesy eventually characterized the intercourse of the two parties.

Dr. Osgood died in 1862, and it is rare that the death of a minister, or any other citizen, leaves so wide a gap in a community. He always was prompt to lend a helping hand to the suffering poor, and his hospitality was unstinted, though often severely taxed. The position he occupied as minister of the first parish of the largest town in western Massachusetts, at the confluence of travel from every quarter of the compass, made his house preëminently a ministers' tavern. He was a genial man, fond of conversation, and ready to take an active part in it, and he had an immense fund of anecdotes with which he interested and amused those in whose company he chanced to be. He enjoyed a most robust health, and in reviewing his ministry at the end of forty years, he claimed that he never had been detained from his

THE OLD SPRINGFIELD DEPOT

pulpit a single Sabbath on account of sickness. It was said of him in his prime that he was the most athletic man in Springfield. The sermons that he wrote numbered more than two thousand. The old inhabitants treasured many stories of his wit and sound sense. He was brave, original, clear-headed and earnest, and he had a love of humanity and picturesque methods of oratory. Men remembered his wit, but better than that was his sterling worth.

Dr. Osgood once, while in the pulpit, struck at a horn bug and hit the lamp, which fell to the floor. He coolly waited until it was picked up unbroken and said: "Good glass! Let us pray."

While preaching one day he suddenly asked: "Who's asleep?" It was suggested that the noise was not snoring, but came from the ducks under the building, and he went on. Again he stopped, saying: "Some one is alseep." But profound silence reigned and the sermon went on. A third time he stopped and asked: "Will somebody rouse that young man in the gallery?" The young man was roused and proved to be the minister's own son.

When the old Universalist Church on State Street was being built, Dr. Osgood accosted Mr. Trask with: "Well, Brother Trask, what are you building here?" Mr. Trask replied: "A house where the truth will be preached." "If it is," was the response, "there will be a scattering among the Universalists."

Mr. Bacon asked: "Why is it, Mr. Osgood, that they call the head of a hog a minister's face?" The doctor did not relish the slur on his profession and said: "I don't know. Perhaps for the same reason they call the other end the bacon."

A worthy gentleman who used to be the terror of the boys at Dr. Osgood's church was Elijah Blake. Another was William Hatfield, a constable of the town, who sometimes took care of the boys that made fun at the church. Once when a missionary spirit was prevailing in Springfield everyone was very much interested in the mission of Mr. Armstrong at the Hawaiian Islands. The Sunday school frequently made contributions for his and other missions, but Mr. Armstrong's mission received more than any other, for he was known, and he sometimes sent curiosities to the Sunday school scholars of George Merriam. A contribution was to be taken up one Sunday afternoon for this mission and the Saturday evening before, the boys met, as was their habit, in front of a well-known store which did considerable business with Mr. Cooley, who made soap and candles. The agreement between the firm and Mr. Cooley was that they should take their pay in pennies and, as a result, they had under their counter a large dry goods case almost filled with pennies—big old-fashioned cents. That evening the boys changed their ninepences and quarters into cents at the store. The next Sunday afternoon they all sat in the old square pew, at the corner of the gallery, and in due time Constable Hatfield rose to begin taking up the contribution. He wore an old-fashioned white wool hat, one of the kind that you can blow on and make windrows, and one that had been worn long enough to have the edges somewhat tender. He went first down to Charley Childs' pew, which was in the front row, and took his contribution, and then he came up to the pew where the boys were and they began to unload their pennies into the hat. They chucked them in with considerable force, and after the contribution from that pew had been taken up, the constable went down the aisle to take up other contributions farther on. As he went along the top of the hat opened and the pennies began to drop out, and soon the hole became so large that down went all the pennies on the floor with a tremendous crash. Dr. Osgood spoke and said: "If Mr. Hatfield will wait where he is now standing I will pronounce the benediction." The benediction was pronounced and then the question arose among the boys as to how they were to get out. They could not jump from a window, and they waited and waited to help pick up the pennies. By and by they made a dash for the door, but the constable was ahead of them on one side and Blake on the other, and before they could pass either of them their ears had a fine twisting and some of them, after they arrived home, wished that their trousers had been reinforced.

One of the Pynchons long remembered was John as he appeared on the streets with cocked hat and small clothes. The boys were his friends, and they used to ride his horse without needing to ask permission when it was turned out to pasture. John was the brother of Major William. He lived on the other side of the street and died at the age of eighty-four.

Harvey Sanderson, merchant, was born in Springfield in 1797 and was apprenticed to Jonas Coolidge to learn the hatter's trade. Afterward he went to Newark, New Jersey, where he worked as a journeyman hatter for some time and then returned to Springfield. In 1824 he was taken into partnership by Mr. Coolidge and engaged in the hat and fur business. The shop for the manufacture of hats was in a wooden building on Main Street, and at that time Garden Brook was open to Worthington Street.

Mr. Coolidge was often seen washing sheep skins in the brook in front of his shop. He made a dam by putting a wide board across the brook to collect the water, and then by fastening the skins to a hook at the end of a long stick he would throw them into the water and souse them around until cleansed.

Calvin Shattuck was born in Hawley in 1790 and reared in Charlemont. He came to Springfield at the age of twenty-two years, and in 1814 he went into the United States service at the armory, where he continued for nearly thirty years. Afterward he engaged in farming and carried on a livery business. Besides, he went into the mulberry and silk culture about 1838 and was successful. At one time he fed 300,000 silk worms, said to be the largest number anyone ever had in the State. He was one of the original owners of the Hampden Brewery located on Myrtle Street, and through his interest he persuaded his partners to give up the business.

Zebina Stebbins, born in 1755, was a merchant with a store on Main Street, where he sold dry goods, drugs, medicines and various other wares. He lived on the northwest corner of that street and Ferry Lane, now Cypress Street. One of his enterprises was a cordage factory on the lane. This was a long, low building, which tumbled down in 1839.

Thomas Stebbins carried on the dyeing business and here is his advertisement:

"BLUE DYEING

"Zebina and Thomas Stebbins having commenced their blue dyeing, those who may wish either cotton or linen yarn dyed may have it done on the usual terms. Springfield, May 23, 1810."

A famous incident in the annals of Springfield has to do with Zebina Stebbins' horse. On Sunday the family used to ride to meeting in a one-horse shay and were prompt to start at the ringing of the bell. But one Sabbath they got ready to go as usual and then were long delayed. So serious was the occasion that they left the horse without hitching, and what did he do when the bell leisurely rang, but walk off with the empty shay to the meetinghouse, where he stopped for a few moments to let his imaginary passengers alight. Next he went to his familiar horse-shed and stayed until meeting was over. Then he backed out, made the usual stop at the meetinghouse door, went home to his master's house and returned to his yard. It was said in those days of whoever showed intelligence above his fellow-beings that he was as smart "as Zebina's horse."

William Ames for many years made two visits to the town annually, and so timed his visits that he came with the arrival of shad in the spring, and the celebration of Thanksgiving. Many persons are said to have continued doubtful as to the exact time of these events until the presence of Mr. Ames in town was known to be a certainty. Another character was Eleazer Williams, prince of innkeepers, and famed for his politeness to everyone, but specially to ladies. It was said of him that on one occasion when he came unexpectedly on a "setting" hen and perceiving her to be disturbed by his intrusion, he took off his hat gracefully, bowed respectfully, and speedily retired with the remark: "Don't rise, madam; don't, I pray you."

In October, 1844, Springfield was visited by a serious fire, which started at Main and Sanford streets. Five buildings were consumed. The fire spread because there was no water in the town brook. A mill owner had shut it off during the night to get water for the next day, and the fire gained a lively start before the gates were opened. Three or four small fires which followed led to the general belief that a fire-bug was at work.

It was said, in 1841, that ten years previous Cabotville had been "a wild spot, the habitation of frogs, quails, snipes, rabbits, and similar untamed life." Now, at the end of that period, there were six cotton mills, eighteen boarding houses for operatives, a forge and two machine shops, a cannon foundry, and several small mills. N. P. Ames came to Cabotville in 1834 and was one of the founders of its commercial prosperity. He was a dignified and generous man and he gave $5,000 to build a Congregational Church.

The concert of Jenny Lind in July, 1851, has been a treasured memory. Dr. Osgood's church was filled with music lovers, and Mr. Goldschmidt, whom she married shortly afterward, was her accompanist.

Chester W. Chapin, once the driver of an ox team, but in 1851 the wealthiest man in Springfield, was the president of the Connecticut River Railroad and had made the town a railroad center. An important industry was added when the Wason car works started in 1845.

Holyoke was incorporated as a town in 1850, and its factories attracted many new nationalities, which was bound to make some difficulties. As an example: On a June evening about nine o'clock an outbreak occurred between rival nationalities at Springfield, near the Hibernian, "a sort of rumhole below the depot." A riot developed, and from ten o'clock to twelve the church bells rang and a big crowd gathered. For an hour no carriage could pass along the street, nor could a foot passenger do so without serious danger. Finally, Sheriff Caleb Rice arrived on the scene and dispersed the mob.

The men at work on the canals at Ireland Depot, as Holyoke was then called, struck on New Year's Day, 1848, because their pay had been reduced from seventy-five and seventy-seven cents a day to seventy cents. For a week the works were at a standstill. Then a dozen men went to work at the reduced wages under protection of the company's engineer, Anderson, and Constable Theodore Farnham. The strikers, "armed with clubs and other weapons of Irish warfare," promptly attacked them, and the constable, while attempting to arrest some of the leaders, was knocked down and trampled on until nearly senseless. Mr. Anderson was struck with a rail and received a bad gash in the cheek. The windows of a temporary grocery were smashed, but the shanties were not torn down as had been threatened. At last one of the ringleaders was captured and sent to Northampton jail on a train that happened along opportunely. As soon as the news reached Northampton, Sheriff Wright, with twenty-five men of the militia company armed with muskets, hastened by special train to the scene of disturbance. They, however, found all quiet and returned at two o'clock in the morning. Early Tuesday, Sheriff Rice came from Springfield with a Catholic priest, who guaranteed there would be no trouble that day nor the next night. Promptly, on Wednesday, Sheriff Rice returned with a posse and made three arrests, and in the afternoon Sheriff Wright arrested another man at the depot.

In 1852, Kossuth, the famous Hungarian statesman and patriot, visited Springfield and there were fully five thousand people at the depot to welcome him. The constables had much trouble in clearing a passage to the Massasoit Hotel, on the balcony of which Kossuth presently appeared and made a short speech. Next day there was a public reception in Dr. Osgood's church. His name, as it appears in the registry book at the Massasoit is "L. Kossuth and Lady," and under the column of residence he wrote "Nowhere." Then followed the names of his six other companions, each accompanied by the word "Homeless." George Merriam and two members of his family gave Kossuth substantial aid.

Springfield used to have a flourishing organization known as "The Club," It met every alternate Monday night, and was a medium of discussing public topics among prominent citizens. Reuben Chapman, a United States Commissioner, is credited with the honor of having originated the club. He was John Brown's attorney there in the wool business and was always enthusiastic in his tributes to Brown's integrity and sense of justice. At a meeting of "The Club" during the troubles in the western border region, a member asked: "What is to be done with Kansas?" And Mr. Chapman said: "We will send on emigrants, and we will send rifles with them. I will furnish one gun." "And I another," said Samuel Bowles. "And I another," said Daniel Harris. "And I another," said the good Dr. Buckingham. Thus the offers went round the room.

Mr. Chamberlain, Chapman's law partner, hesitated for some reason, and Mr. Chapman said, with as much vigor as he ever displayed on any subject: "And I will give a second gun for the credit of the firm." The rifles were all duly furnished, taken apart, and sent in separate boxes and by various routes to Kansas.

When John Brown was finally in the hands of the law in Virginia, his first thought was of the cool, judicious Reuben Chapman, of Springfield, and he appealed to him for legal assistance in the following letter:

CHARLESTOWN, VIRGINIA, October 21, '59.

"Hon. Reuben Chapman, Springfield, Mass.

"DEAR SIR:—I am here a prisoner with several sabre cuts in my head and bayonet stabs in my body. My object in writing is to obtain able and faithful counsel for myself and fellow-prisoners, five in all, as we have the faith of Virginia pledged, through her governor and numerous other prominent citizens, to give us a fair trial. Unless we can obtain such counsel from outside the slave States, the facts in our case cannot come before the world nor can we have the benefit of such facts as might be considered mitigating in view of others at our trial.

"I have money in hand to the amount of $250, and personal property sufficient to pay a most liberal fee to yourself or to any suitable man who will undertake our defense, if I can have the benefit of said property. Can you or some other good man come imediately for the sake of the young men prisoners at least? My wounds are doing well.

"Very respectfully yours,

"JOHN BROWN."

Mr. Chapman was about starting on court business and could not go to Virginia, but he gave his imprisoned friend what advice he could by letter.

Judge Chapman called to order Springfield's first grand war rally, in April, 1861. He exclaimed with a vigor quite uncommon to him: "I believe in nothing but the unconditional surrender of the rebels. I would have that, or hang every man of them." The city government promptly voted $30,000 for volunteers. Springfield was an active place, and the whole community kept a sharp watch on government property. Strangers were seen prowling about the watershops, and a guard sent a bullet whistling by their ears. In June, 1861, Hampden Park was turned into a military camp, and there was the usual friction between the raw recruit and the mess room. One hundred volunteers mutined on account of inferior rations. On one June Sunday, Dr. Tiffany's Unitarian Church was filled with soldiery. Muskets were stacked in front of the pulpit and decorated with flowers. The building shook with the thunderous strains of the "Star Spangled Banner," and Dr. Tiffany's sermon was pitched on that same patriotic key. The matrons and sisters of the community were soon enlisted in the task of contributing to the comfort and convenience of the soldiers. It was a time for picking lint, knitting mittens, and furnishing extra clothing. The destruction of the Harper's Ferry Armory left the Springfield Arsenal the main resource of the government for a time, and it was turning out three thousand five hundred muskets each month, with some of the departments running the full twenty-four hours.

Four   Unusual   Citizens

CHAPTER XXI

Four Unusual Citizens

One of the most unusual characters connected with old-time Springfield was Johnny Appleseed, whose real name was Jonathan Chapman. The family, which was of Scotch ancestry, came to this country about 1710 and settled near Boston. One of the sons, Nathaniel, who later became the father of John, was apprenticed to a carpenter. Nathaniel's first wife was Elizabeth Simonds, and records show that "John" was born in Leominster on September 26, 1774. Tradition says that this event occurred on the eleventh of May, just when apple blossoms were the most beautiful, and that ever afterward John was happiest in apple blossom time.

John's gentle mother had one more child, which probably was born while the father was still serving in Captain Pollard's company of carpenters in New York State. She died in Leominster, July 18, 1776.

A letter is still in existence which Mrs. Chapman wrote to her husband just a few weeks before she died. It was written in Leominster and sent to him in New York State. In the letter Nathaniel's wife speaks of "our children," but the new baby did not long survive her. The letter is quite religious in tone and shows a rather beautiful personality in the writer. She hopes for grace to "patiently bear" her afflictions, but without complaining of her lot. She tells her husband of the health of their neighbors and friends and expresses a desire to be remembered in his prayers. She wishes him not to worry over her condition and states that she has as much money as she needs.

Nathaniel Chapman served some of his time as a soldier in Springfield and eventually brought Johnny there. The young carpenter was frugal and hardworking and in a little while married Lucy Cooley, the daughter of a neighbor. After their marriage they lived on her father's farm in Longmeadow and had five sons and five daughters.

Tradition again gives us the interesting tale that Nathaniel was able to send John to Harvard, where he graduated with honors, and that while there, or soon after, he became interested in the teachings of Swedenborg. The tale is completed with an account of how he was sent out as a missionary from the headquarters of that sect in Boston and so made his first trip to the Potomac.

Apparently Jonathan Chapman was something of a reader and was especially attracted by books of a religious character. The New Testament interested him particularly and in some manner he came in contact with Swedenborg's beliefs and ever afterward was a disciple and, in a limited way, a missionary. His sister, Perces, said of him, later, that he was never happier than when he was wandering in the woods or had animals about him.

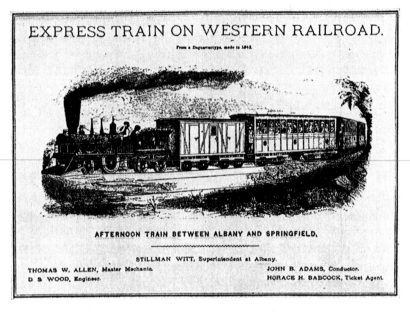

EXPRESS TRAIN ON WESTERN RAILROAD.

From a Daguerreotype, made in 1842.

AFTERNOON TRAIN BETWEEN ALBANY AND SPRINGFIELD.

STILLMAN WITT, Superintendent at Albany.

THOMAS W. ALLEN, Master Mechanic.   JOHN B. ADAMS, Conductor.
D. S. WOOD, Engineer.   HORACE H. BABCOCK, Ticket Agent.

The movement to the westward from the Connecticut Valley was already started when John Chapman was a young man, and his love for the open country, as well as the fullness of his father's house, furnished reason enough for his leaving home. The probability is that he planned to go up the Allegheny from Pittsburgh and visit an uncle near Olean, New York. It was a long and weary journey on foot over the mountains, the trail was hard to follow, and lodging was only to be had in settlers' houses, or rude taverns, and sometimes in the open. Pittsburgh seemed a barren place to John and he especially noticed its lack of fruit trees, for he had spent a number of previous summers caring for the large orchard of a man named Crawford in Springfield and had come to be fond of the work.

He bought a canoe in Pittsburgh and paddled up the river, but when he reached his uncle's cabin he found it deserted, and learned that the uncle had gone with his family to settle on lands near Marietta, Ohio. It was probably while at his uncle's deserted farm that the idea came to John Chapman of being an apple missionary instead of a religious one. The plan he developed was to go to cider presses in the fall and winter, wash out the apple seeds from the pomace, place them in bags for carrying about, and through the spring and summer plant them along the rivers and near the cabins wherever he could get permission. Bags were made of any materials at hand and twenty-five were filled the first winter. A small horse was bought to assist in transportation, tradition says, but he served John badly by kicking him in the head one day, with nearly fatal consequences. The first orchard of about half an acre was planted with a quart of apple seeds, and a brush fence built about it on the farm of Jesse Winrote, near the uncle's deserted cabin. This was the beginning of Johnny Appleseed's work in making the west blossom with fruit trees and it continued for fifty years.

Fifteen miles from the first planting, on a plot of land near Salamanca, the second quart of seeds was put in the ground, the prospective orchard roughly fenced, and a man agreed to take care of the trees as they grew if he could have some for his own use. By the time the seed-loaded canoe reached Pittsburgh a few more nurseries had been planted. At this place we can be pretty sure that John sent a letter to Sarah Crawford, daughter of his former employer, with whom John had fallen in love, but whose father did not approve of the suit. It may be that John's wanderings toward the West were started because the Crawfords had migrated to some unknown region and he had a hope of finding Sarah again.

For the next four years John Chapman worked around New York State, western Pennsylvania and eastern Ohio, planting his nurseries wherever he saw the need and supplying thousands of seedlings to farmers. He made friends all along the way and although often ragged and barefoot he was welcome everywhere. To children and animals he was especially kind. At night in the cabins where he stayed he would read earnestly from the New Testament and set forth the glories of the New Jerusalem.

In 1792 John Chapman built a four-room log cabin on land which he owned near Pittsburgh and there he had a flower garden, as well as a nursery of plums, cherries, peaches and his favorite apples. For a number of years this was his headquarters, but his longing to see his old home and his family finally led him to put his property in care of a neighbor, and start the long journey back to Springfield dressed in a new suit of buckskin.

Before long John Chapman returned to his lonely home and his orcharding and Bible reading. By this time some of his trees had grown to good size and he had many farmers handling them here and there, selling when possible, but giving them away in case of the needy. Some of his nurseries were so far away from his regular travels that he put up a sign saying: "Help yourself to the trees, but guard the fence."

When the region near Pittsburgh seemed pretty well covered, John Chapman sold his farm, and with more bags of apple seeds on his horse, set out armed with a hoe, hatchet and corn cutter for new regions. He was again ragged and barefooted, long-haired and bearded, and as he did not have any other convenient place to carry the pan he cooked his corn-meal mush in, he placed it on his head and started for Ohio.

There, in spite of his odd looks, he received a warm welcome on his travels and started his nurseries at convenient intervals. The fertile soil made him think of his father and finally the whole Chapman family was settled on a farm not far from Marietta. Johnny did not stay with them, but kept on with his work. Several anecdotes are told about his peculiar beliefs. Once when he had a smudge to discourage the mosquitoes that were swarming about, he noticed that they were perishing in the flames, so he put out the fire rather than destroy any of God's creatures. He was always careful not to put a stick on the fire if he thought there were any worms or ants in it, and once when a hornet crawled up his pant's leg he gently forced him downward, preferring to be stung rather than kill the insect. He was stoical about pain and when he had a bad bruise or snake bite would sear it with a hot iron. The Indians regarded him as a medicine man and never molested him.

All this time John Chapman carried the memory of Sarah Crawford with him and made inquiries as he went about, hoping to find the family, for Sarah was not uninterested in him. One story is that he finally located them below Louisville and made his appearance at their home dressed in a new suit and shoes and hat. They were in poorer circumstances than when he worked for them in Springfield and Mr. Crawford's attitude toward him was changed, so that a wedding was quickly arranged for the next day. But Sarah never was a bride, her wedding dress was her burial robe, and Johnny Appleseed once more went his lonely way.

This often took him among the Indians, whose language he learned and who treated him with respect. He was able to warn the settlers of approaching danger from the redskins and was a skilled woodsman and scout. One story about him tells how he ran barefoot and hatless through the night with only a coffee sack for covering, crying at the cabin doors: "Behold the tribes of the heathen are about your doors and a devouring flame followeth after them." At one time he went about wearing a woman's long Mother Hubbard gown. He usually had money which he received for his trees, but he gave it away to the needy as fast as it came to him.

Still he was far from being penniless at his death and it is estimated he left between five and ten thousand dollars' worth of property. He must have owned or leased hundreds of nurseries in the states of Ohio, Indiana, Illinois, Iowa, Pennsylvania, New York, Virginia, Michigan, and Missouri, which he traversed for over forty years. The latter part of John Chapman's life was spent largely in Indiana and for about fifteen years he made Fort Wayne his headquarters. His sister, Perces, lived near there and he had many friends in the region. His death came on March 11, 1847, at the home of William Worth, to which he had been carried after he was found exhausted in one of his young orchards, and friends buried him at the foot of a pine tree in the Archer cemetery.

When news of Johnny Appleseed's death reached Washington, General Sam Houston, of Texas, rose in his place on the floor of the Senate and said: "This old man was one of the most useful citizens of the world in his humble way. He has made a greater contribution to our civilization than we realize. He has left a place that can never be filled."

Several monuments have been erected to the memory of Johnny Appleseed in the region which he traversed. One of these is at Ashland, Ohio, and the Fort Wayne Johnny Appleseed Memorial Association of Indiana is creating a memorial park of one hundred and sixty-five acres located where the Saint Joe and Saint Mary rivers come together to form the Maumee River. The simple stone recently placed on John Chapman's grave bears the inscription: "He lived for others." An apple is carved above the lettering and an open Bible below.

Springfield is making a memorial to Johnny Appleseed in Stebbins Park and received six apple trees from the Fort Wayne Association to set out. So Johnny Appleseed's good works return to bear fruit in the valley where they originated.

Springfield was still a town when the rumblings of the slavery issue began to disturb the national peace and, situated as it was on a highway to Canada, it was inevitable that it should be a station on the underground railroad. The traveling was done at night for secrecy and the stations were the homes of the friends of freedom. The most active station seems to have been the home of Samuel Osgood, minister of the old meetinghouse. It was on Main Street, just below Howard Street. When a runaway came before daylight, he was given a breakfast and put to bed in a little back room which the minister called "the prophet's chamber." At night, the man seeking freedom resumed his journey. In one year as many as fifty slaves were sheltered by the minister.

But the most notable of Springfield's anti-slavery citizens was none other than John Brown, who, however, at that time was not famous.

On Franklin Street, a few doors from North Main, stood a plain, substantial, two-story house as late as 1900. It was painted white and had a veranda across the front, supported by four heavy pillars. As a matter of boards and timbers the house was not marked among its fellows, but here lived for some years one of the world's heroes— John Brown—and to those who have been stirred by the story of Brown's brave, self-sacrificing life, the house was approached with a certain feeling of veneration.

Just across from where the post office used to be on Worthington Street was a little restaurant. Within the door one found a small room with two or three counters at the sides and a variety of shelves and cupboards along the walls, and in the open floor space were a few

JOHN BROWN

chairs and a table. Other rooms half curtained off opened back at the rear. There the hungry were served, but the front room was a place to sit and talk, and if the individual's taste ran that way, to smoke and chew and sip the small beer the place afforded. One afternoon I called at the restaurant and became acquainted with its proprietor,

Thomas Thomas, one of the more elderly of Springfield's colored men. As he sat in his arm chair and between whiles read his newspaper, or served the occasional customers who dropped in, I questioned him as to his knowledge of John Brown, with whom he was connected when Brown lived in the city. His replies are contained in the following:

Brown was the agent of the "Association of Wool Growers." It was like this: The manufacturers of woolen goods used to buy the wool in bulk of the farmers, without any sorting. The farmer couldn't judge exactly as to its quality, and the manufacturer always managed to get it at ten or fifteen cents a pound less than it was really worth. After a while the farmers found out that if they had the wool sorted they could get a higher and fairer price. Then they went to work and formed this association and chose John Brown as the fittest man to oversee the sorting and disposing of the goods. Headquarters were established in Springfield and all the vacant lofts in town were hired for storing places. There was millions of pounds of wool sent here. There'd be enough in town at one time to make a pile bigger than our new post office. Brown had the wool sent him here from all over, and he sold it on commission of two per cent. They sorted the wool into seven grades. The coarsest and poorest sold for twenty-seven cents a pound and the finest for eighty-five. I worked in the sorting rooms all the time John Brown was here. He came in 1847 and stayed two years and a half. They say Brown was no business man, but I never see a better. His only fault was that he didn't succeed. George Washington himself would have been thought a poor stick if he hadn't succeeded. That's the way people have of measuring character and ability. But the only true way is to know the man and know what he had to fight against. Brown was a vigorous, pushing man, and he had good sense and he attended to his business, but he was crushed out by the manufacturers. He was preventing their making that ten or fifteen cents extra on a pound, and they went to work and squelched him.

When he was here he was smooth-faced and had black, heavy hair brushed straight up from his forehead. He always dressed in plain browns, something like a Quaker. He wasn't tall, nor anything of a giant, as some represent, and he wasn't at all fierce or crazy looking.

He was medium in height and he was quiet and agreeable to talk with. He was a gentleman and a Christian.

I met his son on the street the year before his father came. He had just got into town and he asked if there was a colored church here. I took him around to it and he came to my house and spent the evening with me. We had a long talk over the slavery question and he told me the plans of the wool association and engaged me to help in it.

There were quite a good many colored people in Springfield, and most of them had been slaves who'd taken French leave of their masters. I've been a slave myself. That is, there were those said they had a claim on me. I never acknowledged this though, and I never have bowed to but one master, Him, God. But we were in no danger here. Runaways were all the time going through to Canada, mostly stopping with us colored people. They went about openly enough usually, but once in a while there'd be a timid one, or one would fancy he'd seen his master on the street. Then they'd keep dark. But after the fugitive slave law was passed, and some men were carried back from Boston, we all got pretty well scared and a good many went off to Canada. After a few years most of them came back. There was intense excitement here over the slavery question and we had the greatest speakers there were in the country at different times. Sometimes they wouldn't let the Abolitionists have a hall, and then they'd come to the colored church and speak. They were stirring times. The whole town would come out to the meetings and the largest hall in the place wouldn't hold the crowds.

John Brown attended the colored church. He was a Presbyterian and had been educated for a minister. He often spoke in the evening meetings. He was a very earnest speaker, but he traveled a great deal and whenever there was an Abolitionist meeting anywhere near his stopping place he was sure to be there. And when he was there he couldn't keep still.

Brown had a large family and there were five boys and three girls here in Springfield. Some of the boys worked in the wool and the younger children went to school. You'd see the boys some cold Saturday night in winter carrying things to some poor family. One would have a handful of flowers and another would have a basket of food. Brown always looked after those that were in want. He often would send around coal or a barrel of flour to some one he knew was suffering, but he made no show of it and there was no name went with it. The family gave me a chair that I've got now down at my house. I've got besides a lock of John Brown's hair that his wife cut from his head and sent to me after he was hung at Harper's Ferry.

Yes, John Brown was a big-hearted man. There was nothing about him that was wrong. He was the honestest and truest man I ever knew.

Among the earliest and most influential of Springfield's settlers was Deacon Samuel Chapin. He came from England with his family in 1642, and after serving as magistrate and other important offices, died here in 1675. The bronze statue on the library grounds, representing a Puritan settler of New England, was erected as his memorial. Saint Gaudens was the sculptor and this is one of his most famous works. Numerous descendants of the deacon have helped to populate the valley and like him have been "useful and highly esteemed." The heredity was of the best. One descendant died in 1833 at the age of ninety-one. He had served as an ensign during the Revolutionary War, and always was called Ensign Chapin. In this same War for Independence another of these Chapins was present at the battle of Stillwater, and also at the surrender of Burgoyne.

A later example of the Chapin quality was Ethan in this same family line. He was unusual in various ways. For instance, he never was fond of sports and seldom took part in games with children of his own age. While the other boys played he was trying to make something with whatever tools he could find. At about the age of ten he made a little water-wheel which he set up in a stream near his father's house. He was unusually mature and delighted in poring over books and in thinking out some novel theory for what he saw about him in nature. He lived on a farm and had to do his share of work, but his father failed as a farmer when the boy was nine years old. As there were eight children in the family, the situation was serious and it was necessary to make new plans for each one. The misfortune fell most heavily on Ethan, who was sent to live with his grandfather. He was allowed to attend school a part of the time for three years, but as he was given no school books, he was unable to make any satisfactory progress in his studies. At the age of nine his schooling practically ended.

As soon as possible Ethan left his grandfather's farm and went forth to seek his own fortune. There were no longer the restraints of home life, and he was without friends to aid or guide him. He went to work in a factory at Chicopee, which was then called Cabotville, and he experienced all the disadvantages of extreme poverty. Often he went hungry to bed and suffered cold for lack of sufficient clothing. However, he learned in this hard school habits of patience, industry, economy and self-reliance, which in time made him a man of rare quality.

The Cabotville mill operatives began work before sunrise, as soon as there was light enough to see, and spent fourteen and a half hours a day at their task. The work started so early that they all went to the workshops before eating and were allowed twenty minutes for breakfast. Those who were a trifle late were locked out.

Young Chapin was one of three boys who worked together. It was their duty to draw boxes of bobbins by means of ropes attached to three boxes. The box was divided in two compartments, one for the empty bobbins, the other to receive the full ones. In speaking of the work long afterward, one of Mr. Chapin's bobbin-boy companions said, "I can hear the rattle of those old looms today, and see in imagination the three young boys dragging their boxes along, and the women scolding because we didn't come sooner. I remember we were very tired every night. Ethan, at that time was a tall, slim boy, kind-hearted and good-natured. We were both poor, and our small earnings went to our parents."

Later Chapin worked at the Ames arms factory in Chicopee, and in a gun shop. He was constantly devising something new, and his services as a designer of ornamentations for swords and for the handles of guns and pistols were highly prized. Although never taught the engraver's art, his hand seemed naturally to take to it, and when he left the Ames factory he was considered its most skillful workman. While still less than nineteen he was made an overseer. At about twenty he came into possession of Comstock's "Natural Philosophy," and afterward of a book on chemistry. These two books were fairly consumed, they excited such interest and enthusiasm in his mind. He kept them near by while at work, and read them as opportunity offered.

The year 1836 was a landmark in Mr. Chapin's life, for he made an entire change in his congenial occupation that so well fitted him, and when he turned from it his friends were exceedingly regretful. His brother, Marvin, had bought the old Cabot House at Cabotville, and such was his need for help that he sent for Ethan to join him in the venture. Ethan was anxious to be of service to his brother, and he was aware that his eyes were being injured by his present occupation. Immediately he left the Ames factory and joined his brother in the care of the hotel. At one time or another all the four brothers shared in the responsibility of the Cabot House. The conduct of these brothers toward each other was very interesting, for there was an unusual spirit of family loyalty among them. Each one seemed to regard the interests of the others as his own, and it was largely due to this spirit that Ethan Chapin became a hotel keeper and business man, instead of a mechanic and inventor. Mr. Chapin lived six years at the Cabot House, and while there married Louisa Burns, of East Windsor, Connecticut.

The building of the Boston and Albany Railroad through Springfield, in 1838, assured the future growth and importance of the city. Those who foresaw this growth and took advantage of it soon reaped the benefit of their wisdom. Hitherto, Court Square had been the center of the town, as it had been the center of business. All the leading taverns, such as The Exchange and the Hampden Coffee-House, were in that vicinity.

In 1842 the property south of the railroad and west of Main Street was offered for sale. This property contained an acre and a half and measured one hundred and eighty feet on Main Street. Without question, it was the best site in Springfield for a hotel which hoped to catch the growing railroad traffic. Mr. Marvin Chapin foresaw this and, in partnership with a Westfield man, bought it at auction for eight thousand dollars. Then a contract was promptly made for the erection of a brick block to be used as a hotel. The undertaking was a large one for those times, and neither of the partners had money. Therefore, the property had to be mortgaged in order that the purchase might be completed and a new building erected. Meanwhile, the Westfield partner became alarmed at the risks assumed in the enterprise and withdrew. Then, as on a former occasion, the oldest of the Chapin brothers sent for Ethan, who immediately came and filled the gap. He took over the Westfield man's interest and the brothers became the sole members of the firm.

While the construction of the new building was being carried on as fast as possible, various names were suggested for it. Before anything definite had been settled, two barbers who had rented the basement room on the corner of Main and Railroad streets practically decided the question. They hung up their sign and advertised in the Springfield "Republican" that they were ready to receive patrons at their new shop under the "Massasoit House."

The friends of the Chapins were generally much disappointed in this choice of a name. They remonstrated, saying that many could neither spell nor pronounce it; also, it could not be remembered by those who had been pleased with the hotel on a first visit and wished to come again. The critics were likewise agreed that the name was odd and awkward, but experience showed that this unusual name helped to secure for the hotel its unusual success. There have been all kinds of hotels, but only one Massasoit House. Looking back now, it seems very appropriate that the famous Bay State Indian chief should have been thus remembered. The hotel was opened in June, 1843. In general the management of the house was in the hands of the younger brother, who gave himself with enthusiasm and patience to the oversight of everything. The building was enlarged three times, and each time the details of building had the careful oversight of Ethan Chapin. His inventive genius and mechanical skill were frequently put to use in improving the arrangements of the hotel. The laundry, the kitchen, the engine room and other parts of the building were fitted up with various devices of his own for lightening labor, saving expense, and for furthering the comfort of both guests and employees. He was always on the lookout for new things, and his mechanical skill enabled him to see with great shrewdness their probable utility.

He treated his help with friendly consideration, and on several occasions when he found the man who was in charge of a basement engine too ill to do his work, he ordered him to go home and sent word to the office that he himself was occupied and could not be seen Then he pulled on some overalls and went to work in the midst of the oil, steam and dirt of the engine room, with an earnestness that seemed to imply this was his regular employment. There are few hotels whose proprietors either could or would have done this service. Another thing Mr. Chapin did with thoroughness was visiting the best hotels and examining their management to get suggestions for his own.

During the Civil War the owners of the Massasoit House proved themselves to be among the most loyal citizens of Springfield. When the first Massachusetts troops passed through the city, the entire north end of the hotel was beautifully illuminated, and hot coffee with other refreshments were distributed to the men. The same was done when the 2d Regiment was in Springfield on its way to the front. Later, when the veterans began to return, great attention was always given them, and none, no matter what his circumstances, was allowed to go unserved. But what was less well known was the part Ethan Chapin played in helping negroes escape in the unsettled days before the war. On more than one occasion, with the knowledge of but few in the city, he concealed on his own premises, or nearby, parties of these negroes, whom he fed and cared for until arrangements were completed for sending them farther North. Thus the Massasoit House was one of the stations of the "Underground Railroad" which safely conveyed hundreds of fugitive slaves from the South to Canada and freedom. Those were the days when the principles and the courage of anti-slavery men were put to the most severe test. As for Ethan Chapin, he never wavered. His principles did not vary with circumstances.

Although money matters in connection with the hotel were largely in the hands of Marvin Chapin, yet Ethan also was a very shrewd and successful business man, and at the same time he was trusted implicitly by all who knew him. As one of these said: "The city owes a great deal to such men as Ethan Chapin and the Merriam brothers." It was his opinion that as a result of the stand taken by them and others of their stamp, certain kinds of business that had a doubtful character could not enter the city.

Mr. Chapin was always interested in public affairs and bore his share in every scientific, philanthropic and religious movement. When the city library was organized in 1857, he took a lively and practical interest in it. The library first opened in a room on Main Street, but was moved to the City Hall in 1860. At that time the books were few and ill-kept. In 1871 Mr. Chapin aided in buying the present site, and he continued to have a deep interest in the library's growth and success; but his most personal interest, the one that absorbed the greater portion of his thought and time, was science, and in that connection he wrote several very unusual books.

The Chapin family long occupied rooms at the Massasoit House, but in 1869 he bought a beautiful place on Chestnut Street, which he thoroughly enjoyed, not so much because it was more comfortable and convenient than the Massasoit House, but because it was more truly a home, and was therefore a better place for the family. He took great pains in remodeling and furnishing the house, studying to adapt everything to the comfort of the household and trying to make each part suit the needs and tastes of the one who was to occupy it. Many testified to the genial atmosphere that pervaded the place, the chief element of which was Mr. Chapin's unselfish spirit.

Mr. Chapin's natural tastes showed themselves in the books he chose for himself and his children. He never read anything trivial. Ordinary stories and novels gave him no pleasure, and he used to say, "I haven't time for those things," which simply meant he did not think them worth reading. If their contents had seemed valuable, he would have found all the time needed for reading them—and that with care. He often remarked of books: "I don't like to wade through so much to get so little."

In addition to scientific works, he valued histories, biographies, books of travel, and standard poetry. Sir Walter Scott's "Lady of the Lake" was a great favorite. Among his books was a small well-worn copy of this poem, which, like his Bible, was often carried about in his pocket, and was a much-prized companion. He often quoted from it with enthusiasm passages he had memorized. He was born in 1814 and died in 1889.

One noted man associated with Springfield is Charles Goodyear, whose name has a worldwide renown, and though he started his enterprise elsewhere, he succeeded in bringing the manufacture of India rubber to a high state of perfection in a shop that stood on Mill River. He was born at New Haven in 1800. His father was an inventor of farming implements and a leader of that great company of inventors who have lined the streams of the Connecticut with their mills.

While engaged in business with his father in 1824, he married Clarissa Beecher, who in every way was fitted to be the companion and comforter of his life. In 1826 he removed with his wife to Philadelphia and opened a hardware store.

In the winter of 1829 and spring of 1830 the health of Charles, who was the life of his firm, entirely broke down. He had a sudden attack of dyspepsia, a disease that pursued him to the grave, scarcely relaxing its hold on him for a day during the remainder of his life, and often confining him to his bed, so that at times the bed was his only workshop and was often covered with the implements of his experiments.

For ten years after this failure in business Mr. Goodyear was repeatedly imprisoned for debt and at the same time was trying to develop unfinished inventions, so that his creditors might in the end be paid. In after years when he began to receive returns for his long self-denying studies, the first appropriation of money above what was required for the development of his invention was made to these creditors, although time and law had released him from the obligations.

Gum elastic was originally brought from South America and used for the removal of lead pencil marks from paper. This was its first practical use and gave it the name of rubber.

A firm in Roxbury, Massachusetts, became interested in the improvements that were being made in the manufacture of rubber goods and conceived the idea of spreading rubber on cloth, thus producing a waterproof article. A great variety of goods were made of this product and several million dollars were invested in buildings, machinery and stock. Large stores were opened in the principal cities and much attention was given to the new material in the newspapers. These accounts met the eyes and aroused the curiosity of Mr. Goodyear.

Soon afterward, while in New York, he happened to pass the store of the Roxbury Rubber Company and stopped to make inquiries about life preservers, and it occurred to him that he could improve the construction of the tube. Some months later he exhibited to the agent of the company his improved tube. The agent was struck with the skill displayed in overcoming difficulties and told Mr. Goodyear that the whole business was on the edge of ruin; that twenty thousand dollars' worth of goods had been returned to them decomposed and emitting so offensive an odor as to make it necessary to have them buried in the earth. Other companies were in the same condition and large rewards awaited the man who would devise a way to overcome the difficulties. People became disgusted with an article that melted in the summer and stiffened to a stone hardness in winter and they would not buy the goods.

It was significant both of the fortune and of the character of Mr. Goodyear that his first experiment on rubber was made in prison.

A man in the city who asked how he might recognize Mr. Goodyear was told: "If you meet a man who has on an India rubber cap,

FOREST PARK, SPRINGFIELD

stock, coat, vest and shoes, with an India rubber money purse without a cent of money in it, that is he." About this time he obtained a patent for some of his work and medals were given him at some of the fairs in 1835. Improvements in the manufacture of elastic goods secured him such a degree of confidence in the community that he found no difficulty in getting a partner with enough capital to start work.

Success now appeared certain. A building with steam power was hired and shoes, life preservers, articles of clothing and a great variety of useful and ornamental goods were manufactured. The trials of this long-suffering and persevering man seemed to be drawing to a close, and an almost unlimited opening for successful business seemed before him. He moved his family to Staten Island, where he might once more enjoy the comfort of his own home.

An unexpected trouble now broke over him and swept away all his prospects of success. The general failure in business which occurred at this time and made new enterprise impossible, took away the entire fortune of the partner with whom he had recently been associated. This disaster left Mr. Goodyear penniless. However, he finally secured a small loan of money and started for Roxbury, Massachusetts, with a package of his best specimens. In that city immense amounts of money had already been invested and lost in the business, but again prosperity seemed to smile on the persevering inventor and he removed his family to that city with all his accustomed enthusiasm, both in the manufacture of goods and studies for further improvement in the process.

His beautiful articles had attracted so much attention that the government gave him an order for one hundred and fifty India rubber mail bags. It was valuable advertising of his manufactures and he seemed on the road to complete success. The mail bags were finished in the summer season and were exhibited in the factory. They were beautiful in form and color, and excited great admiration from the many visitors who saw them. His business called him away for a few weeks and when he returned great was his consternation to discover that his admired mail bags were decomposing and dropping from their handles. This misfortune led to the discovery of the vulcanizing process, but not until after he had once more gone through a complete business failure. He had spent four years in fruitless attempts to make the improvements he sought and an immense amount of capital had been sunk. Besides, the community had become exasperated by the losses. He took his family to Woburn and they started making rubber shoes in their own home. While working in his kitchen one night a piece of gum mixed with sulphur, which he held in his hand, accidentally came in contact with the hot stove. To his astonishment he noted that it charred like leather without dissolving and no portion of it was sticky. He nailed the piece of gum outside the kitchen door in the intense cold and in the morning he brought it in exultingly. It was found to be perfectly flexible, the same as when he put it out.

This great discovery of the vulcanization of rubber was the turning-point in Mr. Goodyear's life, though terrible years of want were still before him. His friends regarded his important news with complete indifference. Fifty times before he had run to them rejoicing in some new discovery, and fifty times had they been disappointed. It was only after two full years of experiments that he was able to convince even one person of its value.

The invention was submitted to Mr. William Rider, an enterprising merchant, who agreed to furnish sufficient capital to carry on the manufacture to their mutual benefit. The Goodyear family was now placed beyond want and they were never again brought to the verge of actual suffering. But before the difficulties in the way of preparing the rubber for manufacture were overcome, the strange misfortune that had attended Mr. Goodyear in his whole career was illustrated again in the failure of Mr. Rider and the loss of his capital.

Before this occurred he had begun manufacturing operations in Springfield and had succeeded in securing a simple cast-iron machine by the use of which he prepared sheets of the vulcanized rubber and also the shirred goods out of which suspenders and elastics were made. These immediately attracted the favorable attention of the public. Three years after this Goodyear felt safe in taking out his patent.

It was at this time, in Springfield, that he had his last experience of a debtor's prison in America. He was still very poor, and one day was arrested for the non-payment of a debt and put in the jail limits. A suit of clothes was being made for him in a Springfield tailor shop and on Saturday night, when the clothes were to be delivered, one of the firm said that Mr. Goodyear was at Sheriff Foster's. But he said to the trotter-boy in the shop, "When you go home take Mr. Goodyear's suit of clothes to him and tell him he can pay for them at his convenience." The boy on his way to the jail stopped at his home for supper. A barrel of fine red apples had been delivered that afternoon at the boy's house, and his mother asked him to unhead it, which he did, and took out of the barrel one of the largest apples. That one he put in his jacket pocket, and then he started for the jail, which was near by. To his surprise he found Mr. Goodyear reading in Sheriff Foster's office, and he was not behind the bars, but only in

Hampden—24

the jail limits. He delivered the clothes and the message of his employer and then it occurred to him that perhaps the red apple would be to the liking of Mr. Goodyear. He took the apple out of his pocket and handed it to Mr. Goodyear, who thanked him very kindly.

On the first of January, 1854, this young man was in Paris. It was on Sunday and a holiday. Lord Palmerston and other notable Englishmen were there conferring with Napoleon about the allied army. The young man sat down to read some letters that had been received by him, and after he finished he saw in the next room, Mr. Goodyear. He was writing at a desk, but soon looked up and recognized the young man. "You are from Springfield," he said, "and used to be a clerk for the tailors. Do you remember a red apple which was once given me?" The young man replied that he did, and that he was glad circumstances had greatly changed. Also, he remarked that he had noticed with much interest what had been said of Mr. Goodyear in regard to the India rubber pontoons, which he was then making for the French Government. After a pleasant conversation, Mr. Goodyear asked the young man to step around to his hotel at twelve o'clock. He did so, and was invited to drive with Mr. Goodyear to the Bois de Boulogne. The only persons to drive that day up and down the avenue behind four horses were the Emperor and one other distinguished party—Mr. Goodyear and the young clerk from the Springfield tailor shop.

The famous inventor showed the young man marked attention later, and they were constantly talking about Springfield and Mr. Goodyear's connections with the town.

Thousands have found employment in Hampden County because of Goodyear's efforts, others have built up large fortunes; the whole world was benefited by his inventions, but he died with a debt of $200,000.

His last home was in Washington, where for a short time he lived comfortably and happily, carrying on his experiments with greater ease and success than ever before. The career of this great inventor, who besides living and working for a time in Springfield, also went to jail in Springfield, ended July 1, 1860. His discoveries added over five hundred useful articles to the world.

Some Interesting Items

CHAPTER XXII

Some Interesting Items

One of the Merriam school books was "The Village Reader," published in 1841. Its only illustration was a full page engraving of Springfield's town pump. The pump had curbing, a stout handle and spout, and besides it supported a tall lamp-post. The source of illumination was probably whale oil. The pump was in the town square, where there was a background of trees and substantial buildings. Among the buildings was a meetinghouse.

Human activity in the scene was furnished by an old man waddling past supported by a cane, and by a man who had one hand lifted while he drank. Also, there was a farmer in a smock frock wiping the sweat from his brow. The only person in a hurry was a running boy. In the distance a lady was parading with a parasol, and a yoke of oxen were patiently waiting with a load of grain. Lastly, a dog was eagerly lapping his share at the town pump.

The text that goes with the wood cut is in the middle of the book, and we are informed that the scene is at the corner of two principal streets where the town pump is talking through its nose. The time is noon, the sunbeams hot. "I am the head of the fire department," the pump says, "and I am one of the physicians of the board of health. As a keeper of the peace, all water drinkers will confess me equal to the constable. I perform some of the duties of the town clerk by displaying public notices when posted on my front. Summer or winter nobody seeks me in vain; for all day long I am seen at the busiest corner, just above the market, stretching out my arms to rich and poor alike; and at night I hold a lantern over my head, to show where I am, and keep people out of the gutters. At this sultry noon-tide, I am cup-bearer to the thirsty public, and like the dram-seller on muster-day, I cry to all in my plainest accents, and at the very tip-top of my voice: 'Here it is gentlemen! Here is the good liquor! Walk up, walk up, walk up, walk up, gentlemen, here is the superior stuff! Here is the ale of Father Adam—better than strong beer or wine of any price; here it is by the hogshead or the single glass, and not a cent to pay! Walk up, gentlemen, and help yourselves.' Who next? Oh, my little friend, you are let loose from school, and come hither to scrub your blooming face and drown the memory of certain taps with the ferule in a drink from the town pump. The Indians formerly drank here from time immemorial until the fatal deluge of firewater swept away the entire race of the red men."

Endicott and his followers came next, and often knelt down to drink. The richest goblet then was of birch bark. Governor Winthrop, after a journey on foot from Boston, drank here out of the hollow of his hand. For many years it was the watering-place and washbowl of the vicinity, whither all respectable folks came to wash their faces and gaze at them afterward in the mirror which the water made —at least the pretty maidens did.

One of the notable visitors to the Springfield Armory in its early days was Jacob Abbott, famous for his "Rollo" books and other literature for young people. His popularity was widespread, and deserved to be.

The armory interested him, and about 1840 he made it the subject of one of his mildly adventurous and informative juveniles. The title of the book is "Marco Paul's Adventures in Pursuit of Knowledge—Springfield Armory."

Marco and an older cousin named Forester were going from New York City to Vermont by way of Hartford and Springfield. It was early in April, but there were mountains in sight still covered with snow. On their way they concluded to stop and visit the "great National Armory at Springfield," where, as Forester said, "the government of the United States had a wonderful building that manufactures muskets for the national armies, and it is a very curious and interesting place to visit."

At Hartford, where they stopped for the night, they were told there was a great freshet on the river and they went out in the evening to get a view of it from the Statehouse cupola. There they had a grand sight of the river expanding over the valley, with groves, farmhouses, orchards and even the streets of the city rising out of the water.

After looking for a while they went down and walked toward the bank of the river, but long before they got there they found the streets filled with water. Barrels and boxes were floating about; piles of merchandise, which had been taken out of submerged cellars, were arranged along the sidewalks, where they were out of the water's reach, and men were busy getting other goods to places of safety. By this time it was becoming dark and Forester and Marco returned to the hotel.

They were called the next morning at six o'clock and told that a boat was going to start at seven for Springfield. So they dressed with all speed, ate breakfast, and had hardly finished when the coach was at the door to take them to the boat. They got in and soon came to a street full of water. Next there glided into view a little skiff from behind a block of brick buildings. There was a man in it rowing, but he soon disappeared.

The horses had now reached the brink of the water, and to Marco's surprise they did not stop, but advanced slowly into it, drawing the coach after them. The water grew deeper and deeper until the horses were up to their knees, but now Marco could see the end of the bridge that led across the river. That was some relief, for he did not like navigating in such deep water in a carriage.

Just before they reached the bridge the water grew shallower, and they stopped where there was a piece of dry land big enough for them to stand on. Here, too, a little steamer came in sight that was to take them up the river. By scrambling through a store and over planks and along the edges of piers, they succeeded in getting on board. The steamboat had a great paddle-wheel at the stern and two small ones at the sides. It had a small forecastle, which was below the level of the main decks, and there was a little cabin near the bows. The ladies' cabin was toward the stern. It sheltered them from wind and rain, but the several who were passengers on the boat did not stay there long. They wanted to look about and see the effects of the flood and the strange aspect which was given to all the surrounding region by such a deluge of waters, in which everything seemed submerged.

Presently the crew began to push off the boat from the pier and the great paddle-wheel at the stern began to revolve. Then they were swept out into the stream just above the big wooden bridge which stretches across the Connecticut at Hartford. Some of the men said it was very fortunate that no ice was running.

"Why?" Marco asked. And the man replied: "Because it would soon make a jam above the bridge and carry it away."

Marco went forward to the forecastle. The wind was northeast and it blew the cold rain into his face. He tried to hoist his umbrella, but a sudden gust caught it out of his hands and swept it along the upper deck. Marco scrambled up the steps and ran after it. Fortunately, it lodged under the bows of a small skiff which had been placed on the deck in order to be taken up the river. If it had gone over into the water, it would have been so hopelessly damaged it would not have been worth while to detain the steamboat for it.

When Marco got his umbrella again he went back to the forecastle, but was careful not to open the umbrella so the wind would get under it. There he sat peeping out to see the wide waste of waters which extended as far as he could see. It was a melancholy sight to see the farmhouses, some with the water up above the floor, or even to the windows, and others located on a little spot of ground, which the water seemed just ready to cover, and the family standing at the door gazing while the steamboat crossed their mowing fields. Everywhere the water was deep enough so the boat was not obliged to confine itself to the ordinary channel of the river, but made a straight course over fields, fences, yards and gardens.

At some of the farmhouses men were busy saving their goods and furniture; at others, they were gliding about in skiffs, and in one case Marco saw a man and his boy going out to the barn to take care of the cattle on a raft made of barn doors.

Halfway between Hartford and Springfield is a fall where boats cannot go either up or down. Going up is impossible, because even when the water is deep enough they cannot stem the current; and they cannot come down, because the current would sweep them along too swiftly and dash them against rocks on the shore. So they made a canal around the fall to take the boats up, or let them gently down, by means of locks. However, the canal was now submerged and the steamboat had to stop below it at a little village called the Point, and from there the passengers were to be taken the rest of the way by stage. On arrival at this village they sailed along in front of the principal street, and then turned into another at right angles in which the tavern was situated. The helmsman guided the boat to the piazza of the hotel, as if it were a wharf, and the passengers stepped out on it. The piazza was covered with people of the village who had collected there.

Around the tavern on every side was water, and from there a large part of the village could be seen, with streets, yards and gardens entirely submerged. Barrels, boxes and planks were floating about. Everyone stood on steps or piazzas watching the scene. First, a wheelbarrow came slowly drifting into the tavern yard. Then a boy came on a raft made of two planks. Next was a little boat full of children going home from school. There was a bridge made of a series of planks leading across from the platform to the land behind the tavern, and the ends of the planks were supported on horseblocks for piers. Marco ran back and forth across this bridge several times until at length the stages were ready. They were backed down through the water to the step of the piazza and the baggage was put on. Finally the stages were driven out on dry land and the passengers, one by one, went over the long plank bridge, took their seats, and all proceeded to Springfield.

Most New Englanders disclaim a belief in signs, yet a confidential acquaintance is apt to reveal some that their own inner consciousness or their experience have convinced them are true. The person who is not affected at all by these old sayings is the exception. A few of them, as for instance, certain of those about the weather, sometimes have a scientific foundation, but it is not always easy to decide which sayings have truth to back them and which only fancy. If you listen to the relation of them, some of the most fantastic will be told with such detail and so stoutly championed that you are tempted to question if the days of miracles really are past. A man will tell you about horse hairs turning into snakes, and you will hear of wart cures and of the good or ill effect of one thing and another, till you begin to think that your own knowledge of the supernatural is very narrow and bigoted.

Perhaps none of the current signs and sayings of the past are natives of New England by right of invention. Yet if Yankee cuteness did not share in the originating of them, it has given its peculiar local twist to a large number.

There are many believers in the significance of dreams and they can give plenty of instances in their own experience and that of others to show a good foundation for their faith. The moon, too, is seriously given credit for a good many things. Yet how its phases could affect the weather, or the crops, or the pork of hogs that are killed probably no one can explain. Luck and snakes and charms have believers as well as quoters. Love signs are repeated and futures forecast usually for the humor of the thing, though there are those who find even these oracular.

At the old-time apple-paring bees a favorite stunt was to take an apple and pare it round and round so the skin would come off in one continuous piece. Swing the paring around your head three times and then throw it over your shoulder. Where it falls it will take the form of some letter of the alphabet, or it ought to. That letter will be the initial of your beau's last name. On account of the curliness of the paring the rounded letters, and particularly S, occur oftenest. However, an imaginative person can usually make something satisfactory out of the paring.

Nowhere in the enlightened world have ghost stories been related so historically and believed so implicitly as in New England. Even in sensible Springfield a desirable piece of real estate, not far from Mill River, lost its market value for years because it was supposed to be inhabited by the ghost of a murdered man.

The following story has a local setting: "My father," said the narrator, "worked for a man in Longmeadow who was a doctor there. One day the doctor said he guessed he'd send some rye to mill, but the wind didn't blow none so't they could winnow it. In them times they used to have to shake it outdoors somewhere so't the wind'd blow the chaff away. There warn't a mite of wind stirrin' that mornin', and so the doctor, he and my father, sot there in the kitchen a talkin', and guessin' they'd have to let it go till next day. While they was a-doin' o' this in comes the doctor's wife, and says the wind was beginnin' to blow up a little. And sure enough! when they come to go out the wind was blowin' considerable, and my father went right to cleanin' up the rye. There might not be nothin' in it but my father always thought that woman was a witch. 'Twarn't nateral the wind should come up sudden that way, without no help. That woman she wanted the flour, and so she just went out and made the wind blow up the way it did."

A clergyman named Hooker was traveling on horseback, when one evening night overtook him at Springfield and he sought an inn.

Other travelers were before him and the landlord informed the reverend that he had only a single vacant room left and, unfortunately, that room was haunted. The clergyman said he did not mind that, and took the room. He had retired and everything was still when twelve o'clock came, and with it the witches. In they flocked through keyholes and cracks until they filled the room. The visitors brought with them many shining dishes of gold and silver and prepared for a feast. When everything was ready they invited the clergyman to partake. Although he knew very well that if he ate with the witches he would become one, he accepted the invitation. "But," he said, "it is my habit to ask a blessing before eating," and at once began it. The witches couldn't stand blessings and fled helter-skelter, leaving feast and plate in possession of the preacher. Whether or not he ate the whole feast himself is not related, but Mr. Hooker secured the gold and silver dishes. The next morning, while continuing his journey, a crow flapping along overhead shouted to him: "You are Hooker by name and Hooker by nature, and you've hooked it all."

Once in a while there is a rare person who is said to be endowed by nature with the power to discover where it is best to dig a spring or a well. This person, if you employ him, walks about your premises with a branch of witch hazel in his hand. At such spots as water can be struck without deep digging the hazel branch droops downward, even if the medium attempts to prevent its doing so. By the way the twig twists and turns can be determined the exact spot where it will be best for you to dig. A witch hazel crotch is the favorite instrument of the water-finders, but there is a variation in preference. Some claim it doesn't matter what sort of a tree the crotch comes from. One man used an apple tree crotch. He demonstrated he could locate water pipes at the farm where he worked with no previous knowledge of where they were. Every time he passed over a pipe the crotch bent downward. He was able to tell just where the pipes were in spite of their crooked curves. He was a reliable worker and not to be suspected of sleight-of-hand. He said he couldn't prevent the downward inclination of the crotch if he tried to, but had no explanation to offer of the queer performance of the twig in his hand.

A water-finder who used an elm crotch said anyone can find water in this way who has warm hands. This man was something of a professional, and his charge was three dollars for each time he was employed. He says he has never failed but once in his water searching and that was when the man didn't dig where he told him to.

Many a child when ill in the past was dosed with queer remedies or wore a bag of sulphur or asafetida to ward off disease. A red string around the neck was guaranteed to prevent rheumatism, and a cotton string tied around the ankle would prevent cramps. The croupy child was put to bed with a piece of salt pork bound round his neck with red flannel, or a hot bag of onions on his chest. But, oh how stiff that pork was in the morning, and how cold and clammy the onions! Mud was used to cure bee stings and cobwebs, no matter how dirty, were laid on a cut to stop bleeding. Having the ears bored as if for earrings was believed to make one's eyes stronger. Every properly brought up child was told that eating its crusts of bread would make its hair curl.

Soon after the Civil War it was discovered by a physician that certain rays from the sun possessed marked curative qualities. The blue rays, in particular, were supposed to have great virtue. This gave rise to what was known as the "blue glass craze." For a few months a great deal was published in the papers on the subject, and it was a common topic of conversation. People had blue panes of glass put into their windows, or covered some window panes with blue tissue for the light to fall through. Some had glass summer houses made all in blue and lived in them much of their time. Many marvelous cures were affected, but the interest in the "blue glass" passed away as quickly as does a summer shower.

Among the superstitions of Springfield is remembered the belief that a consumptive would find relief by the burning of the remains of a relative who died of the same disease. In 1814 the remains of a woman named Butterfield were dug up from the old cemetery. It was four in the afternoon and school being out all the boys were present. The vitals were carried down to the river bank and burned. The ashes were not applied to the person, but perhaps a whiff of the smoke helped the cure. It was believed that "white swellings" in the knee could be cured by passing the hand of a dead man over the affected part, and it was often tried. Ministers usually discountenanced such practices, but belief in grave medicines and tombstone tonics lingered long.

When clocks were scarce the length of a person's shadow helped to indicate the time of day and in haying time the man in the field knew it was noon if he could "step on his shadow," that is, on the shadow of his head. When the cuckoo called, or the bob white said "more wet, more wet," or you heard the tree-toad croak, or the cat ate grass, it was a sign of rain. If the sun shines while it is raining "the devil is whipping his wife." The severeness of the coming winter was foretold by the thickness of the corn husks, or the duck's feathers, and six weeks from the song of the first katydid frost was expected.

Springfield Is Made a City

CHAPTER XXIII

Springfield Is Made a City

Springfield was organized a town in 1636, and it became a city in 1852. On the latter occasion the government was vested in a mayor, eight aldermen and eighteen common councilmen. No member of either board received compensation for his services, but the mayor was accorded a salary of "four hundred dollars, and no more." However, if the city council were to appoint him commissioner of highways they might "allow him a suitable compensation therefor."

A fire department was established and provision was made for a police court "to consist of one learned, able, and discreet person, appointed by the Governor." It was further decreed that the appointee should "take notice of all crimes, offences, and misdemeanors committed within the city."

A court was to be held by the justice at some suitable and convenient place provided at the expense of the city on two days of each week, at nine of the clock in the forenoon, and as much oftener as necessary. The justice was to keep a fair record of all proceedings in said court, and annually, in the month of January, exhibit to the mayor and aldermen a true and faithful account of all moneys received by him.

"The annual town meeting, which by law is to be held in March or April, is hereby suspended, and all town officers now in office shall hold their places until their successors are chosen and qualified.

"All officers of the town of Springfield having the care and custody of any records, papers, or property belonging to the town, shall deliver the same to the city clerk within one week after his entering on the duties of his office."

Thus, as indicated in condensed form, Springfield the town became Springfield the city, and elected for its first mayor Caleb Rice. At his intervening farmhouses, and when night arrived the weary workers returned with empty dinner pails. Every house in the city was stowed full of humanity from basement to attic; and boarding houses sprang up like Jonah's gourd in a night, and were ready to take "boarders" in the morning. Prosperity reigned on all sides.

When the war ended, and the occasion for more arms had passed, many of the armory workers found means for becoming permanent residents, and the building of houses, stores, and blocks, the improving of streets, and the successful development of industrial interests, have been almost constant since that time.

Three or four years before the outbreak of the Rebellion the manufacture of the Smith and Wesson pistol was begun in hired apartments on Market Street and prospered marvelously, finally overshadowing the armory, both in amount and value of its productions. It made great wealth for its projectors and secured to the city a remarkably prosperous industry.

Springfield was noted for being the home of one of the earliest and most successful paper mills of the country. The name of the firm was D. and J. Ames, and their works were on Mill River. As for their product—it went to every city and village of our civilized country, and their name and fame were spread all over the world. For many years in the long ago it was difficult to find a sheet of foolscap or letter paper—which were the only kinds of writing paper made in those days—that did not have the stamp of "D. and J. Ames" on it.

Springfield was fortunate in being one of the first railroad centers of note in the country. The Western, Hartford and Springfield, and the Connecticut River railroads all ran regular trains either through or into the Springfield depot several years before the town became a city. The Western, now the Boston and Albany, was opened for travel and traffic from Worcester to Springfield on the first day of October, 1839. The Hartford and Springfield Railroad, now the New York, New Haven and Hartford, preceded it by only a few months.

During the Civil War, and when photograph albums were in the height of fashion, Springfield had the largest album manufactory in the country, and it had a similar experience when paper collars were first introduced as wearing apparel. Springfield men were early in the field and at one time four large and profitable paper collar factories were in the full tide of success; but these by means of combination reduced the number in the "survival of the fittest" process until only one remained, and when fashion changed, that one finally faded away.

Springfield put a handsome feather in its cap of notoriety the first year after its incorporation by originating the "Simon-pure horse show business." Mammoth three-sheet posters, with two spirited horses' heads for illustrations, were sent out far and wide, and attracted large crowds to the first horse show ever known. Hampden Park had its origin in that horse show; and although Henry Ward Beecher, at its first public opening dedicated the park to horse shows, it has since often been crowded with people who came to see bicycle races, circuses and ball games. In 1936 the city council voted to change the name of this historic old park to Pynchon Park in honor of the founder of Springfield, and the tercentenary pageant was held there in May, 1936.

At least seventy-five clubs which once were active in the city of Springfield have gone out of existence, but their names impart a sense of the times in which they flourished. The Young Girls' Sewing Club and the Young Men's Literary Club suggest a discreet and cultural atmosphere with sober and worthy pursuits. The Atlanta Boat Club conjures out of the imagination mustached men in striped blazer jerseys ready to step into their boats on the river and row for dear life and glory, when boating was a popular Springfield sport. In the archives of the Connecticut Valley Historical Society there are admission cards to the social and dance of the Coachman's Aid Society, pictures of the Kamp Komfort's cakewalks, records of the doings of the Volcanic Research Society, of the Amabelish Fishing Society, and the Society for the Protection of the Ashes of the Dead.

As the need for these clubs lessened with the changing of the times, they disappeared one by one, and more modern ones came in. The old Hampden County Horticultural Society, for example, turned its tables and vases over to the Garden Club, and donated what remaining funds it had to beautify the grounds of the Shriners' Hospital for Crippled Children. The last meeting of this "lost" society took place in March of 1935, and it officially passed out of existence at the Natural Science Museum. There were only two members present when Joseph Aumer, of Walnut Sreet, called the last meeting by paid advertisement of this old society, which was organized in 1861.

A club that recalls to many old men days of keen sport was the Rod and Gun Club. Organized in 1874, it had a membership of prominent citizens in Springfield, and enjoyed an enviable reputation as a sportsman's club, sponsoring every kind of popular sports activities. The Rod and Gun Club is credited with organizing the third sporting dog show held in the United States. It existed for eleven years until it was organized into what is now the Winthrop Club.

The old Rod and Gun Club in a way was really symbolic of the Springfield of that day, for this city enjoyed a fine reputation as a center of sporting activity, as did West Springfield. The first trotting horse program in connection with a fair took place in 1853 on the grounds of the Springfield Armory, and at that time the public was made aware of the first formal horse show in the United States. P. T. Barnum was the judge and there were a number of witty and eloquent orators of the day who spoke on this occasion.

In the same vein of sport, Springfield lays claims as the home of the famous "Morgan" strain of horses. Justin Morgan was born in 1747 "in or near Springfield," and later located in West Springfield. His horse known as "Justin Morgan" after his master, was foaled in that town. Within fifty years after the death of that horse his descendants were found in practically every state of the Union, and at that time over half the light harness horses could be traced to him, either through dam or through sire. Many of the leading trotters of today show in their pedigrees that they carry a far-removed trace of Morgan blood.

A society of interest was the Springfield Society for the Protection of the Ashes of the Dead, organized in 1828. To the resident of modern Springfield the very name itself would suggest something facetious or perhaps a burlesque of some kind, but in those days it was a recognized organization of worthy men with a practical object. There really were grave-robbers and scavengers then, and they stole valuable jewelry and dissected limbs from the dead, although the tales have probably been distorted into fantastic legends as they came down through the years. The constitution of this "lost" society stated that its purpose was "to use every exertion to detect and apprehend all persons suspected of violating the sanctuary of the grave for the purpose of obtaining subjects for surgical dissection, and shall have the disposal of the funds of the society for that purpose. Also, it shall offer a reward of $5 to be paid to any person who shall make it certain that any grave has been robbed, provided the offenders are detected and brought to justice."

A milestone of progress was indicated by the formation of the Benevolent Society for the Propagation of Cremation among a number of Springfield German citizens. This club was of fairly recent origin, being organized in September, 1906, in the old Turner Hall on West State Street. The organization immediately sponsored a series of lectures and some amount of literature to show how cremation was so much more hygienic and natural than burial. There was, as is the case with any radically new idea, a great deal of opposition, and the club considered that at last it had reached the peak of success when the Springfield Crematory was opened in 1910 and one of the deceased members cremated there.

As a strictly religious organization with a serious purpose, there was none stronger than the Hampden County Temperance Society, which was organized about 1832. Its second annual report, published by G. and C. Merriam, leaves no question in the reader's mind as to the "pernicious" effect of "ardent spirits," and in the appendix are two examples outlining the society's views, the first maintaining that cholera was due to the demon rum, and the second exploiting the herculean strength and fine bodily health of a man of ninety who never drank of spirits. The pledge of the society reads: "Every member of this society hereby engages to abstain from the use of ardent spirits, except when rendered necessary as an article of medicine; also to use his influence to restrain others from a habit so pernicious."

Up to 1873 there were no women's clubs in Springfield and at that time there was but one woman's club in Boston, which had grown up from the days of the Abolition movement, and which later was called the Saturday Morning Club of Boston. In that year "The Club," or The Dorcas, as it was called, was founded, the only woman's club in this part of the State. Its membership was composed of worthy young women who met afternoons every fortnight to make and repair clothing for the deserving poor, at the same time to chat to their hearts' content. It was later that one of the members felt that the time was wasted in mere gossip, and set about to organize a literary club for the purpose of reading original essays and selections from accepted authors. Today, many other women's clubs of every description have followed in the wake of these pioneers.

These clubs are "lost" perhaps as far as present existence is concerned, but their influence has never really disappeared. Most of them did much good in their day, and the good was perpetuated in many of the modern clubs of Springfield which now serve worthy purposes. They have contributed, too, in great measure to history, furnishing perhaps in better style than any other record a clear cross-section picture of the life and tempo of their period.

In September, 1892, groups of business men headed by Reuben Currier asked a Salvation Army captain, Julius Cummings, who had formerly been in Springfield, but at that time was doing splendid social service work in Lynn, to return to Springfield and open a social agency. Captain Cummings agreed, and the Springfield Rescue Mission was born.

Captain Cummings had few educational advantages, but was an intelligent man and an ardent churchman. He had a real vision of helping his fellowmen, and it is due mainly to his efforts that the mission became such a worthy institution. The mission's first home was in a single room over a laundry on Sanford Street. This room contained only a few broken settees and an old stove, but it was a warm shelter and a place where a helpless man could get hot soup and friendly treatment. Under Captain Cummings' fine leadership the work grew, and the agency moved to Elm Street, where an old French boarding house was torn down and a new refuge built on the site. With the expansion of the street, the Elm Street place had to be sold by right of eminent domain, and the mission built a place on Court Square, where the Department of Welfare now stands. In 1909 it bought the land at the corner of Cross and Willow streets, and built the red brick building which has been its quarters since that time.

The Springfield Rescue Mission is one of the finest social agencies in the city. It is an independent agency, in the sense that it is not affiliated with any social agency of national scope. It is supported by funds from the community chest, by contributions of a private nature, and in a small measure by funds received from the lodging department, where some of those who come are able to and insist upon paying a small amount of money for their keep. The staff consists of a group of paid workers, and a group of volunteer workers, all under Superintendent E. L. Smith, who is also a clergyman, and who took over the administrative duties of the organization after Captain Cummings' death a few years ago.

The setup of the building is simple, yet efficient. In the cellar is the dining hall and the kitchen. There are brown wooden tables and chairs, the brown walls are free of adornment, and the whole place is immaculately clean. On the first floor is the chapel, a large roomy hall with its furnishings painted white. On the first floor also are the superintendent's office, and a well-kept recreation room. The second floor consists mainly of separate sleeping rooms, and the third contains the large dormitory and shower baths.

The idea behind the Springfield Rescue Mission is to take men who have gone astray and reclaim them in the spirit of Jesus for normal Christian living; to assist the needy and unfortunate with a view toward physical, spiritual, and mental rehabilitation; to assist homeless men to secure self-supporting employment, and in general to give them a new outlook on life.

The clock in the city hall tower of 1883 used to be kept at Boston time, which was nearly five minutes earlier than true time. For convenience this was generally used throughout the city, but in 1883 the new standard time was adopted. Not until a few years afterward was the old custom abandoned of ringing the bell at the hour of nine in the evening, and on such momentous occasions as the straying of a child away from its mother.

The Irish monks who, in the sixth century, founded bishoprics in Iceland, and, later on, moved to some greater Ireland on the mainland, to make way for Norwegian newcomers, may have visited what we know as New England.

When the Catholic Acadians were driven into exile, the pathos of which our poet Longfellow immortalized in his beautiful poem Evangeline, one of the group settled in Worcester, and this is the first Catholic of whom we have any record in the heart of the Commonwealth.

At the close of the Revolutionary War Catholics in Massachusetts were not numerous and they were not welcomed. Banishment was what the law prescribed for them. In or near Boston were twenty-five or thirty Irish families with a few French and Spanish residents.

These were the only Catholics in Massachusetts at that time, though the State is now fully half Catholic.

It was about then that the first sturdy Catholic missionary sought out the scattered groups of Catholic laborers along the railroads and canals, to give them the consolations of religion. Fitton, of blessed memory, blazed the pioneer trail of priestly activity and we can visualize that lone figure, on foot or on horseback, on hand car, or freight train, covering the vast area from the confines of Boston to the New York line, and from the borders of Vermont to Hartford. As we read the thrilling tales of priestly journeyings before the days of easy travel we marvel at the ground covered, the obstacles overcome, and wonder if they had a home and when they visited it, for at that time one priest covered the whole State.

That lone pioneer established missions and stations from Worcester and other towns on the east, to Springfield and towns on the west as far as Great Barrington. It is only justice, a century later, that we lay this wreath of gratitude to the memory of this great worker, who at Worcester built the first Catholic Church in western Massachusetts, and said the first mass at its temporary altar amid a terrific thunder storm which failed to hinder the priest or scatter the flock. Famine in Ireland, oppression in Poland, industrial necessity in Canada, sent large reinforcements to Catholic ranks.

The laborers were few but energetic to the point of being tireless, and not a canal was built, not a railroad constructed, not a mill operated but a Catholic priest appeared. With the return of peace after the era of construction, came permanent structures of brick and mortar to replace the frame buildings. A lion-hearted pastor at Chicopee established the first Catholic school in charge of religious teachers, and in little more than half a century Catholic schools sheltered fifty thousand pupils in these counties.

From small and humble beginnings the Roman Catholic Church in Springfield has grown in a comparatively short time to wonderful proportions, with churches, schools and institutions, with bishops and priests and religious organizations.

In 1847 an archbishop from Boston helped in the dedication ceremonies of St. Benedict's Church in Union Street. A great change has taken place in the religious life of this community since then. At that time you could almost count the Roman Catholic churches of New

England on the fingers of one hand. The people were mostly poor emigrants from Ireland in a community strongly opposed to their faith and church.

The following account of the March blizzard of 1888 was written by Charles Goodrich Whiting and appeared in the "Springfield Republican": "The storm now upon us (March 12), which in its course up the Atlantic coast reached this region late Sunday evening, and has brought pretty nearly all the concerns of men to a standstill will be remembered in history as the greatest of a generation. No middle-aged man can recall its parallel. It began with a light snowfall with a deceitful gentleness, and people said it would probably turn to rain as soon as the sun rose. The wind was northeast, and chilly, but not very cold. As the night grew toward morning the wind increased in strength and velocity, the snow came faster, and the drifts began to pile. It was already so much of a storm as nine o'clock approached that mothers felt apprehensive as their children started for school. By this time, too, the railroad trains were giving up the contest. And so it went on; the wind becoming a gale from the north, the snow continuing to fall, and drifts to grow, all paths to close up; all means of locomotion were withdrawn from the streets; there were no trains run and consequently no mails received or dispatched; there was no business done in shops or stores for few ventured abroad, and they only persons who had work to do.

"Those who had come to their daily tasks in the morning could not get home at night, and the hotels were crowded with men and women whose employers had to house them there; while business men who could not join their families were added to the homeless throngs. There were many rumors of missing children who had not reported since their schools were let out, even into the evening. There was much reason to fear that some of the rumors might be true in a tempest so fierce and unceasing, where besides the fine, light snow that the wind bore in its fury, a keen sleet that cut the face was driven sharply. The wind was of such fury that every breath seemed to tear the lungs, and this trebled the labor of the walker, contending against snow mid-thigh or waist deep, so that an ordinary three-minute walk in a side street would consume a quarter of an hour. This was in the middle of the afternoon; by night the side streets were given up as impassable by anyone, the sidewalk drifts covering the fences from sight except for an occasional gulch scooped by the arctic winds.

"There was no such thing as getting a view of the storm during the day; the vision could reach but a few rods, the clouds could not be seen, all the air was a mad whirl of flakes, and to look up Main Street was to see an ominous moving wall, frayed and tossed at the edges, of a sort of dull brown color in the height of day, deepening as the unseen sun dropped below the blocks.

"How far the storm reaches no one knows at this writing. It took from between nine and ten o'clock Sunday night until eight o'clock

MASONIC BUILDING, SPRINGFIELD

yesterday morning for it to reach Lowell, which is not very rapid traveling for such a coast gale as this. In the evening, about twenty-four hours after it began, the snow had apparently almost ceased falling here, and the temperature was less exasperating, though the winds still blew swiftly, heaping up the snow, whistling and wailing around the eaves and down the chimneys, and making life out of doors about as undesirable as it ever is.

"The appearance of the city (the next day) was unprecedented. In the unbroken quiet of the morning hours it lay, except for Main

Street, as trackless as the forest. Like the forest there was the exception of its lesser animal life, for as the rabbits and foxes mark the woodland with paths, so had the cats and dogs streaked the wilderness of the streets and gardens with their tracks. Gradually as the day grew toward noon the streets became curiously diversified with trails, those who had to pass through taking the middle of the road as far as it might be, but describing long curves or sharp diagonals, to take advantage of the lowest grades; and sometimes, confronted by an absolutely forbidding drift across the whole highway, the trails led directly over miniature Alps and White Mountains. Fences were largely not matters of faith but pure supposition, and great drifts rose even to second-story windows, covered hen houses in sepulchral mounds, or combed up like ocean waves twelve to fifteen feet high— poising there as if a moment more might dash them to break in foam against the assailed houses.

"Main Street was a marvelous sight in the morning, nor less so when the cleaning of the sidewalks had heaped the sides of the streets as they were never heaped before. Up Harrison Avenue a long notched ridge, a veritable Sierra Nevada, reared its imposing bulk; Market Street up to noon was a wild stretch of mountain and valley. The Hill showed the freakish mischief of the gale that swept out gullies and canyons where no one wanted to go, to pile full the household pathways and the public walks.

"The fall was three feet on the level, and the nearest approach to that in the memory records is the twenty-two inches that fell in the storm of January 31, 1882. William Smith, of Pine Street, remembers a snowfall of four feet in the last part of March, when he was a boy in Dalton, almost eighty years ago, but then it did not blow. A lesser fall with such a wind produces on the hills as great drifts as we have now in the city and, moreover, pounds and presses the snow so close that oxen draw sleds over the drifts.

"Here the drifts were nowhere solid enough to bear even boys upon their surface, and on snowshoes alone could one traverse the wild scenery with freedom. If we are to have old-fashioned winters as a regular thing, we shall have to practice the aboriginal craft of snow-shoe locomotion. Such winters will be very unpopular, however, and everyone will be content to look back upon this March storm as unrivaled, unapproachable, unique and ideal."

Boyhood Memories of a Springfield Mayor

CHAPTER XXIV

Boyhood Memories of a Springfield Mayor

I was born in the village of Wales, twenty-five miles east of Springfield. My mother died when I was two years old, and my grandfather took my two sisters, both older than myself. The name I bore was Fordis, a hard and unusual name for a great many people to remember and write, as shown in later years by the weird addresses on much of my mail. I would not think it possible so many errors could be made with six letters of the alphabet.

My earliest memories are of a comfortable white farm house in a peaceful little valley where my grandfather's home stood on a low knoll near the road with many great maple trees near by. Directly back of the house rose a long, low range of hills, and for miles to the west there were no habitations. Instead, were just forest, wilderness and hills. The road through the "Hollow," as it is called, ran north and south for about three miles, keeping to the western side, and finally climbing out at the south and over Dimmock's Hill into the skirts of Wales. Our house had in front of it across the highway a great meadow and fields extending easterly about a third of a mile to the East Hill, and a large brook nosed its way through the meadow to the delight of the trout fishermen.

Somewhat to the North of us, near a wooded bend in the road, were the ruins of a good sized gristmill, and there the water wheel and remains of the dam gave mute testimony of days when the "Hollow" was of some importance. Crossroads were lacking, and the valley was very much shut in. The nearest we came to getting a distant view was the northern hills, whence from our valley we could see Tower Hill and Steerage Rock about three miles away.

It is not to be expected that a little lad of four or five years away back in the country would have an exciting life, but the activities on our farm were interesting. Haying was fun, and sometimes the men would have a race to see who could mow a long swath quickest; how the scythes would rip through the fresh green stems, after which that jug of water, flavored with plenty of ginger and molasses, would be dug out of its resting place wrapped in cool damp grass.

When it came to getting out the grass from the wet swampy ground, it was the oxen's turn to perform. They stood still while being loaded, but sank lower into the swamp and sometimes the great brutes would only reach the uplands by wallowing through water almost up to their flanks.

My people made maple sugar, and the great maples were made to contribute their sweet sap, but it was something like trying to build up a bank account—it took an awful amount of running and boiling and smoky tears to get a little sugar.

The days of butchering were very bad days, and I shall not go into details, but it seemed just too bad to see creatures that you had known, and perhaps named and fed, stagger up and down the lane bleeding to death. It was one of the first demonstrations to me that all was not ideal with the plan of things.

Among the most delightful places I remember was my grandmother's dairy. It was built into a small side hill and walled up at one end. The cold spring water oozed copiously among the dark stones and was drained away. There were two rooms, a small and a large, but there was little daylight in the large one. The person fortunate enough to get into that room on a hot afternoon was treated to a draught of cold cream or buttermilk.

My school days at the little box of a schoolhouse were few, because I left the valley while quite young, but I remember two exciting incidents in connection with it. The teacher was a fine young fellow and we little people were his first charges. Among the larger boys was one by the name of Works, who was allowed a little schooling in the winter. One day during recess the big lad got gay with a dirty broom, and when he had whacked everybody else with it, he stuck it in the teacher's face. Of course, the teacher couldn't "laugh that off," and so I witnessed my first battle by big fellows. Right prevailed, but the teacher had to carry the fight out of the schoolroom into the yard, and his Works did follow him.

The other incident meant great delight to a little chap of four years. It occurred one morning when we went to school in a snow storm. The storm grew worse and the snow accumulated fast, so that by four o'clock it was quite deep. Just before school closed my grandfather appeared with the oxen yoked to the big sled, and with bundles of straw before the runners to "break out" the road. We children greatly enjoyed riding home through the deep, white snow, drawn by those powerful, wallowing cattle.

That same winter we had a fine Christmas. My father came out from Springfield and brought a friend, and an uncle and aunt drove up from Southbridge; we had a grand time in the big room, with food enough for a small regiment, and pleasing presents.

My next sporting event was when old white Billie, the driving horse, ran away with me in the sleigh, as an observer. My sister and another big girl of thirteen winters and myself started for the post office more than two miles from home, with my sister driving. On Brimfield Plain a horse came up behind us and his heels rang too loud, I think, to suit Billie. Anyway, Billie took us for a mile ride that made me proud of him. When we got to the post-office good old Bill realized that he was at the end of the line, and he slowed up and turned into the Wales Road. Some of the hard workers usually found around the post-office stove ran out and caught the reins, and that was all the excitement the town had that day.

The murder of Jim Fisk was my introduction to newspapers. Our weekly contained large pictures of Fisk, Stokes, and Miss Mansfield, and told all about what had happened. I didn't think it was a nice thing for Mr. Stokes to kill Mr. Fisk. The whole affair was certainly news to me.

My people were quite religious, and my grandmother was a Second Adventist. About this time a preacher of the sect came to work on the farm. He was a good man, and he prayed long and loud. I was interested in my small way and tried to do my part. One of the hymns we used to attempt was worded "All I want, all I want is a little more faith in Jesus."

Another interesting newspaper experience was the sensational story of the assembling of the Second Adventists on Terry Island in the Connecticut River, near Windsor Locks, for the purpose of taking off from that point to meet Christ on the occasion of his second coming. The news was thoroughly illustrated in our weekly paper. The story, as it was told to me, while it was consistent with my grandmother's belief, did not enthuse me because I had only gotten started down here on earth. I was much relieved when the fateful days passed and no newspaper reports came stating that people with wings had been observed flying over the Connecticut River.

One of the important daily events in our little town was the passing of the four-horse stagecoach as it traveled from Southbridge to Palmer, a twenty-mile run. The Post Road was one mile north of our house, and it was something of an event to go up to the turn on an errand for the stage driver. Stage drivers were important persons representing contact with the outside world. They cheerfully did favors for the farmers and farmers' wives, shopping for them in the larger terminal towns; it might be matching a piece of cloth, buying a box of pills, getting a tool, or taking care of an express package.

I remember some strange characters who lived in the town. An uncle and aunt of mine conducted the town farm for several years, and I used to go to see them. The inmates were not numerous, but three of them were certainly unfortunate exhibits.

"Tom" was just plain crazy, but was harmless, and allowed to walk about the farm. No matter how hot it was he covered his head with a blanket, and stumbled about beating the air with a bundle of sticks trying to keep devils away. Another case was a creature who was quite a giantess, well over six feet high, with the squarest shoulders I ever saw, strong, well proportioned, with no excess of fat, hair kept short, and she wore dresses, and was called Hannah. The poor thing was pleasant and easy to manage, and would sit on a rock and jabber smilingly. The voice was changeable, but mentality almost lacking. The third case was that of a half-witted man who was usually smiling, and he wanted to please. When directed he could do some farm work. He was about forty years of age, and for short intervals pleasant and amusing. His great obsession was the stagecoaches, and he seemed to live to see the stage come into town. If he was allowed to lead out one of the horses, or if the driver spoke pleasantly to him, he was proud and happy.

I was still a small boy when my father announced that he would take me to Springfield with him for a visit; so I, who had never been farther than Palmer Depot, emerged from the hills and vales of Brimfield and saw Springfield for the first time. The armory, surrounded by what seemed miles and miles of high iron fence, interested me. The soldiers came out all dressed up and fired a big gun, but didn't hit any-thing.   I was taken to a museum, where I saw a tiger with glass eyes, also some dead birds, some spotted eggs that didn't look very fresh, and a great fish, all bones, with an awfully long nose.   It was a sword fish, and there were many other exhibits that I do not remember. After a happy week I returned to the Hollow with more knowledge of the wonders that existed beyond Foskits Mill and Palmer Depot than I would have thought possible.   I hadn't had any idea that North America was such a big place.

A few months later we moved into Springfield to live, and my father rented a small cottage on King Street.   After that I had little connection with Brimfield.   Most of my schooling I got in the Oak Street schools.   In my studies I think I did fairly well, although never a keen student.   I could not memorize easily, and had to work hard for a commendable recitation.   Most of my recitations were in Mr. Barrows' grammar school.   "Daddy" Barrows was very well liked. He always wore a long-tail coat which provided an ideal place of concealment for his very practical strap.   I enjoyed especially the hours devoted to writing and music lessons.

As to music, I was supposed to be very good.   In fact, for one brief period I threatened to be a singer.   I sang a solo at an exhibi-tion in the school hall and had a tryout for a solo to be sung in the city hall at an important festival, but alas, a top note or two caused my "undoing."   I was rejected.   I took the decision peacefully enough, but my grandmother never really had much confidence in the judg-ment of the school authorities after that.

The "Eighties" were a decade during which several emotional efforts were put forth on a large scale.   Moody and Sankey, a Rev-erend Mr. Earle and Elder Lutz visited the city and caused much religious excitement.   Music and organization were relied on greatly to make these drives a success, and many people were advertised as "having been brought into the fold."   Francis Murphy held great temperance meetings in the city hall, and it was a feature of the temperance movement of the period to make a widespread use of pledge-signing.

Elder Lutz was rather in a class by himself, and was severely criticized by many.   He came under the auspices of a good man, but eventually drifted down and out.   He was rough and sensational, and admitted he had been a very "tough egg," a drunkard, gambler, fake, adventurer, and he certainly showed signs of extremely hard wear, including a glass eye.   My impression is that the Elder's converts were rather disappointed in his moral accomplishments.

I was always fond of animals, and at various times took on small pets.   I kept rabbits, guinea pigs, white mice, pigeons and chickens. They did their best to make me prosperous, and they certainly could multiply.   I once set thirteen eggs under a hen, and in due season thirteen chickens arrived, and of these, twelve fine, barred Plymouth Rock chickens grew to lusty youth.   I traded them to my father for a watch, and he got rid of the chickens by trading them for a cord of wood.

I picked up quite a few pennies one way or another, and some of them I saved without any great effort.   One of my best jobs was distributing insurance circulars for my friend, Colonel Warriner.   I used to do this sort of work for him on a Saturday now and then, for which he generously paid me a dollar a day.   I would pay ten cents for a lunch in a restaurant, and feel that I was a regular business man.

My first contact with politics came during a presidential campaign. Colonel Warriner hired a big two-horse dray, filled it with little kids, including myself, furnished us with red, white and blue capes and caps, and put us in a big torchlight procession.

What with the bands, the drums and fifes, the redfire, the miles of lanterns, the hundreds of men marching to music, I was thrilled beyond all telling.   When the great parade was over the colonel took us to his offices and served us with doughnuts and coffee.   After that I had no use for Democrats.

One of the interesting spots we boys used to enjoy was "Goosy" or Goose Pond.   It was located just east of Sherman Street and covered a few acres south of Bay Street.   The pond was very shallow and made safe skating in winter and fine wading and "polly wogging" in summer.   To go swimming we used to travel over the rough land south of King and east of Hancock Street to Watershop Pond.   It was wild land and some of it adjoined the slaughter houses of Perkins and Nye.

The only traveling I did was between Springfield and Wales and Southbridge.   We had many relatives in those towns, and on the occasions when my father gave me a trip I was filled with joy.   Sometimes we would take a lunch and eat it on the way under the Washington elm in Palmer or some other big tree.   My father loved horses and if his horse had any speed, and the opportunity presented itself, we would have one of those quickening experiences—a horse race.

I had only two vacations in my early days, the first when I was ten or eleven years of age and was visiting an uncle in Wales.   He announced he was going to Martha's Vineyard and invited my sister and me to go along with an aunt and cousin.   This was one of my first big experiences.   We left very early one summer morning, in a high three-seated wagan drawn by his horses Sam and Bill, who understood they were allowed one hour to make ten miles.   That ride down the hills, through the valleys, following the brooks, and passing through charming woodland was a great treat, but I leave the trip to your imagination.   The second vacation was entirely different.   I was large for my age, and when I went to visit relatives on Tower Hill, at Brimfield, they allowed me to take part in the farm activities, no mistake about it; also, they allowed me to do work that required the use of a horse, and that delighted me.

I remember going alone to the Warren cheese factory with the milk, starting at six in the morning and driving grey Dan, a beautiful and gentle horse bred on the Parker farm.   I was allowed to drive the hay rake; and with my small cousin take a one-horse cart and get in hay all on our own.   I certainly felt important, and was delighted to work in this way to the limit of my strength.   I picked quantities of berries and brought home a half bushel for canning.   It was a hard-working vacation, but a happy one.

As a smaller boy, I occasionally saw three rather weird acting chaps who made an impression on me.   They were "Pop Corn" Paige, "Soapy" Allen, and Daniel Charter.   All elderly men.   "Old Pop Corn" had one short leg, and he used to rest the foot attached to it on a bracket of the crutch.   Sometimes he would suddenly rise on this bracket with the aid of his cane, and yell "pop," looking as if he was going to swoop down on you.   He had a little cart drawn by a donkey, and in that he rode to town.   His habit of yelling "pop" or "corn" in the ear of some unsuspecting person as he went up and down Main Street was unusual advertising.

"Soapy" Allen was a member of a well-known firm of well diggers. I don't know how he got the name of "Soapy."   He had the look of a little monkey, and sometimes he wore clothing that was far too large for his meager frame. Much of the time he was full of firewater, or nearly so, and crept about the streets of the hill, talking to himself, eyes nearly closed, and given a wide berth by the boys. When he was really at his worst, he sometimes preached vociferously to fallen humanity. A good deal of the time he went about barefoot, which was partly accounted for by his occupation as a well digger.

Daniel Charter was a farmer and a good citizen. He was an ardent temperance advocate, and though usually reserved, he would

SPRINGFIELD POST-OFFICE

occasionally burst forth on a street corner and tell the world where he thought rum drinkers would finally land. It wasn't in the frigid zone, I assure you. His sturdy figure was clad in overalls, and the fact that he was sober used to sometimes draw him listeners.

Primus Mason was another unusual man. He amassed a considerable fortune, some of it in rather strange ways. Probably the business most talked about was that of undertaker for horses. I recall his telling me of his experiences as a "Forty Niner," and about his passage around the "Horn," on his way to the gold fields of California. He was black, weighed about three hundred pounds, and talked in a high squeaky voice. One couldn't possibly think of him as a "no 'count" darkey. He had too much poise, and talked too intelligently to be considered that. We all know of the monument he left—the Old Men's Home.

One of our great winter sports was the horse racing on State Street, between Oak Street and Winchester Park. From three to four thirty almost every afternoon when the sleighing was good the "horsey" men enjoyed themselves, and the street from Hancock east would sometimes be lined with spectators. Springfield's ponies that possessed speed, or whose owners thought they had it, raced over the course. It was a gay sight and many of the horses were beautiful with wonderful style and action. Many of the sleighs were gaily colored with fine fur robes within and without, and the sleigh bells rang musically on the sparkling winter air.

Unless a person has lived in Springfield during the 70's or 80's, he has no idea of the importance and magnitude of the events staged on Hampden Park. Later days have had nothing that approached it excepting at the Eastern States Exposition Grounds. Springfield was one of a league of four cities that initiated grand circuit horse racing in the United States. About all of the fastest trotters and pacers and noted horsemen helped make the Springfield meets among the biggest harness racing events in the country. In 1882 Springfield became internationally famous on account of bicycle racing. It had the world's champion in George M. Hendee, and a little later was accounted as having the fastest track in the world. Still later, in 1889, the great Harvard-Yale football game was played here, and repeated every year until 1894, when the grand Harvard-Yale row spoiled everything.

Schools and Teachers

CHAPTER XXV

Schools and Teachers

The first building erected in the town for a high school was on School Street. Later it was used as a dwelling and the bell has long ceased to summon pupils. It was on a day in April, 1827, that the town voted to choose a committee to report some plan for establishing a high school, and where it should be kept. In due time the committee recommended that the town build a schoolhouse of brick two stories high, with a woodhouse under it, and a cupola and bell on one end and with a proper outhouse attached. The house was to be fitted up in plain, strong style for one school room on each story, and the ground fenced in. August 2, 1827, School Street was opened from State to Union Street. The first instructor of the school was Storey Hebard, a native of New Hampshire, and a graduate of Amherst College in 1828. He took charge of the school, soon after his graduation, and successfully conducted it until he resigned in 1830 because his annual salary of seven hundred and fifty dollars was reduced. After leaving the school he went to Syria as a missionary and died at Malta when not quite forty years of age.

The attachment of the pupils to Mr. Hebard was so strong that the boys rebelled against David Sheldon, of Suffield, Connecticut, who was hired in his place. They took advantage of the new teacher's ignorance of their names when the roll was called and answered to wrong names or did not answer at all. When his back was turned some of them crept out of the room on their hands and knees, and every sort of device was used to embarrass him. The monitors who were appointed to be on the platform with the teacher and notice any who were delinquent and report the same did not do so, as they were rebellious also. Mr. Sheldon resigned owing to the disobedience of the boys, but it seems that afterward he became a successful Unitarian minister. One of the scholars was in later life a Boston merchant, who writes of his school days:

"There was at one time considerable disobedience, especially among the older boys, and this state of things made it necessary that the school committee should be informed. One day an officer called at the school to address the scholars on the matter. He said to them that if a change for better order did not speedily take place it might be necessary to call out the militia. This seemed to have the effect of awing the boys into a state of respectful obedience and unusual attention to their studies."

The securing of a live hen and placing it in the teacher's desk, its sudden flight when he opened the desk, surprising him as much as it delighted the boys, was one of many diversions.

The school committee, in 1831, secured Simeon Calhoun, a graduate of Williams College in 1829. Mr. Calhoun was a man of much worth and great sincerity of purpose and was held in high esteem by the community. When he became the teacher, he was wise enough to have present at roll call one of the committee who knew the names of most of the students, so that the boys who ran out of school were caught. After a few days in which he let the boys have their own way, Mr. Calhoun said: "Boys, you have ruled long enough and now it is my turn," and with determined and severe treatment he brought the school into subjection. The school became harmonious and united. The teacher was loved and obeyed and during his administration a revival of religion took place.

Mr. Calhoun was a man of much religious fervor and kindness, and drew the scholars to him with great affection. He taught two years in Springfield, and later went to Smyrna as a missionary. Next, we find him transferred to the Syrian Mission, where he established a seminary on Mount Lebanon for the education of native teachers, and after long service abroad he returned to the United States, where he died at the age of seventy-two.

One of Mr. Calhoun's scholars, who went to live in Ohio, said of him: "I remember well the morning of his advent, and how we all saw at once he was not to be trifled with, and how he said: 'Boys, I am going to teach this school; if you obey the rules, all is well; if you don't, I shall flog you!'"

A qualification that always appeared necessary for teachers in those days was that they should be orthodox in religion.

A lad who used to live in the city recalls what follows: One cold winter morning one of the boys who was fond of making chemical experiments put on the hot cast-iron box-stove a quantity of brimstone, which in melting sent forth a peculiar, suffocating odor and smoke that filled the room, and the windows had to be opened for ventilation. Before that could be accomplished the teacher arrived and the scholars hurriedly took their seats; but a considerable time elapsed before the windows could be closed. After the school was quiet the teacher asked who caused the breach of peace, and it soon was evident that a boy named Jim was the guilty one. The teacher ordered him to come forward and hold out his right hand with the palm up. On that he struck two or three hard blows with the ferule, which Jim received with Spartan firmness, and then smilingly took his seat.

Sardis Morley, of Otis, Massachusetts, was the next instructor. He fitted himself for college and supported himself by preaching and teaching. In his ministry he was blessed with many revivals and conversions. When roused he was capable of speaking with great eloquence. One of his scholars recalled an occasion in the old high school. On the north side of the school room the wall was painted black between the windows and used as a blackboard, and it so happened one noontime that a boy drew the grotesque figure of a man and forgot to do the erasing. When Mr. Morley came it was at once the object of everyone's interest, and Mr. Morley began a careful process of questioning that on his part left no doubt of the picturemaker.

This and previous pranks seemed to justify heroic treatment, and the boy with his coat buttoned around him was ordered to come forward with his hands held out of range of three twisted withes. Then the teacher struck three blows that brought the withes around his body with a loud crack. Not a word was uttered and the boy submissively took his seat.

Another Springfield youth remembered a summer morning before the teacher arrived, when some of the boys were very busy digging a pit directly in front of the steps at the south entrance to the school room. After completing this task they covered the top with light material and on that put a layer of dirt. Then they took favorable positions under cover and awaited the coming of the teacher. He soon appeared, but only to disappear with startling suddenness, all but his head. By his own efforts, and those of some of the boys, he was brought to the surface without much delay and very little injury. The expression of the teacher's face as he entered the school room gave the impression that if he could find the boys that dared to do such a thing he would give them a severe flogging, but his efforts to discover them were of no avail.

One of the Springfield boys makes this confession: My brother George and I stole out of the school room by crawling under the seats, in order to see the first train from Worcester in 1839, and after seeing the event we came back to school without being missed by the teacher. We thought it quite an exploit. One lad tells of a boy who sat next to him who came to school one day with a striped snake in his bosom, inside his shirt, and it gave him a chill which he thought had always clung to him.

In November, 1830, the town paid Caleb Hopkins seven dollars for taking care of the schoolhouse, and Joseph Bull was paid five dollars for ringing the bell at twelve o'clock.

One school instructor had a habit of wearing green goggles, which prevented the boys from seeing whether he was looking at them or not. If they made any noise or were not in their seats he was quick to detect it, much to their surprise.

A boy who became a successful merchant in Michigan tells how he entered the high school under the tuition of Mr. Vaille:

> "He was a lovable person except to evil doers, and he had a faculty of taking kinks out of boys. He took several out of the writer. I hailed from the upper Watershops and was one of some ten or twelve who trailed through mud and snow from there to the high school. We had room enough for travel in those days for the houses were few in that region. We made our own path in the snow and on our return at night found it much the same as we left it in the morning.

> "The high school gathered its pupils from different parts of the town, which at that time included the present limits of Chicopee. In those early days in the winter season the out-of-school hours were scenes of fierce snowball fights between the 'hillers' and the 'streeters,' as the scholars from the different localities were distinguished. One of the bright boys who

later became a resident of California, tells of the floggings Mr. Calhoun used to give him, saying he thought he deserved them. Calhoun's successor, a most excellent man, taught only one term, during which the boys made things uncomfortable for him. During this term he organized an evening school 'in order to improve our minds,' and there a Jack-o-lantern was placed on top of the mineral case, ink stands and bullets were thrown about the room and through the windows, the old box-stove near the door was covered with tallow, and several lengths of stovepipe which ran the entire length of the room were let down on the desks, causing the school to be dismissed and giving us a half holiday. Once brick-bats were hung under the floor suspended by strings from various stools. One boy would pull up a brick which would strike the floor from underneath with a loud thump. The teacher would start out to find where the noise came from and as he neared the spot a loud noise would again be heard across the room. Then he would start for that locality and when he arrived there the noise would be repeated from some other part of the room. Finally, as the noise seemed to come from below, the teacher visited the cellar and there saw to his amazement several bricks suspended by strings to the floor above."

One of the pupils who attended the old high school from its opening in 1829 until 1831, when he left to follow the sea after the example of his father and grandfather, was Charles Emery. His first voyage was made as a boy on the ship "Eclipse" from Salem to Manila and Canton. He sailed on his fifteenth birthday and was gone thirteen months. Other voyages he made took him to the West Indies, Liverpool and Calcutta. In 1836 he was offered the command of the brig "Swan," fitting out for the west coast of South America, and made the voyage around Cape Horn as captain when but three months over twenty years of age. After spending two years on that coast and visiting all its principal ports, he returned as passenger on the whaling bark "Columbus," of New Bedford. He afterward bought the brig "Wallace" and took out a cargo of naval stores for the United States fleet on the Rio Janeiro station, sold this vessel to the Russian governor of Kamchatka and came home by way of

Peru and the Isthmus of Panama. After remaining at home about two years he bought the brig "Grand Turk" and loaded it with material for a British shipyard in Hong Kong, China. He arrived there after a passage of one hundred and sixty-four days, sold his ship and came home to Boston.

Captain Emery was later agent of the New England Coal Mine at Portsmouth, Rhode Island, and for several years was interested in Lake Superior copper mines. In the winter of 1878 New York parties were interested in exploring the Amazon River in order to obtain cedar and mahogany and other desirable woods of the tropics, and Captain Emery agreed to take charge of the expedition. He sailed for Para, Brazil, and proceeded up the big river carrying the United States flag where it had never been before. On another voyage to Para he sailed farther up the Amazon to establish a branch for a rubber house, and there he remained two years. Captain Emery's later life was spent in the eastern part of the State, where with other old shipmasters he delighted in recalling the old days when they sailed the high seas before steam supplanted the sailing ships.

Another pupil of this old high school was Thomas Dale, who went on a whaling voyage and was absent three years. On his return he engaged in the business of selling buttons and tailors' supplies, and soon became the leading tailors' trimming house in the United States. As an importer he went to Paris, where he had an elegant mansion and dispensed a princely hospitality. He owned a residence in New York and a beautiful villa in Newport.

George Tannatt went to California in 1849, sailing from Boston. At the outbreak of the Rebellion he enlisted as first lieutenant and was later captain on the staff of General Prince at the battle of Cedar Mountain, where he fell, and was taken to Alexandria, where he died of his wounds. James Harding, who was on the staff of General Sterling Price of the rebel army, saw Captain Tannatt when he was taken prisoner in one of the battles in Missouri and Tannatt helped him to pass through the Union lines. He told Harding that he would much prefer to see him in a different suit from the one he had on.

David A. Wells, the well-known economist, a graduate of Williams College, was on the editorial staff of the "Springfield Republican" and suggested the idea of folding newspapers and books by machinery in connection with the power printing presses. The first of these machines ever built was at his expense and was operated under his direction in the office of the "Republican." He was later a special pupil of Louis Agassiz and graduated from the Lawrence Scientific School of Harvard.

Horace T. Draper, a member of the school during Mr. Vaille's administration, left Springfield for New York in 1842. He shipped for a voyage to China and followed the sea for twenty-three years, filling all positions from cabin boy to captain. He was in the United States Navy during the Rebellion and was on board the flagship "Hartford" with Admiral Farragut at the capture of New Orleans.

Ralph W. Kirkham, another graduate, was also a graduate of West Point, served in the Mexican War and was brevetted captain for gallant and meritorious conduct in battle. He assisted in the capture of the city of Mexico and was honorably mentioned in General Scott's dispatches. While in Mexico he was one of a party of six American officers and an Englishman who reached the summit of Popocatapetl. The original number that set out on the expedition was about one hundred. This mountain had never been ascended since the time of Cortez in 1519. He participated in the frontier Indian wars and was commissioned major in the Civil War. His grandfather had been a soldier in the Revolutionary War.

Francis Potter, when the "gold fever" broke out in 1849, embarked on a vessel bound for California by way of Cape Horn and was six months making the voyage. Later he was chief engineer on one of the steamers running between San Francisco and Panama.

Horace Fern was another California "forty-niner" and it took him seven months to make the trip around the Horn in the bark "Strafford." After the bark was towed up the Sacramento River to Sutterville he went to the mines and later was the first regular express messenger between Sacramento and San Francisco. In October, 1851, he started an express line from Sacramento to Nevada City for Freeman and Company, afterwards Adams and Company, and was superintendent of the line for some years. This was followed by a period of quartz mining.

In 1831 the proprietors of the "female seminary in Springfield" bought a lot of land on Maple Street and soon erected a three-story building. This was heated during the winter by placing cast-iron box-stoves in the cellar and running tin pipes up through each floor to conduct the heat from pine wood used as fuel. The first principals and teachers were women and the school was run for girls only, but after

George Eaton, a Harvard graduate and a gentleman of scholarly attainments succeeded to the principalship, boys were permitted to enter. It was not agreeable to some of the boys to be obliged to attend school where girls were to be their schoolmates, but they soon became reconciled to the change under the encouraging sympathy manifested by the girls for their bashfulness. Children of parents living on armory grounds were not allowed to attend the town schools, and in consequence many attended this private school.

CHRIST CHURCH CATHEDRAL, SPRINGFIELD

One of the students at this school was Edward Flint, who later was superintendent of the Pacific Mail Steamship Company. In July, 1862, he started homeward for a visit by way of Panama, being a passenger on the steamer "Golden Gate," which took fire fifteen miles off shore and was burnt to the water's edge. About two hundred persons perished in this disaster and among those who were lost was the genial Flint, then only thirty-five.

William Dwight attended West Point Military Academy, but resigned before he graduated. When the attack on Fort Sumter was made he was commissioned captain and was soon made a colonel. At the battle of Williamsburg he received three wounds and was left as dead on the field, but was found alive by the rebels and was taken prisoner. On his release he was made brigadier-general for his gallantry in that battle. He was General Banks' chief of staff in the Red River campaign, and later served under General Sheridan in the Shenandoah Valley. He rendered valuable service at Winchester when the Union Army rallied and defeated the rebel forces of General Early. At the close of the war Dwight's division was a conspicuous feature in the final grand review at Washington.

James Dwight Orne, a civil engineer, entered the Union Army and was three times promoted for gallant conduct in battle. He took part in thirty-six battles and was reported dead and left as such on the field in the second battle of Bull Run. At Chancellorsville the back of his saddle was shot off, and at Gettysburg a piece of shell nearly cut his hat into two pieces. He went through the whole Peninsular campaign and took part in nearly all of its battles.

Horatio Sargeant went west, where he was a railroad ticket agent and also superintendent of a Baptist Sunday school. He was instrumental in starting several mission schools in Toledo, Ohio, and did a great amount of work for the cause of Christianity. While he was private secretary to the superintendent of the Lake Shore road, he was requested to sell tickets after midnight on Saturday. This he refused to do and tendered his resignation, which, however, was not accepted, and instead his salary was increased. He was ordained as a minister in 1864 and was later pastor of a church in the town of Huntington.

James Scutt Dwight, when but seventeen went to sea, and before he was twenty-five was made master of a vessel. He took command of the vessel "Cutwater" after the captain had been swept overboard during a heavy sea. He was master of the ships "Charger" and "Springfield," the latter having been named in honor of his native town. His friends presented him with a set of colors as a compliment. Among the sons of Springfield who have gone forth to win fame and fortune none had brighter prospects or was more highly esteemed than Captain Dwight. While on the voyage from Calcutta to New York he was crully murdered at midnight in his cabin on board the ship by the cook and steward, who were Malay Chinese.

The Spanish-American War

CHAPTER XXVI

The Spanish-American War

The men of Springfield, and of Hampden County, have never been backward in responding to the colors when the call came to take up arms against the enemy.

Back in the very early days, when this region was little more than a succession of clearings in the virgin forest, the first settlers fought the hostile Indians who swooped down into the valley to dispute the right of those pioneers to establish their homes and till their land in peace. Springfield blood was shed in the Colonial wars, and when the roll of the drums came to announce the revolution of the Colonies against England, the men of the county were foremost in joining the ranks of the nondescript army that fought so bravely and finally emerged victorious. In the Civil War, too, Springfield, Holyoke, Westfield and other towns in the county filled their quotas with many to spare, and it was the 37th, in great measure composed of men from this valley, which played a prominent part along with a New York regiment in turning the Southerners away from Washington aftei their victory at Bull Run.

When the call came for men in this section to again take up arms against the enemy the response was just as immediate and just as enthusiastic as it had ever been in the musty years of the past.

The first company to leave Springfield for the war was H Company, Naval Brigade. The navy was far better prepared than the army at this time, and it was the belief of military experts that the war would be fought largely on the sea, leaving the army forces to do little except garrison duty. On the sixteenth of April, 1898, Lieutenant J. K. Dexter, the commander of the brigade, arrived in Springfield with official orders and immediately began to assemble his detail by the alarm list signal, telephone and special messenger. This detail went to New York, marching to the Union Station amidst a tremendous ovation.

There was still a number of H Company men left under Lieutenant Henry S. Crossman, and they were designated for duty aboard the "Prairie," formerly the fast steamer "El Sud," of the Morgan line. This contingent assembled at the Armory on the afternoon and evening of April 23. Relatives, friends, well-wishers, wives and sweethearts gathered in thousands to see the "jackies" off, so-called because of their naval jackets. The boys of the company rolled their dunnage and gathered together their equipment, every bit as excited as the cheering crowds about them. It was 1:30 A. M. when the men, fully armed and dressed in regulation uniform, marched through the Main Street to the Union Station, but despite the lateness of the hour, it seemed as if every local citizen who could walk or ride was down in the cheering mobs which lined the streets and shouted themselves hoarse.

Rockets, colored lights and flares lit up the night. Laughter and tears, shouted farewells, and good wishes followed the men as the train pulled out of the station. And it was these sons of Springfield, and also those of outlying towns attached to the company, who served their country on the high seas, some of them on the monitor "Lehigh" and some on the auxiliary cruiser previously mentioned. Part of their service included sinking a Spanish transport and a gunboat.

On the twenty-ninth of April the call came to this region for land troops and Colonel Embury P. Clark, of the 2d Regiment, was designated as one of the six commanding officers to raise a regiment of volunteers. At that time there were three companies of army militia here, and the men of the militia were given the first chance to enlist in the volunteer regiment, the remainder to be made up by the enlistments of residents other than those already members. Applications for enlistment far exceeded the quota desired. Twice the required four companies could have been filled with ease. Officers actually took it upon themselves to dissuade citizens with families and other heavy responsibilities from entering the rolls, pointing out that there were plenty of single men with less obligations. Many of these men, eager to be of service, dropped their regular business to work day and night in the armory, where the personnel had trebled.

On May 3 the three companies formed in the big drill shed of the armory, their uniforms spick and span, their knapsacks packed and their overcoats rolled up on top of the knapsacks. As the sharp command came from the officers and traveled down the line, the men wheeled and marched out in almost perfect precision.

There was not quite as enthusiastic a reception awaiting them as had been given the naval brigade some days before. It was a dismal, dreary morning with the rain falling at intervals, dampening to some extent the spirits of the awaiting populace and at the same time serving to bedraggle the fine uniforms. Then, too, the people had come to realize the seriousness of war, and the early eager anticipation of conflict had toned down to a rather grim, determined outlook. This realization came home to people here even before a single shot was fired in actual battle.

Still the demonstration was all that could be asked for in comparison with any during a time of peace. Outside the armory hundreds of spectators had gathered and prominent among them were members of the E. K. Wilcox Post, the G. A. R., the Veterans' Corps and several other military and patriotic organizations, headed by the 2d Regiment Band, to provide an escort to the station.

Thousands of people massed in and about Court Square as the men marched down Main Street, then around the square in front of the city hall, where Mayor Dickinson and the city officials reviewed them. Perhaps the first shot of the Spanish-American War was fired a few minutes later, so far as Springfield was concerned, when men from the fire department headquarters on Pynchon Street saluted the boys with a shot from a small cannon!

The station was packed, but the cheering was more subdued. There were more tears than cheers, especially from the women, when the train pulled out of the station bound for the camp in South Framingham. To have the men in the city, even if the atmosphere was martial, was one thing. To see them step into waiting cars, perhaps never to come back, was quite another.

The records of the war tell their own story of the bravery and soldierly bearing of these men of the county, both in battle and in the fever-producing climate of Cuba. It was these men who fought at El Caney, a battle where the infantry, without any appreciable artillery support, managed to seize a heavily fortified town, a feat in itself stupendous and unprecedented. It was these men of Springfield and other parts of Hampden County who were instrumental in bottling up the city of Santiago so that the Spaniards ultimately were forced to surrender. Only partially trained, in fact virtually rookies, they went into battle with all the coolness and bravery of veterans who had many times before advanced into a hail of bullets, and emerged with honor.

Some of the men died on the field of battle. Some submitted to the ravages of fever after lingering illness. Still others died later on the way home from the effects of wounds or the weakening of their resistance by hardships and disease in the field. About twenty-five men in these three companies answered the final muster.

Prominent among Springfield's dead heroes was Henry C. Bowen, major and surgeon of the 2d Regiment. He was the son of Charles W. Bowen, of Westfield, and studied in public schools in that city and later at Wilbraham Academy, finally completing his medical education at New York University. He enlisted while on the surgical staff of the Mercy Hospital, where he was headed for a brilliant medical career. Men still relate that when the regiment was in front of Santiago, in terrible physical condition because of the ravages of Cuban fever and poor diet, it was Bowen, who virtually alone and working hour after hour without rest, took care of over eight hundred sick and dying men to the best of his ability. Unable to procure medical supplies of any description for his men, and faced with insurmountable odds, he was still responsible for their welfare and indirectly gave his life to the cause. The very disease that he fought against, Cuban malarial fever, finally overcame him and he died in the 2d Division Hospital near Santiago, every bit as much of a hero as the soldier killed in action on the field.

The death of Sergeant Richard, "Dickie," Bearse brought grief to hundreds of his friends back in Springfield, as well as to his comrades. His patriotism was of the highest. He was rejected twice in physical examinations by the surgeons, but wheedled himself into the service by sheer, dogged persistence. Always good-natured and cheery, Bearse was a wonderful influence on the morale of the men in their hardships, although his own body was somewhat less equipped to meet the vicissitudes of rigorous campaign life. He died of the dread calentura, and his body was brought home and buried in the family plot at Oak Grove Cemetery. Hundreds of saddened residents of the city followed the casket in the mournful funeral.

Others died facing the Spaniards on the field of battle. Robert Kelly was shot in the left cheek in front of Santiago, the bullet passing through and lodging in the muscles on the other side. John Malone, of B Company, was fatally wounded at El Caney, and Arthur Packard, who had been employed in the "Homestead" office, was killed instantly in the same encounter. George A. Richmond, in Lieutenant Leyden's squad (later sheriff of Springfield), was shot through the head early in the battle, and was carried to an improvised field hospital nearby, where he suffered horrible agonies before death came, and Chaplain Fitzgerald, of the 22d, administered the last rites. The others who died, whether from fever or from enemy bullets, inscribed their names just as deeply on the scroll of honor as these men did.

Perhaps the strangest and most tragic casualty of all was that of Thomas C. Boone, who came to the front with K Company, but later transferred to the Signal Corps. Boone did not die on foreign fields, but in the Massachusetts General Hospital. An expert telegrapher, he was finally detailed to code and observation work. On July 2 he was aloft in a war balloon at San Juan at a height of about 2,700 feet, making observations of the Spanish lines along with Colonel Drew and Major Maxfield. As they floated over a creek the gas bag was pierced by jagged shrapnel from the enemy lines and fell. The basket lodged in the top of a tree and Boone was caught in the anchor with the iron hook stuck in his side. He hung suspended over the creek before he finally fell into the water, badly hurt. He might have recovered even then, but on a journey to a hospital by mule team, the vehicle overturned and the old wound was aggravated. Through an error on the part of some officer, he was accused of desertion, but the truth finally came out and he received an honorable discharge from the army before death from his wounds overtook him.

The Springfield contingent, after the armistice was made and the victory won, returned home on the "Mobile," appropriately called "the death ship" by the men. It had lain in the harbor of Santiago under the worst of sanitary conditions, and was overcrowded with men who slept in any spot they could find, in the hold, or on the deck. The food was poor and meagre, and several were sick or had festering wounds. On this voyage Second Lieutenant Harry Vesper and Wagoner Paul Kingston, both of Springfield, passed away, and they were lowered over the side, their bodies draped in American flags. The "Mobile" was in actuality a "death ship" with a toll of nine men and one officer on the trip from Santiago to Montauk Point.

As the ship came into Montauk a group of Springfield newspapermen tried to get near the "Mobile" in a small boat, but were ordered away, even though the ship had passed quarantine. The first Springfield man to reach the regiment aboard was Dr. David Clark, a Springfield surgeon, who for many years had been associated with the militia. Dr. Clark had spent many weary hours hidden under the wharf at Montauk, so that he could be inside the guard lines when the "Mobile" came in. He was immediately surrounded, and some of the men had tears in their eyes, so hungry were they for the sight of a face from home, and for news of their loved ones. The next day the men were allowed to disembark, and those who were able to walk down the gangplank put up a semblance of order and precision as they were transferred to a quarantine camp.

The return of the soldiers to Springfield was not a gay and glittering pageant, replete with parades, the ring of martial music and the roar of thousands. Like the day they had left, the morning was rainy and generally miserable. News had come home that most of those men who had marched so gallantly away were now wasted and emaciated from fever and hardships, weary of war, and looking only for rest and recovery, and were in no shape for a riotous and exhausting welcome. Officials emphasized to the public that the less strain placed upon the men the better, and the Union Station was roped off and patroled by officers.

The crowd numbered about 10,000, and among them was Governor Wolcott. The welcome was subdued, so far as noise went, but it came from the hearts of the citizens.

On October 3, 1898, the men of the 2d Massachusetts Regiment were mustered out of the United States Army. The local companies marched to the station at first to receive the other companies from the Second who were to be mustered out in Springfield. The men were without rifles or equipment, and were dressed in nondescript uniforms of militia blue and campaign khaki. Between the sporadic cheering from the crowds on the streets there was wonderment and stares. People had been accustomed to see soldiers on parade marching with precision and fire and many of them were a little disappointed at the rather sorry military bearing of the veterans. But to those who fought in Cuba under the worst conditions possible, pomp and glory were only empty manifestations, and it was their desire to forget it as soon as they could.

Many of the returned soldiers were members of clubs and secret societies of various nature around town, and banquet after banquet was given. Private Morris Grenowitz, of B Company, the only Hebrew in the Springfield contingent, was given a public reception by the Young Men's Hebrew Association, and presented a medal and a small amount of money. Many of the others received gold medals, rings or watches, including Private Peter Boyer and Private William Ferrier. A number of the veterans resided in West Springfield or Mittineague, and the residents there arranged a large celebration resembling an election night, with red fire and salutes, and plenty to eat and drink.

Perhaps the largest public celebration of them all was that held in the old city hall on November 3. The place was packed to the doors, and cheer after cheer resounded as the colors of the regiment were brought into view. The Governor gave a speech, as did many prominent citizens of Springfield.

Soon afterward there was an organized movement to send a delegation down to Cuba to bring back the bodies of those men who had died in the foreign land. The movement gained impetus, and a number of meetings were held in Springfield, attended by delegates from nearby cities and towns. In January, 1899, the expedition left for Cuba, and after some delay, the bodies of the dead heroes were located with one exception. A thorough search failed to reveal the remains of Private R. Kelly, who was shot in action.

Justice and Law

CHAPTER XXVII

Justice and Law

The present Hampden County Courthouse on Elm Street, facing Court Square, is the third building of its kind to be erected in the county. The first county courthouse was a plain structure, built about 1740, which stood in the path of Sanford Street, its front projecting into Main Street. For years it was the only public building in Springfield, and was used by town and county jointly, not only for court proceedings, but also for singing schools, conference meetings, and all other gatherings of a public nature. In August, 1812, Hampden County officially came into existence, and after nine years of agitation, another courthouse was built in Court Square, which served until the present structure was erected.

The architectural style is Florentine, as suggested by the buildings of northern Italy, and part of the tower follows closely the Palazzio Vecchio in Venice. The courthouse is constructed of Monson granite, a rugged looking and substantial material, and the entire building gives the impression of quiet solidity.

The new courthouse was not built in 1873 without a struggle. The cost was the subject of much grumbling and opposition from the smaller county towns, although over half the expense fell on Springfield itself. The argument of the smaller towns was that they could not see the justification for erecting a building to beautify Springfield with part of the money coming from their own treasuries. It was further argued that the old courthouse served its purpose well enough, and there was no need of a change. Opposition also came from some of the members of the Hampden Bar Association, who declared that neither the site nor the building were satisfactory, and a distinguished judge, A. M. Copeland, was one of those who declared publicly that the site was poor and that the building had been constructed only with regard to the external appearance.

THE CAMPANILE, MUNICIPAL GROUP, SPRINGFIELD

Despite this opposition, the contract was made with Norcross Brothers for $142,000, and the courthouse was completed in December of 1873. The dedication services were held the next year, and William G. Bates, the president of the old Hampden Bar Association, gave the dedication address. The courtroom on that April afternoon was well filled, and the members of the bar and their friends sat attentively as Mr. Bates proceeded with the address. It was a lengthy piece of oratory, and Mr. Bates, who was then over seventy, became exhausted and could not finish it, so E. B. Gillett finished it for him in fine style. There were galleries in the new courthouse at first, but these were taken out later when it was found that people entering them and moving into their seats caused a great deal of disturbance, which upset the routine of the court.

In the early days the court lasted only a month during various parts of the year, where today it sits practically all of the time. There were the October Civil Court, the March Civil Court and the June Civil Court to take care of cases of this nature. There were also the May Criminal Sessions and the December Criminal Sessions. Today the district courts are housed in a new building on Vernon Street, but at that time these were included in the regular courthouse, which is itself virtually a superior court in function.

Interwoven in every way with the county courthouse is the Hampden County Bar Association. This was permanently organized in 1864 under the presidency of W. G. Bates, although an association less formal in character had existed as far back as the very early years of the nineteenth century. The members of the bar had no entrance fee to pay then, and there was a strong bond of fraternity, due to the fact that there were fewer lawyers and the profession was more distinctly separated from the rest. The bar gathered often to pay tribute to distinguished visitors, to solace heartbroken widows of their deceased members with sympathy and money, and in a way acted as a sort of mutual benefit society.

The bar association was presided over for many years by William H. Brooks, who was one of the leading men in its progress.

The fundamental object of the bar association is to investigate and prohibit illegal practice of law. The grievance committee is probably one of the most potent functions of the association. To this committee any member within the bar can enter a complaint concerning unethical tactics by a fellow-lawyer, and the privilege for complaint is extended to any layman also. Some of the work done by the bar in cleaning its house was the elimination of so-called "ambulance chasers," or lawyers who arrived at the scenes of accidents or shortly afterward in hospitals and gained the representation of the client before the patient was aware of what he was doing. Another practice which the association is trying to eliminate is that of illegal collection agencies, and many of these have already been eliminated.

The Hampden County Courthouse has had its share of cases which have attracted nation-wide attention. Although there were many of a sensational nature, it is generally agreed that the trial of Bertram G. Spencer, in 1910, gained the widest publicity.

The events leading up to the famous trial of B. G. Spencer are in themselves extraordinary. In 1909 the people of Springfield were terrorized as reports came that some mysterious person prowling in the night was attacking women and breaking into homes with intent to rob. Conditions reached such a point that people would not venture along some of the more isolated streets after dark, and windows were locked, despite warm weather, against the mysterious terror. Events came to a dramatic head when a school teacher was shot to death at her home on Round Hill. This woman had just settled in her home with two of her friends, ready for a quiet social evening, when a man suddenly appeared with a black mask over his face. The women ran screaming in terror from the room, and as they did so the man whipped out a revolver and fired, killing the school teacher.

By this time the city was thoroughly aroused, and all the forces of the police were employed to track down the murderer. Despite the vigilance and efficiency of the authorities, they were continually baffled by the apparent shrewdness of the mysterious killer, until one day the police were set on the trail of a man named Bertram G. Spencer, who was later captured.

On one of his housebreaking expeditions he had, in descending a ladder from an upper story, dropped a small locket. This locket was later found by an old man, who at first did not hand it in to the authorities. The son-in-law of this old man finally brought it down to the officials, explaining that it had been found on the scene of the robbery, and detectives immediately went to work to trace it.

An enlargement was made of the locket and the police discovered the letters "B. G. S." on it. A search of the "S" section of the city directory for any name having the initials B. G. S. resulted in a blank, but the West Springfield directory, then a separate unit, yielded the name of Bertram G. Spencer. There were in the locket two women's pictures and these were enlarged until they were clear and unmistakable. These pictures were connected with Spencer and he was arrested.

The man was obviously guilty and confessed to having killed the school teacher. There was only one defense available, and that was on the grounds of insanity. Spencer was sent to Bridgewater for observation, and then returned to be tried in the Hampden County Courthouse. Every available seat was jammed, and crowds waited outside, almost rioting as they were prevented from entering. Correspondents from the big cities of the country were present to cover the trial, and well-known cartoonists sketched the prisoner and the other principals as the trial progressed.

A remarkable feature of the trial was that the prisoner almost fooled the alienists in feigning insanity. Now and then he would break violently into tantrums and fits, so that he had to be controlled by force. The trial stretched on for days, but Spencer was finally convicted of murder in the first degree and afterward executed.

The Hampden County Jail and House of Correction is lofty, well-lighted and airy, and its entrance hall, if it were not for the iron bars in plain evidence, would look somewhat like the lobby of a small hotel. The windows run almost the entire height of the inside walls, and giant fans in the basement sweep in a large volume of clean air.

An iron fence encircles the grounds, which are divided into small vegetable gardens. The prisoners, who from the street can sometimes be seen working in the gardens, wear grayish trousers and blue workmen's shirts, and if it were not for the fence and the steel-barred building in the background, they might easily be mistaken for ordinary laborers.

The prison theory is that idleness for men in confinement breeds trouble and discontent. Years before the labor unions came into being, the men worked at the manufacture of boots, shoes, or cane chairs, and the products were sold outside. These, however, were important industries furnishing a means of livelihood to free laborers, and labor unions objected strenuously. Finally, the industries were divided so that no two jails should manufacture the same thing. To the Hampden County Jail went the manufacture of umbrellas for a number of years, and the men were kept busy at their appointed tasks of folding, cutting and stitching. A bill was passed by the Legislature in May, 1913, permitting the authorities to employ prisoners in reclaiming and cultivating the land, as long as the products were used for the maintenance of the institution itself, and not sold outside in competition with free labor. Only a few years ago the Hawes-Hooper Bill was passed, preventing interstate sale of prison-made goods. The Hampden County Jail, however, through its prison labor, solves its own problem of maintenance in every department, workshop, kitchen, bakery, and gardening, and its per capita cost has been the lowest of any county jail in Massachusetts.

Both men and women are admitted to the institution, but kept separately. Practically the sole manual occupation of the women is the laundering of prison clothing. At times there are three hundred inmates behind the red brick walls, and as each is allowed three face towels a week, this item in itself reaches sizeable proportions.

There is a routine procedure for every prisoner admitted to the jail. First he is led through a preliminary door at the entrance, which is unlocked by a guard who has the key for that door only. Then another door is unlocked by another guard, admitting the prisoner to the lobby. The first step is to take the prisoner's record for offenses, his aliases if he has any, the term of his sentence, identifying marks and other information. The prisoner is searched and all personal property is laid aside. He is then led through the "detector door," which is perhaps the newest thing in prison equipment in New England. The detector door is magnetized and built in such a way that if the prisoner has any ferrous metal in his possession, such as a steel knife or weapon which has eluded the search of the guards, this fact is immediately indicated by the door. The prisoner is then stripped and his clothes placed in a bag, which will be kept for him until his sentence has expired. He is next subjected to a thorough physical examination by the doctor, bathed, and given fresh and fumigated prison clothes.

The prisoners are separated into two distinct classes: those who are already serving sentence, and those who are being held pending action of the Grand Jury or as witnesses. The latter group is given every possible freedom within the prison. Brief conversation is permitted. The discipline, while not harsh, is still strict enough to maintain perfect order. The prisoner's lot is easier than it was a number of years ago, and the results accomplished have shown that firm but fair treatment is by far better than the old-time lash and stripes method.

One of the most famous sections of the jail was that known as "The Chicopee House," so named by a trusty, formerly a frequent prisoner, but later reformed. This section was used to discipline unruly or vicious prisoners. There was an old-time padded cell, and several larger cells, an ideal place for the treatment of men afflicted with delirium tremens, and the cells were large enough to place an armed guard with every prisoner. The beds were simple board frames raised a few inches from the floor.

General Embury P. Clark, who was sheriff for more than thirty years, was responsible for much which has contributed to the high standing of the Hampden County Jail. It was in 1893 that he entered on his duties as sheriff, and hung Wallace W. Holmes for murder three months after he went into office. In 1899 he executed the murderer Krathofski, who was the last man to die by the hangman's noose in the State of Massachusetts. Clark distinguished himself as colonel of a regiment of militia which went to Cuba during the Spanish-American War, and later was given the rank of general. General Clark, although a firm believer in discipline, was to a great extent responsible for softening some of the harsh measures formerly used. Besides his duties as a sheriff, he was registrar of the water commissioners, chairman of the Holyoke school board for five consecutive three-year terms, and ardently interested in music. His activities in music were numerous; he was president of the old Chorus Union of that city, sang in the choir of the First Congregational Church of Holyoke, and was instrumental in organizing the Connecticut Valley Music Society.

Escapes have not been frequent from the Hampden County Jail, due in part to the barriers in the way and the vigilance of the personnel, but mainly due to the fact that the terms are so short. In comparison with State and Federal prisons, the terms served at the jail are "temporary," and it is far wiser for the inmate to serve his term out and emerge a free man, than foolishly to attempt escape and be hunted down in the end. Those escapes which have been made were mostly on the part of men who were being kept in the jail temporarily, awaiting trial for serious misdemeanors.

In 1904 an escape occurred which attracted considerable attention. Hoffman, a confidence man of international reputation, broke out of the jail and escaped, despite the fact that he had a crippled leg and used crutches! A man with this physical disadvantage could be easily remembered if seen, but it was considerably later that the authorities caught up with Hoffman as he was riding through Vermont using hired horses. It was found that Hoffman had in some ingenious manner made keys to fit the cell doors, and had calmly left the jail. Sheriff Clark paid from his own pocket the money for the great Hoffman manhunt, which extended through Massachusetts, New York State and Vermont. From time to time there have been other breaks, in one instance resulting in the escape of three men who waited their chance and then sawed their way out of chapel.

The most sensational prison-break and manhunt ever staged in Hampden County took place in 1933 and 1934 in the notable "Kaminski Case," when for many days the countryside was terrorized as the robber and murderer, Alexander Kaminski, roamed loose constantly eluding the large number of police on his trail. On this occasion two men died, another was slightly wounded, and a total of about $25,000 was spent before the criminal was finally apprehended, sentenced and executed.

The amazing series of events strung throughout the case started mildly enough on the night of September 14, 1933. Two Springfield officers stopped a car on Vernon Street occupied by two men, one of whom was Alexander Kaminski, and the other Paul Wargo. Not satisfied with the appearance of the two men or their explanations, and suspicious of the car, the policemen on investigation found firearms in their possession, and booked the young men for appearance in court the following morning.

Wargo pleaded guilty on the charge of illegal possession of a revolver, but Kaminski pleaded not guilty and the case was put over for a few days. Neither of the men could provide bail. They were both finally found guilty and sentenced to six months in the Hampden County Jail.

Kaminski, at the age of twenty-three, was already an accomplished criminal. When he was but nineteen, he had been sentenced to a year in a Florida prison for breaking and entering and larceny. After he had finished that term, he came north and soon after was sentenced to the Connecticut State Prison at Wethersfield for burglary, and from there he was later paroled. It was at Wethersfield that he met Paul Wargo, a gunman and robber, and the two young men decided to join their fortunes.

On the night of October 22, 1933, Kaminski and Wargo escaped from the Hampden County Jail in a spectacular manner, beating Guard Merritt W. Hayden severely in the process. This, in spite of the fact that their sentences would have expired in March of the following year, and the two men would have then walked out of the jail free. Police immediately began an intensive hunt for Kaminski and Wargo, and while this was going on Hayden died. The escaped criminals were no longer merely robbers and gunmen; they were murderers.

Wargo was captured a short time after the break, but Kaminski disappeared. The Governor of Massachusetts, Joseph B. Ely, offered a reward of $1,000 for his capture. In November, a young man who called himself "Robert Laroy" was arrested for robbery at Lynchburg, Virginia, and his fingerprints taken. He was then identified as Kaminski and was brought back to Springfield.

The trial of these men, and the events that followed, received national attention. In the Superior Court trial, the courthouse was jammed with curious onlookers, and many were turned away from the doors. Wargo was found guilty in the second degree, but Kaminski was convicted in the first degree, the difference hinging on the fact that although Wargo was legally an accessory to the murder, it had been Kaminski who had clubbed Hayden with unnecessary violence and with intent to kill.

A sensational and near-disastrous event came about at this trial, one that nearly caused the ruin of the courthouse and the loss of several lives. The murderer's brother, John Kaminski, had hitch-hiked from Connecticut to make a desperate attempt to rescue Alexander. Hidden about his person there were a homemade dynamite bomb wrapped in paper, five hundred bullets, two revolvers, a pair of wire cutters, a hacksaw, and two hand grenades. The story went the rounds later that when John Kaminski had received a ride from New Britain to the city, he had cautioned the driver to "take it easy over the bumps."

Court had just adjourned. The spectators were pushing their way out through the center doors. A preliminary incident had set the crowd in good humor when the knob of Judge Nelson Brown's gavel had flown from the handle and bounced harmlessly from the head of one of the spectators. There was no premonition or warning of anything dangerous to come.

John Kaminski edged into the courtroom just as the crowd was pouring out. Sheriff David Manning, who was sitting in the sheriff's box, glanced at the man coming in and then rivetted his attention on him, recognizing him at once. There was something in Kaminski's face and demeanor that boded no good, and the sheriff leaped toward him. Alexander Kaminski, in the prisoner's box, saw the drama enacted and cried frantically: "Don't do it, John!" But it was too late. John Kaminski threw the bomb down, while those in the court room stared paralyzed with fright. He whipped out a revolver, and as Sheriff Manning was almost on him, he fired. Luckily, the sheriff had reached him soon enough so that as he seized the barrel of the gun, the shot was deflected down and hit the sheriff in the leg. An army of police then descended on Kaminski and bore him to the ground.

Meanwhile the bomb was lying there, and people frantically fought to get down the stairs and out of the building before the explosion came. But there was no explosion. The bomb, later examined, was a very good homemade one and had enough high explosive to wreck at least part of the building, but something had been wrong with the contacts. A State trooper picked it up while it lay in the court room, and with exceptional bravery carried it out and threw it in a snowdrift, and the few minutes of drama were over.

John Kaminski was given several years in prison, and his brother Alexander was convicted of murder in the first degree, a sentence which was finally carried out after he had made a second escape from jail and was caught again. But had the bomb gone off, there would in all probability have been some fatalities and injuries, and certainly a portion of the Hampden County Courthouse would have been destroyed.

Alexander Kaminski was returned to the Hampden County Jail to await the mandatory death sentence. About four-thirty on the morning of Monday, September 17, a little more than a year after his original arrest here, Kaminski again broke out of the jail, apparently under the very noses of the guards delegated to watch him. A special guard who was seated in the corridor of the jail, about four feet away from Kaminski's cell, did not know that his prisoner had escaped until he was so informed by one of the regular guards.

The effect of this second sensational escape on the part of the desperate criminal can readily be imagined. Inspection of the cell showed that the lower bars of the door had been sawed through and then bent aside, allowing Kaminski to get out. The special guard had not looked into the cell because of a blanket which had been hung over the door at the criminal's request, so that the light would not shine in his eyes as he tried to sleep. The blanket had been there for several nights.

Authorities declared immediately that the job was an "inside" one and that Kaminski could never have escaped without receiving help from someone within the prison. The three special guards from the reserve force of the Springfield Police Department were discharged and subjected to repeated grillings by the district attorney and other officials, without appreciable result, although one guard said that he surprised Kaminski in the kitchen of the jail, but made no attempt to stop him.

The first definite clue came from Thompsonville, Connecticut, when Kaminski's prison cap was found in a home which had been broken into, and an automobile was also stolen. At West Stafford gasoline was siphoned from several trucks, presumably for the stolen car, and milk was taken. The authorities tightened their net about every highway.

It was next decided that Kaminski was trapped in the Tolland-Coventry-Willimantic woods, and State troopers and police were concentrated there, but the wily fugitive was not to be found. The automobile which had been stolen from Thompsonville was found at Coventry Lake, and bloodhounds were put on the trail across the tracks and on to the Hartford-Willimantic Highway, but the trail was lost, due to the heavy rain which came at that time.

The rumor that Kaminski had somehow escaped the cordon and gone to some other part of the country was refuted when police caught the trail of an automobile at Manchester, Connecticut, and chased it for a mile. The end of the chase came when the automobile, which had been stolen, was found smashed against a pole on the Middletown Road. In it was a double-barreled shotgun, but Kaminski had escaped into a swamp. Residents in the vicinity were urged to be on the lookout, and at the same time asked to keep any weapons in their possession concealed to minimize the danger of the criminal again being armed. A cottage on the South Bolton Road was entered, however, and a revolver stolen, which heightened the tension.

It was at this point that another life was lost in the dramatic hunt, although Kaminski this time was not directly responsible. Police had received a tip that Kaminski was in the railroad yards in Manchester, and several officers hurried there. The culprit was nowhere to be found, but Willard Mack, a Manchester negro, was arrested and later committed suicide by hanging himself in the Manchester jail.

A definite clue came when fingerprints on a soup bowl belonging to the Vernon House and found a short distance away proved to be the fugitive's. The following day, on September 24, a garage in East Hartford was broken into and shortly afterward a safe opened in the offices of a coal company there. A Massachusetts fingerprint expert identified the fingerprints as those of Kaminski.

From here on the trail of the murderer completely disappeared. Baffled police searched everywhere in vain, without an inkling of a clue.

It was at Albany that the long manhunt ended. Kaminski, after escaping the ring of police at Manchester, had gone to Hartford, dyed his mustache and hair, and had proceeded to Danbury, Connecticut, in a stolen car which he later abandoned. From there he went by foot and auto to New York City and later took the bus for Kingston, New York, staying there at an overnight camp. In taking the bus for Albany, he accidentally left his bag on a bus line at Kingston, and when it was opened Kingston police found burglar tools and a pair of blood-stained gloves. They immediately notified the Albany police, who laid a trap for Kaminski and captured him there. When the murderer was found, he was well-dressed, had $350, and police found hacksaw blades sewed into the soles of his shoes.

Kaminski ultimately paid the supreme penalty for his crime. He was undoubtedly one of the most desperate criminals ever to be housed in the red brick building on York Street, and his pursuit marked the greatest manhunt ever held throughout this section. For many days his name occupied the headlines in bold-face type, and had it not been for that one mistake at Kingston, he might have disappeared entirely, leaving his name a legend as one of the few to escape from the Hampden County jail, and the only one to escape twice.

An outstanding judicial figure in the District Court of Springfield was Judge Wallace R. Heady, who resigned from the bench in 1936 after twenty-two years of service.

On January 30, 1914, Judge Heady qualified as justice of the Police Court, now the District Court, and the following morning presided at the sitting of the court. He was appointed to the bench in 1914 by Governor David I. Walsh to succeed Judge William Hamilton, who vacated the Police Court bench by virtue of his appointment as a Justice of the Superior Court.

Judge Heady gave up private practice of law after his appointment in order to devote his entire time and energy to the dispensing of justice in the Police Court. For many years he continued to sit alone on criminal or civil cases without calling in special justices except on rare occasions, during periods of illness or vacation, but as time went on, he paid most of his attention to criminal cases.

The new District Court Building was erected a few years ago, largely on recommendations and specifications by Judge Heady. He is responsible for establishing the Domestic Relations Court for the private hearing of non-support and domestic cases. He had unusual ability in straightening out family troubles, and he devoted one day a week to the hearing of domestic relations cases.

His reign on the bench saw the inauguration of the small claims procedure in 1920, and the Appellate Division of the District Court in 1922. Judge Heady was for some time a member of the administration committee of the Appellate Division, but resigned because of pressure of court duties. After being admitted to the bar in 1890, he served as master and auditor in more cases than any other Hampden County lawyer up to the time of his appointment to the bench.

Judge Charles L. Long, who died in 1930, was an honest, fearless and upright Justice of the Probate Court. He served a term of thirty-four years, from January, 1896, to October, 1929. Judge Long applied his brilliant intellect and profound knowledge of the law to the problems which came before him, and his legal opinions were classics of their kind. A portrait of Judge Long now holds an honored place in the Hall of Records.

Racial Groups in Hampden County

CHAPTER XXVIII

Racial Groups in Hampden County

The Armenians came to America in large numbers just before the turn of the century. The reason for their exodus from their native land was the same as that of so many other inhabitants of Asia Minor—to escape oppression at the hands of the Turks. And of all the races, these tall, dark, broad-headed people from the slopes of Mt. Ararat have perhaps suffered most from the warlike scavengers who marched under the banner of the Ottoman Empire.

There are now about two hundred and fifty foreign-born Armenians in Springfield, consisting mostly of refugees who escaped from the terror that cut down so many of their countrymen. About sixty Armenian families live in Springfield proper, and about fifty families in Indian Orchard. These peace-loving people have entrenched themselves here in a security which they never experienced in their native land. Their interest in Armenia, however, has not waned because of their new home. Today Armenia is a socialistic Soviet Republic created in 1918, but the American-Armenian will tell you proudly that Armenia was an important land far back in biblical times. It was on the crest of Mt. Ararat that Noah's Ark was supposed to have perched after the flood which lasted forty days and forty nights.

Archie Bedrossian, of Maynard Street, who now is employed at the Van Norman Company, and B. H. Markarian, who conducts an oriental rug shop on State Street, were among the first Armenians to settle in Springfield. Mr. Markarian, who came to this city in 1895, established a residence in the old Young Men's Christian Association and opened up a rug store near the old Victoria Restaurant, with the intention of remaining here but a short time. Noticing a fine museum nearby, he took a number of his best rugs there with the idea of showing them to Mr. George Walter Vincent Smith, then director of the museum. Mr. Smith refused to see him at first, but the Armenian immigrant persisted and finally won an audience. It was the close

friendship he later enjoyed with the museum director that convinced
Mr. Markarian of the virtues of this city as a permanent residence!
His sister joined him here in 1904 and attended Mt. Holyoke College.
She then occupied herself for a time in Near East relief work, and
ultimately married an Episcopalian minister.

Mr. Markarian is proud of the fact that he was the first to send a
wireless telegram from midocean, about thirty-five years ago. On
a return trip from abroad, the boat he was on passed a vessel
which was headed for England. He sent his message across to
the other boat and it was relayed to England when the ship was two

SPRINGFIELD HOSPITAL

hundred miles away from Liverpool, that distance being the maximum
for wireless reception at that time. The message was then cabled to
New York and sent to Springfield, where it was received by Mr.
Markarian's business partner.

From 1899 on, there was a slow but constant influx of Armenians
into Springfield and Indian Orchard. Of a total of 55,057 Armenians
who came to the United States since 1899, 14,192 settled in Massachusetts, this number being exceeded only by the 17,391 who established permanent residence in New York State.

The Armenians here, as well as elsewhere, have gone about their
business quietly, taking little part in civil, political, administrative or

social affairs. They are content to live in peace, as useful and industrious citizens. In Springfield such names as Keuleyan, Emerzian and Piligian have come before the public occasionally, but in the main these people are self-effacing. The Armenians living in the city proper are primarily business men. The art of weaving oriental rugs, in which the people of the Ararat have no superiors, finds its expression in the sale of these rugs in the various Armenian shops on State Street. Other businesses in which the Armenians are engaged are candy making, grocery, shoe repairing and dry cleaning. In Indian Orchard the majority of the Armenians work in mills, or cultivate farms and truck gardens. The local members of the race are scattered about the city, but in the Orchard most of the Armenians live in a colony in the vicinity of Healey Avenue and Beauregard Street.

The majority of the Armenians are Orthodox Catholic Christians, and the rest Protestants of various denominations. There is no Armenian church in Springfield or in the Orchard, but occasionally services are held in Christ Church on State Street, under the spiritual leadership of a visiting bishop from one of the large cities. In Indian Orchard there is an Armenian school, where classes are conducted for children whose parents wish them to be familiar with their native tongue, and religious services are sometimes held there also, under the auspices of what is called the Apostle Church of Indian Orchard.

The Tashnag, Hoc, and Hunchag are three organizations within the Armenian group concerned with religious or political policies. These organizations, which correspond faintly to the Chinese Tongs, have no relation to the American life of these people. A few years ago there was open bitterness between the Tashnag and Hoc groups, which finally culminated in a complete separation when a prominent Armenian bishop was assassinated in New York.

There are two classes of Chinese in the city of Springfield: The ordinary, uneducated people who live here more or less permanently, and who are in the main engaged in the laundry or restaurant business; and the students, who are here temporarily in quest of an education, and are conceded to be the flower of Chinese culture.

The history of the ordinary Chinese in Springfield is hazy. These people establish no citizenship, take part in no activities, and do not mix in any great degree with the Occidental races here. When the Chinese laundryman feels that he has accumulated enough money, he quietly closes his shop and moves out of the city as silently as he came, presumably to go back to China and there end his days. The Oriental here has no intention of becoming Americanized to any great degree. The customs of Mother China are observed by him just as faithfully here as they are in Shanghai or Peiping. Now and then there have been outbreaks here during the Tong wars between the On Leong and Hip Sing factions, and only a few years ago a violent affair of this sort was staged in a Chinese laundry on Liberty Street by hatchetmen presumably imported for this purpose.

The second group, or the Chinese students, really have a history behind them. They are picked youths sent here for the worthy purpose of acquiring a knowledge of western ideals, manners and customs to take back to China. It is pleasing to note that all of the Chinese students educated here later filled positions of distinction in their own country, and took their places as leaders in the overthrow of the Ming Dynasty.

The first Chinese student came to this city in 1847, thirteen years before Japan consented to open her gates to travelers from the West. His name was Tung Wing, and some years later he became Dr. Tung Wing. Originally, he had contemplated a career as a Christian missionary, but finally decided to serve his people in another rôle, a decision which cost him the support of some of his patrons. He persisted in his studies, however, despite his meagre financial resources, and was helped along by Dr. and Mrs. McLean, formerly of Bliss Street. Later he graduated from Monson Academy and Yale University, and in 1867 he persuaded the Chinese Government to appropriate $1,000,-000 for the education of Chinese youths in this country. He was appointed Minister of Education for Chinese in America and established his headquarters at the home of Dr. McLean and later in Hartford. As commissioner he supervised the education of the first group of Chinese students sent to this country in 1867. He died in 1912, having lived to see his activities materialize in the form of the new Chinese republic.

Another eminent Chinese who received the ground work for his education in Springfield, and later in Northampton, was Tong Kwoh On, who came here in 1873 with the second batch of thirty picked students. After a short residence Tong became the pupil of Mrs. Sarah Matthews of Northampton, who later was the second wife

of Dr. McLean. He graduated with honors from both Exeter and
Yale, and on his return to his native land was appointed Commissioner of Education at Shanghai.

Perhaps the most brilliant representative of the Chinese students
here was Chung Mun Teow, who came with the 1872 group, and also
made his home with Dr. and Mrs. McLean. He later graduated from
the Stebbins Classical Institute and the Hartford Latin School, where
he distinguished himself as a student of exceptional merit. In 1879
he entered Yale, where he gained great popularity, being initiated into
the Delta Kappa Epsilon Fraternity and holding down a berth in the
varsity crew as coxswain in 1880 and 1881. He returned to China in
1891, and five years later was called to this country as secretary-
interpreter to the Chinese Legation at Washington, District of Columbia. A few years later he was chosen as Chinese representative at
Madrid, and in 1904 he became consul-general in the Philippines, a
highly important post. He named his son Daniel McLean Chung,
after Dr. McLean.

Many of the French-Canadians crossed the southern border of
Canada down into the Connecticut valley simply because of a restless, adventurous spirit. There was, too, the desire for gain and
the hope of still better opportunity here than that afforded in the
provinces. The French-Canadians in Springfield are second only to
the Irish group in population among the various racial elements.

They merge quickly and easily into the rest of the population,
instead of colonizing. Manners, customs and speech change in a few
years, and often even names. Rousseau become Brooks, LaForce
or Fortier becomes Strong, DuCharme becomes Beach, and Courte-
manche becomes Shortsleeves. At present there are about 19,000
people of French descent in Springfield and Indian Orchard, some
of whose ancestors fought at the side of Montcalm on the Plains of
Abraham back in 1759. Only a few hundred people came directly
from France; the vast majority crossed the border.

There were a few French-Canadians here before the middle of
1800. A Mr. LaPierre lived in the city and also a Mr. DuMontiers,
who kept a blacksmith shop in the south end under the name of Das-
sett. A leading figure of the time was Mr. Proulx, who enjoyed the
trust and confidence of his people here as well as in Holyoke, where
there were a score or more of his countrymen. There were a few

other French-Canadians here besides these three, mainly employed as brickmakers and gardeners. These early settlers came from Sorel, between Montreal and Quebec, and they were objects of curiosity at first with their tasseled hats, half-moccasins, and their soft speech. When the novelty of these quaint strangers wore off Springfield people noticed how hard-working and industrious they were, and welcomed them into their midst.

The great movement of French-Canadians into the Connecticut valley began in 1850. There was plenty of work and a prosperity far exceeding that of Sorel, and the few pioneers wished to share their prosperity with their countrymen. Mr. Proulx was an important factor in starting the immigration. He traveled to Sorel and brought back across the border a large number of his people in big vans resembling prairie schooners. The men tramped the entire distance beside the horses, while the women and children of these migrating colonies rode. It was by far the most picturesque and spectacular cavalcade ever to come into the valley.

The majority of these early French-Canadians were "habitants" or small farmers. They came here at first purely as a speculative trip, in much the same spirit that our ancestors went West during the golden days of '49. Many of them intended to return to Sorel in a short time, but once here found this city much to their liking and resolved to stay. The ringing of the ax was superseded by the whirring of wheels, but they quickly adapted themselves to the change from farming to manufacture.

In those early days the French turned to cotton and textile mills. While a number settled in the city proper, many more found their way to Holyoke, Ludlow, Ware and Three Rivers, where there were factories that were short-handed. A few went into brickmaking and a number into carpentry and cabinetmaking. Woodworking was a favorite vocation, a heritage handed down from the "coureurs du bois," who had traveled through hundreds of miles of dense woodland, built huts with no more tools than an ax and a knife, and to whom the working of wood came almost as second nature.

Those in the mills later worked themselves up, some of them ultimately becoming managers or members of the firm. Practically all of them raised large families. With eight or ten children working in the mills and earning from $4 a week up, plus the additional income taken in from boarders, the head of the family could finally relax on money coming in weekly and reflect how good life was. In those days every child was a distinct asset.

From 1850 to 1860 the influx of French-Canadians into this city was gradual but steady. In the next ten years there was a decided increase and from 1870 to 1890 about three-quarters of the total number of French-Canadians took up residence. They came usually in the spring, just after the big snows disappeared, and went to work in the mills or for building contractors. For a time there was a certain amount of resentment on the part of the local working men who saw in this great flood of immigrants a distinct future menace to their jobs, but work was so plentiful that this fear soon died down. No questions were asked at the border of these people coming down from the provinces, and no papers nor red tape were necessary. The short-handed mill owners were glad to get extra help. A large number of the French-Canadians settled in Holyoke.

One of the most prominent of the early French here was Napoleon Byron. He came to New England in 1863, first settling in Chicopee and finally coming to Springfield in 1880. His people regarded him as their spokesman, and he handled many of their affairs in communal life. Byron went into the contracting business, as did many of his kind, and one of his outstanding buildings was the handsome residence of Nathan D. Bill. He later became active in politics with the support of the French-Canadian group, and gained a position on the common council in 1900, and from there went to the board of aldermen in 1902. During the following two years he was president of the board, and in 1904 ran for mayor on the Republican ticket, but was defeated by F. W. Dickinson. Later he entered the undertaking business and devoted most of his attention to that until his death.

Another leading French-Canadian settler was Octave LaRiviere. He was prominent in the business and political life of Indian Orchard, and in that ward fulfilled much the same public functions as Byron. He was in the contracting and insurance business and also served three terms on the board of aldermen. Other French-Canadian notables then and later were Christopher I. Gagnier, builder and real estate agent; J. G. Roy, another builder; and E. R. Normandin, a painter. Prominent, too, in the building line was Napoleon E. Russell, who came here in 1879. He practiced his vocation as a carpenter, and after work went to evening school.   Later he worked for the Wason Manufacturing Company, and finally entered the building and contracting business.   He built many houses in the Brightwood section, and almost entire streets there may be traced to him.   In 1901 he established the Brightwood Woodworks, and later devoted much of his time to public life when Mayor William P. Hayes appointed him fire commissioner.

One of the oldest French-Canadians in Springfield today is Pierre Angers, who is now retired and lives at 116 Ingersoll Grove.   In 1886, at the age of seventeen, Mr. Angers ran a combination sawmill, planing mill and machine shop in his native Langegardien, twenty miles from Montreal.   During that year his mill burned down, and while Mr. Angers was considering rebuilding, a Springfield man named Ciouci made his appearance in Langegardien and began to lend money left and right on various enterprises.   The youth was greatly impressed by this show of opulence and prosperity, and resolved to migrate to this section in search of real wealth.   On his arrival he lived first on Franklin Street and went to work for John Provost, one of his countrymen and a well-known contractor.   Mr. Angers rose from cabinetmaker to foreman, and finally started his own building business in partnership with C. I. Gagnier.   The firm of Gagnier and Angers, until its termination in 1926, put up eight hundred and thirty-seven buildings in Springfield alone and 1,017 throughout the State.

Mr. Angers relates that when he came to Springfield in 1887 he found Main Street a succession of small wooden buildings, punctuated by a church here and there.   The French-Canadians then in town lived mostly in the south end.   He remembers several of the better known French-Canadians here.   There was a Mr. Fredette, a printer on Dwight Street, whose establishment is still maintained there by his descendants.   A Mr. Parenteau ran a cabinetmaking shop on Taylor Street, and a man named LeFevre, who lived on Linden Street, made a specialty of building churches.   The Potvin brothers on Taylor Street were well known as manufacturers of tools for stonecutters. There were also a few professional men among the French-Canadians here: Dr. Fagnent had an office on the corner of Howard Street and what is now Columbus Avenue, and a man named LePierre was an attorney on Main Street.   It was not until later years that the French-Canadians produced a large number of professional men, because the rank and file of the earlier settlers felt the need to earn at once and went into the mills or contracting with as little delay as possible.

The French-Canadians of the 'seventies and 'eighties were strong churchmen, just as their ancestors were and their descendants are now. The majority are Roman Catholics, although there are a few Protestants. The French-Canadian participates in the religious holidays with great enthusiasm, making them occasions to be remembered. From January 1 to January 6 the "Day of Kings" is celebrated, a ceremony commemorating the story of the Three Wise Men. Then comes Lent or "Careme" and finally Easter, during which a great church festival takes place. Another great occasion comes on July 26, when the "Festival of St. Anne de Beaupre" is celebrated. On these holidays the festive board fairly groans with quantities of delicious food, including pea soup, which may be called the traditional French-Canadian dish.

The church building in the provinces of Canada was the center of communal life, and the same condition held true here. Once the early French-Canadian settlers gained a foothold in this city, they immediately went about to fulfill the need of a church in which to worship and hold meetings, and many were the discussions at their popular gathering place on the corner of Bliss and Main streets on how to go about gaining this end. Previously the French-Canadians had been attending the church in Chicopee every Sunday, but from October, 1869, to July, 1870, services were held at a hall on Main Street, where the old Gilmore Hotel used to be. The first pastor was Rev. Magloire Turcotte, and after him came Rev. Augustine LeVerdiere, who stayed here until April, 1872. Services in this year were held in a small church at the corner of Willow and Main streets, known as "the little white church."

The leading figure in the movement for a French-Canadian religious center was Rev. Louis G. Gagnier. On March 9, 1873, he said his first mass in the old city hall, and began at once the task of raising funds for a church. The French-Canadians organized a bazaar in May of that year under his direction, raising $2,500, and bought the land at the corner of Howard Street and Columbus Avenue, which was valued at $20,000. The basement was completed in June and the first mass in the edifice was said by local French-Canadians in November. Four years later St. Joseph's Church was completed, Father

Gagnier being its pastor for thirty-five years, until his death in 1908. A mission was maintained for a time on Bliss Street, for the French Protestants, the services of which were conducted by various local Protestant ministers, but it later disappeared and the French-Canadians of this denomination attended other Protestant churches. A few years after the turn of the century another French Roman Catholic church was built in Brightwood, the Church of St. Thomas Aquinas.

The French-Canadians, while merging with their neighbors with ease, still kept some national unity within their own group through the medium of organizations. There were the Ligue des Patriots, Councils of the Union St. Jean Baptiste, Société des Artisans Canadiens Française, Court Levis of Indian Orchard, Courts Frontenac, Marie Antoinette and Iberville, French Foresters, and others.

In the first half of the 1800's a number of liberal Germans, finding little fertile ground for new policies in their native land, came to the United States. Some of them settled in Massachusetts, and their intellectual effect on the educational life of this State has been profound.

Among these cultured Germans were Carl Beck and Carl Follen. These two men, exiled from the Fatherland because of their political activities, came to this country on Christmas Day, 1834. Shortly afterward, both Beck and Follen went to teach at the Round Hill School, in Northampton, where, under the supervision of Beck, the Round Hill Gymnasium was started, probably the first of its kind in the United States. This gymnasium may be considered the forerunner of the present-day Turn Verein, and it soon became a well-known institution throughout the valley.

Although records fail to show any Germans actually taking up residence in this city at that time, there were several well-known immigrants from the Fatherland in Springfield as early as 1849. Peter Platt conducted a blacksmith shop and he was known as "a good blacksmith with a good shop." A year later, in 1850, Francis Traps opened a furniture shop here. The Gemeunders, however, was the best known local German family at this time. All the male members of this extraordinary immigrant family achieved world-wide reputations as manufacturers of musical instruments. George, the youngest of the brothers, was an expert violinmaker and was awarded first prizes for several of his instruments at the Crystal Palace World's Fair at London in 1851. The first organ in Springfield was made by Albrecht Gemeunders for the Universalist Church, and August, another brother, was noted in this country as a premier bass viol-maker.

Up to the Civil War there were few Germans in Springfield. They came in small groups and their colony was located down on Cross Street, for in those days Springfield had its share of old Yankee intolerance. This state of affairs did not continue very long, however, and the local Germans began to spread. The immigrants of this nationality were in the main educated men, but the primary reason for their coming here was the opportunity for better wages, rather than the desire for intellectual freedom that prompted their predecessors to leave the Fatherland twenty or thirty years before.

At the outbreak of the Civil War, the work in the armory shops attracted many German mechanics. The hostility of local landlords which was at first evident to these strangers from a far land soon vanished when it was found that the Germans were honest and industrious and paid their bills promptly. The old gathering place and center of entertainment for local Germans was the United States Hotel, later torn down when the city widened Cross Street. The center of activity for the new immigrants was Gilmore's Hall on Main Street, and following that the old Turn Verein rooms on West State Street. These people attended the German Evangelical Lutheran Trinity Church.

Skilled labor was highly prized during those stirring days of the Civil War and the Germans had no equals when it came to mechanical ability. Scores of them came to work here, producing the firearms used by the Union soldiers, and the United States Armory ran day and night. In the thirty years following the war, the local German population reached the thousand mark, and in the next two decades nine hundred and seventy more settled here. Fewer Germans came to America than any other significant race, yet Springfield attracted numbers of them like a magnet.

In the days of the little German colony on Cross Street, a well-known figure was Mrs. Elizabeth Gruendler. She ran the United States Hotel, and on Saturday night when the German tobacco workers came in from the Hook farm in Feeding Hills and other locations, the upper floors of the hostelry used to bend under the weight of the dancers as they clumped about the hall in the familiar steps of the old German dances.

The German is by nature a genial and jovial host, and it is not at all surprising that local Germans took kindly to hotelkeeping. Old Maurice Conrad, familiarly known as "Dutchy," was a well-known host of his time, and in 1875 his little basement restaurant at Main and Sanford streets was the rendezvous of Springfield's gay young men. His real reputation as a host and dispenser of good food and drink was gained, however, in his restaurant at Sanford and Market streets, to which place he moved in 1882 and which for years was one of the city's most favored eating places. Dietrich Sievers was a later manager of the United States Hotel, but in 1901 started his life career as manager of the Highland Hotel. With the assistance of his wife he gained an enviable reputation as a provider of the best in food. The Langes, Lubolds and Henckings were all Germans in the business of selling food and drink, and the name of Schroeder is a familiar one to old-time Springfield diners.

The Germans also branched out in other forms of business. The old Kalmbach and Geisel brewery, which was established in 1869, was probably the forerunner of all the local German business enterprises. It was located on Boston Road at the end of the old horse-car line, and it was thoroughly German in its efficiency and the quality of its product. Then Jacob Lutz, the German lithographer, who had started out in the Goodrich block with a little hand-press as a nucleus, just two years before, began to make tremendous forward strides and built a good business which was housed in the Taylor and Ray block on West Worthington Street. Jacob Lutz turned out the finest work in this section of New England for many years. With the decline of lithography as an illustrating process there, of course, came a corresponding decline in business, but not in the quality of work turned out.

The Dickinson Manufacturing Company, producers of rubber articles, and once an enterprising firm, was directed by Kurt R. Sternberg. Mr. Sternberg took a public-spirited interest in civic affairs and exerted his best efforts in the political field to bring about reforms for the well-being of local citizens. He was a member of the municipal planning commission, and did splendid work for that board. He had also a thorough knowledge of chemistry, and is credited with being one of the co-inventors of bakelite and condensite.

Other German business men came into prominence as the years went on. Otto Baab was well known as a piano dealer. The firm of Guenther and Handel became one of the leading delicatessen establishments. Herman Buchholz was Springfield's main costumer and decorator. Every time there was an amateur theatrical performance his services were likely to be in active demand, and he could supply everything from a monk's cowl to a Satan's costume. Another well-known local German of the same family was Phillip H. Buchholz, before whose big camera hundreds of Springfield people have taken their turn.

In the field of hotel management, a number of other Germans attained prominence. Gus Hencking was manager of the Hencking Hotel on Lyman Street, where the Crown Hotel is now located. Herman Lange, who lived in Springfield, owned and operated the Park Square Hotel in Westfield. Robert Jahrling succeeded D. H. Sievers at the Highland Hotel, and is still there to maintain the excellent reputation of that famous hostelry. One of the first German barbers in Springfield and a man active in singing and dramatic circles of the Turn Verein is Paul Hofman, who still plies his trade in the barber shop of the Highland. Hofman was a barber for a number of years on the North German Lloyd before coming here.

Probably one of the finest examples of German thoroughness, efficiency and perfection of system was the Bosch magneto factory. This was a stronghold of skilled German workmen, and most of the superintendents were Germans also. There were German machine workers, tool and diemakers, and assemblers in most of the other Springfield plants, but it was at the Bosch that the same system which might have been employed at the Krupp factories in the Fatherland was used.

By 1900 there were 2,516 Germans in Springfield. In the next ten years the rate of immigration fell off greatly, but picked up from 1910 to 1914. Many of the local Germans took up residence in the Hill section, although others were scattered everywhere throughout the city. The Germans represented all forms of endeavor: there were skilled machinists and diemakers, business men, cabinetmakers and woodworkers, and a few in politics and the professional world.

In the field of music Emil Janser was a well-known violinist and orchestra leader. His brother Arnold was a singer; while Margarethe Von Mitzlaff made a name for herself in opera.

The center of German activity here as well as elsewhere is the Turn Verein. This famous and unique organization concerns itself with the physical, social and educational welfare of its members, and its "gymnasium" method of teaching has been adopted by practically our entire school system throughout the country. Prominent in the organization is Chris Neubauer, instructor in charge of gymnasium classes. Always an earnest Turner and a strong gymnast, Neubauer received his early training in Germany in this phase of physical culture. Emigrating to America as a young man, he worked in a factory days and taught gymnastic classes in the evening, finally entering the Normal College of the American Gymnastic Union, from which he graduated in 1893. From then on he taught in several Turn Vereins throughout the country, and came to the local organization, then on West State Street, in 1897. Under his able leadership the local club became well known for its gymnastics, fencing and basketball classes, as well as its singing and dramatic divisions. The present-day Turn Verein is located in palatial quarters on Round Hill. Another organization, the Shuetzenverein, was popular some years ago. The Shuetzenverein encouraged amateur marksmen to test their eyes and hands in revolver shooting, and a crack shot was developed in Theodore Geisel, who won many prizes and who became prominent in local militia circles.

In Springfield today there are about 5,000 people of German descent, and of these about 1,200 were immigrants from the Fatherland. The Germans for the most part are Protestants, attending the German Lutheran Church or other Protestant churches throughout the city.

The Greeks are comparatively new to Springfield as well as to the rest of America. A large percentage came from regions other than Greece proper: Turkey, eastern Thrace, northern Epirus, Pontus and other parts of Asia Minor. Some came because of a love of travel and adventure, coupled with a hope for material wealth. But the vast majority of Greeks came because of an intense and passionate love of freedom, which was stifled by Turkish persecution and domination in Asia Minor.

Long before the first Greek came to this city the people of Spring-field were sympathetic with the Hellenic fight for freedom against the Turk. On December 13, 1823, according to the "Hampden Patriot," a local newspaper of the time, a meeting was held at the Peabody assembly hall, "led by many of the most respected citizens and with-out distinction in support of Greek freedom and independence in every possible manner." A committee of eleven was selected out of Spring-field's 4,000 citizens, including Rev. Dr. Samuel Osgood, Rev. Wil-liam B. O. Peabody and others to further this cause. Another impor-tant event was in 1827, when a big mass meeting was held with O. B. Morris presiding and Rev. Mr. Bezaleel Howard giving the address, with the aim of sending munitions and supplies to the Greeks, while Samuel Bowles, editor of the "Republican," wrote at this time: "We revert to the affairs of Greece as of the first importance to the cause of freedom and liberty."

Fifty-seven years later the first Greek immigrant settled in this city. His name was Eleftherius S. Pilalas, and he went to work for the Kibbe Brothers Candy Company, where he ultimately became a manager. Mr. Pilalas, the "father of the Greek Colony," was well liked and respected. He was the man who brought the candy manu-facturing business in this city to its zenith. His brother, Stavros Pila-las, followed shortly afterward, and worked for the Kibbe Company for twenty-four years. He put his evenings after work to good use, attended night school for five years, and soon became well enough versed in English to be employed from time to time as a Greek inter-preter in local courts.

Theodore Carelas followed the Pilalas brothers in 1886. Mr. Carelas was a young giant from Sparta, whose massive frame made it easy to imagine that one of his ancestors fought in the sturdy band which held the pass at Thermopylæ many centuries ago. Like his predecessors, he went to work for Kibbe Brothers and stayed with that firm for sixteen years. John D. Cokkinias opened the first candy stores in the city up to 1900, when the Greek population of the city reached some five hundred.

In 1908 the Greeks began to leave their native land and come to America in large numbers. The incentive for the movement was fur-nished in that year by the young Turks who had seized control of the

Ottoman Empire from the Sultan, and passed a law making it compulsory for every male of military age to serve in the Turkish Army for a term of years.

Many of these people, rather than serve under the crescent banner of the Porte, left their homes. Large numbers of them came to America, but some were forced into military service before they could flee. According to Greek leaders here, at least half of the male Greek immigrants in Springfield have escaped the Turkish Army at the risk of being shot if caught. Stephen L. Efthymion, now dead, but formerly proprietor along with E. Janetis of a tobacco store on Main Street, was representative of this group. While standing with his platoon at the Smyrna waterfront, he took a sudden plunge into the water and swam two miles out into the bay to an American liner and made a successful getaway.

Today there are about 3,500 Greeks in Springfield, settled in all parts of the city, instead of close together in a Greek colony. You will find them in the north and south ends, in the Forest Park section and on the Hill.

Hesiod, more than seven hundred years before Christ, preached the doctrine of moderation. This sentiment the ancient Greeks made the ruling principle of their way of living, and their descendants still follow it. The Greeks make free use of wine, but the sons of Hellas in Springfield make the proud boast that never has one of their race been arrested for intoxication, and very rarely for any other infraction of the law.

There are about one hundred lunch rooms and restaurants owned and operated by Greeks in this city. The Greek in Springfield is a man of business. If he has brought enough money with him from abroad, he opens a store of his own or in partnership with another of his own kind. If he hasn't the money, he goes to work and saves until he has enough to start on his own. Candy and fruit stores, tobacco and news shops, shoe shining and hat cleaning establishments are among the lines of business endeavor favored by the Greeks, although the race has representatives in practically every other type of business.

Since the influx of Greeks in this city was most pronounced between the years 1910-25, this element in Springfield's population is of too recent origin to have produced many professional men. Dr. Socrates J.

Paul, now dead, was a graduate of Tufts Medical College and the first Springfield physician of Greek extraction. Today Dr. L. G. Spelios, of 63 Langdon Street, is a well-known local doctor. In law, Dimitrius V. Constantine is the sole representative of the race.

Probably one of the most famous Greeks in America, as well as in Springfield, is K. P. Tsolainos, formerly of 37 Sargeant Street. Educated in the American School at Smyrna, and later at McGill University in Canada and at Columbia University, he was chosen by American Greeks to represent them at the Paris peace conference some years ago. It was in the French capital that he attracted the attention of Venizelos, the great liberal of Greece, who thought so much of Mr. Tsolainos that he appointed him his secretary. Now he occupies a high position in the National City Bank of New York and for three years won a substantial prize for selling more foreign bonds than anyone else.

Other local Greeks have won distinction in various fields. Nicholas G. V. Nestor, besides being president and editor of the "National Union," the only American Hellenic news magazine printed in the English language in this country is also the American representative of all the Greek newspapers abroad, and is one of the founders and past Supreme Warden of the National Order of Ahepa. George Bacopoulos served for a time as Greek Minister of the Interior. Elias Janetis headed the Ahepa national excursion to Greece in 1930, while Nicholas Cassavetes founded the Pharos Tourist Agency, originating the Greek-American excursions abroad. Charilaus Lagoudakis, formerly of Springfield College, became director of Athens College in Athens, Greece, and Anestis Fanos worked himself up to be editor of the "Atlantis," oldest Greek national daily newspaper in New York City.

One of the Greek leaders in Springfield today is John Michalaros, President of Ahepa, the best known of all the Hellenic organizations. Besides his numerous other communal activities, he is chairman of the Greek committee chosen to arrange for the participation of that race in the tercentenary activities. His history reads almost like fiction. Twenty years ago he left Smyrna for this country, but during the war was interned in France. After some time, however, he was able to come here through the efforts of the American Ambassador, whose interest in Michalaros had been gained through the efforts of

Miss Lawrence and Mrs. Mallory, both Springfield women associated
with the American School at Smyrna. He enrolled in the American
International College and later he was sent some money and eight
hundred bales of Greek tobacco by his family, who had learned of
his whereabouts through the Red Cross. With this start he set up the
Ionian Importing Company. In 1923 he returned to Smyrna to open
a branch of his company there, and being of military age, was immediately seized by the Turks.

Mr. Michalaros still carries scars from the beatings he was subjected to by the Ottoman soldiers. While a prisoner during the Greek
disaster in Smyrna, a Turkish officer approached him and offered to
help him escape in return for money. This officer had charge of several ambulance trucks, and Michalaros, his face completely bandaged,
was dressed in a Turkish uniform and carried, disguised as a wounded
Turkish soldier, to the docks at Smyrna. From there he managed to
attract the attention of two American sailors in a small boat, who
took him to their vessel lying out in the harbor. Mr. Michalaros
liquidated every resource at his command and paid the Turkish officer
about $13,000 for a short ride in a truck as his part of the bargain!

The Greeks in Springfield are proud of the showing their young
men made in the World War. Constantine Veniopoulos Nestor, of
Springfield, who was killed in the Argonne, won high praise for valor
in battle. Hercules Gorgis, who, although from Lynn, spent considerable time in this city, received the highest honors from Congress.
True to his mighty namesake, he captured two hundred and fifty-seven
Germans single-handed.

The great majority of Greeks in Springfield are adherents of the
Greek Orthodox Church, to which their ancestors bore allegiance.
Rev. Christos Manopolous is the spiritual leader of the Church of
St. George on Patton Street, and Rev. D. Pappaleonidas is the leader
of Holy Trinity Church on Carew Street.

The social core of Greek life is the Ahepa Club. Its primary
purpose is Americanization and its name is derived from the first
letters in each word of the following: American Hellenic Educational
Progressive Association. There are more than three hundred and
sixty chapters in the union, the Springfield branch being organized in
1924 by Nicholas Nestor. The Springfield Ahepa is located in the
Young Building at 1653 Main Street, and here one may see an assem-

bly hall, billiard tables, library and other social rooms. The Greeks, who are inclined toward the Republican party politically, thrash out the merits or shortcomings of various candidates in these quarters, and should a passerby on our busiest thoroughfare step into the Ahepa Club just before election time, he would be treated to as rare a battle of words as it has ever been his privilege to hear.

The Gapa is another noteworthy Greek club. Its purpose is the preservation of Greek ideals in American life. Clubs for the younger generation include the Junior Order of the Sons of Pericles and the Maids of Athens, both under the jurisdiction of Ahepa. The Philoptohos is exclusively a woman's organization devoted to charitable work and is under the auspices of Saint George's.

The Greeks, for the most part, are here to stay. Like the members of many other races, they have found Springfield a haven after the bitterness of oppression abroad. Their intense love of liberty has been fully gratified here, and they make sober, industrious and hardworking citizens. It is to the credit of the Greeks that they have never asked or received a single penny from any outside charitable organization or the community chest, their own organizations assisting at all times in taking care of their own group in time of emergency.

The Irish are the largest individual portion of Springfield's population, outside of the native born Yankee and the later settlers of English descent. They number about 21,000, or one-seventh of the population of the city, and of these about 5,600 are immigrants directly from the old country.

It was on the seventeenth of June, 1643, only twenty-three years after the "Mayflower" landed at historic Plymouth with its one hundred passengers, that an Irish immigration took place that put the small Pilgrim colony in the shade. The American colonies needed population and economic and political conditions in Ireland favored migration. The Commissioners of Ireland, in September, 1642, contracted with Captain John Vernon, William Leader and Daniel Sellick to supply them with two hundred and fifty women of the Irish nation, between the ages of fifteen and fifty, and three hundred young men, to be found in the country within twenty miles of Cork, Kerry, Waterford, Wexford and Tipperary, to import into New England. Here, then, we find at the very beginning of the American colonies in New England, five hundred and fifty Irish men and women in the prime of life, brought in to mingle with the English stock. It is fairly certain that some of these found their way to Springfield a few years later.

The early records show that Henry Chapin sold to "John Riley" sixteen acres of land along the west side of the Connecticut River, the property being described as "West of the Connecticut river and north from the Riley tract," which would indicate that the purchase was in addition to some land previously owned by some member of the Riley family. The sale was witnessed by Miles Morgan, and the deed recorded by John Holyoke. This was a part of the territory known as "Ireland Parish" and is the present site of the home for orphan children at Brightside.

Besides John Riley and his wife, Grace O'Dea, who settled here in 1649, there were Jonathan, Mary, Grace, Sarah, Jacob, and Isaac Riley born to this couple, according to the senior Riley's will of 1671, and also a nephew of Mr. Riley and a sister of Mrs. Riley's, Margaret O'Dea. It may be said, therefore, that in all probability the Rileys were the first people of distinct Irish descent in Springfield during the pioneer days, and their names keep occurring in the records through the years.

In the year 1712 an organized movement of Scotch-Irish to New England took place after a petition to Governor Shute, of Massachusetts, was signed by three hundred and twenty leading men from the north of Ireland and presented to Reverend William Boyd as intermediary. The petition, couched in respectful language, was acted on and these Scotch-Irish landed in Boston, many of them later finding their way to this vicinity. Of these men a celebrated writer has said:

"They were men of pluck and muscle who hewed down the trees which built their frontier homes and churches, men who coveted no fine linen for their tables and were contented if they had enough of cornbread and potatoes, and yet imbued with such a thirst for learning that they became the founders of many of our foremost schools and colleges."

These settlers came in families, parents and children with all their worldy goods, and bound together by race, kindred and creed, determined that their posterity would live from their beginning. These early Irish pioneers brought with them the potato, a vegetable then unknown to New England, and it was an important article of their food supply, as it is today.

In later years they figured conspicuously in the establishment of this government, and did much for freedom of thought and in saving the institutions of the government when in danger. In the very early years the Irish settlers in Springfield were more or less looked down on by the rest of the inhabitants, partly because of prejudice still lingering from abroad, partly because of religious differences, and in some measure due to the natural suspicion of the early pioneers toward those different from themselves. An Irishman later became known simply as "Paddy," or he was called by his last name and designation: "Kelly the Irishman," or "Burke the Irishman."

The Irish, because of their inherent love for freedom of thought and hatred of political shackles, were practically all on the colonies' side during the American Revolution. They were also prominent in the various Indian wars and in Shays' Rebellion. The official records of the battle of Bunker Hill show that of the 2,000 men on the patriot side, two hundred and thirty-four had distinctly Irish names, and of this number many were from this region. There were others from the valley, including Patrick Nugent, of West Springfield, who played a prominent part in Colonel Timothy Danielson's regiment of minutemen.

From 1832 to 1850 large numbers of Irishmen came to Springfield to work on the railroads. They were strong men and willing workers, and their presence here as laborers was urgently needed at a time when the country was beginning to awake to the immense possibilities of railroad transportation. These Irish settled on Ferry, Liberty and Sharon streets, and also in "Mechanics' Row," which was a short, alley-like street at the foot of Bliss Street near the river, and adjacent to the Boston and Albany Railroad. The Irish living in the Row itself had to live frugally; in fact, dangerously close to the ragged edge, as wages for laboring were from three to five dollars a week.

In 1846 there were perhaps three or four hundred Irish in Springfield, and probably less than a thousand in the whole county. The local Irish in the middle of the nineteenth century held no public positions of eminence, and few had even a semblance of ordinary wealth.

One of the most important problems to arise with the constant influx of Irish was the establishing of a place of worship. From 1846 to 1856 three priests, the Reverends G. T. Reardon, John J. Doherty, and William Blinkensop had ministered to the spiritual needs of the Irish here. The history of active Catholic faith and the spiritual progress and prosperity of the Catholics of Springfield may be said to date from the coming of the Reverend M. P. Galligher from Boston. Father Galligher founded a small church on Union Street, which soon became inadequate for the growing population. Instead of having one pew to a family, several families would crowd in, each contributing a small share of money to cover the total expense. Father Galligher began to organize his people, and so successful were the united efforts of pastor and flock that in about four years from the time of his arrival the splendid church property was purchased on which now stand St. Michael's Cathedral, the bishop's residence, the Catholic rectory, and the convent of the Sisters of St. Joseph.

Through the untiring efforts of Father Galligher, the property was entirely free from debt and the church consecrated by Bishop Williams, of Boston, on September 28, 1867. Worn out by his labors and respected by the whole community, Protestants as well as Catholic, Father Galligher died on June 1, 1869. The patriotic stand which he took during the Civil War, encouraging the enlistment of Catholics for the Union Army, and the particularly active part he took at the time of President Lincoln's death, endeared him to every citizen.

The diocese of Springfield was created by Pope Pius IX in July, 1870, and the Reverend P. T. O'Reilly was appointed first bishop of Springfield at St. Michael's Cathedral, the consecrator being Cardinal McCloskey, archbishop of New York, and the sermon was preached by Bishop Bacon, of Portland, Maine. After twenty-two years of useful service Bishop O'Reilly died, to be succeeded by the Right Reverend Thomas D. Beaven and others up to the present time. With St. Michael's as the Catholic center other small parishes developed throughout the city, especially with the advent of Catholics of other races.

One of the oldest Irish residents of Springfield today is Thomas E. King, father of Attorneys Raymond and Albert King. He was born here in 1850, attended a few grades at the local schools, and finally went to work in the millinery establishment of a man named Fallon, in

Besse Place. Young King received $1.50 each week for sweeping out and doing odd jobs. A short time later, he worked at the United States Armory straightening gun barrels, and it was while he was engaged in this arduous task that the Civil War broke out.

King was far too young for military service, but the music of the band and the sound of marching feet got into his blood, and he almost succeeded in stowing away on a troop train ready to head south to the front, before his anxious and worried mother finally located him and took him off. In 1882 he entered the meat business and bought considerable property, and finally retired, a successful business man, to his home on Mulberry Street.

During the Civil War, according to Mr. King, almost whole families of Irishmen from Ferry and Sharon streets and Mechanics' Row enlisted in the Union Army. Hugh Donnelly was captain of a company in the 37th Massachusetts, and through the brilliance of his service returned a colonel. Captain Malloy was another local Irishman who headed a company in this regiment and distinguished himself. It was the 37th, in which many local Irish enlisted, that was partly instrumental with a New York regiment in turning back the victorious Southerners from Washington, after their victory at Bull Run. Mr. King remembers making the huge sum of five dollars selling "Republicans" on the fateful day of Bull Run!

Another incident besides the Irish patriotism which softened local hostility toward the Irish was a banquet given by a group of young Irishmen to Ben Shields. A prominent and eminent citizen of Springfield, Judge Shurtleff, who was then a member of the common council, was invited. He was amazed at the keenness and fine manners of the young men there, and when he returned to his affairs in the city government he promptly entered the names of fifty of the men as eligibles for jury duty. Up to this time no Irishman had ever sat in a local jury box, this privilege being reserved exclusively for those who belonged to certain select lodges. This incident, according to Mr. King, marks the start of the local Irish into politics!

Another of the old Irishmen living in this city today is Edward A. Hall, of Bliss Street, now an official of the Springfield Coöperative Bank. His father was a blacksmith, who worked at the United States Armory, and the family lived where the Boys' Club is now located on Chestnut Street. After Hall graduated from the public schools in

Springfield, he entered the clothing business on the site of the old post office. He moved to the corner of Main Street and Harrison Avenue when the government bought the post office property. After twenty-five years in the clothing business, Hall became a parole and probation officer for the State and finally entered the banking business. He was a scholar as well as a business man, and has written several books and papers on the Irish for historical societies, all of which have been the results of long and exhaustive research.

One of the important Irishmen here before the Civil War, according to Mr. Hall, was James Bannon. In the days when the armory was privately owned instead of by the government, a man named Charles Stearns employed a number of Irish and sold land to them. The Catholics had just begun to make excavations on the property for a Catholic church when local citizens protested violently, and a trial was held at which James Bannon was a prominent witness. Bannon, who had previously served under Robert Emmet, the great Irish patriot, raised a large family here, and lived on Walnut Street. One of his sons, Robert Emmet Bannon, became the first Irish letter carrier of Springfield; another, one of the first Irish in the city council, and a daughter one of the first Irish women to teach in a local school.

During the Civil War many of the Irish worked in the armory, and there was some migration up to points nearer their work in the Carew and Armory Street sections, commonly known as the "Hungry Hill" district, where many Irish live today. Prominent among the Irish was Florance Donahue, the father of John W. Donahue. The elder Donahue rose to be superintendent of construction on the Boston and Albany Railroad, and played a prominent part in the building of many of its bridges and depots. He was also one of the first local Irishmen to become a member of the common council.

Dr. Edward Fitzgerald was the first Irish doctor here, about 1860, as far as old residents can remember. An Irishman named Luke Hart was the first Irish policeman. The Burke brothers ran a combination tea shop and undertaking parlor on the corner of Worthington and Main streets, and Phillip J. Ryan ran a Catholic book store on Taylor and Main. Tom Sampson ran an undertaking parlor and is still in the same business. A man named Burns was in the hotel business, as well as Charles Shean, who later became prominent both in his business and public life. A local Irish citizen whose name became a great one in the American theatre was Jerry Cohan, himself an actor, and the father of the great George M. Cohan, famous the world over. According to Thomas King, every member of the Cohan family was an actor or dancer. The senior Cohan blacked boots and sold papers as a youth, and then worked as a servant for Dr. Otis on State Street. Later, he took his family and went on the road to give theatrical performances, and the world knows the result. The family was billed as "The Four Cohans," but it was George who wrote the show and was the guiding genius behind it. Another local Irishman who became nationally famous was William J. Hynes, who lived on Mechanics' Row. After the Civil War he went to Arkansas, became a Congressman, and later a distinguished criminal lawyer.

There is an interesting sidelight on that famous Mechanics' Row, which has long since disappeared. In former days, when the river overflowed its banks, the Irish tenements and homes were among the first to be submerged. There were no relief agencies to speak of, and the suffering was acute, many of the Irish living out in the open until the waters had subsided. The great fear that hung over the people then was a disease that we little think of now. That disease was malaria. The floods turned the river banks into swampy, muddy, morasses, forming excellent breeding places for the tertian mosquito, carrier of malaria. The danger was accentuated by the cramped living conditions of the Irish, and when the people crowded into their little church to say mass, this spectre hung over them constantly, and in one year several died of the malady.

Starting from 1870, when the Irish began to achieve their places in public life, up to the present time, the people of Erin who became prominent are too numerous to mention. The Irish devote themselves to no one activity, but may be found in business, in skilled and unskilled labor, in the professions, and particularly in politics. James B. Carroll is perhaps the outstanding local Irish public figure of the 'eighties. Carroll, through a remarkable gift of oratory and individual capability and brilliance, rose to become a member of the Supreme Court of Massachusetts. Other men who might be mentioned are Captain Henry McDonald, a war veteran and probably the first Irish chief of police; William P. Hayes, who became mayor at the turn of the century; Captain Hugh Donnelly, a prominent local man and a Civil War veteran, who later became clerk of the Supreme Court. Today many city and county officials are of Irish descent.

In the colorful mosaic of nationalities which make up Springfield are the dark-eyed, vivacious and industrious people whose native land is the country of the olive grove and the vineyard. That country which through the centuries has produced the finest in art, music, and architecture, is today under the rule of a Fascist dictator, and across its terrain march thousands of uniformed men who nominally, at least, march with a singleness of purpose under one leader. Yet it is probable that the Lombard will always differ from the Neapolitan, and the Genoan from the swarthy Sicilian, as Italy differs within itself—a checkerboard of provinces with distinct individualities, varying customs, puzzling dialects and opposing temperaments.

The members of this complex and fascinating people number about 15,000 in the city of Springfield, and of these about 4,500 are immigrants born in Italy. The different classes of society as well as the different provinces are represented here, and those from similar home locations are naturally found living close to each other. In "Little Italy" or the south end section of the city, most of the people are Southern Italians, and comprise in great measure the working class. About sixty per cent. of the Springfield Italians are from the north of Italy, however, and their tendency is not to colonize, but rather to spread to all parts of the city. These northern Italians are engaged in various retail and wholesale business enterprises for the most part, or have taken up professions. The first Italians who came to Springfield came from that northern part of their native land which gave to the world the man who discovered America. The Genoese have always been noted as adventurous and daring sailors, and have traditionally emulated that greatest wanderer of them all, Christopher Columbus. Not only were they the first to come to the United States, but they were also the first Italians to settle in Central and South America.

The first Springfield Italians were not laboring men. The Genoese, besides their flair for travel, are noted as shrewd and able traders and business men, and it is rather a rare occurrence to see a Genoese working with his hands at unskilled labor. The early Italian settlers here had business ability or were men with a trade, and they engaged immediately in profitable callings of this nature, despite the handicap of being totally unfamiliar with the language.

Francis Denegri, as far as can be ascertained, was the first Italian to come to Springfield, and his name appeared in the city directory in

1864. Denegri went to work for the Kibbe Brothers Candy Company. The following year his son came and worked for the same firm. Both men, with characteristic aptitude, did well in their occupation. Francis eventually became an expert candymaker and rose to the position of foreman before the family moved to Canada in 1875.

From this point on, Italians straggled into Springfield in small groups. A noted family was the Papantis. The sons, all skilled technicians, worked in the armory, Smith and Wesson and the E. H. Barney companies. Luigi Papanti, the father of these men, though his English was broken and his manners strange, in a very short time became a well-known musician and dance teacher throughout New England, and was the leader of the Southland Orchestra at the old Gilmore Theatre, which was then Springfield's opera house. During his residence he also taught music and dancing at Smith and Mount Holyoke colleges.

The Italians who came in the 'seventies were, in the main, small business men, opening groceries and fruit stands, the latter until then unknown in Springfield. An outstanding Italian who settled here in the 'seventies was Joseph Bardelli, who made a name for himself not only in Springfield but throughout the country. Before his coming to America, fancy paper boxes were imported from France and Germany. Bardelli learned his trade in his native city, Milan, and later in Paris, and finally developed into a clever designer of novelties in fancy boxes. He came into Springfield in 1875, and is really the man responsible for introducing fancy boxmaking in this country. In Springfield, Bardelli made a small fortune at his trade, and he spent it lavishly in expensive living and entertaining his friends. Old men relate that when Bardelli was connected with the Morgan Envelope Company he lived in a large house, kept four fast horses, employed two coachmen and two servants, and that in 1877 he gave a banquet at the Gilmore block, where every kind of food, domestic and imported, was available for the table, besides every variety of wines and spirits then known. The most prominent citizens of Springfield, including Mayor Wight and the members of the city government, sat at this magnificent banquet, which is reputed to have cost Mr. Bardelli $1,700, a lot of money in those days.

These first Italians, contrary to the later custom of the people to colonize, lived in different sections of the city. Every Sunday, however, they gathered in the house of one of the members, enjoyed Italian food and the opportunity to talk their own language to those who would understand, and helped each other whenever possible in the difficulties encountered by a small group of strangers in a strange land.

Toward the end of 1873 the first Sicilians and other southern Italians came to Springfield. Until 1890 there was an influx of these people and they immediately colonized. The newcomers established themselves in the houses along the river bank at the foot of Court and State streets, which marked the beginning of "Little Italy." In 1885 there were over a hundred southern Italians here, most of them laborers. It was near this time that the contract to build the Hampden County Jail was awarded to a Boston contractor named Nye, and he brought about twenty-five Italians to the city. Most of them liked this locality so well that they adopted it as their permanent home.

The southern Italians have produced their share of prominent men in business, in the professions and in art, although not as many as those from the north. But in those early days, handicapped as these people were by their complete ignorance of American language and custom, there was nothing for them to do but work at unskilled labor here, despite the fact that many of them were artisans of one sort or another in Italy. Many of them worked for Sackett and Reynolds and J. R. Driscoll in excavating, and many also on the railroad gangs. It was a common sight to see groups of Italians coming down the railroad along the river working furiously at the handles of the hand-cars and eating their lunches as they went.

The leader of the early southern Italians here was John Albano. He opened an Italian bank on Union Street, and later a steamship agency and office which was really a clearing house for sending money and mail to relatives in Italy. If an Italian of this period went to one of the regular banks in the city, it was impossible to make himself understood and he had no knowledge of the strange ways in which American business and banking was conducted. At Albano's his affairs of this nature were taken care of with ease and in a manner understandable to himself. Albano rose to prominence among his people as the years went on, and was called "The King of Little Italy." For years he was a professional bondsman for those Italians who were so unfortunate as to fall afoul of the law, and he was prominent at festivities in the colony and also as one of the founders of the Patria Society.

There are many Italian barbers in the city today, but a man named Carlo Florio was the forerunner of them all. He had a small shop at 26 Bridge Street, and was a real expert at his trade. Every Italian who was desirous of learning barbering went to Florio's for his instruction, and there are many in the modern shops of today who, as young men, learned their trade under Florio's guidance.

Along with the small business men and the hard working laborers among the southern Italians came a few who by the nature of their work were looked down upon by their fellow-countrymen. Springfield, at this time, was a mecca and a headquarters for organ grinders, especially during the winter, when they could get their organs repaired and tuned by a Yankee doctor of music who lived here. The organ grinders as a class, however, were distinctly out of repute with the Italians throughout the city, who considered them on the lower rungs of the social ladder.

Many of the laborers worked for the city then, as they do now. At that time the average wage for labor was about $1.50 a day, and yet the Italian with characteristic thrift, managed to save a little from his pay envelope every week. There was an Italian boardinghouse on the river bank at the foot of Bliss Street, where many of the laborers boarded, and when times were good enjoyed ravioli, pignoli, pignolatta and the inevitable spaghetti and macaroni. When times were bad, however, the main and sometimes only item on the bill of fare was soup.

The south end area along the river was a colorful and bizarre place, especially in the cool of the evening. The Italians, when the weather was fair, spent most of their hours in front of their houses in chairs, or on the porches. In Italy, the poor had linen in their wooden chests as did the rich, and they used and bought only the finest. The women brought their hand work with them across the water, and it was a common sight to see the housewife crocheting for hours. Practically every Italian woman was an expert with the hook and needle. Another colorful sight was that of red stockings. In "Little Italy" they were very much in evidence, being preferred by Italian women, old and young, instead of the rather drab greys, browns, and blacks of the descendants of the Puritans. Each woman owned several pairs of them, and they made patches of real color along Columbus Avenue.

The observer, as he walked down through this section, could not fail to catch the distinctive odors of strange cooking. The Italian housewife, besides being handy with the needle, is also an expert at the culinary art. On holidays there were special foods to tickle the palate —ravioli, a suggestion of our chicken fricassee with chicken sauce combined in some mysterious way with tomatoes; pignoli, a Christmas sweetbread pastry with capsule-shaped nuts; foglia, consisting mostly of shortening and eggs and fried in olive oil; and pignolatta, peanuts mixed with honey and resembling very much our peanut brittle. There were a variety of others, including green salads with olive oil used instead of our dressing, and onions baked instead of raw or fried.

In the year 1888 the first mutual benefit society was founded and named the Societa Unione e Fratellanza Italiana, which provided for the services of a physician and also a sick benefit. Eugene Metelli, an influential and well-to-do Italian was the founder. It did some splendid work among the Italians then as well as later.

There was a wave of immigration to America toward the turn of the century, and the number of Italians in Springfield increased considerably. By 1893 there were 2,000 Italians here, and three years later there were thirteen fruit and confectionery stores, two wholesale fruit stores, eleven grocers and seven liquor stores run by them. The colony expanded southward along the river bank until lower Union Street became the center of the Italian quarter, invading the domain of the old Irish residents, who gave way and moved elsewhere. Before the Italians came to Springfield, the city directory did not contain such words as "fruit dealer," "peanut vender" or "bootblack." In 1894 there were no bootblacks registered, but the next year seven of them made their appearance and did a thriving business.

One of the greatest Italian celebrations ever to take place in the city occurred in 1892 when the four hundredth anniversary of the discovery of America by Columbus took place. Amidst scenes of the wildest enthusiasm, a parade marched down Main Street led by the Lafayette Band, and later came a dance at Turn Hall, followed by banqueting and general celebration everywhere. The Italians are by nature demonstrative, and the annual Mt. Carmel celebration is something that we may view even today, when Columbus Avenue is bedecked with arching colored lights, the streets teem with humanity in a holiday mood, and fireworks light up the sky. There was another tremendous celebration shortly after the war when Enrico Caruso came here and sang.

An Italian worthy of mention as the new century came into being was P. A. Breglio. He was a communal leader here, always striving for more recognition for his race, and was instrumental in organizing the Italian-American Protective League. After some years in the grocery business, Breglio went into construction on a large scale, and was especially influential in the building of the Little River water system, which now supplies Springfield. It was Breglio who furnished the labor and to some degree directed it, and a large number of the workers on this tremendous engineering project were Springfield Italians. Another Italian worthy of mention was Silvio Origo. Like many other Genoese, he had been a sailor, serving for many years as an officer in the Italian Navy, and he could speak French, English, and Spanish fluently besides his native tongue. It was Origo who made the speech of welcome when Cardinal Martinelli came to Springfield in 1898, and later he became the official interpreter for the Police and Superior courts here. After some years he became an ardent Socialist, and the National Socialist committee sent him out twice on speaking tours.

The Italian population in 1900 was upward of 3,000. The colony then extended all the way from Bliss to Mill Street between Main and Water streets, now Columbus Avenue. Some years later there was a definite exodus into the smaller towns of Hampden County, especially to West Springfield, Agawam and Feeding Hills, where many Italians established small garden and truck farms, bringing their produce to the city each day. The World War had a radical effect on the Italians here, many of them becoming factory workers instead of laborers, especially at the Springfield Armory, which had been the stronghold of the Yankees, Irish, Germans and Scandinavians, and there were many young Springfield Italians who took up arms for their native land.

The Italians, who are Roman Catholic almost without exception, were without a church or chapel for many years. An attempt was made in 1892 by Joseph Bardelli and others to raise funds for a small church, but the attempt failed, and the Reverends Kelley and Conaty, both of whom spoke Italian, ministered to the spiritual needs of the people. In 1906 the Reverend Anthony Dellaporta came to Springfield and began his hard and discouraging task of raising funds for the building of a church. For several years the Italians gathered in a little impoverished structure on Union Street for religious worship, until in 1911 enough money was raised for the building of the Mount Carmel Church on Williams Street and Columbus Avenue.

The Italians are inclined toward social activities, there being roughly eleven societies and two clubs formed by the race here. In the world of art the people of sunny Italy have produced many local musicians and artists of distinction, as well as a generous number of professional men.

Louis Rittenberg, as far as old men can remember, was the first known Jew in Springfield. He moved here, in 1881, from Holyoke, where he maintained a dry goods establishment, and opened a store on Worthington Street to dispense peddlers' supplies. Jews alive today who patronized that store will tell of the sterling qualities of this man, who rose to be a millionaire "woolen king" in New York City from his humble start here. He trusted impoverished Jewish peddlers; shared with the neediest of them his bed; and constantly sought to relieve his friends in distress. Like him in charities, a few years later was Henry Glickman, the father of Dr. Alfred L. Glickman.

Philip Cohn, who died three years ago, is considered by many the "Pioneer of Springfield Jews." When he came to this city, in 1883, there was but one other Jew here, Louis Alpert. In 1885 there were three Jewish families in town beside that of Mr. Cohn: Henry Glickman, H. Winitsky, and Abram Abrams.

These first Jewish families all lived on Liberty Street. The men were humble peddlers, and it was only natural that they lived close to each other. It gave them a feeling of kinship and prevented a solid front of resistance to the hoodlums who sometimes made sporadic excursions into that neighborhood, and who delighted in taunting the newcomers. Mr. Cohn still has scars on his forehead that were caused by stones thrown at him during his peddler days. But the police swung their clubs menacingly and brought a much-appreciated protection to this minority group. Mr. Cohn was always a staunch admirer of the Springfield police, and this is one of the reasons he gave:

One night, in those early days, young Cohn, laden with eggs, ink, molasses and kerosene, was attacked by a half dozen roughnecks with no great respect for the beard he wore. The provisions and supplies were destroyed and the culprits fled. But the police rounded up the guilty ones a few hours later by detecting the odor of kerosene on their clothes.

Cohn and Rittenberg headed the parade of Russian Jews who flocked to this city immediately after Ignatief, the Russian Secretary of the Interior, issued an edict expelling them from Russia. Springfield was then merely an enterprising country town with a population of about 37,000 people. White Street was a fruitful hunting section, while the Forest Park district was a dense wood.

Although Mr. Cohn is dead, his son Frederic is a well-known attorney here. As his father was called the "Pioneer," his son may well be called the "Historian." Last year he made a thorough study of the Jews here, over a fifty-year period (1885-1935), and presented his results in two lectures to the local B'nai B'rith.

By 1887 the influx of Jews in Springfield became more pronounced. Louis Lasker, the father of Attorney Henry Lasker, was a prominent newcomer of that year, and shortly afterward came Benjamin Bearg, who is still alive and a well-known merchant on Main Street. Mr. Bearg will never forget the day in 1889 when he made a clear profit of $2 from his peddling. He remembers, too, how amazed Springfield people were, during the course of his peddling route, to find out that he was a Jew. After surviving the shock, they would press the peddler curiously for an account of himself and listen intently while he spun a woeful tale in rather unusual English.

The files of the "Republican" for January 22, 1888, reveal a story with the headline, "A Genuine Jewish Synagogue," which reads, in part, as follows:

"In the upper story of Patton's Block, on the corner of Main and Hampden Streets, is a room of fair size which goes by the somewhat dignified designation of a Jewish Synagogue. Here the Jews of the city are wont to gather at stated intervals and hold simple and yet devout services.

"The furnishings of the room are rather disappointing to those who expect before entering to see an elaborate miniature temple. The walls are plainly whitewashed, simple settees give ample accommodations, a table in the corner, covered with cloth and bearing two candles is the altar, and a curtain placed behind, shields the most sacred portion of the apartment from the view of the unholy.

"There are perhaps in this city twenty Jewish families, who, with the well-known characteristics of the race speedily took measures to secure a place of their own. . . . . "

Historically anything that comes first is of prime importance. In 1888 William Gelin was the bridegroom in the first Jewish wedding in Springfield. Harry Greenberg opened the first Jewish grocery on Ferry Street in 1889, and Benjamin Rosenstein became the first Jewish shoemaker. In 1890 Selig Manila, Felix Cohen and Ferdinand Haas made names for themselves by opening the first Jewish-operated brewery.

The year 1892 is an important one for these people. The first Jewish lodge of Springfield was formed: "The Commonwealth Lodge of the Sons of Benjamin." Other significant events this year were that the Jews, slightly more opulent, moved their synagogue to more palatial quarters in a room over Graves Hall, the present Carlisle Building, and a Jewish burying ground was bought in West Springfield. Prior to the purchase of the burying ground, bodies of Jews who died were shipped either to Boston or New York for burial. The Beth-El Cemetery was the answer to that sad and at the same time expensive procedure.

By this time the Jews were rapidly instituting themselves in various businesses, drawing away from the simple peddling that had been the chief means of livelihood. In 1892 Max Weiner became the first Jewish baker. Jacob Dorenbaum entered the field as the first Jewish barber and still plies his trade in this city! A welcome addition to the business world took place when Samuel and Julius Goldstein opened the first Jewish meat market. Formerly, it was necessary to get Kosher meat from New York, again an inconvenient and expensive procedure.

Moses Ehrlich came to Springfield during this year and a short time later started an iron and metal business on Liberty Street. Along with Philip Cohn and M. J. Aronson, he is considered a prime mover in the advancement of Jewish life here, religious, social, and charitable. The beautiful Kodimoh Synagogue on Oakland Street was due mainly to his efforts, and he was its president for several years before his death in 1924.

Events and personalities crop up here one after another. The first separate and distinct Jewish synagogue on Grays Avenue was dedicated, and Philip Cohn, the "Pioneer," was its sexton for forty-five years until his death. Max Weiner opened the first Turkish baths. The Young Men's Hebrew Association was instituted at 118 Worthington Street and later moved to Sargeant Street. Julius Kingsburg became the first Jewish jeweler in town, and Charles Henin the first Jewish doctor. And it was in 1896 that the Jews first came to be recognized in quite another way—in what was considered a wonderful political manœuvre, a job was obtained for Hillel Levine as a street cleaner!

The women organized the first women's society called the Hebrew Ladies' Relief Association. Two years later, Morris Grenowitz became the first Spanish War veteran. The field of municipal education was entered when Frederic Cohn, at the age of sixteen, became a teacher in the Elm Street Evening School, where the present Registry of Deeds now stands.

At the turn of the century, Jewish community life here was firmly established. It is possible only to touch on the high-lights of the multiple and numerous local Jewish activities. Samuel Rapaport was the first rabbi in Springfield in 1904. Ida Singer the first Jewish dentist. In 1911 a great event in Jewish life came when the B'nai B'rith Lodge was instituted in Odd Fellows Hall.

Henry Lasker was the first Jewish lawyer in Springfield and later became prominent in civic affairs. As president of the board of aldermen, Mr. Lasker acted in the capacity of mayor on several occasions, and in 1909 his vote decided the question of building the municipal group. It was Lasker, who as a student in high school, brought the great Israel Zangwill here to lecture. He was also founder of the Springfield Lodge of the B'nai B'rith and was the first president of the Congregation Beth-El. Another prominent civic figure a few years ago was Ezekiel M. Ezekiel, who was appointed by Mayor Ralph N. Ellis as police commissioner in 1902 and served two terms of three years each.

At the time of the World War, two hundred and fifty Jewish boys enlisted or were drafted. Six were killed in action and two subsequently died of their wounds. Abe Flesher was outstanding in performing deeds of heroism while with the American Army in France. At this time the Jews in Springfield raised $25,000 for war relief, exhibiting a splendid spirit of patriotism to the Nation.

The negro in Springfield goes far back into the dusty pages of history. There were negro slaves in this city as early as 1680, not long after William Pynchon and his followers came. Slavery at that time was still in its infant stage in America, but was a recognized institution in the North as well as in the South. It was not until 1808 that the last Springfield slave was purchased and freed by local citizens.

Several years before the first gun boomed at Fort Sumter to open the Civil War, this city became an important temporary stopping-place for colored men. They came under the cover of night, slept the daylight hours through in cellars or behind barred shutters and left the following night, as silently and mysteriously as they had come. These negroes were escaped slaves from southern plantations, and their destination was Canada and freedom. For Springfield was a station along the famous "Underground Railway," and here there were agents ready to welcome the fugitive with food and shelter, and arrange for his dash to the next station. And here it was that many an irate slaveowner from Virginia or the Carolinas came to look for his human property, only to turn back baffled by that crude yet strangely efficient system of stations strung from Philadelphia to the border. The "station" might be a house hidden away in the hills; it might be an innocent-looking barn with enough hay to conceal a man; or it might be a cellar or tunnel dug in the earth to shelter the freedom-bound negro from prying eyes. Many of these runaway slaves passed through this city in their dash for freedom.

About 1840 a few of the fugitives, finding friends among the whites, decided to run the risk of being caught and settled here in Springfield. They found employment as cooks, domestic workers and helpers, and soon became numerous enough to start the Colored African Congregational Church on what is now Sanford Street. Six years later two men, one colored and the other white, carved deep niches for themselves in local negro history.

The colored man was Thomas Thomas, a runaway slave from eastern Maryland. And the white man was John Brown, whose name is immortal as the great Abolitionist of American history—the same John Brown who schemed and planned for the negro's liberation for over twenty years; whose famous foray at Harper's Ferry came to a disastrous end; and about whom a song was later written which swept the country like wildfire and was sung by Union soldiers in wild chorus as they marched into battle against the Johnny Rebs.

John Brown came to Springfield in 1846 and planned many of the details of his insurrection while here. He was a member of the wool-dealing firm of Perkins and Brown and he opened a warehouse in the old John L. King Building, at the present location of Columbus Avenue and Railroad Street. Among the residents of Springfield, John Brown had the reputation of being a quiet, peaceful citizen and a religious man. There were not many aware of the passionate hate he had for slavery and the schemes he turned over in his mind to end once and for all this institution.

The Reverend Mr. Conklin, of the North Congregational Church, who separated himself in great measure from the other ministers in Springfield because he thought them indifferent to slavery, was intimate with Brown and sympathized with him in his ideas. Brown and his eldest son, John Brown, Jr., attended the little African church, and there met Thomas Thomas. Learning something of Thomas' upright and courageous character, the Browns invited him to join in their liberation enterprises. Thomas accepted, and during that time was sent by Brown to look up Madison Washington, the leader of the brave slaves of the vessel "Creole," whom the Abolitionist wanted as a leader for his colored recruits. Thomas formed the Springfield Gileadites, an order among colored people to resist capture of fugitives. Later he opened a small eating place near the site of the present Bijou Theatre, which he ran for years until his death in 1895. Among Thomas' colored lieutenants were B. C. Dowling and J. N. Howard, and all these men were intimate with Fred Douglass, a nationally known negro, who was one of the originators of the Underground Railway.

Brown left this city in 1849 to draw the strings of his scheme together and also because of business failure. While he was very neat and exact in his accounts, he never kept track of his checks and as a result rarely knew his bank balance. A great man with a great purpose, he was obstinate and stubborn in business, refusing to take the advice of his associates, and he is reputed to have lost $60,000 here. It is interesting to note that a tunnel was found in Brown's former home on Cypress Street when the house was torn down, and that many years later his old iron safe was found in a barn in Indian Orchard. This safe had a concealed keyhole hidden under a panel which slid to one side when a certain rivet on the front of the safe was pressed. Brown kept his papers dealing with the Abolitionist movement in this safe.

A prominent local negro in the 'fifties along with Thomas and the others was Primus Mason, who went West to California in the gold rush and accumulated a small fortune. He lived on the corner of Mason and State streets, and later contributed the land and much of the money for the founding and maintaining of Springfield's splendid Home for Aged Men on Walnut Street, which also has negroes on its board of directors. A nephew of Primus, Henry Mason, lives today on Bay Street.

Immediately after the Civil War there was an influx of negroes in the North, and many of them found their way to Springfield. One of them, Henry Clay, was well known here at that time. A former slave, he served his master as a body servant in the war. His master was shot and Clay escaped into the Union Army, where he enlisted, serving in a Rhode Island regiment. At one time he was commissioned by his commanding officer to enter the Confederate lines as a bread and pie vendor, and in that manner secured much valuable information. Later he was captured by the Confederates, but escaped and lay in abandoned trenches for some days, with nothing to eat but grass and roots and nothing to drink but rain water which had fallen into hoofprints left by horses. He received an honorable discharge at the close of the war, and came here and established a small furniture business on Worthington Street. His widow still lives in their tiny home at Hancock Street.

Another prominent negro during the years immediately following the war was William Hughes. He was an importer of colored domestic help, and brought from ten to fifteen negroes on each of five trips to his native Virginia. As a result, quite a large colony of Virginia negroes settled in the vicinity of Willow and Cross streets. Hughes, who was born in the State of Virginia, in 1825, was sold from one master to another until he became the property of James C. Spott, of

Richmond, with whom he remained until the surrender of Lee at Appomattox. It is interesting to note that Hughes was called "By the Way" Hughes by his colored friends, because of his peculiar habit of starting practically every sentence with that phrase.

One of the oldest and best known citizens of Springfield is Alexander Hughes, who, incidentally, is not related to William. Mr. Hughes is now blind and lives in his own home on Monson Street, and he has an interesting story to tell of the early days. As a child he was a slave on the plantation of John B. Young in Henrico County, three miles north of Richmond. When the master returned from the war, he gave Mr. Hughes' father five days to leave the plantation, but young Alexander stayed on and worked about the place.

While still in his teens, he left the plantation and went to work in a tobacco factory in Richmond, later leaving there to drive a grocery wagon. In September, 1881, he came to Springfield, arriving on a Sunday. On Monday, Mr. Hughes relates, President Garfield was assassinated, and for the first time in his life the colored youth saw in amazement that negroes marched side by side with white men in the funeral parade held here. That day marked also the first time that he sat down beside a white person.

There were, according to Mr. Hughes, three colored churches in Springfield in 1882: the Sanford Street Congregational Church, the Lawrence Street Methodist Church, and the Pilgrim Baptist Church, which was located on the second floor of the old town hall on the corner of Market and State streets.

A day or so after Hughes' arrival here, he went to work for the grocery firm of West and Stone. During the evenings he attended the old Elm Street School, where he learned to read and write, something that was unknown to the Southern negro of that time. Later John Hall, of the Massachusetts Mutual Life Insurance Company, hired Hughes to work in the shipping department of that company, and he remained there until he was forced to retire on a pension when his sight failed him.

Mr. Hughes proudly relates that he entertained Booker T. Washington in his home when that famous negro visited Springfield. He is proud, too, of the fact that the Young Men's Christian Association, which he joined in 1882, awarded him a life membership, and also of the prizes he received from the "Springfield Republican" some years ago for having the most attractive and best kept flower gardens around his home. One of the things he wanted to do when in the South was to vote, a privilege there denied him. In 1882 he cast his vote in an election here, and has not once missed going to the polls since then, voting the Republican ticket every time. He is seventy-nine years old, is owner of his home, and asserts smilingly that he hopes to live to be a hundred, secure in a happy existence despite the loss of his sight.

Shortly before the war, large numbers of negroes came to this city. The acute problem to be faced was the renting of homes to these people. However, the prejudice which has operated so long and so keenly against colored tenants served as an incentive to the possession of homes among them. In those years they lived in colonies in the Willow Street area and in the Hancock and Eastern Avenue area. Today, while the negro density is still large in the latter section, there has been a definite tendency to move toward the north end. There are about 3,000 colored people in Springfield, numbering over seven hundred families, and the assessed value of real estate owned by negroes is in the vicinity of a half million dollars.

The World War had an almost revolutionary effect on the economic and industrial status of the negro of the North. Previous to this the colored man had in practically every instance been an unskilled laborer, a "hewer of wood and drawer of water," but the war opened new doors of vocational opportunity for him. While the great majority of negroes in Springfield are still engaged in common labor, there has been a pronounced tendency to move into the skilled trades, and many of these people recently became machinists, masons, tailors, barbers and carpenters. A large number also are engaged as janitors, porters, hotel workers, clerks and elevator operators. In the local professional field there are Dr. B. T. Bowens and Dr. H. P. Kennedy in medicine; William H. Martin and J. C. Clarkson in law; and in dentistry, Dr. W. H. Jones, Otis B. Byrd, and O. L. Fraser.

Practically all the negroes are Protestants of various denominations. Two of the churches in this city which are attended by whites sprang from humble negro churches. There are about six organized negro churches in Springfield at the present time, and at least three other religious missions conducted by negroes. A local branch of the

National Association for the Advancement of Colored People is maintained here and exerts a wide influence.

One of the finest negro social agencies in America is maintained here in the Dunbar Community League. This non-sectarian organization is an outgrowth of the St. John's institutional activities and Dr. William N. DeBerry, the outstanding leader in the local negro community resigned from the pastorate of St. John's Church in order to devote his entire time to the league as its executive officer. The Dunbar Community League, in its work toward the social betterment of negroes, is divided into several valuable departments. The Dunbar Home, at 643 Union Street, was built for the accommodations of working girls and women. The Dunbar Club for Boys and the Club for Girls at 620 Union Street are social centers encouraging wholesome entertainment for the colored youth of the city. The league also maintains classes for adult women, a playground and a free employment service. A housing project was started under the league auspices which involved the purchasing of several tenement houses, the apartments of which were let to colored families at modest rentals and on a plan of mutual benefit. A summer camp for boys, Camp Atwater, in East Brookfield, is still another league activity.

The colored man is social by temperament and character. He takes keen interest in organizing into groups of his own for various purposes. The oldest organization of colored people here is the Springfield Mutual Beneficial Association, founded in 1864. In 1866 the Sumner Lodge of Free and Accepted Masons was formed and seven years later the Golden Chain Lodge of Odd Fellows. In more recent years the Elks Lodge, the Knights of Pythias, the Good Samaritans and the Galilean Fishermen were started.

By far the most outstanding negro leader in Springfield is Dr. William N. DeBerry. Receiving his early education in the South and completing his theological course at Oberlin, Ohio, he came to this city in 1899 and since then has been the moving spirit in practically every line of endeavor undertaken by his people. Besides being pastor of St. John's Church for twenty-five years, he is on the board of directors of the Home for Aged Men, is the executive director of the Dunbar League, an officer in the National Association for the Advancement of Colored People, and holds positions of responsibility in a host of other organizations throughout the city. Dr.

DeBerry is largely responsible for bringing the Springfield negro up to the standing he now enjoys.

The main problem of the negro here as well as in the rest of America is, according to Dr. DeBerry, his place in industry. The depression set the colored man back several years in economic security, as it did the white man, and he believes it will take the Northern negro a long time before he can get back his hard won gains. Then, too, there is always the problem of prejudice, although Springfield is as free from racial animosities as any other American city with as many negro residents. The solution to this condition is, of course, education for all racial factions, and from this phase the outlook is bright. The rate of negro illiteracy has dropped very sharply in the last fifteen years, due to the adequacy of the schools in the North. A number of years ago, very few negroes knew how to read or write, but today it is difficult to find one here in Springfield who does not have at least the rudiments of education formerly denied to his father and grandfathers in the days of slavery.

It was economic pressure and the hope for better living conditions that was behind the migration of most Poles to America. Springfield has about 3,500 of these Polish residents, a number that is almost trivial compared with the Polish population in some of the other places in the county, particularly Chicopee. The local people are mostly Russian Poles, while those in Chicopee came in great numbers from that part of Poland nearest the Austrian border. Like the French-Canadians, the Poles almost automatically settled in the mill cities and after the first of them obtained work and saved a little money they wrote home to friends and relatives to follow them here.

The beginning of the large Polish population in Chicopee was by accident. In the early 'eighties, a New York train stopped at the Springfield station for a short time, and aboard it was a group of six Poles. These men, being weary from their trip, decided to stretch their legs for awhile, and took a short walk around the main streets of Springfield. When they returned to the station, they were dismayed to see their train disappearing in the distance, and carrying with it their railroad tickets which they had left on the seats. Unable to speak English and left in a strange town, they were in a quandary as to what to do. The men finally spied a familiar figure in the person of a Catholic priest, who turned out to be Father Healey, of Chicopee.

He took them back to that town with him and the next day the men went to work in the Dwight mills!

The first Polish settler in Springfield was Kazimir Misulis, who came here in 1893. Mr. Misulis was a laborer, as were the majority of the early Poles here, and came directly from the old country. His first job was working in the Collins coal yard at Spring and Lyman streets, and he stayed there five years. He later worked in the Boston and Albany roundhouse, for the Bartlett Brothers' mason's supply organization, the Springfield Coal and Wood Company, the Fisk Rubber Company, and finally at the Indian Motorcycle, where he stayed for eighteen years before his retirement.

From 1893 until 1908 the Polish influx into Springfield was slow, as most of these people went directly to Chicopee, Chicopee Falls, Holyoke, and other surrounding towns. In 1908, however, a significant number of Polish people came to Springfield. That year the Boston and Albany Railroad was in the throes of a strike, and a number of Polish families were imported from Worcester to work on the railroad. Some went back to Worcester after the job was completed, but the majority liked Springfield well enough to make it their permanent home, and in 1909 there were about sixty Polish families.

In 1910 the Polish group was numerous enough to start the first organization, a mutual benefit society called the Society of John Sobieski. At this time, too, there was some discussion of bringing a Polish priest here to minister to the spiritual wants of the people. This was of tremendous importance, since the church has always been the center of Polish life, and the Polish priest a leader and adviser in every phase of business, social and spiritual life.

The early Poles traveled to Indian Orchard or Chicopee for worship, and up to 1916 a Polish priest came every year for Easter confessions. In 1916, after some debate, a committee was elected to arrange for the organization of a permanent parish. This committee was taken from the Society of John Sobieski and was composed of four men: Martin Debrowski, Kazimir Misulis, Peter Shulc, and Joseph Kowalcyzyk. These men gained an audience with Bishop Thomas Beaven, and the bishop advised them to take a census of Polish residents to determine whether there were enough to justify a parish. The results of the census showed that there were seven hundred Poles in Springfield, and Bishop Beaven promised that a Polish priest would come every Sunday to conduct worship.

Father Joseph Tomikowski, a pastor of the Immaculate Conception Church of Indian Orchard, was commissioned to come, and it was decided to use the Syrian church on Liberty Street as a temporary place of worship. Services were held there for a year and a half until the attendance became so great that it was impossible to accommodate all who wished to attend. On July 15, 1917, Father Stanley Orlemanski, then assistant pastor at the Immaculate Conception, was appointed resident pastor of the parish, and he immediately entered on the all important work of raising funds for a permanent Polish church in Springfield. At this time there were 1,500 Polish residents.

Through the tireless and patient efforts of Father Orlemanski and several of the leading Polish citizens, enough money was raised to buy land at Leonard, Franklin and Underwood streets. Building operations were delayed in 1918, due to the severity of the winter, but in May of that year the corner stone was laid and the ceremonies were attended by a large number of Polish people, including many of the clergy from surrounding parishes. The local parish was called Our Lady of the Rosary, and a year later a school for Polish children was instituted on the same land, and the Sisters of Nazareth came here to teach.

Our Lady of the Rosary may justly be considered the hub of local Polish life. Besides the church and the school, there are recreation rooms, large and roomy club rooms adequately equipped for every function of a social center, and the parish house, formerly the old Vinton home. The church property, including all units, is valued at about $175,000. There are also several societies: the St. Joseph's Society, which is the same as the Sobieski organization; the Polish Citizens' Club; the Polish Alliance, the Polish Women's Alliance; and the Rosary Guild.

The Polish people, due to their lack of knowledge of the language and customs of this country, were at first handicapped to great extent and of necessity went into manual labor. Of late, however, they have been making rapid strides through the benefits of education, and many Poles have started small businesses as well as gone into training for the professions. One of the best known Polish leaders in Springfield is Aloysius Lasek, and Anthony Medeski, who runs a furniture manufacturing establishment, is prominent in business. Attorney Paul Flak is representative of the Polish people in the professional world.

The Poles are peace-loving, yet sensitive to encroachment on their liberties. They are thrifty and industrious and in time of distress do not enlist outside agencies for help, but go to their own organizations. The Poles are also sticklers for tradition and native customs, and enjoy demonstrations. One of the most important ceremonies during the year is at Easter time, when the priest goes to the individual homes and blesses the food which will be consumed on Easter Sunday, the same food being available for the poor as well as the rich.

Springfield played host to Russians as far back as 1871, when no less a personage than the Grand Duke Alexis came here with his entourage and visited the Smith and Wesson factory. He evinced keen interest in the manufacture of these famous firearms, and his delight was marked when he was presented with a revolver of exquisite craftsmanship made especially for him. Later this business was stimulated to great degree by the Russian orders which came in for firearms.

The Russian immigrants, however, are the most recent people to settle here as permanent citizens. These settlers are from Kiev, Grodno and Minsk for the most part, and they came here because of poor economic conditions at home and the lack of social and educational opportunities under the Czar. They were woefully ignorant, most of them could neither read nor write, and for a time they were given a rather cold and suspicious reception by local citizens. The majority of them finally found work as manual laborers on the railroads and roads.

Two men, Tomenko and Kosak, are credited with being the first Russian settlers, about 1900. Tomenko obtained employment as a window cleaner and Kosak went to work as a laborer on the railroads. Until 1904 there were few additions, but in this year the attention of local people was attracted to the small Russian group because of the Russo-Japanese War in the East. This had the effect of solidifying the local group and at the same time stimulating migration from Russia, and by 1910 the colony had increased to about four hundred members. The people continued to stay in the laboring class, working in the Boston and Albany gangs, and the Hendee and Knox factories.

The Russian social life here was rather riotous. The Slav is given to heated and long debate, and the local Russians met in eating houses in the north end, particularly on Liberty, Chestnut and Carew streets, and argued their favorite problems far into the night. Besides being decidedly clannish, these simple people lived frugally on a peasant diet of cabbage, fish and rye bread in their homes on Ferry, Sharon and other streets. Much of the money they made here was sent home to less fortunate brethren in the Russian Ukraine, and the distress among the local Russians was great when the United States immigration laws of 1915 practically eliminated the Russian quota. Worry over the fate of Russian relatives abroad reached a high point during the war, and the local people often met in the banking establishment and clearing house of Joseph Goldin, at 4 Ferry Street, to wait for news and delayed letters, and also to send money abroad. This money was a godsend to the Russian peasants who received it, for the salary of the Russian soldier during the war only amounted to about twenty-five cents a month!

The war had the effect of changing the Russian attitude toward the United States also. Many of the immigrants had expected to stay for a period and then return to their native land with the fruits of their toil. However, they quickly saw that America was a safe and secure country, and they settled down to the business of becoming American citizens. In recent years a few have broken away from the laboring group and entered small businesses, and almost every Russian here eagerly participated in the opportunity for education so rigorously denied them in the old country.

The beginning of the local Russian church in 1916 was indicative of the growth of Russian population and the solidity attained by these people. The Russian orthodox church was started by a pastor named Chervinsky. Following him came a clergyman named Dmitriev, and finally Bishop Klimowicz took over the duties of administering to the spiritual needs of local Russians. The Russian orthodox church here from 1916 to 1928 was called St. Nicholas Church, but it broke up and was reorganized under the name of the Church of St. Peter and St. Paul.

Today there are roughly between five and six hundred "pure" Russians in Springfield. Accurate figures are unavailable because immigration figures have placed Russian Jews in the same category. Among the leading local Russians are Anatole Bourman, the dancing instructor, formerly a member of the Russian ballet, and Dr. Peter Karpovich, professor of physiology at Springfield College.

The story of the Scandinavian anywhere one goes is essentially a story of steel. Before each foray in those days of long ago, the ring of steel against steel was a familiar sound throughout Scandinavia as the Viking swords and battle-axes were forged, weapons that were far superior to those of the southern people. Today the descendants of those ancient warriors in Hampden County still carry on the traditions of being foremost in the working of steel. The Swedes, Norwegians, and Danes are now for the most part skilled machinists, toolmakers, diemakers and forgers of metal, true to the tradition of Thor, whose hammer, Miolnir, could crush the hardest of objects.

There are over 4,000 Scandinavians in Springfield, and of these about 1,600 are immigrants. The Swedes are far in the majority, the local Danes, Finns, and Norwegians aggregating only about five hundred. Most of the immigrants came from central or southern Sweden because, like their hardy ancestors, they loved travel and adventure; also, they desired better economic conditions than those offered by the small farms and factories in their native land. Most of the Scandinavians did not stay in the eastern part of the country, but migrated into the Middle West, where they became both farmers and factory workers. The ability of the Scandinavian is by no means limited to skill in the metal working trades. Those who stayed in the eastern part of the country either settled in the coastal towns to engage in the fishing industries along the seaboard, or entered the factories in the various industrial towns. It is for the most part the skilled tradesmen who settled in the industrial areas within the confines of the county.

The first Scandinavians in the vicinity came in the early 'seventies, and settled in the town of East Longmeadow, just outside of Springfield. They came mostly from Portland, Connecticut, and worked for the Norcross people as stonecutters in the sandstone quarries. Fashions in buildings changed and the industry died a natural death. Today the Scandinavians in East Longmeadow cultivate small farms or work in Springfield factories. But evidences of their craft still come to light now and then. Boys diving into the waters which now fills most of the quarries occasionally bring up sharp cutting tools, relics of a bygone industry and a bygone day. Yet the descendants of these people live on in East Longmeadow, and Lars Olson, an old stonecutter, still remembers when lanes were cut through thick forest so that huge blocks of sandstone, hewed from the mother rock, could be hauled out to the road leading into Springfield.

The first Scandinavians came to Springfield in the early 'eighties. They were two brothers, John and Edward Stromwald, and they went to work in the railroad roundhouse. There was little intolerance shown by Springfield citizens to these newcomers, because they were hard working and industrious, and above all, ardent churchmen. They later became active in local Scandinavian societies, especially in those of the Swedish Congregational Church.

A prominent Swede to follow the Stromwalds was John Hanson. He came to Springfield about 1884 and worked for a number of years as a foreman at the Springfield Provision Company. Hanson was prominent in Congregational Church activities, and no one was more sympathetic or charitable than he toward his fellowman. When a new Scandinavian from distant parts came into the city, he almost automatically went to Hanson's house if he had no relatives or friends. Hanson would give him a bed, shelter and food and keep him until he found a job.

Several Swedes came to Springfield in the middle 'eighties and became permanent settlers, although a large proportion stayed only for a short time and then journeyed out into the Middle West. Among those who established their homes here was Charles Gustafson. Gustafson knew steel, and he knew the workings of machinery. He is credited with having a great deal to do with the development of the motorcycle of today, and he was one of the leaders in establishing the Hendee Manufacturing Company, producers of the far-famed Indian Motorcycle. Gustafson, when the industry was still in its infancy, traveled to England and other parts of Europe exhibiting his motors at various industrial shows, and the famous name "Indian" became known wherever motorcycle enthusiasts gathered. Along with Gustafson came many other Swedes into the plant, most of them skilled toolmakers and diemakers with an innate knowledge of machinery. Oscar Hedstrom achieved a high position in this line, and invented some of the later models used.

In 1892 there were probably about eighty Scandinavians in Springfield. For some reason or other, the majority of them settled up on the "Hill" in the Wilbraham Road section. Some of them went to work in the Springfield Armory and rose to high positions there, being particularly adapted for the accuracy of making gun barrels and other delicate working parts of the famous Springfield rifles. The same situation held true at Smith and Wesson, where small arms of great precision were manufactured. There were at this time other Scandinavians scattered about throughout the county in the factories of Holyoke, Westfield, Chicopee and the smaller towns.

A Springfield Scandinavian, Gabriel Carlson, was responsible for the manufacture of candy in commercial quantities. Carlson came here in the early 'nineties, and may be considered perhaps the most outstanding Scandinavian in the city of Springfield. He came from Minneapolis, and his inventive genius and knowledge of machines quickly became evident here. Previous to Carlson's various inventions, candy making involved a laborious and awkward hand process, somewhat like the work of "taffy pulling." Carlson started in a small way on Liberty Street, using a few of his original ideas in candy manufacturing, and spent the evenings poring over drawings or laboring over models of new machinery conceived by his nimble brain. Later he moved to what is now the corner of Hampden Street and Columbus Avenue, and finally as his inventions became more widely known, he assembled every resource at his command and established the National Equipment Company. In time his machines became world-famous, and his plant expanded as new machines for the manufacture of ice cream were invented. Carlson brought many Scandinavians here and gave them jobs in his factory, and today the personnel of the National Equipment Company, both in the shop and in the executive departments, is filled with Swansons, Johnsons, and Olsens.

In those early days the social life of the Scandinavians here was simple. There were church socials, picnics at the old Maple Grove, and occasionally a street car ride to Forest Park, which was considered quite an excursion then. These were all-day affairs, usually held under the auspices of the Swedish church, and old settlers delight in recalling the happy hours spent among those who spoke their own language, and where Swedish food and drink was served in the good old way. Unlike some of the other peoples, no beer or any intoxicating beverages were used at these outings. The main drink was coffee, and the coffee pots and cups were as vital a part of the picnicking equipment as all the food put together. The Scandinavians, as a rule, are frugal in their use of alcoholic beverages, preferring coffee, which is almost a national Swedish institution. And it is a matter of record that a temperance lodge, called the Tegnic Lodge, was established in 1895, under church auspices, to combat the "demon rum."

Another favorite form of recreation for local Scandinavians was the singing society. The Orpheus Drangei, better known as the "O. D.," was a social club formed in the 'nineties, and is still in existence. Practically every Scandinavian in the city could be found at the rehearsals of the O. D. when they took place, and often when the windows of the hall were open, people of Springfield would stop and listen raptly to the strains of the sturdy voices as they eddied out into the warm night air. Several singing societies in addition to the O. D. were formed later, under the auspices of the separate churches, and they met on Sunday nights in the churches for their rehearsals. A Scandinavian of Springfield prominent in singing activities was William Sederlund. He was somewhat of a leader among his people, especially in social events, and it is due to his efforts that the first lodge was established in Springfield in 1893. This lodge was called the "Braga" and still exists as a branch of the Vasa Lodge. The "Braga" was a mutual benefit organization, and whenever one of the local Scandinavians was unable to work or sick or injured, or died, arrangements were immediately made by the "Braga" to furnish the necessary funds.

The Scandinavians, who are in the main Protestants, are good churchgoers and take an active part in both the spiritual and social life offered by their religious centers. Almost the first concern of these people as they settled in East Longmeadow, Springfield, Holyoke and elsewhere throughout the county was the establishment of churches. As early as 1883 the Reverend Vickberg, of South Manchester, Connecticut, made occasional visits and preached to the handful of Swedes in the locality. A few years later the Reverend L. P. Ahlquist, of Portland, Connecticut, visited both East Longmeadow and Springfield. A large number of Swedes had by this time settled in East Longmeadow and a congregation was finally organized there numbering one hundred and forty-two communicants, six months before any congregation could be founded in Springfield.

First among the Swedish churches to be established in Springfield was the Congregational church, now on Johns Street. It was but a short time later that the Lutherans began their movement for a center of worship. This movement was started by the Reverend Augustus Olsen, pastor of the Swedish Lutheran Church of South Manchester, Connecticut. On May 28, 1891, a mass meeting of Swedes was called in Springfield, and this was attended by fourteen men and eighteen women, who formed the present Bethesda Lutheran congregation. It was decided that all single members should contribute fifty cents a month to the support of the church, and the families seventy-five cents a month. In January, 1892, the congregation was incorporated through the efforts of the Reverend Johannes Franzen. The congregation met first in the old Odd Fellows Hall on Court Square, later in the Guild Hall on Main Street, and then on Union Street, and finally on the present site. Later a Swedish Methodist church was organized, and a Swedish branch of the Salvation Army, as well as a Baptist church.

The Scandinavian of today in the largest city of the county is a lover of peace and law and order. The old days of the roving warrior have long faded into the musty past, and the Scandinavian countries abroad are particularly noted for their abstinence from war. Police officers and judges alike assert that the Swedes, Norwegians and Finns are almost never haled into court for any criminal infraction of the law, and rarely indeed for any civil disputes, it being a characteristic of the descendants of the once aggressive Northman to settle his disputes amicably, peaceably and fairly. A Swedish newspaper is maintained, under the local editorship of Carl Rehn, and this paper circulates throughout the county as well as in other parts of New England.

As time went on, and the position of the Scandinavian became more and more secure, a large number of Scandinavians came into Springfield and the surrounding regions, particularly at the turn of the century. Prominent among these was Axel Dahl, a moulder. Dahl was a huge man of marvelous physique, and one of the finest Swedish athletes in the city. Invariably, in the friendly wrestling bouts he engaged in after his day's work, he threw his opponents with almost ridiculous ease. He was also proficient in boxing and various other sports. The beginning of the century was marked by the entrance of several Swedish Finns into Springfield. These people differed from the Swedes in the language they used, but otherwise

resembled the Swedes closely.   At the present time there are about
a hundred of them in Springfield and the Order of Runeberg, Nord-
vakten Chapter, is an organization of the Finns on Braeburn and
Johnson streets.   There is also a Danish brotherhood in the city,
although this branch of the Scandinavians in Springfield has less than
a hundred representatives.

Many of the Scandinavians in the vicinity are active in public life.
Tyco Petersen, a Dane, is prominent in the Legislature.   Dr. John
Granrud is superintendent of schools in Springfield, and S. J. Johnson
is secretary of the Massachusetts Mutual Life Insurance Company.
A man who has gained an enviable reputation in quite another field is
Dr. Luther Anderson.   Dr. Anderson was war correspondent in two
Chinese revolutions for the Chicago "Daily News," and has traveled
extensively into other parts of the world.   He has an insurance business, he teaches at Springfield College, and is an active contributor to
several national magazines.   But the rank and file of the Scandinavians, in and around Springfield, may still be found in their skilled
trades in numerous factories, practically all of them carrying on the
ancient tradition of their ancestors in the working and manufacture of
modern machines—and the knowledge of steel and other metals.

There are about two hundred Syrian families in Springfield,
descendants of an ancient and once powerful people.   They are
divided into three religious groups, although the people are in effect
Arabs who have become domesticated, and their language is the
Arabic-Aramic.   The Druses are warlike Syrian Arabs who follow
the precepts of Mohammed, and are in the main nomadic by preference.   The second branch follows the Syrian orthodox forms of worship, and the third is the Syrian Roman Catholic, to which the
majority of Springfield Syrians belong.

The first Syrians came to this city in 1895.   Peter Karam, the
original settler, lived on Ferry Street and conducted a small dry goods
business.   Shortly after him came Steven Halon, who lived near
Karam and did odd jobs around the city.   Following Halon came
Mansour Elim, a peddler, who now lives on Greenwood Street.   With
Elim came Joe Shilby, who lived in Springfield for a number of years,
but later moved to Feeding Hills and took up farming.

Among the early Syrian settlers were two well known in local
business circles.   Peter Frangeia, before his death, conducted a large

dry goods business, and A. Josephs is now the head of a prosperous dry goods manufacturing business on Chestnut Street. From this it is easy to see that the manufacture and sale of clothing is the favorite vocation of these people, although some are small tradesmen in other lines, and a few are farmers or factory workers. The Syrians take kindly to business, and the reason for their coming here was mainly because Turkish domination and consequent lack of opportunity limited activities in their native land.

There are two Syrian churches in town. The Roman Catholic Parish of St. Anthony on Liberty Street was founded in 1905 by the Reverend Monseigneur Paul A. Saab, and later the Reverend Michael took over the active duties as spiritual leader. It is to the Roman Catholic Church that most of the local Syrians belong. Those who believe in the orthodox precepts attend the Syrian church on Carew Street. These churches are the very centers of Syrian religious and social life. Originally, the members lived in a colony on Ferry Street, but later extended outward somewhat and now are scattered throughout the north end.

Dr. Fred Ziter and Dr. Albert Ghourayeb are representatives in the field of medicine, and Attorney John George in law. As in the case of the Greeks, the Syrians are too recent in Springfield's population to have produced many professional men, but there are a number of the American-born younger generation who are studying medicine or law in various universities. The largest number of Syrian immigrants came to this country in 1913. Of 3,708 Syrian immigrants entering this country in that year, five hundred and two gave their destinations as Massachusetts, ranking this State second only to New York.

The Syrians are a quiet, unobtrusive people who, in the case of the immigrants, do not mix much with the rest of the people. The sons of these immigrants, however, are thoroughly Americanized, adhering to the standards and customs of this country rather than the country of their fathers. The Mt. Lebanon Girls' Club, the Karam Society and the St. Anthony's Young Boys' Club are representative of the social activities of the young Syrians in Springfield.

There is only one Turk in Springfield who has made this city his permanent residence.

He is Redjeb Ahmed, of 39 Seventh Street, and he came here from Stamboul in 1911. A good-natured individual, Mr. Ahmed has the knack of making friends easily, and it is no uncommon sight to see two or three men sitting in his little establishment near the corner of Sharon and Main streets and whiling away an hour or so in talk. Mr. Ahmed has maintained a gas station on that spot for some years, and he will tell you in his broken English that the money he takes in will not make him a rich man, but at the same time it is enough to take care of his simple requirements, and that is all he wants.

When a youth, he plied the fisherman's trade in Stamboul, but tired of the monotony and set out for travel and adventure. He went through Greece, Italy, and later through the eastern part of the United States before he decided to settle here after his thirst for seeing new places had been slaked. Mr. Ahmed is a Mohammedan, and there is no mosque in this city which he can attend. This he will tell you is no obstacle, since the Moslem can pray anywhere at anytime, and his words will still be heard by Allah.

Mr. Ahmed decries the old régime under the Sultan, and is entirely in sympathy with the present administration in Turkey. He is a great admirer of Mustapha Kemal Pasha, who, according to this Turkish resident has done wonders in modernizing Turkey, and who is a soldier, politician, statesman and idol of the people all rolled into one. A picture of that militant-looking Turkish leader occupies a prominent place on the wall of his small station.

There are not many Turks in this country. Springfield has occasionally played host to a few of them at a time, but these swarthy people are in the main transients, never staying very long in one place. Mr. Ahmed has occasionally contacted a few of them, but these meetings have been so rare and so casual that he cannot even remember the names of his countrymen who have passed through here in their travels.

Industrial Springfield

CHAPTER XXIX

Industrial Springfield

The early history of the Springfield Armory is closely interwoven with that of the early history of Springfield itself and has been given in former pages. Since 1865 the armory has settled down to a definite policy, both the army and the civilian having learned through hard experience what are each other's rights and duties, and probably never again will there be disturbances of the peace, civil suits and courts martial as there were previous to that date. The civilian employees are occupied with production and administration and the executive positions are filled by ordnance officers, while a detachment of enlisted men performs the military duties about the plant. The trade of armorer is a highly skilled trade and tends to be handed down from father to son. It has been said by some that the armory mechanics gave to the world the main contribution of America to industry, namely, the idea of interchangeable parts, which has made possible the Elgin watch and the Ford car, as well as the Springfield rifle. With interchangeability established and the coming of machine methods of production, a new era opened for the armory. The steam engine released it from the dominance of uncertain waterpower, and steamboats on the Connecticut and later the steam engine on the railroad cut down costs of transportation. In war time work was speeded up and skilled laborers drawn into the city, and when the war was over many of the skilled men remained to be drawn into other industries. The products of the city have always reflected this overflow from the armory. Revolvers, machine guns, skates, magnetos, motorcycles, street cars, airplanes are all commodities which an expert gunsmith could easily learn to produce, but which could not be turned out except by skilled labor.

Besides supplying arms to the United States in time of war, and serving as a storage plant in times of peace, the armory has been of

great service to the Nation through the experiments in arms manufacture carried on there. It has contributed quality to both the industrial and social life of the city, and must be considered as more than
a factory.

The armory today owns nearly three hundred acres of valuable
property. The oldest building now in use dates back to 1808 and is
known as the West Arsenal and used as the enlisted men's barracks.
Building after building has been constructed since that date to line the
quadrangle. Besides various arsenal buildings they include a model
shop, an interesting small arms museum, a hospital and machine and
woodworking shops, as well as quarters. Expansion in the watershops plant has accompanied that on the hill, and in 1900 an act of
Congress provided the necessary funds for new buildings and machinery. During the period of the World War the experimental building
in Armory Square and the chemical laboratory in Federal Square were
erected and equipped. In 1918 manufacturing activities at the armory
reached the highest point in its existence. In June, 1917, the average
daily production of rifles was one hundred and seventy-five, but by
November of the next year it had reached the enormous total of
1,500. This included spare parts and assembling and packing ready
for shipment. 5,381 employees were on the payroll. If war comes
again to the United States the armory is prepared to play its part as in
the past and in the meantime its peacetime activities in manufacture
and experiments will be carried on.

Springfield has been a marked and significant railroad center ever
since the Civil War. The earlier railroads which established themselves here were not parts of a vast railroad chain, but rather individual railroads. The original Boston and Albany started with a capital of $20,000,000, and to the north the Connecticut River Railroad
began with a capital of only $2,370,000. This road, long out of
existence, traveled from Springfield to South Vernon, with short
branches at Chicopee Falls and Easthampton. The New York, New
Haven and Hartford Railroad, so important today in passenger and
freight transportation through Springfield, started with a capital of
only $15,500,000, but with able management later absorbed most of
the smaller roads.

The old Western Line was the first railroad to link Albany to
Springfield, back in the middle of the last century. Trains left Spring-

field in the morning, reached Albany after a five-hour trip, and returned in the evening. This old line, although primitive and crude compared to our modern stream-lined, air-conditioned trains, did its work well.

All coupling was done by hand. Mail bags hung on metal frames built near the tracks and as the train approached it slowed down, so that some one could lean out and pluck the bag of mail from the frame. Another danger, particularly to brakemen, was that the bridges were of wood and their roofs low. There were no warning tassels hanging in front of the bridge as there were in later times, and on a foggy or stormy night, when vision was poor, the brakeman ran a good chance of striking his head against a wooden beam.

There were many snow hazards on this Springfield-Albany line. The few wooden plows available were almost wholly inadequate to clean away the snow, and along the road were wooden fences designed to keep the snow from drifting onto the tracks. There were no cozy cabs for engineers and firemen. These men stayed in the open, rain or shine, and even the conductor was unprotected at times since the cars did not open into each other, and he passed from one car to another by means of a wooden plank.

When the line first opened, the cars were heated by small wood stoves. Protests on the part of the chilled passengers forced the company to place a stove at each end of the car, instead of only one in the middle. The baggage car was not heated for fear of fire, and the baggagemaster and express messenger often ran races around the car in order to keep warm.

Wood was the fuel used before coal came in, and there were wood stations all along the line. At each station a woodchopper was employed by the company to saw and split wood so that the trains could proceed without delay. The train employees had no distinctive uniforms, but wore ordinary grey suits, their official positions being designated by tags on their hats. The old Western had four cars to a train, a baggage car, then a first-class coach, and finally two second-class coaches. On this line were carried at one time or another President Van Buren, Horace Greeley, and "Commodore" Vanderbilt.

In 1886 most of the engines used on railroads through Springfield had been made in the old Eddy shops located in the city, and Wilson Eddy, since the late 'fifties, had turned out some three hundred engines

in all for the Boston and Albany Railroad alone. Mr. Eddy gave
each engine a name, starting with countries, then states, until he finally
had to get down to officers and other men in the shops.

A change felt by many occurred in 1908, with the abandoning of
the free ride to Boston to attend the annual stockholders' meeting.
This free ride was anticipated by hosts of women, who felt it their
duty to "show their passes to the railroad" on the pretext of going to
the meetings, but their real object was to attend the fall style openings
in Boston and spend the period in a shopping orgy. For many years
"Stockholders' Day" meant a free excursion for a gala holiday of buying, and when this disappeared forever the disappointment was keen.

In 1889 the east side depot was built. In many respects this depot
was not a model one, for with a platform crossing the tracks between
the two buildings, life was in constant danger. In the spring of the
following year the stone arch over Main Street was built, and there
was some agitation at first because it was feared that when horses on
the road heard the rumbling of trains overhead they would become
frantic and run away. Instances of this nature did happen, but after
a few trips beneath the structure under a tight rein and firm bit, the
horses became used to the noise.

Some of the crack trains of America, with their air-conditioned
cars, luxurious drawing and smoking rooms, and exactness as to
schedule, pass through Springfield. Among these are the famous
Twentieth Century, which runs from Boston to Chicago in twenty
and one-half hours. There are names which are famous, too, at least
in Springfield railroading. Lucius S. Storrs was for several years executive head of the great Springfield railway system. Another deserving
of mention was Colonel James Rumrill, an able corporation lawyer, and a recognized leader in railroad affairs. He was for a long
time vice-president of the Boston and Albany Railroad, director of the
Chapin and Agawam banks, and one of the founders of the old Springfield Club.

Some of the railroads in Springfield were small in scope, springing
up like mushroom growths and then disappearing. One of these was
the Springfield and Longmeadow Railroad, boasting of only a few
miles of track, and its directors were Springfield men. A railroad
venture with a strange ending came when a company began to lay
track for a Springfield to Providence railroad, but the project was

abandoned before it was completed, and has left behind miles of unfinished railroad.

In the later 'seventies Springfield had shaken off the effects of the Civil War and begun an accelerated industrial development. Factories, once merely a room or two rented in buildings, now branched out and built places of their own. Smith and Wesson, Milton Bradley, the Wason Manufacturing Company, and many others made products which traveled far beyond the limits of the city. Smith and Wesson revolvers were used in the Civil War and later by the military forces and police of countries across the sea, as well as throughout America. Its founder, Daniel Baird Wesson, is really responsible for the perfection of modern small arms. It was Wesson's ingenuity and mechanical skill that made possible the metallic cartridge commercially, as well as the breech loading rifle and revolver. He also developed the tubular magazine action which later became the famous Winchester repeating rifle.

Springfield is credited with having produced the first sleeping car, T. W. Wason and Company, later the Wason Manufacturing Company, having built it several years before the Civil War. T. T. Woodruff, of Alton, Illinois, is supposed to be the inventor, but the same claim is made for Asa Hapgood, a native of Massachusetts. George C. Fisk, former president of the Wason Company, said Woodruff came into the company's office one day with his model, upon which he had received a patent, done up in a bandana handkerchief. The Wasons built a car for him, having twenty-eight seats which could be thrown into couches, for a cost of about $4,000. That was in 1857, and in 1890 the famous palace car "Boston," costing $50,000, was built by the same company. Other outputs of the same car manufacturers are motor boats and steel framed dining cars, followers of the old horse-drawn lunch cart, which also originated in Springfield. In 1860 the Wason Company built what was called the "most beautiful car in the world" for the Viceroy of India.

Everett H. Barney, founder of the Barney and Berry Company, skate manufacturers, was an accomplished skater from his early youth. He was born at Framingham, December 7, 1835, the son of a locomotive builder. He disliked the cumbersome wooden skate with its binding straps and when only a boy of fourteen invented and made a metal skate with a clamp. This was operated at first with a key, but later he did away with that and invented the lever. Mr. Barney was a fancy skater as well as a swift one, and could make grapevines, Maltese crosses, balls of twine or any ice figure known. On his seventieth birthday he is said to have complained because there was no ice to skate on.

Mr. Barney formed his skatemaking company in 1864 and induced his old friend John Berry to join him in the venture. They made five hundred skates the first season in their little shop and by 1878 were turning out 80,000 pairs a year, which included all sorts and styles.

Other forms of athletics interested Mr. Barney, especially canoeing and camping. In 1882 he bought a large tract of unimproved land on the edge of the city overlooking the river and built his home. A part of his purchase belonged in the town of Longmeadow and so anxious was he to have all his property included in his beloved Springfield that he induced the Legislature to change the city boundaries. On this estate were set out trees and shrubs from many foreign lands.

Mr. Barney's only son died of tuberculosis in 1889 and was buried on Laurel Hill, where his father had planned to build him a house. The mausoleum there which contains also the bodies of Mr. Barney and his second wife was designed by Mr. Barney himself. The loss of his son was a great blow to Mr. Barney and was perhaps the main reason for his deeding his estate of one hundred and nine and one-half acres to the city. He reserved the right to use his residence as long as he or his wife lived, but that, too, eventually became Springfield property.

It was not until he was about fifty years of age that Mr. Barney became interested in canoeing. He built, according to his own ideas, the canoe "Pecousic," and against the advice of friends sailed it in the international regatta at Thousand Islands and won the race. It was later split in half and one side mounted in the Springfield Yacht Club and lost when their building burned, but the other half is owned by the Connecticut Valley Historical Society.

The showy and spectacular always appealed to Mr. Barney and he enjoyed going out on the river in his canoe and tipping over when he knew he had an audience on the bank. For years a salute of three shots were fired from the Barney property whenever a boatload of picnickers went up or down the river.

Mr. Everett Barney died in Florida, March 31, 1916, reputed the richest man in Springfield. In January, 1935, twelve buildings of the old skate company, once the scene of great activity, were razed on Broad Street.

Milton Bradley came to Springfield in 1856 as a young man looking for work. His first position was as draftsman at the locomotive works of the Wason Company.

With the training that he received on that job, Bradley later opened his own office for doing mechanical drawing and securing patents. Bradley, however, did not wholly sever his connection with the Wason Company at that time. One of his best known accomplishments was to make the mechanical drawings and superintend the construction of a $10,000 car which the company had contracted to build for the Pasha of Egypt. It had three separate apartments, and was an elegant affair in those days, attracting considerable attention far and wide.

It was a lithograph made of this car by a Hartford firm that stimulated Bradley's interest in lithography. He negotiated with a firm in Providence to buy a press, and traveled to that city to learn how to run it, paying an old Scotchman ten dollars for personal instruction. He came back to Springfield and set up the press, but immediately had trouble with his pressmen. One of them, Jack Riddle, went off to the Civil War during a slack business period and returned with shoulder straps, but with one arm missing. Another, Jack Kelly, was an excellent pressman when he was sober, which was rarely, and this man quit Bradley's employ when he discovered that work interfered with his drinking. This event placed Bradley in rather a difficult situation. Good pressmen were rare, the business of lithographing being only in its infancy, and the instruction that Bradley had received from the old Scotchman was meagre. Bradley had to make a number of prints of "Christ Blessing Little Children" for Gurdon Bill, and he worked the press himself, with Bill hinting that the quality of the prints didn't seem to be anywhere near as fine as they had been previously.

One of the most profitable moves was to lithograph the portrait of Abraham Lincoln, who had just received the nomination for President. The original picture from which the prints were made was brought to Springfield by Samuel Bowles, and copies of the picture are still treasured in the company's office as representing the first really important Bradley lithographing job.

The widely-known game industry of the company got its start from a visit which Bradley paid one evening to the home of G. W. Tapley, then a bookbinder in the employ of Samuel Bowles, but later for many years the president of the Milton Bradley Company. The two men were engaged in a simple game, when the idea came to Bradley of getting up a new game which could be lithographed. Bradley originated "The Checkered Game of Life" and took a few samples through New York State, where money was a little more plentiful. Because of his expert salesmanship and the novelty of his merchandise he was able to sell all his goods and was flooded with orders for more. They continued to grow until in 1870 a new building for the firm was erected at Harrison and Dwight streets.

An item in the rapid expansion of the company was the rise in popularity of croquet. The sale of the sets was enormous and Milton Bradley and Company were among the first in the field. It was Bradley who devised the permanent wooden wicket holders, and also issued the first manual for croquet players. Another game which the company could not turn out fast enough to fill its orders was the "Terrible Fifteen Puzzle," a mind challenging game which caught the popular fancy. And it was Bradley who developed the "Zeotrope" or "Wheel of Life," the original motion picture machine. This was a scientific toy, which caused simple figures on strips of paper to become animated. In 1878 the Milton Bradley Company received genteel and yet enthusiastic plaudits from two of the best known and most popular magazines of the day, "The Eclectic" and "Godey's Ladies' Book."

A neighbor of Bradley's, Edward Wiebe, a German music teacher and an educated man, wrote a book on kindergartens and wanted Bradley to print it for him. This type of child-education work was practically unknown in this country and was just beginning to gain a foothold in Europe, and Bradley was uninterested in it at first. An early pioneer in this new education delivered a lecture on it in Springfield, which Bradley and his father attended. When the two men walked out after the talk, Bradley was thoughtful and preoccupied, and a short time later he published Wiebe's manuscript, "Paradise of Childhood and Practical Guide to Kindergartners." Soon Bradley began to manufacture kindergarten supplies, a procedure which people thought was a bold and rash venture and could end only in financial disaster. But gradually public interest in this new educational trend increased, and the illustrated guide to the kindergarten received an honorable mention at the Philadelphia Exposition for being the first of its kind ever published in the English language.

A development rising out of this unusual industry was the extensive manufacture and use of water colors. Colored paper in great quantities was needed. Milton Bradley experimented with various pigments, grinding them at first on a small scale in a chemist's muller and mixing them in an ice cream freezer. Orders for the new colors kept pouring in, so that the freezer was abandoned and regular paint grinders used to meet the demand. From this start came the famous Bradley water colors, of which "Bradley Blue" is best known.

In 1881 the company moved into the large building it now occupies on Willow, Cross and Park streets, and in this building are contained all the various types of businesses which Milton Bradley made famous in those early days.

The Chapman Valve Company, incorporated in 1874, soon made extensive enlargements of their factory space in order to handle the rapidly increasing business. The Chapman Company, then as now, had the finest type of cast-iron and brass foundries, and its valves are in a host of dams, locks and sewage systems everywhere.

Elisha Morgan, a direct descendant of that rugged pioneer, Miles Morgan, was the founder of the Morgan Envelope Company on Harrison Avenue. They were the original contractors for furnishing the United States Government with post cards and started the papeterie industry in Springfield which grew to such proportions that the city produced more than any other city in the country. In 1898 the business was merged in the United States Envelope Company and Mr. Morgan became vice-president. Springfield now has the general offices of the company, as well as the P. P. Kellogg division, in their big plant on Cypress Street.

The first postal card in the United States to go through the mails was printed by the Morgan Envelope Company of Springfield and mailed on May 12, 1873, by S. S. Bumstead, coal dealer, to Henry M. Burt, founder and editor of the "New England Homestead." The card was lost to sight for many years, but was exhibited recently by a son of the recipient at a meeting of the Springfield Stamp Club.

In conjunction with industry, the city's business activity prospered. The stores were for the most part not specialty shops, but general stores, carrying stocks as great in items, although infinitely less in quantity, than the modern department stores. There were, however, a number of stores that were taking on a modern tinge, and slowly confining themselves to specialties. Smith and Murray, and Forbes and Wallace, were making names for themselves in dry goods; D. H. Brigham and Company carried a fine stock of men's wear before they went into ladies' clothing in 1888; and O. D. Morse's "Great Family Shoe Store," later called the "Central Shoe Store," occupied the new Shaw and Kirkham building on Main Street. This store, in 1895, developed into the present Morse and Haynes, with a long tradition of carrying the finest in shoes and boots.

It was a familiar sight in Springfield, in the 'seventies and 'eighties, to see farmers come in from the country once a week or twice a month to do their buying, and the advertisements carried in the newspapers of the time directed their publicity to these country people quite as much as to those who lived in Springfield. An advertising circular put out by the Central Shoe Store includes "some special features designed to promote the comfort of our 'Country Trade,' including a quiet corner where you can discuss the merits of your good wife's little lunch should you desire." Serge buskins and serge congress shoes were a big item in the "Central Shoe Store" stock, and later gave way in public favor to ladies' wear. Kid and calf boots and brogans were worn by the dandies of the city, and button shoes for both men and women were long a standard of merchandise in this establishment.

In 1877 Franz G. Jensen, Sr., a young man of twenty-five, went into the candy retailing business with George Hartman, with a joint capital of $400. Despite his youth, Jensen was a progressive business man, and knew well the value of a firm name when it was associated with only the highest quality of merchandise. There were other stores in Springfield selling candy at the time, but Jensen took care that his confections were always richer and tastier than those of his competitors. The business gradually prospered and finally Jensen bought Hartman's interest.

An outstanding characteristic of Jensen was that he always tried to keep pace with what was new. He was the first to introduce wax paper in Springfield for the purpose of wrapping confections. Previous to this the customer had great difficulty in peeling the paper from the candy, especially on hot days.

In the early 'eighties, when the incandescent lamp was new, Mr. Jensen installed the first electric generator to be used in lighting a retail store in the city, many people making their purchases in the store so that they could observe the new lighting system.

Shortly afterward, Mr. Jensen made further use of electricity by using it in the manufacture of ice cream. Up to that time the heavy work of making ice cream had been done entirely by hand power. He further gained the gratitude of his employees in his work for better working conditions by establishing a model candy factory on Temple Street.

When the company's candy store in the Springfield National Bank Building was destroyed by fire in February, 1932, Mr. Jensen decided to reopen on Bridge Street, and today the store, with its gleaming mirrors and fountain, attractive luncheon tables, and long counters filled with rich confections of every kind is still foremost in its field in Springfield.

Both the founders of the Forbes and Wallace department store emigrated to this country from Scotland. Wallace came to Boston during the spring of 1867. He stayed there for three years and then started out for himself in Pittsfield, joining in a partnership with John M. Smith, who later became a partner in the Springfield firm of Smith and Murray. It was in March, 1874, that Mr. Wallace came to Springfield and went into the dry goods business with Mr. Forbes. The store then sold dry goods exclusively and was housed in a red brick building. The floor space of that humble store occupied but one-tenth of an acre, while the Forbes and Wallace of today has eight acres.

In 1876 the Barnes Block, in which the original store was opened, was bought at auction by the firm for $80,000. The business was conducted in the two stores north of the main entrance to the building, and on the south side of the entrance were the Third National Bank and the Shredd and Knight concern. The three upper floors were occupied by lawyers, dentists and other tenants.

The residents of Springfield took kindly to the progressive policies pursued by the store and in 1884 a lot was purchased on Vernon

Street and a five-story building erected. With the trend of the times, the store expanded its merchandising policies, and added books, shoes, bicycles, kitchenware and other specialized items.

It was in 1907 that the beautiful Observatory Restaurant was added, on the top floor, where a panorama of Springfield could be seen far away from the dust and noise of the street below.

In 1919 and 1920 the present eight-story building was constructed. To walk completely through the store would entail a trip of about four miles, a distance longer than the average golf course.

It was Andrew Wallace's leadership that brought the firm to its present enviable position, as Mr. Forbes retired in 1895. Always progressive and always aware of the needs of his customers, he watched every department closely. Mr. Wallace was a lover and a student of art. Part of his personal collection of etchings and paintings are exhibited in the store, and the rest have been given to the City Library Association. He took great personal pride in the store, and it was only in the later years that he relaxed somewhat and gave the reins of management over to his sons, who have continued to maintain the store as one of America's finest. At his death in 1923 most of the stores in the city closed for an hour, and the flags were placed at half mast. At Ormond Beach, Florida, some of his elderly friends, including John D. Rockefeller, did not play their usual round of golf that day out of respect to his memory.

Another event in the mercantile history of Springfield came in 1906, when Albert Steiger opened his store in Springfield. Forbes and Wallace was at that time well established on Main Street, and Meekins, Packard & Wheat was known as one of the best furniture stores in the country. Mr. Steiger, through the help of some of the city's bankers, made some important real estate purchases, and his large store on Main Street soon was a solid and established institution. In 1930 business forced an enlargement of the original store, and Mr. Steiger bought out the Charles Hall store and built a handsome new establishment adjoining his Main Street property, where the Hall galleries were housed.

A little over a hundred years ago a mutual savings bank was incorporated. The first year it received forty-six deposits totaling $1,200. A hundred years later the transactions for the year totaled over 170,000, involving over $20,000,000. The one man who, more than any other, was responsible for the growth of the Springfield Institution for Savings was Henry S. Lee. In 1858, when only twenty-three years old, he was elected treasurer. For forty-four years, until his death in 1902, he led the bank safely through years of panics, wars and financial disturbances. Next to Mr. Lee stands John W. B. Brand, the present head, who has been with the institution longer than any other officer in its history.

The Springfield Five Cents Savings Bank in the late 'seventies moved into a handsome structure of granite and brick at the corner of Main and Court streets and there conducted its business, maintaining the policy that even the smallest sums were welcome. The first treasurer of this bank was Dr. Joseph C. Pynchon, a direct descendant in the sixth generation of William Pynchon, founder of Springfield.

The Third National Bank and Trust Company, which occupied the Iron Block, where now is Meekins, Packard & Wheat, experienced a remarkable prosperity. In 1907 the bank had spacious quarters in the Lyman Building, and later a ten-story building, combining both utility and beauty, was erected on the corner of Main Street and Harrison Avenue, where the bank is still a financial Gibraltar.

The Springfield Safe Deposit and Trust Company brought the first safe deposit vault systems into the city for rental to the public. When it opened in the old Massachusetts Mutual Building on Main Street, later known as the Hall Building, its capital was $200,000, its deposits zero and its surplus zero.

The Springfield Fire and Marine Insurance Company started in 1849, mainly through the efforts of Marvin Chapin. Mr. Chapin had already made the Massasoit House of Springfield one of the best known in New England, and was a public-spirited citizen in every way, especially where his adopted home of Springfield was concerned. Mr. Chapin carried a large amount of insurance, and most of the money he paid out in premiums, as well as money paid out by other Springfield people, went to Hartford. It seemed to him that if Hartford could maintain insurance companies, Springfield could, and the money would then stay in the city.

He approached a well-known resident of Springfield, Chester W. Chapin, and Mr. Chapin suggested that Marvin go down town among the business men and solicit funds for stock in an insurance company. At first he was unable to get anyone to invest a dollar in such stock. Chester Chapin was now enthusiastic and urged him to try again, with the object of getting ten men or firms to take $10,000 worth of stock so as to insure a capitalization of $100,000. Each man took a share himself and worked zealously among the business men until all the shares had been taken up but two, and these were apportioned out to those who did not want or could not afford to take as much as $10,000.

The Springfield Fire and Marine Insurance Company was incorporated from this beginning in 1849. Real business began in Novem-

THE FIRE AND MARINE INSURANCE BUILDING, FLANKED BY THE CHURCH OF THE UNITY

ber, 1851, with the first loss by fire, when Enos Parsons, of Northampton, holding policy No. 24, met with damage amounting to about three hundred dollars. One more trifling loss was sustained at the close of the year, and the company was well started.

An ambitious search for business marked the early years of the company. Industries were beginning to awaken and extend their activities, and the company engaged their first traveling agent, Mr.

Edwin Ray, of Springfield. The first major insurance problem came up in 1852, when the company was undecided whether to take a marine risk on the new steamer "Yankee Blade." It was finally voted not to take insurance on the hulls of steamers running south of Savannah, Georgia, because of the danger from tropical storms. It was also voted to discontinue insurance on woolen mills, with the exception of those making white flannel blankets and "fulling" cloth. These mills were without much fire protection, and once they were ignited the flames were almost impossible to stop.

The company expanded, making a home office necessary. A lot was purchased on the corner of Main and Fort streets from the heirs of William Pynchon. In 1858 the company moved into its new quarters.

The company showed forethought in its insurance policies in those early days of its existence. Just before the Civil War broke out it was decided to discontinue all marine business except inland lake and river risks. After the Civil War times were difficult for fire insurance companies, but the Springfield Fire and Marine held its own and even prospered, while such strong companies as the Massasoit and Hampden Fire Insurance companies, both of Springfield, went out of business.

In 1871 a calamity came which ruined several strong fire insurance companies. This calamity was the great fire of Chicago, which raged with fury through the southwest part of the city and then fed by a strong wind, drove directly through the heart of the business section. Hundreds of buildings were completely destroyed and millions of dollars' worth of grain, furniture, machinery and merchandise went up in smoke. The Springfield company suffered the staggering loss of $450,000, and for a time it teetered on the edge of bankruptcy. But almost before the flames in the great western city had died down, a special meeting of the board of directors was held, and it was proposed that the corporation repair its capital by assessing the stock sixty-five per cent.

Out of seventy-five stockholders there was not a single "no" vote! Thus, in positive fashion, the men behind the company signified their faith in it, and this unswerving loyalty through several reverses has made the company the strong and worthy institution it is today. After this fire, business looked toward the Springfield company for their

insurance with full confidence, knowing that the company would pay
dollar for dollar, no matter what the calamity.

On November 9, 1872, a great conflagration swept Boston.   It
started at the corner of Summer and Kingston streets, in the business
center, and raged for an entire day.   The wholesale district, thickly
congested with stores and warehouses, was destroyed, and the aggre-
gate loss from the fire amounted to $80,000,000.   The blow to Mas-
sachusetts companies was a terrible one, and twenty-six were forced to

THE MASSACHUSETTS MUTUAL BUILDING

close their doors.   The Springfield company, in the same manner as
after the Chicago fire, voted to assess their capital stock thirty per
cent., as their loss in the Boston fire amounted to about a quarter of a
millon dollars.   Again there was not a single negative vote cast among
the stockholders!   The company emerged stronger than ever.

The history of the company from here on is one of constantly
increasing prestige and financial stability.   Expansion progressed
steadily until now the name of the Springfield Fire and Marine
Insurance Company is known clear to the Pacific Coast.

The Massachusetts Mutual Company, whose first president was Caleb Rice, a citizen of the highest type, who became mayor of the city, did a prosperous business on Main Street, in what was considered one of the handsomest buildings. At the end of the century the company erected a modern eight-story structure, which was believed sufficient for the future needs of the company, but its business ran up into staggering figures, and in less than two decades it became apparent that larger quarters were necessary. Twenty-seven acres were purchased two miles out of the center on State Street, and there a building was erected from plans by Kirkham and Parlett, that today is accepted as one of the finest insurance buildings in the eastern part of the country. The great building, with its trim and dignified lines, its wide well-kept lawn, its many shining windows and great clock represent a landmark of Springfield.

On Thanksgiving Day, 1895, an automobile or "gasoline motocycle" ran though the snow and slush of Chicago streets to win the first auto race ever held in America. The average rate of speed of about five miles an hour was considered phenomenal and the newspapers reported exultantly that the first eight miles of the course had been covered in a single hour.

The car which easily defeated its four competitors was made in the city of Springfield, and its designer was J. Frank Duryea, who lived in the city at the time. It was called a "gasoline motocycle," despite the fact that it had four wheels. It covered the entire distance of fifty-four miles, from Jackson Park to Evanston and back, in ten hours and twenty-three minutes, and won the prize of $5,000 offered by the Chicago "Times-Herald." The nearest competitor to the Duryea was a Benz, especially imported for the occasion. The Duryea led all the way, although at one time the steering wheel broke and a stop had to be made at a roadside blacksmith shop for repairs.

Duryea is generally credited with being "The Father of the Automobile" and the maker of "America's First Gas Car," although this has often been disputed. It was in 1892 that the first American automobile factory was established by Duryea in this city, and in the succeeding year he produced fifteen motor cars. His very first car was built the year before that and was equipped with a one-cylinder motor. Duryea's two-cylinder motor-driven vehicles were the first to be placed in the hands of the public by any manufacturer.

The Duryea record is a record of progress through many obstacles and adverse conditions. The policy was first and foremost to expand along conservative lines, not branching out until automobile standards had become settled and basic. Duryea never put experimental cars on the market and was never obliged to retrace a single step in the evolution of the motor car. It was this painstaking thoroughness and strict attention to practical detail that gave the later Stevens-Duryea motor cars the highest reputation.

As Duryea made that first great change in the motor from a "one-lunger" to a "two-lunger," he also made a radical change in the body. Where his first efforts had been on the high-wheel buggy type, he changed the model so that it became a moderate-sized pneumatic-tired wheel affair, thus providing an easier running and shock-absorbing vehicle. A feature of Duryea cars was his carburetor, and this the whole automobile world soon copied, as its qualities for regulating the mixture were far superior to those of other pioneers in the field.

It was in the early 'nineties that William M. Remington, who was chief draftsman for Mr. Duryea, was made a partner and the concern set out with the object of producing the best road-wagon for a moderate price suitable for American roads and requirements. These early cars of Duryea's, sold in Springfield, had twelve horse-power water-cooled motors, and the two cylinders were cast integrally and placed horizontally side by side. These were the first cars that were efficient at varying speeds, due to the superior carburetor action.

It was one of these same "gas-wagons" that won another notable victory in the Ardsley Casino Decoration Day race, from New York City to Irvington-on-the-Hudson, in 1896. This was the second road race run in America, and the Duryea this time was awarded a cash prize of $3,000. The model of 1896 again won distinction when it was exhibited and run on the floor of the Charitable Mechanics' Fair held in Boston in that year, marking probably the first authentic automobile show in the country. The first annual automobile show held in Springfield was in 1904.

Constantly looking for ways to better his product, Mr. Duryea next added various improvements to the motor, increasing the speed, durability and appearance of his cars as he went, the result being a vehicle which received high commendation when shown at an exhibit in New York in 1897. About the same time, a Duryea car, driven by Mr. Duryea himself, ran through rain and mud to win the London-to-Brighton race in England. It bettered all previous records for the distance by an hour, and was acclaimed as the speediest car ever raced on British soil.

In 1900, the Duryea Motor Wagon Company, as it was called, became the Stevens-Duryea Company, when Irving H. Page, president and treasurer of the J. Stevens Arms and Tool Company, affiliated himself with Mr. Duryea. This company, which was located at a manufacturing plant in East Springfield, was at first the only recognized auto manufacturing concern, although later other competitors in the field came fast, and this city was a mecca for early automobile enthusiasts.

The Knox Automobile Company, now out of business, but formerly located on Wilbraham Road, was one of Springfield's noted manufacturing concerns. It was founded in 1900, and its plant occupied about 5,000 square feet of floor space, with a production capacity of one hundred and fifty cars a year. The Knox became popular for its durability and general efficiency, and the business increased many times with the coming of W. E. Wright as general manager. This company at the time of its inception in Springfield was one of the few, and possibly the only factory in America, to make and assemble every part of its cars within the walls of its own plant.

The American Bosch Company in Brightwood is one of Springfield's industries under the leadership of President Murray. Its beginning was in the Bosch Magneto Company, a firm run almost wholly by Germans and engaged in making auto magnetos, but when the World War came, the plant was taken over by a "regulator" and later became the American Bosch Corporation, with its principal article of manufacture today the famous "Bosch" radio. Shortly after the war, when the company was manufacturing magnetos, business dropped. The firm, however, bought up a number of interests and went into other channels of manufacture with considerable success.

A development of national and international import came in 1901, when George M. Hendee built the first motorcycle in America, and thus Springfield has the double honor of having both the first automobile and first motorcycle in America built within its limits. This two-wheeled contrivance, a mechanical version of the former foot-driven bicycle, excited great comment, and was considered a dangerous vehicle in every respect, too dangerous to be manufactured and sold commercially. But the great plant of the Indian Motocycle Company, located near Winchester Square, was the outgrowth, and the famous red "Indian Motorcycle" became known everywhere here and abroad.

Industry profited when the Fiberloid Corporation moved to Indian Orchard from Newburyport and began to manufacture its many colloid products.

In 1900 the population of Springfield was 62,050, almost double the number of people here fifteen years before. Court Square extension was made possible through public subscription, a significant geographical change in the city of Springfield. This early part of the decade of 1910-20 is significant of a building boom to accommodate the increased demand of new population, the building permits of 1912 amounting to $6,250,000, an increase of forty per cent. over the previous year! It was in 1904 that S. Z. Poli built one of the first of the modern theatres here, and this amusement house is still in existence under the name of the "Poli Theatre," although the ownership has changed. Springfield has a group of theatres well equipped for the needs of the public so far as motion pictures go, and the Court Square Theatre, itself an institution of long standing, still supplies the legitimate stage to the city.

The coming of the New England Westinghouse plant to this city in 1915 added strong impetus to an already favorable industrial situation. This great plant, which covers a large area of land in East Springfield, manufactures refrigerators, fans, and all sorts of electrical equipment which is sent throughout the country.

Municipal Springfield

CHAPTER XXX

Municipal Springfield

Water has always been a prime factor in the migration and location of peoples. Where there is water, men settle and build their homes, until finally populous cities grow. Areas without it are today barren of human population, as they were a thousand or ten thousand years ago.

It was the abundance of water, in the main, which led the hardy pioneers to establish their homes in Springfield plantation some three centuries ago. Here there were broad and fertile meadows, nurtured by the wide river which cut through it. And here there was a brook, later called the Town Brook, which coursed across the plantation and could provide water for all purposes, including convenient and adequate fire protection as well as a natural laundry for the plain rough garments of those sober Puritans. But even William Pynchon, visionary and dreamer as he was, could not have foreseen that those who succeeded him would take their water from the hills eighteen miles away, first through the very heart of a mountain and then through many miles of underground pipes to every home.

The first man to become actively interested in a system of water distribution was Charles Stearns, in 1843. Mr. Stearns, an enterprising business man with the courage to carry out his own convictions, suggested the establishing of a system of water works, but was generally laughed at and politely ridiculed by other citizens, and he could get no financial aid for his scheme.

Finally he secured permission from the selectmen to go ahead with his idea of constructing a general water system for the business section of Springfield. In August of 1843 he began the work on his own resources, and laid wooden main pipes from what is now known as Van Horn Reservoir through the various streets to the

Western Railroad depot and from there down to Main and Bliss streets, supplying dwellings, stores, hotels and other buildings, to the number of about one hundred and fifty, with pure and wholesome water at reasonable cost. Stearns, as he saw his dream coming true, increased the speed of his work and soon nearly all the principal streets in the business center were supplied.

It was true that this pioneer water distributing system was crude and almost primitive as compared to our systems of today. Yet it was tremendously useful to the people of that time, and from every angle was a successful and remunerative investment. Those who had laughed at Stearns at first, hurried to buy stock in a proposed company for an even better water system.

Five years after Stearns had completed his layout, a petition was formed for the incorporation of the Springfield Aqueduct Company, and it carried the names of eighty-three solid citizens of the community. There was some opposition at first, but finally the bill blossomed into a law, and the Springfield Aqueduct Company was duly incorporated, with Stearns, Festus Stevens, George Hastings and "their associates" succeeding to the properties and interests formerly owned by Mr. Stearns. This company almost immediately became a real instrument of public improvement.

The reservoir capacity was enlarged as population increased, and the old wooden logs were replaced by cement-lined conveyors. Yet there was the fear among the residents of Springfield that the improvements in water distribution would not be sufficient to keep pace with the rapid increase of people establishing their homes in the city, and the water supply, while not yet taxed, became a serious topic of discussion and consideration. It was about this time, too, that a well for fire prevention purposes was sunk at the corner of State and Stebbins streets, and proposals were advanced to construct a system of wells, connect them by pipes, and carry the water by gravity to the lower part of the city for general use.

The pressure of public opinion toward the installation of the wells became stronger, a feasible plan was at last reported by engineers, and the City Aqueduct Company was formed, replacing the old Springfield company. Water was taken from wells on the hill and conveyed through pipes to the business section, and immediately a loud cry of indignation arose from residents on the hill. Being public-spirited was a fine thing, within limits, but when it came to draining private wells and creating an acute danger of the trees and vegetation drying up because their nourishment was being carried away, it was time that something was done. As the situation became more acute, the Legislature finally authorized a million dollar bond issue for the purpose of creating an adequate water supply, with the source either in the Connecticut or Chicopee rivers. Under this Act of 1872 the first board of water commissioners in the city of Springfield was formed.

The combined franchises and interests of the old Springfield Aqueduct and City Aqueduct companies were purchased, the systems united, and a new and temporary system was established, the source of supply coming first from Garden Brook and later from a pumping station on the banks of the Connecticut in Brightwood. After some time the commission purchased more than eight hundred acres of land in Ludlow for the source of the necessary water, and Ludlow Reservoir was built. Like the various systems which preceded it, this, too, became inadequate as the city continued to grow.

With the problem becoming more serious, Little River was considered, but rejected as too expensive and almost impossible. With the adverse reports concerning Little River before it, the city government began to consider the Westfield River in hilly Huntington, where already a project had been made at considerable expense. But no sooner had Springfield brought the Huntington water bill before the Legislature than an overwhelming opposition arose from all directions. The city of Holyoke came forward with the assertion that Huntington was the only future source of water supply as far as that city was concerned. And on the heels of this barrier, the town of Westfield also protested with great vigor. The result was that the petition presented by the city of Springfield was thrown out of court.

At this time it seemed that the water question would never become settled. Suggestions flew thick and fast, engineers presented report after report, and hours were spent in futile conference. Finally, the special commission which had indorsed the Westfield River scheme turned a right-about-face in 1904 and advocated the development of Ludlow, which they reported, with increased sources of supply and with regulated and economical use of the water in Springfield, would be adequate for ten or fifteen years. And since there had been various experiments, all without signal success, for the purification of Ludlow water, the city council decided to build a filtration plant at Ludlow through which the water of the old reservoir, tainted with abundant animal and vegetable growth, would be made sufficiently pure and palatable for drinking. This order, carrying an appropriation of $300,000, was passed by the council and Allen Hazen, of New York, an expert engineer, was brought up to supervise the construction work.

But there was one man who had faith in Little River. That man was Mayor Everett E. Stone. Impressed with Little River and convinced of its feasibility from the start, and despite the official order for the Ludlow Reservoir, the mayor instituted a private survey of the Little River possibilities through Hazen. To Mayor Stone goes much of the credit for our splendid water system of today, since through his insistence the idea was not allowed to die a natural death, but instead was constantly before the city government and the people of Springfield.

The report of Engineer Hazen, sponsored privately by the mayor, stated that it probably would be possible at some expense to get satisfactory water from Ludlow, although no water of this character had as yet been made satisfactory for any city by any method of treatment. But where there was good water, available at no greater and possibly less expense, the continued use of the Ludlow supply could not be recommended, and the sources appearing most worthy of consideration by the city were the tributaries of the Westfield River, especially the east and middle branches, and the Westfield Little River. The board of health, always a potent force, backed Hazen up in his decision concerning Ludlow.

After this report, there was bitter strife in the city government, and various contentions between officials and experts. The experts, outside of Engineer Hazen, ridiculed the idea, saying either that it couldn't be done, or that if it were it would cost so much that the city of Springfield would be steeped in debt for many years to come.

But through the dogged fight put up by Mayor Stone and the influence he exercised, the city council finally reversed its stand again and this time ordered an investigation of Little River. On May 2, 1905, the findings of the investigation were submitted to the city government and acceptance insured, and this date marks the beginning of the present splendid water system of Springfield. Mayor Stone, the leader in the movement, at the close of his mayoralty term was elected chairman of the water commission, and Mr. Hazen was retained as advisory engineer.

More than 3,000 laborers were employed in constructing the system from the beginning of the work in September, 1907, to the completion in 1909, although at no one time were there more than 1,000 employed. The system constructed then included the Borden Brook Reservoir, the Mundale filtration plant and the Provin Mountain pure water storage.

The skilled labor for the great part came with the working forces of the contractors, but the common labor was furnished by P. A. Breglio, head of the Springfield Labor Company. The workmen in Springfield were given first preference, and at this much joy was evidenced in the south end of the city, where lived a large number of Italian laborers. Work had never been too plentiful, and now came the big job in the hills with prospects of steady pay for a few years. Practically every available laborer in the city was snapped up, and then Breglio, through his agents in Boston, New York and various other cities, secured many more. This work was not merely the routine of hiring a number of men and letting it go at that. The first requirement was sturdy men who had the stamina to labor in the rock and earth excavations. Then there were concrete workers to be secured for the big dam and the filter plant and the storage basin—men who lived with cement and water and sand, and knew their proportions in terms of yards and gallons, as a chemist knows his in terms of grams and cubic centimeters. Tunnel workers, men who lived much of their lives in darkness below ground, were necessary for the bore through the hill, and many of these had cut through the hearts of mountains in Italy and Switzerland, and some had worked in the great Simplon Tunnel. Then there were expert choppers to cut down tall trees, carpenters to build the bunkhouses and bridges, metal workers to set the girders and a host of others. It was no easy task for the commissioner of labor of the Little River project to house, clothe, and feed these men.

There were four camps in all. The common laborers lived in bunkhouses or "sleeping shacks," housing anywhere from one hundred to three hundred men each, while the skilled workmen lived in private rooms and had separate dining accommodations. In this respect the army of a labor camp is no different from a military army, with varying degrees of prestige and varying privileges. It was a credit to the labor supervisors that there were very few cases of sickness during the two years, men being detailed to keep the camps clean and in good sanitary condition.

At each camp large ovens were constructed, where expert bakers turned out hundreds of loaves of bread each day. To add variety there was a daily meal of spaghetti or beef stew cooked in the open, over rude fireplaces, and there was also considerable canned vegetables and fruits included in the diet. The skilled workmen, mechanics and so-called "regular boarders" had a different daily bill of fare and paid a weekly amount of money for both food and lodging, but the laborers paid only for food, as their bunks were provided free.

Goods were bought by store checks given by the company, and the amounts deducted from the pay envelopes at the end of the week. The prices, despite the great expense involved in transporting supplies from the city to the remote camps, were the same as in the city, and any effort to raise them above this level to take care of the added overhead immediately brought an aroused contingent down on the heads of the storekeepers.

The men held up admirably against great difficulties. An illustration of their fortitude may be seen in the experiences they went through at Borden Brook Reservoir. It was in March, and the snow was waist deep in many places, when the pioneer squad of workmen traveled up the wild mountain road to the site of the dam for the purpose of building the shacks and bunkhouses for the great army of laborers who would come with the spring to start active work. It was bitter cold, with a sharp biting wind. On this wild mountain the men were entirely dependent on themselves, for the nearest town was miles away over a difficult route.

A shipment of supplies had preceded the workmen, but through an error in the order, there was no bread in the shipment. They immediately set to work building a rude shelter for themselves and as a substitute for the missing bread they opened a barrel of corn meal, which they cooked over open fires. With no means of communication, they stayed there a week, cutting trees and setting house frames, and during this time had nothing to eat but corn meal and a limited supply of canned food. Each morning they would eat their "mush" with the hope that a relief expedition was coming up the mountainside with a load of fresh, soft bread, but it was a week before it arrived. During that terrible mealy week the workers lived in a rude lean-to of brush and loose boards, with the cold ground for beds.

As is inevitable in any large group of working men, there were scattered evidences of dissatisfaction, often from the most trivial causes. Some of the laborers were "floaters," men with the blood of wanderers in their veins, seldom staying on a job for more than a month. Others were over-particular as to what was coming to them in the way of food and housing, and some were just lazy. On one morning an entire gang of twenty-five men laid down their tools and quit because a foreman, perhaps loudly and profanely, objected to one of their number lighting his pipe on the windward side of a dynamite shack. Instead of taking the reasonable view of the matter, and listening to persuasion to stay, the men packed their belongings and started down the trail, believing that their rights had been imposed on, but they were quickly replaced through the medium of a telephone call by the labor commissioner, and their successors probably left Boston or New York that night bound for the dam, so that the digging and blasting could go on uninterrupted.

An important part of the entire Little River system is the Mundale filtration plant. The pure mountain water which comes in is really fit for consumption as it is, but it is put through a cleansing process that makes its purity absolute. The water first flows into a reservoir, where it settles, giving it a chance to clear itself of soil. It is then conducted through a central powerhouse, from where it is directed into one of the six filter chambers, and between the powerhouse and the filters the water gushes up like a huge fountain in the center of a large circular concrete basin, in order to give it an air wash before it is passed through alternate layers of crushed rock and sand.

The pipes used to convey the water in the Little River system are made of steel. This was considered an innovation in New England at that time, since previous pipes had been made of cast iron, but the steel since then has demonstrated its superior value time and time again. There are twelve miles of pipe line, some of it forced through rock, but the majority through earth, for which a steam trenching machine was used, saving the labor of hundreds of shovelers. The most difficult job faced by those laying the pipe was in crossing the Westfield River, which although ordinarily calm, sometimes becomes a raging torrent. A coffer dam was constructed half way across the river, and inside this structure the pipe was laid in a solid concrete base on the bed of the stream.

Laying pipes across the Connecticut River was another difficult feat, but was accomplished by the use of a whole fleet of floating machinery, including a dredger, pile-driver, barges and diving floats.

The Borden Brook Reservoir covers an area of two hundred and thirteen acres and has enough water to furnish Springfield with a full supply for about five months if all other sources were cut off. The great volume of water, coming from Borden Brook, Alder Brook, and Sugar Cane Creek, is held back by an earth dam that is one of the largest of its kind in New England. From here the water runs through a concrete tunnel in regulated volume down through the valley into Little River, where it is caught by the diversion dam.

One of the best views of Springfield may be obtained from the top of Provin Mountain Reservoir, and with a pair of field glasses the time on the clocks of the municipal tower may be clearly seen. This reservoir is in effect an equalization basin that gives uniform pressure to the city's water supply, and is located in the Feeding Hills region of the town of Agawam.

The Cobble Mountain Dam is located at the foot of the northern slope of Cobble Mountain, in the narrow gorge of the Little River. This great earthen dam, at the time of its completion in 1932, was the highest dam of its type in the world, the height of its center being two hundred and forty-three feet above the original river bed. It was built to conserve water in the streams of the Little River watershed, no matter how heavy the rain on the watershed nor how deep the snow in the hills during early spring. The new reservoir made by it occupies the site of a glacial reservoir of some millions of years ago, and this reservoir has a capacity of 22.83 billion gallons and an area of 1,134 acres, both staggering figures well in accordance with this tremendous undertaking, which came to successful completion under the able direction of Chief Engineer Elbert E. Lochridge.

Aside from this great conservation of water, the building of the dam made possible the creation of plentiful hydroelectric power and the distribution of this power from the potential energy of the water stored in Cobble Mountain Reservoir throughout western Massachusetts by the Turners Falls Power and Electric Company. This company made an agreement with the city of Springfield whereby it was given under a thirty-year lease all the power it could generate at the power plant from a storage capacity in Cobble Mountain and Borden Brook reservoirs amounting to a maximum of 2.9 billion cubic feet, agreeing at the same time to allow to come through the power plant sufficient water for the city's daily consumption, and not allow the water level in the reservoir to drop below certain stipulated points each month. The hydroelectric plant built near the reservoir for Springfield by the power company cost $1,100,000 and is leased by the company at approximately $270,000 a year. The pressure tunnel alone cost $651,000.

The great dam was created by sluicing some 1,800,000 cubic yards of material into the valley between two natural mountains. The Cobble Mountain Dam today is one of the scenic attractions of the section. Its width is 50 feet at the top, on which there is a roadway, and this tapers out to a width of 1,510 feet at the base. The length at the top is seven hundred and thirty feet, in proportion to the whole mammoth enterprise. Among the other features embodied in the construction of the Cobble Mountain Dam was a great spillway, discharging water into Little River, a half mile below the dam, and a diversion tunnel cut through the base of the mountain and measuring over a mile in length, the shape being not cylindrical but like a horseshoe. In the construction of this passageway the muck from the tunnel was removed by narrow-gauge cars hauled by two locomotives to the site of the division dam, and used to form the upper toe of the Cobble Mountain Dam.

The dam, built at a cost of millions of dollars, but expected to pay for itself in a reasonable time, both through the provision of ample water and ample hydroelectric power, was started in 1927 and completed five years later, by the Springfield Board of Water Commissioners, with E. E. Lochridge as chief engineer, the late Allen Hazen as consulting engineer, and H. H. Hatch the division engineer in charge of construction.

A wave of intense excitement spread through Springfield when, in 1879, it was announced that the first public demonstration of Alexander Graham Bell's invention would be made. Everyone apparently wanted to know what the curious toy was like, and both the few believers and the many skeptics went to the city hall for the demonstration. Receivers had been put up in the main room and chairs were arranged for the skeptics, who waited grimly for the fantastic dream of communication to fizzle. Presently there was a click, followed by a buzz, and the amazed listeners heard a weak voice say "Pittsfield on the wire!" Following this startling announcement, came the faint but unmistakable strains of a waltz played by a musician in the hill town over fifty miles away. After this performance, many subscribers signed on the spot, and others took out subscriptions later.

A few months after this initial demonstration, Moody and Sankey, the famous evangelists, visited the city. They were escorted to the city hall, and Sankey, his imagination aflame with the possibilities of the telephone, sat on a sandpile in the cellar of the big building and sang "Nearer, My God to Thee" through the 'phone to eager listeners in towns about Springfield. This marked what was probably the first revivalist meeting ever held by wire.

The pioneer telephone operator of Springfield was Frederick G. Daboll, of Harvard Street, who interested the city in this new and wondrous device only ten years after Bell invented it. A switchboard was located in a little room on Pynchon Street, and from this switchboard Daboll ran fifty wires during the first year of its installation. Henry Denver, who was connected with the Western Union Telegraph Company, became interested and obtained the first hundred subscribers, and it was W. J. Denver who got the Western Union authority from New York to subsidize the adventure to the amount of $3,000.

The telephone then was a luxury, costing in the vicinity of seventy-five dollars a year. Several of the more affluent citizens had private lines outside the jurisdiction of the Springfield company. Among these was E. S. Bradford, of State Street, who could talk after a fashion with his associates in his woolen mill in Holyoke. The livery stable owned by Oliver Marsh was also a pioneer telephone station in the business section.

John Fitzpatrick was the first telephone lineman in Springfield. He installed the first switchboard and trailed most of the lines over the housetops for the new subscribers. Outside the Pynchon Street room there were two long wooden arms set up and supported over the sidewalk, and places for eighteen wires were fixed. When the telephone manager for Massachusetts visited the city for a field inspection trip, he was overcome at the extent of the service contemplated and wanted to know "where they were going to get enough business in a hundred years to fill up eighteen wires." Today the city has several thousand separate wires at the exchange.

The original switchboard, although awesome-looking, was a technical puzzle. Following Fitzpatrick, a mechanic from Bridgeport named Doolittle constructed the board out of black walnut and rigged each of the fifty line terminals with a small nickel bell. Each of these bells rang vigorously, and each had its individual melody. There were no women operators then, and the young boy who was night operator could tell by the sound of the ring which line it was, and in the darkness run to the correct one and plug in. Like the family doctor or lawyer, the switchboard boy became a family confidant and a storehouse of local information. There was often an unmanageable clicking and buzzing on the out-of-town lines, much as our radio static of today, and central was often asked to relay the message. Miss Lizzie Lane, niece of Henry Denver, was the first girl operator.

The telephone was really in a crude state that first year of operation by Mr. Daboll. No efficient transmitter had been invented, and after a button was pressed and a period spent waiting for the bell to jingle down at the exchange, the patient subscriber would have to take time listening to and talking into the receiver. The mouthpiece was a later development.

The wires in particular puzzled the people of the city, and there were some extraordinary reactions from the willing but uneducated public. One old man said he'd be delighted to subscribe and have a telephone line, but he would not permit any wires to run into his home, for fear of lightning. Many persons of a scientific bent carefully examined the wires, looking for the hole through the wire where the sound traveled. The first linemen would clamber over the housetops with reels of wire, fastening it wherever they could with a complete disregard of property rights.

The Springfield company, although crude to start with, improved rapidly. Many local people invested money in it and came out with their original investments multiplied. One story in connection with this relates that Fred Gower, city editor of the Providence "Journal," came to Springfield to inspect the telephone exchange at city hall. Enthusiastic over its possibilities, he remarked to his host, Solomon Griffin, the former managing editor of the "Springfield Republican," that a man could become a millionaire if he invested $10,000 in the venture at once. Mr. Griffin did not invest any money, but Mr. Gower did, with the result that he became a millionaire a comparatively short time after his prophecy.

Transportation in the city at this time was by horse-cars, and the headquarters of the Springfield Street Railway Company were located at the corner of Main and Hooker streets. The first car was run on March 10, 1870, and the first line of track was laid through Main and State streets to Oak. In the 'eighties, as street car traveling became more practical, there was rapid extension of the lines to all parts of the city and outlying towns. There were other municipal improvements. The reservoir in Cherry Valley, Ludlow, was completed for the city s water supply, a forerunner of the magnificent Little River system. The North End Bridge over the Connecticut was built, and two years later the South End Bridge, made of iron at a cost of $100,000, was completed.

Springfield's splendid park system began when O. H. Greenleaf, a member of the first board of park commissioners, in 1884, gave to the city sixty-four acres of land to be known as Forest Park. Two additional tracts were purchased which brought the acreage up to ninety-acres, and a good start was made toward the seven hundred and fifty-seven acres now in the park. This region was heavily wooded with a remarkably large variety of trees and was the home of many game and song birds. It also had an attractive little brook known as Clay Brook, a branch of the Pecowsic.

The following year Forest Park was developed, and the commission acquired Court Square from the county, which paid $500 to the city for being released of its care. By the time the park department was six years old it had obtained sixteen small parks about the city and had come to the conclusion that Forest Park was not large enough.

The most eventful year in the park history was 1890, when Everett H. Barney gave his beautiful estate of one hundred and nine and one-half acres to the city. Mr. Greenleaf added a small parcel to what he had already given, a group of three men gave the Cooley property of forty-one acres, and the city purchased the Dickinson estate of ninety-two acres. During the same year the street railway company extended its tracks to the Summer Avenue entrance and 75,000 people by that means alone visited Forest Park. As many more probably came in other ways.

It was at this time that the city lost the services of J. D. McKnight, a member of the park board, donor of land to Forest Park and many of the small parks, and the one who was principally responsible for the plan and ornamentation of Oak Grove Cemetery, where he was buried.

The next few years were given over to development work. Roads were laid out, croquet and tennis courts started, the ball field improved, white pines planted, and gifts of elk, deer, swans, wild geese and other birds and animals were received. The pheasantry was built, and Bowles Fountain was erected as a memorial to the late Samuel Bowles, by a gift of Mrs. Mary Dwight Bowles. Emphasis was placed on the lotus and lily ponds, and several service buildings were constructed. More donors of land were added to the growing list of those who saw the value of this beautiful piece of property.

The park commission had visioned a possible acquisition of land along the river to beautify the water frontage from Bridge to Howard streets, but finally acquired only the levee, a little tract of less than an acre at the foot of Elm Street. In 1898 the bears' and prairie dogs' cages were built at Forest Park and visitors were becoming familiar with the sight of a shepherd and his flock roaming over the hillsides, and with the herd of many breeds of blooded cattle. The wading pool, built the following year, was the first one ever provided in a public park in the United States. A greenhouse was the gift of Dwight O. Gilmore, and Tilly Haynes gave $10,000 to be used for the Court Square extension.

A stone skatinghouse on Barney Pond, built of salvaged paving block in 1907, was later converted into the useful and interesting trailside museum.

The first large playground in the city, the Emerson Wight, was given by Nathan Bill, in 1908, and he continued in later years to make other gifts of the same sort. The rose garden in Forest Park was started in 1914, but the war period saw other kinds of gardens laid out and in one year 6,000 bushels of potatoes were raised as well as many cabbages, beets, turnips and summer vegetables. When normal times returned a dam was constructed and nearly forty-five acres of swamp were flooded to make Porter Lake, in memory of Sherman D. Porter, who gave $10,000 to the park about this time. Memorial Grove, of one hundred and forty pin oaks, was planted in honor of the soldiers who did not return from the World War.

The iris garden, started in 1923, has since come to be a rival of the rose garden in beauty and interest. Blunt Park was developed about this time and the Franconia golf course, made possible by the gift of $50,000 from Mr. Bill, was a great addition to the city's recreational facilities. The Springfield park system now covers nearly 2,000 acres, scattered well over the city, which has been fortunate in having an unusual number of public-spirited citizens interested and able to assist in the work.

On January 24, 1881, the "Springfield Republican" recorded that the Blair and Fiske Company, which manufactured lawnmowers in the Steam Power Company's building on Taylor Street, experimentally lighted their plant with electric lamps for all night work. Four days later the exterior of the Taylor Street plant was illuminated for about one-half hour by one outdoor lamp, and on March 22 of the same year two lamps were used to illuminate Springfield's skating rink. In April, as a matter of safety, wires were placed underground, the conductors in those early days having been run over the buildings.

The Springfield Electric Light Company, as it was then called, was formed in 1881, shortly after these events. Its capital was $10,000, but an indication of its growth may be seen when six years later it had jumped to five times the original investment. Soon the Springfield Electric Light Company was organized into the United Electric Light Company, with a capital of $100,000. The station, which produced incandescent lighting by means of electric motors, was located in the Steam Power Company's building. It later expanded and the station was moved to its present quarters on State Street, and as the city grew various substations were built to accommodate the added load. It is worthy of note that Springfield was perhaps the first city in New England to have an electric power company. Boston was toying with the idea, but did not have an electric light company until some time after 1881.

The Springfield Gas Light Company was organized as far back as 1847, although gas was not used for lighting purposes until two years later. For years the company lagged because the people had no confidence in the new fuel. It was only when the Gilbert and Barker Company, after a hard struggle, had perfected gas-producing apparatus and the technique of gas utility that expansion came. Gas was not used in Springfield for industrial appliances until 1866.

At that time the consumer using gas in Springfield paid a rate of $3.50 per thousand cubic feet. Its use was a real luxury, far beyond the poor man's purse, and there were no quarter meter machines to bring the fuel within his means. Since then the rates have dropped, and in 1911 they had gone down as far as eighty-five cents per thousand cubic feet. H. Haile was president of the company and S. J. Fowler manager.

In 1901 a utility commission took up the management of the company and made many improvements. A few years later the plant moved into new quarters at its present location, under the leadership of Charles H. Tenney.

Springfield's first great disaster from fire was in June, 1675, when thirty-two of her forty-five dwellings were burned, together with twenty-four barns and the jail, nearly three-fourths of the little settlement's buildings going up in smoke in one day. Regulations for the prevention of fire were early made and the first apparatus consisted of hooks, fire poles and buckets. The first fire company of which we have record was organized in 1794, and each member was required to keep two fire bags and buckets hung up by the front door of his house. An old print shows the burning of the armory in 1824. Two lines of men, possibly seventy-five in each, form the bucket brigade, reaching from a well or cistern to the wildly blazing building, against which a ladder is leaning. One line passes up the full buckets while the empty ones are returned along the parallel row of helpers. The first crude fire engine was named the "Lion" and purchased in 1792. It had five feet of hose and was kept in active use up to 1824, being housed in a shed built for the purpose. In 1827 the town voted to build an enginehouse to properly care for the hook and ladder wagon and one hundred feet of new hose, as well as a suction engine. The first steamer, called the "Monitor," was purchased in 1862. Volunteer companies at first manned the fire fighting apparatus, but the time came when the city was obliged to finance them.

It was an honor in those days to be connected with the fire department and Robert O. Morris recalled with what pride he saw his father in red shirt and white helmet, carrying a trumpet bedecked with flowers, attending a muster on Court Square, where the companies vied with each other to throw a stream over the rooster on the old church.

The most destructive fire that ever visited Springfield broke out on May 30, 1875, and raged furiously for three hours, sweeping through the business section of the city. The fire originated on Taylor Street, the center of planing mills and mattress factories. The wind put the fire beyond control almost at the start and after crossing Main Street to Bridge Street it pushed on down to Water Street. The fire destroyed about forty-five buildings, about thirty of which were homes. Many were made homeless and about two hundred thrown out of employment, but there was no loss of life. Holyoke knew nothing of the fire until news was brought there by a railroad engine, as no operator could be found at the depot to send a telegram for aid. But in thirteen minutes the Relief Steamer and the Mt. Tom Hose companies were on their way. A special train was ordered out on the Athol Railroad to Indian Orchard and brought in a steamer. The steamer from Chicopee, with two companies, arrived in time to render good service. Two steamers were loaded on a train at Hartford and made the run of twenty-eight miles in twenty-five minutes. Alderman Brigham mounted a horse at the Richmond stables and started for Westfield, but the horse was exhausted before arriving there and a woman passing in a carriage galloped her horse to the town and gave the alarm. The Westfield engine was hustled on to a train and made the distance of nine miles in eighteen minutes. People expected the whole city to be destroyed, and a general movement of goods to some safe place was begun and even the river was dotted over with boats loaded down with goods. Upon the arrival of out-of-town assistance, which included police from Chicopee and Holyoke, things quieted down, and before dark the danger was over.

The fire alarm system was installed in 1868, and prior to that time all alarms were given on the city hall bell, different numbers designating the various wards.

In the afternoon of the seventh of March, 1888, about forty employees in the office of the Union Publishing Plant on the fifth floor of the Wight Block on Main Street were making preparations to go home. A volume of dense smoke burst suddenly from the elevator shaft, and as the many windows were closed, the place was quickly filled with the stifling smoke. The occupants at first did not realize the seriousness of what was happening, but went to the elevator and rang the bell. As they waited and the elevator did not come their fears mounted into panic. By a strange coincidence, as was discovered later, something had gone wrong with the elevator only a few minutes before the fire broke out.

The panic-stricken occupants milled about, trapped in the building; they were advised by Managing Editor E. A. Hill to go to the roof and this many did. About fifteen people, however, rushed for the rooms in the front of the building to wait for the firemen, and about eight or nine of these crowded into a front corner room. Smoke poured out of doors and windows as the terror-stricken, white-faced people at the windows cried for help to the crowds far below. The fire apparatus reached the scene, and a ladder was raised as a cheer broke out from the watching throng, but the cheer died quickly into the silence of horror when it was discovered that the ladder was fourteen feet too short to reach the trapped occupants. One woman, in desperation, leaped from the windows and was killed on the pavement. As the tongues of flame came nearer the group at the windows prayed. All hope of escape was shut off.

Carpets and mattresses were spread below by the frantic crowd. Thomas Donohue leaped into a blanket held as a life net, but it did not hold and he was killed on the pavement. Others jumped and were killed in the same way, and before the horrible fire had finished it had taken a toll of eight lives. The cause of the fire was unknown, but the tragedy did have one significant effect. Agitation was immediately started to give the fire department more modern and complete fire-fighting equipment, to guard against any recurrence of the short ladder episode. Today Springfield has one of the finest equipped and best trained fire fighting forces in the country.

The old city hall, in January, 1905, was destroyed by a blaze which started when a monkey in a show going on at the time knocked over a kerosene lamp. The damage to the building, which had been standing since 1853, a year after the incorporation of Springfield as a city,

Hampden—35

amounted to about $100,000. The old bell, which weighed 4,000 pounds, fell and cracked during the fire, and there were thrilling rescues made by the fire department.

The Highland Baptist Church burned in a spectacular fire the following year, and in 1907 came the fire which destroyed the Phelps Publishing Company. This blaze was on a bitterly cold night, which made conditions for fighting the fire almost impossible. The fire had been discovered by a night watchman, in the cellar, and he and another watchman thought they succeeded in extinguishing the blaze. They left the cellar and only a few minutes later returned to be greeted by a hot burst of flame. Meanwhile some outsider noticed the fire and sounded the alarm. The flames seemed to devour the antiquated wooden building almost in a flash, and a withering blanket of heat from the roaring furnace kept the firemen at a distance. Less than fifteen minutes after the fire had been discovered the building was a mass of flames. Another quick fire was that which consumed the Springfield News Company, in 1910. Thirteen persons were rescued by the firemen and the loss suffered was $50,000.

Another fire catastrophe came in 1931, when the East Court Street Hotel Fire occurred. It was in December and a bitter cold wind froze the streams of water which ran from eighteen lines of hose. The ladders, coated with ice, were dangerous to climb and the firemen wore safety belts as they mounted the precarious rungs to fight the fire that was rapidly destroying the hotel. The loss in money was $100,000, a sum that was modest compared to some of the other Springfield fires, but the loss of eight lives in the fire was the tragedy. These people, awakened from their sleep, were trapped in the building, and more than a dozen were carried to safety by heroic firemen. The year following witnessed another terrible tragedy when an explosion occurred in a building on Ferry Street, killing five people.

In 1893 the affairs of the department were placed in the hands of a fire commission and from this time on until 1905 the working force was almost doubled. There were then four engine companies, five hose companies and three hook and ladder companies. The hose wagons were drawn by horses, and Amoskeag steamers were used, as well as Leverich trucks and Babcock aerial ladders.

There are today in Springfield fifteen fire stations, including head-quarters at Court Square, and Chief Root, at the head of the department since 1904, has brought in the most modern fire apparatus available and constantly instituted new and more efficient fire-fighting methods. The two-platoon system came in under Chief Root's administration, which allows two separate shifts of men to work instead of having one shift on duty the entire twenty-four hours. The personnel of the department consists of about three hundred and fifty-seven men, including officers. The Fire Prevention Bureau, an agency for preventing fires through inspection and educational propaganda, consists of a chief and four other inspectors.

A feature of the Springfield fire-fighting force is the department school, first instituted in 1908. This "drill school" was primarily for rookies, but for years every man in the department had to attend, and many of the firemen from the small outlying towns came to the drill school for instruction. The rookie who takes the department school training must come out with a thorough knowledge of fire hazards and the methods of fighting fires before he is given his ranking grade. A drill is held at each station at least once a week, and the benefit of this expert instruction and constant drilling may be seen in the fact that since the turn of the century no fire has occurred in Springfield that was not under control in a very short time.

The Springfield Police Department is the natural successor of the "watch" who made his nightly rounds in the old days, lantern on arm, calling the hours and adding "all is well"; of the "tything man," who saw that Sunday laws were kept; and of the various officers, such as "hog reeves," who protected the highways from being cluttered up with stray animals. Then, those who were brought into court were charged for the most part with trivial offenses, such as failing to "ring" swine, neglecting to maintain fences properly, and absenting themselves from town meeting. Drunkenness, theft, assaults and the like were uncommon.

At first only one constable was needed to preserve the majesty of the law, and "wise and discreet" men were supposed to be selected. Apparently it was not an office which was much sought after for the selectmen attached a forfeit of twenty shillings for refusal to accept it. Miles Morgan, who now turns his back on the police department in Court Square, was once a constable. Men were not obliged to serve in this position two years in succession, and though the pay was small and made mostly in products, few declined to serve.

The constable had to see that no man cut, without permission, a tree suitable for a "canoe tree," or that undesirable persons, who might become burdens on the town, were harbored in the homes. There were parking problems of a sort in those days, too, for drivers who kept teams across the river in the spring of the year to plough there, were forbidden to let them "damnify" other people's property, but must keep them in some house or yard until the first of May or otherwise properly restrain them. Part of the constable's pay came from individuals, as each family was ordered to pay him six pence in wampum or a peck of Indian corn for beating the drum before meetings, and the shilling he was granted later for ringing the bell for marriages and burials was to be collected from those employing him. Elizur Holyoke, of a prominent family in Springfield, was constable at a time when the duties included "ringing ye bell and sweeping ye meetinge house."

During a wave of "unpleasantness" which struck the community, it is recorded that a servant was given twenty lashes for profaning the Sabbath; Jean Miller was summoned to answer to the charge of calling her husband a "fool, toad, vermine"; Samuel Ely was fined for selling cider to the Indians; and Goodwife Hunter was gagged and made to stand half an hour in the stocks for sundry "exorbitancys of ye tongue." Lawless youths gave the constables considerable trouble, and several boys were arraigned on a June day for profaning the Sabbath. These young offenders were fined, and their fines were to be paid by their "Governors," presumably meaning fathers, in default of which they were to be publicly whipped by the constable.

In 1775 the number of constables had been increased to five, and they were quite unable to cope with a force of one hundred and fifty men who broke open the jail and released the prisoners. The constable system was abandoned at the first meeting of the city council in 1852, and from then on there was a police force, consisting at first of only seven men, though eleven more were soon added.

With the coming into force of the civil service law, in 1894, a new era was begun in the police department, and the system of mental and physical examinations became more rigid. A policeman must be at least five feet seven inches in height, and the weight range was placed between one hundred and thirty-five pounds and one hundred and seventy-five pounds. A bicycle squad was an innovation, but an effective one, and finally the police alarm telegraph signal was installed, much to the benefit of both the force and the city.

An innovation in municipal affairs was instituted in 1902 when the first police commission was formed, and five years later William J. Quilty, who died in 1935, at almost eighty years of age, was named first police chief to succeed a line of police marshals. Chief Quilty retired from service in 1932, having spent forty-five years in the department, and twenty-five of them as its executive head. He was outstanding not only from point of long service, but also because of his splendid detective work and his efforts toward maintaining the department on an efficient basis in line with modern and up-to-date police methods.

He was born in Springfield in 1855 and received his early education in the old Elm Street School. He first worked for the Kibbe Candy Company and later as a grocery boy for his brother. After a trip to San Francisco, where he was engaged in the grocery business, Chief Quilty returned to this city, but the wanderlust took him again and he shipped to Africa on an old New Bedford whaler. He was stricken with fever on that continent, but miraculously recovered.

He was appointed to the police force on March 7, 1887, by Mayor E. B. Maynard and in 1891 promoted to the rank of inspector. City Marshal John Rice made him a permanent police inspector the following year and on August 10, 1907, he was made city marshal. At the time of his appointment the Springfield police force consisted of about forty men, and since then it has grown to about three hundred men. Under Chief Quilty a number of beneficial changes and additions took place in the department, and among these was the establishing of a detective bureau and also a vice squad.

Chief Quilty was a shrewd and able detective and took part in a number of exciting incidents. Two of his most notable feats were the capturing of the assailant of Dr. Fred Brigham, who was on his way to a midnight case, and the capture of Palmer and Sheedy, notorious burglars, in 1910.

Not only did Chief Quilty keep in touch with individual members of the force, but he also kept in touch with new methods elsewhere, and in cases where they were applicable used them in his own department. His prestige grew steadily from the day he was appointed city marshal. Recognition of his fine public service came in tangible form when he received the William Pynchon medal for outstanding public service to Springfield. An oil portrait of the chief is now in the Connecticut Valley Historical Society building.

As a traveler approaches Springfield from an elevation so that the city lies before him in panoramic view, his eyes are instantly drawn to the three white buildings in the center, about which the rest of the city buildings seem to be clustered as satellites. Between two massive structures rises a tall straight spire reaching three hundred feet into the sky, and on each side near the top is a huge golden-lettered clock. Plain, yet classic in its beauty and construction, the auditorium, administration building and campanile tower form a municipal group unrivaled in any other city the size of Springfield.

A feature of this group lies in the fact that none of the utility has been sacrificed in the name of beauty. The auditorium, with a seating capacity of 4,000, is a busy center of both business and cultural activity. It is here that great artists and speakers are heard, also that great trade and political conventions gather, because of the ideal conditions it provides in seating capacity, acoustics, ventilation, light, and convenience of location. There are a number of galleries, yet from every seat the stage may be seen clearly and the speaker or the musician heard distinctly. The basement floor is ideal for exhibition booths, for holding banquets, and for other purposes auxiliary to the great hall upstairs. Impressive as the auditorium is on the outside, with its fluted Corinthian columns and its majestic rise of steps, it is every bit as impressive in the interior.

The administration building, from the outside virtually a twin of the auditorium, is quite different on the inside. Here the government of the city of Springfield is housed, and the offices flanking the long corridors contain the multiple municipal divisions of the city. A magnificent flight of marble steps leads to the upper floors, where there are still other offices.

The most interesting and unusual building of the three, however, is the campanile tower. Its design was adopted from the St. Mark's Square campanile in Venice. Like a hollow rectangular tube inside, its walls are sheer and unbroken except for a few tiny windows and a single small balcony. From this balcony just above the clocks, to which the elevator running up the shaft quickly travels, a sightseer may view the entire city of Springfield and the surrounding region. Then there are the great bells in the tower belfry, which chime at every quarter hour, and from which on certain occasions deep and impressive music comes. The sound of these bells may carry eight miles north and south up and down the valley, conveyed on the surface of the river which flows past, and to the east and west a somewhat less distance. At the very top of the tower is a bright yellow beacon light.

The building of the municipal group came about through necessity. The old city hall was destroyed by fire in January, 1906, and the city government was left homeless. The city hall up to that time had not been particularly outstanding as far as beauty was concerned, although it served its purpose well enough, and a movement was started to have the new quarters of the municipal government impressive in design and yet adequate to serve the needs of the city for many years.

There was much opposition in the council toward building a pretentious structure, due to the cost that would certainly be entailed. After much discussion, a building commission was appointed by Mayor Francke Dickinson, in May, 1906, with George Dwight Pratt as chairman. There were eighty-two separate designs submitted in competition, and that entered by Pell and Corbett, of New York, was finally adopted in November, 1908. The contracts were awarded for the foundations and superstructures the following year, but it was not until 1910 that the corner stone was laid. In 1913 the three Indiana limestone buildings were completed.

One morning early in April of 1911 the startling news spread through the city that someone had tried to dynamite the new municipal tower, then still in the early stages of construction, but fortunately, the explosive charge was not sufficient and was so placed that the damage was slight. Watchmen were stationed about the buildings and an investigation followed. There were at that time a series of dynamite outrages all over the country, and it was finally revealed that a man named Ortie McManigal, who was employed by the officials of a structural steel workers' organization, had made the attempt to blow up the tower as a part of a premeditated plan to terrify the employers of such labor throughout the United States. This sensational episode came close to costing a large sum of money and possibly some lives.

It was because of McManigal's lack of knowledge concerning high explosives that the work went on without serious interruption.

In the entire work of construction there was only one fatality, a good record considering the magnitude of the work done. About a year after the McManigal incident, three of the workers were busy fastening the cornice to the northeast corner of the building when a large section gave way. One of the three men who fell was killed, and the other two seriously injured, while still another man who was working below was hurt by falling débris.

The contractors in the process of building were subjected to one delay over which they had no possible control. Skyros marble was used in great quantity in the fine staircase of the administration building and also in paneling the walls of the corridors in front of the city council rooms and elsewhere. This marble, the same which many years ago was used in ancient Asian or Grecian palaces and temples, came from an island in the Ægean Sea, and was imported here at great expense. Trouble broke out in the Near East, when Greece, who for many years had been crushed under the harsh rule of the Ottoman Turk, allied herself with other peoples of the Near East and threw off the yoke. While this was going on there was little exporting of materials and the marble was delayed for some time.

In any large public and spacious building the problem of acoustics invariably rises. In the auditorium of the municipal group, the acoustic situation is a happy one, since there is little or no rebounding of sound through the hall. When Madame Schumann-Heink, the world-renowned singer, gave a concert here, she was delighted with the hall from this point of view, and paid the city a high compliment. Later, Paderewski, the great pianist, declared publicly that the hall was the finest he had ever played in.

The approximate total cost of the municipal group, after its completion, was about $1,900,000, or a per capita cost of about nineteen dollars per person. The buildings are modeled somewhat on the style of the famous Parthenon in Greece. The bells in the campanile are not church bells, but community bells, and Ernest Newton Bagg is the official bell-ringer. There are about a dozen bells in the belfrey, and these were cast by the grandson of Meneely of Troy, who in 1856, cast the old city hall bell. Each of the bells is a gift, the largest being from the city of Springfield. On one side of it is the same inscription as that contained on the old city hall bell, and on the other side is inscribed: "Municipal Campanile, Springfield, Mass., July 4, 1913. 'For a thousand years in thy sight are but as yesterday.'" The other and smaller bells were given by the school children of Springfield and by individual citizens.

On holidays such as Easter and Christmas the song of the bells in appropriate hymns rings out over the city. The bells are also rung when a visiting personage comes to the city. When Marshal Foch came to Springfield shortly after the World War the "Marseillaise" was the principal song, although other military airs, both American and French, were played. It is also the custom for the bells to ring before a convention, and on Sundays various anthems are played.

The campanile bells were the first in the United States to sound an old Hebrew tune, the "Hatikvah," or "Song of Hope." The request for the hymn came from a rabbi, when a Jewish assembly was convening in the city, and the bell-ringer was amazed, when he looked down, to see a number of orthodox and devout Jews bowed in prayer as the sound of the bells rang forth.